# The School Counselor's Preparation and Professional Practice Desk Reference and Examination Study Guide

This third edition of *The School Counselor's Preparation and Professional Practice Desk Reference and Examination Study Guide* is a comprehensive resource for both pre-service and practicing school counselors. It is intended to be used as a school counselor preparation course text, credentialing exam study resource, and comprehensive desk reference.

The text material holistically addresses culturally sensitive practices and the professional, legal, and ethical principles of school counseling in today's public K-12 schools, capturing the past, present, and future of the profession using a personable writing style that engages readers. The material meets preparation criteria for the NBPTS School Counseling National Certification assessment, School Counselor Preparation Comprehensive exams, state-specific school counselor licensure exams, and the Praxis School Counselor exam, which was recently adopted as the exam for earning the ASCA Certified School Counselor (ACSC) credential. The text includes a glossary of important terms, common acronyms, and real-world case studies for enriched discussions and enhanced understanding. Each chapter includes guided reflections and knowledge checks with end-of-chapter exam simulations and case studies to include correct responses and explanations for those responses. A cumulative end-of-text comprehensive simulation exam with responses is also included.

The text covers the requisite information pre-service and practicing school counselors need to be the very best twenty-first century school counselors in accordance with contemporary research, the ASCA National Model, CAEP, CACREP, and NBPTS standards.

**Rita Schellenberg** is a professor in the school counseling program at Liberty University. She is actively involved in the profession serving in leadership roles and presenting at conferences. Dr. Schellenberg is a licensed professional counselor, school counselor, counselor supervisor, and holds several other national counseling credentials and ASCA certifications.

# The School Counselor's Preparation and Professional Practice Desk Reference and Examination Study Guide

## Third Edition

Rita Schellenberg

Routledge
Taylor & Francis Group
NEW YORK AND LONDON

Designed cover image: ©Getty

Third edition published 2025
by Routledge
605 Third Avenue, New York, NY 10158

and by Routledge
4 Park Square, Milton Park, Abingdon, Oxon, OX14 4RN

*Routledge is an imprint of the Taylor & Francis Group, an informa business*

© 2025 Rita Schellenberg

The right of Rita Schellenberg to be identified as author of this work has been asserted in accordance with sections 77 and 78 of the Copyright, Designs and Patents Act 1988.

All rights reserved. No part of this book may be reprinted or reproduced or utilised in any form or by any electronic, mechanical, or other means, now known or hereafter invented, including photocopying and recording, or in any information storage or retrieval system, without permission in writing from the publishers.

*Trademark notice*: Product or corporate names may be trademarks or registered trademarks, and are used only for identification and explanation without intent to infringe.

Second edition published by Routledge 2018

*Library of Congress Cataloging-in-Publication Data*
Names: Schellenberg, Rita Cantrell, author.
Title: The school counselor's preparation and professional practice desk reference and examination study guide : a psychobiography / Rita Schellenberg.
Other titles: School counselor's desk reference and credentialing examination study guide
Description: Third edition. | New York : Routledge, 2025. | Preceded by The school counselor's desk reference and credentialing examination study guide / Rita Schellenberg. 2018. | Includes bibliographical references and index. |
Identifiers: LCCN 2024025289 (print) | LCCN 2024025290 (ebook) | ISBN 9781032634456 (pbk) | ISBN 9781032634463 (hbk) | ISBN 9781032634500 (ebk)
Subjects: MESH: Counseling | Child | Adolescent | School Health Services | Child Guidance | United States | Case Reports | Examination Questions
Classification: LCC LB1027.5 .S2534 2025 (print) | LCC LB1027.5 (ebook) | DDC 371.4076--dc23/eng/20240614
LC record available at https://lccn.loc.gov/2024025289
LC ebook record available at https://lccn.loc.gov/2024025290

ISBN: 978-1-032-63446-3 (hbk)
ISBN: 978-1-032-63445-6 (pbk)
ISBN: 978-1-032-63450-0 (ebk)

DOI: 10.4324/9781032634500

Typeset in Garamond
by SPi Technologies India Pvt Ltd (Straive)

# Contents

**Foreword** .................................................................................... ix
**PAUL HARRIS**
**Preface** ...................................................................................... xi
**Acknowledgments** ................................................................. xiii
**About the author** .................................................................. xiv
**Introduction** ........................................................................... xvi
    Using this resource ............................................................ xvii
    Tips for test-taker triumph ................................................ xvii

**1 Foundations of school counseling** ..................................... 1
    The first hundred years ........................................................... 1
    ASCA and the national model ................................................. 3
    The transforming school counseling initiative ....................... 4
    Professional identity: roles, preparation, unification, and
    certification ............................................................................... 5
        School counselor as educator ............................................ 6
        School counselor as counselor ......................................... 7
        School counselor preparation programs ......................... 8
    Licensure and advanced voluntary school counseling credentials ..... 11
    Ethical, legal, and professional considerations ..................... 12
        Confidentiality ................................................................. 15
        Confidentiality of counseling-related electronic
        communication ................................................................ 19
        Harm to self or others ..................................................... 21
        Child abuse and neglect ................................................. 24
        Scope of practice ............................................................. 27
        Informed consent ............................................................ 29

Student records and counseling case notes ................................ 30
IDEA and Section 504 .................................................................. 33
Homelessness ................................................................................ 35
Research ........................................................................................ 36
Dual relationships ........................................................................ 37
Supervision .................................................................................... 37
Human development, learning, and motivation ................................. 39
Psychosocial development ............................................................ 40
Moral and spiritual development ................................................. 46
Cognitive development and learning theories ............................. 49
Motivation ..................................................................................... 54
Chapter 1 Case conceptualization responses ..................................... 59
Chapter 1 Simulation: Ernesto ............................................................ 64
Chapter 1 Simulation responses: Ernesto .......................................... 68
Chapter 1 Guided reflection ............................................................... 76

## 2 Comprehensive school counseling programs ......................... 81
The ASCA national model and a comprehensive school
counseling program ............................................................................. 81
Define: student standards and professional standards ................ 84
Manage: program focus and planning ......................................... 85
Deliver: direct and indirect student services ............................... 99
Assess: program assessment and school counselor
assessment and appraisal ............................................................ 138
Chapter 2 Case conceptualization responses ................................... 149
Chapter 2 Simulation: Collaboration ................................................ 155
Chapter 2 Simulation responses: Collaboration .............................. 158
Chapter 2 Guided reflection ............................................................. 164

## 3 Primary developmental domains ........................................... 172
Social/emotional development .......................................................... 175
Transitioning ............................................................................... 178
School violence and bullying ...................................................... 180
Internet safety and cyberbullying ............................................... 182
Substance use, abuse, addiction ................................................. 185
Divorce ........................................................................................ 187
Parenting style ............................................................................ 188
Career development .......................................................................... 189
Influences on career decision making ....................................... 190

Career development theory and career counseling .................. 192
Career and college transitions ...................................... 197
Career assessment instruments and career information delivery systems ........................................................ 202
Academic development ................................................ 204
Curriculum development ......................................... 206
Closing the achievement gap ................................... 209
Specialty and alternative education programs ........... 210
Chapter 3 Case conceptualization responses ................... 221
Chapter 3 Simulation: High school career development ... 223
Chapter 3 Simulation responses: High school career development .................................................................. 227
Chapter 3 Guided reflection ............................................. 235

# 4 Theories and techniques for school settings ........................ 242
Adlerian ............................................................................ 243
Behavioral ......................................................................... 244
Cognitive behavioral ......................................................... 245
Gestalt .............................................................................. 246
Person-centered ................................................................ 247
Rational emotive behavior therapy ................................... 248
Reality counseling ............................................................. 249
Solution-focused brief counseling ..................................... 250
Strengths-based counseling .............................................. 251
Play therapy techniques .................................................... 253
Chapter 4 Case conceptualization responses ................... 256
Chapter 4 Simulation: Esther ........................................... 257
Chapter 4 Simulation responses: Esther .......................... 260
Chapter 4 Guided reflection ............................................. 266

# 5 Diversity, equity, and advocacy ........................................... 269
Advocacy and equity ........................................................ 270
Access, attainment, and achievement ............................... 275
Multicultural competence ................................................. 278
Spirituality ................................................................... 283
Chapter 5 Case conceptualization responses ................... 286
Chapter 5 Simulation: The newbie ................................... 288
Chapter 5 Simulation responses: The newbie .................. 292
Chapter 5 Guided reflection ............................................. 298

## 6 Leadership .................................................................. 301
- Leadership attributes, styles, and practices ........................................ 302
- Use of technology ............................................................................. 306
- School counseling websites .............................................................. 308
- School, family, and community partnerships .................................... 309
- Systemic change ................................................................................ 311
- Chapter 6 Case conceptualization responses .................................... 314
- Chapter 6 Simulation: School counselor leader ................................ 315
- Chapter 6 Simulation responses: School counselor leader ............... 318
- Chapter 6 Guided reflection .............................................................. 323

## Full-length practice exam ............................................................. 325
- Simulation One: College readiness .................................................... 325
- Simulation Two: School violence ....................................................... 329
- Simulation Three: Student appraisal ................................................. 333
- Simulation Four: Early intervention .................................................. 337
- Simulation Five: Academic achievement .......................................... 341
- Simulation Six: Assessment ............................................................... 345
- Simulation Seven: Special needs and scope of practice ................... 348
- Simulation Eight: Program evaluation .............................................. 352
- Simulation Nine: Alternative educational programs ........................ 355
- Full-length practice exam responses ................................................ 358

## Glossary ............................................................................. 414
## References ........................................................................ 427
## Acronyms .......................................................................... 436
## Index ................................................................................. 439

# Foreword

An issue that has been debated for decades has been that of the nature of our roles in schools. Are we to be therapists, where individual counseling takes the center stage as our most prominent intervention? Or are we to be considered more as educators who have counseling skills that can inform an array of interventions – assessment, collaboration, information dissemination, etc.? Historically, this has been predicated on the times and what was deemed most needed at the time (e.g., responding to the launch of Sputnik by hiring staff to identify and encourage more students to pursue math and science, etc.). We've shifted back and forth from strictly vocational guides to mental health practitioners to whatever else is sometimes arbitrarily put on our list of duties.

Further, as a profession we have grappled with how best to serve an increasingly diverse population. By the year 2050, it is predicted that there will be no majority race or ethnicity in the US; every American will be a member of a minority group. And of course, these differences are not limited to race or ethnicity. Gender, class, geographical origin, family traditions, sexuality, language, and more will continue to require school counselors and the training programs through which they come to prioritize cultural proficiency and humility in their professional growth. And as the population continues to evolve, school counselors are ethically obligated to acquire the requisite awareness, knowledge, and skills to deliver a comprehensive school counseling program to every student from culturally diverse backgrounds.

That said, significant advocacy efforts by various organizations over decades have propelled the school counseling profession to a place where there is more of a shared professional identity and commitment to equity and access than there has ever been. It is now expected that contemporary school counselors passionately pursue purpose by designing comprehensive, preventive, and developmentally appropriate programs that address the academic, emotional, and career needs of K-12 students. Moreover, there are credentialing pathways that ensure that training and service delivery is as uniform as possible in service to an increasingly diverse student body.

Given the multiple contributors to the advances in school counseling as a profession, it is rare to find any resource that combines the latest information from each. This is especially true of preparatory materials to guide pre-service counselors toward national certification and more. Dr. Schellenberg's study guide fills this literature void by providing a practical guide toward content mastery that not only prepares pre-service school counselors for their exams, but equips them for critical service to their students.

I am honored to write the foreword for this exceptional work. Dr. Schellenberg should be commended for creating a resource that will undoubtedly bolster the careers of many school counselors and transform the lives of students whose services they receive.

**Paul Harris, PhD, NCC, NCSC**
*Founder, Integrity Matters, LLC*
*Professor, Counselor, and Distinguished Keynote Speaker*
*Senior Advisory Board, The Professional Counselor*
*Past Editorial Review Board, Professional School Counseling*
*Past President, Virginia School Counselor Association*
*Past Board of Directors, American School Counselor Association*

# Preface

The growing demand for accountability and enhanced mental health services for children and adolescents has heightened the need for rigorous credentialing requirements, setting you on the path to becoming a credential junkie like myself. Virtually every state in this great nation requires a school counselor specialty exam in addition to completion of the school counseling preparation program in order to obtain licensure/certification in an effort to ensure that school counselors are fully prepared to provide counseling services to minors in K-12 settings. Optimal preparation is critical. Imagine, the school counselor is the only counselor a troubled child or adolescent may ever see.

Preparing for my own credentials, I found myself wading through a shallow pool of school counseling study guides. After a daunting and exhausting immersion, all I had to show for it was saturated, wrinkled feet. So, I turned my efforts toward finding at least one comprehensive but succinct text that would cover school counseling without all the superfluous material—still nothing.

How was this possible? I could not fathom the nonexistence of a dedicated study guide for all exams in school counseling. Nor, could I wrap my mind around the absence of a comprehensive school counseling text that cut to the chase without the redundancy that drives even the sanest of people to madness.

My search led me deep into a forest of textbooks where I plowed through one after another before groping to find my way back out. Having passed my credentialing exam, I obviously managed to pick up what I needed somewhere. Necessity being the father of invention, I accepted the self-imposed challenge to create a comprehensive school counseling text that could be used as a school counselor preparation text, a desk reference, and a study guide.

I am pleased that *The School Counselor's Desk Reference and Credentialing Examination Study Guide* has helped many across the country to successfully pass their School Counseling Praxis exam, as well as other state-required school counseling exams and school counselor education comprehensive exams. Mission accomplished!

I am humbled by those who have hunted me down to thank me and to share your positive testing experience. Many of you have asked that I continue to update the text so you can always have the reference at your fingertips as a practicing school counselor or have it to include as a school counseling course text as counselor educators. Your wish is my command as I now embark upon this third edition.

So, whether you're bending the pages of this text to pass a school counseling exam, to complete course assignments, or to refresh your memory about specific school counseling practices and processes, thank you for seeking to be the very best school counselor you can be! It is my hope that you never stop seeking to improve your skills and snare the advanced voluntary credentials that set you apart as a professional dedicated to life-long learning and providing optimal counseling services. One credential junkie to another—there are worse things! Although, be warned, there may be no treatment for credential addiction!

# Acknowledgments

I owe a debt of gratitude to countless and sensational colleagues, who, over the years and as a collective, have informed, encouraged, supported, challenged, and propelled me forward. This book is not the work of one, but of the many, as demonstrated by the exhaustive references.

I am thrilled to acknowledge my students—past, present, and future. Bearing witness to your sincere yearning for knowledge has pushed me to continue learning so that I might continue to have something more to share. It is my hope that I might encourage you to be explorers of your own world while exploring the worlds of others and to live in the world, not just on it.

I would especially like to express my gratitude to Dr. Paul Harris for writing the Foreword in support of this text. His tireless contributions to the profession are to be applauded. He has helped to strengthen and advance the profession holding important leadership roles in the American School Counselor Association (ASCA) and Virginia School Counselor Association (VSCA). Dr. Harris often serves as keynote speaker at professional conferences across the country—a testament to his ability to inspire and positively speak to the profession.

A special thanks to the outstanding Routledge team, namely my Editor Amanda Savage and the editorial staff. I would also like to extend continued gratitude for a helpful review to Dr. Howard Rosenthal, renowned author of the bestselling *Encyclopedia of Counseling*.

As always, John, the captain of my heart, thank you for the many years of unwavering support. Finally, and *most importantly*, glory to God for the life He breathed into each of us and into this work. Amen.

**Rita Schellenberg**

# About the author

**Dr. Rita Schellenberg** is full professor in the school counseling program at Liberty University in Virginia, where she has also served as both online chair and program director for the M.Ed. in School Counseling program. Dr. Schellenberg is actively involved in numerous professional counseling associations and she has held a variety of leadership roles including School Counseling Representative for the Virginia Association for Counselor Education and Supervision, Positions Statement Reviewer for the American School Counselor Association, Awards Reviewer for the Southern Association of Counselor Education and Supervision, and Research Chair for the Virginia School Counselor Association. Dr. Schellenberg received her training in school counseling from the College of William & Mary in Virginia. She was named outstanding graduate in her PhD program in counselor education and supervision program completed at Regent University. She is a licensed professional counselor, licensed professional counselor supervisor, and licensed PK-12 school counselor. She also holds the credentials of National Certified Counselor, National Certified School Counselor, Approved Clinical Supervisor, and Clinical Mental Health Counselor. Dr. Schellenberg is also an ASCA certified School Counseling Legal and Ethical Specialist and a Bully Prevention Specialist.

Dr. Schellenberg is well-published and presents at numerous conferences across the country on topics related to the contemporary practice of school counseling. With over a decade of experience as an elementary and secondary-school counselor, she has been recognized at the local and national levels for her contributions in education, counseling, and specifically school counseling and counselor education. Tenacity and strength of spirit helped Dr. Schellenberg to overcome adversity faced as a first-generation college student thereby serving as an inspiration to others who may be struggling to find their own versions of success.

# Introduction

*The School Counselor's Preparation and Professional Practice Desk Reference and Examination Study Guide* is a comprehensive text for school counselor preparation and a handy reference for practicing school counselors. It is also the only school counseling specialty study guide that provides potential examinees with one resource for all state-specific school counseling exams, NBPTS school counselor exam, NBPTS school counseling exam, and preparation program comprehensive school counseling exams, and the Praxis II school counselor exam, which is now used by the American School Counselor Association as a pathway to the ASCA Certified School Counselor (ACSC).

Although school counseling exams vary in length and format (e.g., multiple choice, short answer, essay, case simulation, recorded client–counselor interactions), knowledge gained by the discipline specific content of this resource is transferrable. The chapters of this text cover essential information, concepts, theories, approaches, and techniques for developing school counselor competency as defined by:

- The 2024 Council for Accreditation of Counseling and Related Educational Programs (CACREP, 2024) Standards (www.cacrep.org).
- The American School Counselor Association (ASCA, 2019b) School Counselor Competencies (www.schoolcounselor.org).
- The National Board for Professional Teaching Standards (NBPTS, 2012) for School Counseling (www.nbpts.org).
- Council for the Accreditation of Educator Preparation (CAEP, 2022) (www.caepnet.org).

# Using this resource

Information presented in this resource depicts empirically supported strategies for enhancing learning and recall. This resource presents information in tables, lists, clusters, and charts for mapping main ideas, which isolates key points, thereby promoting movement from short-term memory to long-term memory thus aiding in the recall of information. Case illustrations are presented throughout the chapters to reinforce critical constructs. Appropriate responses and explanations for case conceptualizations are provided at the end of each chapter. Chapter knowledge checks also include simulations and guided reflection to reinforce text content in a repetitive manner to aid in memorization.

A glossary of terms supplement the material and serve as an additional learning tool. Paired with the exhaustive list of acronyms presented in the Appendix, this resource will help you to fully grasp the language of the profession. Throughout the chapters, you will view case illustrations and ASCA position statements as they relate to the practice of school counseling. Guided reflection sections at the end of each chapter are grounded in Bloom's taxonomy to test you on a variety of levels: knowledge, comprehension, application, analysis, synthesis, and evaluation. You are encouraged to make use of this section to fully reflect on the material presented in each chapter.

In addition to end of chapter simulations, a full-length practice exam that includes nine simulations serve as a cumulative knowledge check. All simulations consist of three components: scenario, information gathering (IG), and decision making (DM). Each section of the scenarios require a combination of IG and DM responses. Learning is improved when you understand where your thinking may have gone astray. For this reason, all simulations are followed by the correct responses that include explanations as to why responses are deemed correct or incorrect.

My best advice is to revisit each simulation until perfect scores are achieved and to complete each item of the guided reflection sections until you have nailed it! Remember, writing and rewriting helps to commit information to memory.

# Tips for test-taker triumph

Without a doubt, *making the grade* on school counselor exams for licensure and credentialing are important milestones in your career.

Although the enormity of the information needed to prepare for these exams can be overwhelming, please take a deep breath and try to keep in mind that you have already been exposed to most if not all of this information as a part of your school counselor education preparation program courses and clinical experiences. There are, nonetheless, a few tips I can share that may boost your score.

*Repetition is key to retention and lasting learning.* For this reason, consider designing a timeline that allows you to control your study schedule. When it comes to control, you may now bow to the Queen! Both a vice and a virtue, I can micromanage a minute, squeezing every ounce of life out of time. Try breaking up the information into manageable segments and pacing study sessions. Consider mastering one segment before moving on to the next, which will allow the information to move from short-term memory to long-term memory.

*Association has been linked to successful testing outcomes.* Consider associating new information with familiar or easily remembered information. My favorite is using mnemonic acronyms. This is exemplified in Lazarus' assessment strategy, described later in this text, known as BASIC ID (*B*ehavior, *A*ffect, *S*ensation, *I*magery, *C*ognition, *I*nterpersonal, *D*rugs/Biological). Concept mapping and cognitive mapping promotes learning and recall by connecting pieces of information and illustrating relationships with mental visualization.

*Performance improves with a comfortable learning environment.* Studying is just not a part of cultural or intellectual DNA for some of us. However, since a major in channel surfing was not an option, there are still things you can do to reduce study pain. Pairing study time with more desirable activities and studying in an environment that you find personally motivating can make all the difference. For example, you may wish to study in your favorite room by the calming glow of a scented candle that clears your head and gets those cognitive juices flowing while wearing your favorite woolly socks and those sweatpants you've rescued from the trash so many times. Or, if quietude is not for you, music has been found to enhance mood and cognitive abilities. Yep, *Dougie* if you want to! Those delighted synapses will sing harmoniously while those neurons fire at a rate of a million dancing Umpa-Lumpas!

*Performance improves with nutrition.* Shamelessly plate up a scrumptious gallery of snacks to nibble on while enduring the permeation of knowledge. Oh, and by the way, stock up on blueberries and caffeine to boost memory. Also, cruciferous veggies (e.g., cabbage, carrots, broccoli,

Brussel sprouts, cauliflower, kale) improve cognitive functioning and memory, but they come with a warning! Although these super-veggies maximize brain power, in concentration they can induce weaponized gas—*buon appetito!*

*Studying with peeps (not the marshmallow kind) can help.* If you have peeps in your social or academic circle who are willing to help, have them quiz you. Make flash cards using the glossary and acronyms in this text, and have your peeps turn chapter titles and subtitles into questions—voilà!

*Focus on applying knowledge and skills.* The square root of Pi is one of the most familiar and culturally significant of all constants that many have devoted countless hours to memorizing. However, the concepts and information related to school counseling are rarely, if ever, constant. School counseling exams seek to apply rather than recite, so while you may need to recall specific models, theories, and techniques, and how those are applied in a specific case for a particular student at a certain grade/developmental level. Oh, by the way, for those of you with inquiring minds—the square root of Pi (3.14) is roughly 1.7725.

*Apply Occam's razor when choosing the best response in the absence of certainty.* One of the biggest challenges for test takers is following directions—imagine that! I believe Freud would agree that in our unconscious attempt to control the test-taking environment, we tend to distort the truth of the written word. Selecting the "single best response" becomes "what does the author want?" Do avoid this pitfall, take a minute to be sure that we have fully read and understood the exam item. Then, we must think to either select a "best" response, or create a response, based on school counseling standards, best practices, ethics, law, culture, school counselor roles and functions, and the scope of practice within the school setting. Too often we tend to over-analyze exam items making them more complex than needed. So, consider the logic of Occam's razor, or as it is also called, the law of parsimony. In the humblest terms, Occam's razor contends that the simplest explanation is preferable to the more complex in a given context.

*Context really is everything.* Like other counseling specialties, school counselors act in the best interest of their clients. In doing so, are there other relevant individuals or agencies (e.g., parent, child protective services, community counselors) whose involvement may be needed or beneficial when counseling specific minors in a specific situation? What ethical and legal issues need to be considered? What cultural issues need to be considered? What developmental issues need to be considered? Provide responses that are helpful, thorough, and relevant to the specific case (i.e., context) presented at that given time in treatment—no more, no less. If you err, err on the side of less is more.

*Take the anxiety out of timed exams.* Even short-term anxiety impedes recall and cognitive functioning. Allow yourself two to three minutes to stop and do some deep breathing exercises and muscle relaxation techniques before and during the exam. There will be some items that you will blow right through, while others will leave you wide-eyed, sorting through all the possibilities. Do not allow yourself to become overly concerned with the time. In my many experiences with counseling and school counseling exams, I have found the time allotted to be ample, and I am a characteristically slow test taker. Stay focused and just allow yourself to recognize when you are spending an inordinate amount of time on one particular item. Recognize when you're chewing twine and losing your vertical hold *as they say*, which may mean viewing that particular item as expendable. You are not expected to make a perfect score. There is room for error. It is likely that you will not know the answer to every question; and, not every correct response will jump out at you. Like my grandaddy use to say—*you can't always get socks on the rooster!*

*Think like a winner.* Relaxing and remaining positive about your ability to successfully complete the school counseling exam positively impacts your performance. This has been empirically validated! So, should you find yourself loading the wrong wagon, Aaron Beck might say (and I would concur), *use affirming self-talk.* I have been known to hold entire conversations with myself—out loud. However, I would encourage an internal dialogue while in public so as to avoid a clinical enthusiast pegging you as schizophrenic. In my case that ship has sailed, but there's still hope for you! Also, consider what you will gain as a result of passing the exam, like earning your degree, adding a certification to your credentials, and/or becoming a practicing school counselor. Consider the inspirational words of Dr. Seuss—*oh, the places you'll go! (and the students you'll help!).*

*Make use of imagery.* Imagery is a powerful motivator. It can have you charging at hell with a bucket of ice water! So, just sit back for a few seconds and imagine yourself putting those hard-working little fingers on that license—like touching the Shroud of Turin.

*Both triumph and defeat reside within each of us. Triumph prevails with hard work, perseverance, and a belief in our ability to be victorious. Now, go carpe that diem!*

# Chapter 1
# Foundations of school counseling

Some believe that even when we are aware of the past, we are doomed to repeat it; it is part of living. Perhaps this is so; I'm no philosopher. True or not, logic dictates that by knowing the mistakes of the past, we are better equipped to avoid those mistakes in the present and into the future. Based on this logic, it is important to become familiar with the profession's roots, milestones, trends, and current and future direction.

## The first hundred years

The profession of school counseling has been largely shaped by its multidisciplinary heritage that encompasses both education and counseling. With one foot planted in each applied field, school counseling has slowly, but at times not so steadily, morphed into a profession unique it its own right.

School counseling began as a vocational and moral curriculum developed by Jesse Davis, a high-school principal, in 1907. A year later, Frank Parsons, an engineer, university professor, public school teacher, lawyer, author, and social activist, a true *jack of all trade's* kind of guy, established the Vocation Bureau. Interested in helping students transition from school to work, Parsons' work paved the way for the trait and factor theory of career development and earned him the title of "father of vocational guidance."

DOI: 10.4324/9781032634500-1

In the 1920s and 1930s, guidance in the schools grew and became recognized as an area of specialty using a trait and factor model for identifying vocational direction. Together, the progressive education and mental health movements gave rise to vocational guidance and counseling. In the 1940s, Carl Rogers' focus on a nonmedical model for individual counseling resulted in individual counseling in high schools as a primary function of guidance.

In 1952, the American Personnel and Guidance Association (APGA) was established. The work of APGA was grounded in the philosophies of Carl Rogers (1961, 1969) well into the 1960s. The APGA created two divisions: the American School Counselor Association (ASCA) and the Association for Counselor Education and Supervision (ACES). These divisions provide leadership and promote *standards* for training programs and school counseling practices.

In 1957, Soviet satellite Sputnik took a 98-minute celestial stroll around the earth, catapulting our astounded nation into the space age. The United States, perceiving the launch of Sputnik as a display of educational, technical, and political superiority, passed the National Defense Education Act. This legislation was the steroid that instantly pumped up the muscles of the school counseling profession. Funds were made available to create and enhance existing guidance counseling training programs and to hire more *guidance counselors* (as we were called) to provide career guidance and to identify students with a propensity toward the disciplines of science and math. To meet the volumes of post–World War II baby boomers, hiring more guidance counselors turned into an extreme sports version of recruitment and training. We were on our way; and, like Sputnik, our elliptical path was uncertain as we explored, probed, and sometimes wobbled through a mysterious universe.

Comprehensive developmental school *guidance* programs began to emerge to meet the needs of K–12 students in the 1960s and 1970s. Developmental guidance became a global phenomenon, and, in 1985, the APGA changed its name to the American Association for Counseling and Development (AACD).

The impetus behind the shift in paradigm toward a more holistic focus on student development was prompted by an alarming treatise published in 1987 by the AACD, called *School Counseling: A Profession at Risk*. The undeniable realities about a profession that was viewed as nice but not necessary by important stakeholders, incited immediate and unremitting action on the part of concerned school counselor educators and practitioners.

A few years later, with refocused fortitude, the AACD changed its name to the American Counseling Association (ACA). ASCA, taking paramedic responsibility for the resuscitation of a dying profession, created monographs and position statements, revised program philosophies, clarified roles, and provided a series of recommendations to include school counselors as key players in educational reform. ASCA adopted a National Model (ASCA 2019a) and changed the title of *guidance counselor* to *professional school counselor* to define renewed roles and practices more appropriately. Again, in 2016, ASCA official changed our title to *school counselor*.

Over the past decade, there appears to be a slant by ASCA back toward the profession's guidance roots, embracing our role of educator over counselor and re-engaging our emphasis on college and career readiness. The contemporary roles and practices of the school counselor extend beyond the limited functions rooted in vocational guidance. How can a student learn and focus on learning and preparing for post K-12 years, in the face of personal, social, and/or emotional issues? Continuing to recognize a systemic approach to the *holistic* development of all students necessitates the exercising of our counselor role. We are first and foremost counselors in a school setting and sometimes the only counselor students may ever see in their lifetime.

## ASCA and the national model

ASCA is a division of the ACA with a membership of approximately 43,000 school counseling professionals. The ACA is the largest professional counseling association in existence. ASCA is the national *professional association* specifically designed for school counselors and the practice of school counseling. ASCA provides professional development, leadership, advocacy, research, publications, and resources to school counselor educators, preservice school counselors, and school counseling practitioners.

The ASCA National Model (ASCA, 2019a) is recognized by CACREP, CAEP, and the Department of Education as a framework from which to establish accountable, comprehensive, standards-based, developmental school counseling programs that align with academic achievement missions and emphasize systems-focused service delivery as an integral part of the total education program. Due to the overwhelming support backing ASCA, some schools seek to align their school counseling programs with the ASCA National Model in order to become a Recognized ASCA Model Program (RAMP). The ASCA National Model Implementation Guide (2022b) discusses how to achieve RAMP status and provides tools toward this end. ASCA continues to grow and have an epic impact on the profession. In 2019, ASCA created standards for school counselor preparation programs discussed in greater detail below. As the only recognized national comprehensive developmental school counseling program (CDSCP) model that defines our profession, the ASCA National Model is covered in greater detail in Chapter 2 of this text.

## The transforming school counseling initiative

In 1997, the Education Trust with the support of ASCA, ACES, and the ACA introduced the *Transforming School Counseling Initiative* (TSCI). TSCI (Education Trust, 1997) was based on the belief that the prevailing and historically predominant individual- and mental health–focused model failed to align school counseling with the mission of schools and demonstrate an impact on academic achievement. TSCI balked at what they believed to be an outdated model responsible for the exclusion of school counselors from educational reform agendas. TSCI further contended that the model's ambiguous focus on academic achievement gave rise to the misconception that school counseling is an ancillary service in schools.

TSCI, seeking to replace the traditional individual- and mental health–focused paradigm, introduced a new vision for school counseling that emphasizes the importance of school counseling *leadership* and support for a *systems-focused* and *academic-focused* paradigm. TSCI's *new vision school counseling* reflects the school counselor's dual roles of educator and counselor and aligns school counseling more closely with the academic mission of schools while emphasizing the need for counseling in K-12 schools.

Changing the paradigm from mental health–focused to academic-focused and individual-focused to systems-focused was a bold move that positioned many within the profession nose-to-nose in opposition. For devout traditionalists and others who are just not hardwired to change, skepticism hit like a ballistic missile, creating an explosive divide. Nonetheless, as Julius Caesar declared to his army, *alea iacta est—the die is cast*.

TSCI, the brave scout, trudged forward blazing a trail so that the next era of school counselors could find their way in an uninhabited new frontier. Partnering with Metropolitan Life Insurance Company (MetLife) to fund the development of the NSCTI and the NCTSC, TSCI developed and distributed four modules to bridge previous thinking with new ways of conceptualizing the profession.

The modules describe how school counselors can contribute to high academic achievement and obtain educational equity for all students through both systemic and individual leadership, advocacy, and collaboration. Toward this end, ASCA, the Council for Accreditation of Counseling and Related Educational Programs (CACREP), and the TSCI emphasized the importance of identifying and addressing systemic inequities using data, accountable practices, technological competence, and cultural sensitivity by promoting the tenets of *social justice* (Education Trust, 1997), to be discussed in Chapter 5. Some are still chafing against what has now become the contemporary practice of school counseling. Alas, the dinosaurs that continue to practice from what has become a Jurassic model are slowly nearing extinction. Eventually, those dinosaurs will only reemerge as relics in an archeological dig into the proud beginnings of our profession.

We have traveled a great distance and gained much ground over the past century, overpowering the challenges and enduring periods of uncertainty. It says much about the tenacity of the gallant stakeholders of our profession when you consider that we have done more than merely survive but emerge stronger and with the vigor of ten Grinches plus two and a renewed vision for every Who in Whoville—the tall and the small.

## Professional identity: roles, preparation, unification, and certification

School counselors are a special breed. In the past, I recall a conversation I had with a counselor educator. She referred to one of her school counselors in training as possessing the inherent qualities of Saint Francis of Assisi. Specifically, that the student did not so much seek to be consoled as to console or to be understood as to understand. I have seen the same in so many school counselors and school counselors in training whose hearts of service and passion for the profession are marked with an altruistic drive to make a difference in the world. You are likely reading this book at this very moment in time.

School counselors absolutely do make a difference in the world and the lives of children and adolescents by integrating their primary role of *counselor* with the role of *educator*. School counselors live by a succinct guiding philosophy that holds the healthy mind as an educable mind. And, we are best ready to serve when we understand that a healthy mind is not necessarily a mind that is free from physical, mental, emotional, social, and environmental distress.

Operating from this philosophy, school counselors recognize that we all have baggage that we haul around—some heavier than others. In other words, we are all merely a rubber band snap away from complete madness. Okay, so I am exaggerating just a bit. The point is we cannot ignore academic needs in order to only address the baggage. School counselors make every effort to meet all needs simultaneously. Ignoring educational needs in the presence of other issues is detrimental to the student's academic success and perpetuates gaps in achievement. School counselors are called to meet the academic and the personal, social, and emotional needs of students while also preparing them for postsecondary success.

School counselors are trained to move fluidly between the two roles of educator and counselor for optimal and total student development. Meeting the total development of students often requires that school counselors engage in a host of shared functions including *teaming*, consulting, informing, collaborating, leading, advocating, programming, assessing, referring, teaching, evaluating, coordinating, and reporting. Oh, yes, and counseling!

## School counselor as educator

Education and training that distinguishes the school counselor as an *educator* includes PK-12 program design and delivery, classroom instruction, classroom management, theories of learning, standardized academic testing, assessment and interpretation of scores, use of technology for enhanced learning, behavioral theory, disability and exceptional behavior, identifying student competencies and ways to achieve academic competency, identifying and removing barriers to academic achievement, and developing effective learning environments. School counselors work closely with stakeholders, namely teachers, to provide optimal services to students and parents and to accomplish the academic mission of schools.

Because fulfillment of the school counselor's role of educator involves instruction, a few states still require a teaching background or what each of those states deem equivalent in order to become a school counselor. Decades of research have examined the question of whether or not school counselors should be teachers prior to becoming school counselors. In summary, many studies indicate that school administrators, school counselor supervisors, and practicing school counselors do not find previous teaching experience necessary in order to be an effective school counselor (Hobson, Fox & Swickert, 2000; Moyer & Yu, 2012). Research identifies distinct differences between the functions of teachers and school counselors, which necessitates that teachers unlearn previously held dispositions in order to acquire new dispositions that are in some ways contrary in nature to that of the school counselor. For example, the teacher's role is to judge, discipline, and manage. The role of teacher is subject-focused and involves didactic teaching with little or no concern for confidentiality in teacher–student interactions. The school counselor's role is to be nonjudgmental in nature. And, school counselors *do not* discipline students. The role of the school counselor is facilitative and change-focused and ensures confidentiality in school counselor–student interactions. On a personal note, although teachers and school counselors are apples and oranges, I have had the pleasure of working with many school counselors who have been teachers and who have not been teachers prior to becoming school counselors. I have not observed any correlation with regard to the quality of a school counselor and teaching background or absence of teaching background.

## School counselor as counselor

In our role of counselor, the school counselor provides classroom instruction to all students that is preventative in nature and addresses career and academic development and the personal, social, and emotional well-being of students. As mental health professionals, school counselors meet with students individually and in small groups to provide direct responsive services that promote well-being and remove barriers to academic achievement and holistic development. School counselors also work with students to provide appraisal and advising services that promote academic achievement and college and career readiness.

School counselors work with teachers to modify the classroom climate for optimal learning and to develop academic contracts and schedules of *reinforcement*. School counselors consult and collaborate with stakeholders to provide support, information, and referral sources as needed and to promote equity and access to school programs, activities, and a rigorous curriculum.

School counselors understand that the relationship between academic success and personal well-being is a door that swings both ways. As such, school counselors encourage students faced with personal, social, and emotional issues and physical challenges to believe in their ability to change, grow, and overcome challenges in order to achieve academically. School counselors encourage impaired students to embrace academics as an avenue to a promising, self-directed future. Academic-focused channeling can be therapeutic and motivational and it can build competencies, self-esteem, and psychological *resilience*—epitomizing the specialty of school counseling.

Challenges can be our greatest asset, pushing us onward and lifting us up to achieve at higher levels. For this reason, school counselors are dogmatic in their efforts to balance their roles of counselor and educator for optimal student development. While priority is given to the significant role of counselor, counselors embrace and fulfill their dual roles of counselor and educator. After all, this is the role that sets counseling in the schools apart from other counseling specialties and defines our profession.

## School counselor preparation programs

As a spice-of-life consequence to our multidisciplinary dual roles, school counselors generally take a variety of counseling, school counseling, and education courses. As such, preparation programs embrace the school counselor's dual roles of both counselor and educator. This resource addresses the CACREP, CAEP, and ASCA School Counselor Specialty Standards described below.

*CACREP standards for the specialized practice area of school counseling*
Committed to the advancement of counselor education and supervision, ACES began establishing accreditation standards for counseling programs. ACES indissoluble efforts to standardize counselor education and training programs laid the foundation for its successor, CACREP formed in 1978 to standardize training. CACREP began functioning as the primary accrediting body for counselor education programs, which included school

counseling but under the prevailing mental-health focused pedagogy of the time. In 2001, CACREP published standards that reflected the new vision's academic- and systems-focused paradigm. Since that time, CACREP has continued to revise the standards to reflect the academic- and systems-focused school-counseling paradigm. CACREP standards place a strong emphasis on the professional identity of *counselor* and on *quality* underscoring the importance of measuring student learning outcomes as a means toward this end.

CACREP provides counselor education programs with unified, minimal competencies for the optimal preparation of school counselors at the graduate level. In addition to the 19 specific school counseling specialty competencies, CACREP (2024) requires that pre-service school counselors demonstrate knowledge in eight core areas of counselor education, which are: 1) professional counseling, orientation, and ethical practice, 2) social and cultural identities and experiences, 3) lifespan development, 4) career development, 5) counseling practice and relationships, 6) group counseling and group work, 7) assessment and diagnostic processes, and 8) research and program evaluation. Both CACREP (2024) core and specialty standards are covered in the content of the text.

CACREP has become a university magnet with schools across the country seeking its stamp of approval. Indeed, if counselor education was a religion, CACREP would be their Bible, with counselor educators striving to live by the word. The CACREP Standards can be accessed at:

https://www.cacrep.org/wp-content/uploads/2023/06/2024-Standards-Combined-Version-6.27.23.pdf.

## CAEP standards for educator preparation

While CACREP is considered to be the primary accrediting body for counselor education programs, CAEP is considered to be the primary accrediting body for teacher education/educators. Many school counseling programs are accredited by both CAEP and CACREP. Some are not accredited at all—*buyer beware*! CAEP provides standards that address the knowledge, skills, and professional dispositions required of teachers, administrators, and other school personnel (e.g., school counselors). School counseling falls under CAEP's seven advanced level standards as an advanced licensure program, which are: 1) content and pedagogical knowledge, 2) clinical partnerships and practice, 3) candidate quality and selectivity, 4) satisfaction with preparation, 5) quality assurance system and continuous improvement, 6) fiscal and administrative capacity, and 7) record of compliance with Title IV of the Higher Education Act (if seeking access to Title IV funds). The CAEP Standards can be accessed at: http://caepnet.org/standards/2022-adv.

*ASCA standards for school counselor preparation programs*

The newest kid on the block entered the school counselor preparation program neighborhood in 2019, creating the ASCA Standards for School Counselor Preparation Programs (2019c). These standards have been accepted by CAEP and the Association for Advancing Quality in Educator Preparation (AAQEP). Twenty-two competencies are covered under the following seven standards: 1) foundational knowledge, 2) core theories and concepts, 3) instructional and school counseling interventions, 4) student learning outcomes, 5) designing, implementing, and evaluation comprehensive school counseling programs, 6) professional practice, and 7) ethical practice. The ASCA Standards for School Counselor Preparation Programs can be viewed at: https://www.schoolcounselor.org/getmedia/573d7c2c-1622-4d25-a5ac-ac74d2e614ca/ASCA-Standards-for-School-Counselor-Preparation-Programs.pdf.

---

### ASCA Position on The School Counselor and School Counseling Preparation Programs

School counselors are best prepared through master's-level and doctoral-level programs that align with the philosophy and vision of the ASCA National Model (2019a), the ASCA School Counselor Professional Standards & Competencies (2019b), the ASCA Standards for School Counseling Program Preparation (2019c), the ASCA Student Standards: Mindsets & Behaviors for Student Success (2021) and the ASCA Ethical Standards for School Counselors (2022a). These programs emphasize training in the implementation of a school counseling program that enhances student achievement and success.

*Position statement adopted 2008; revised 2014, 2020*

# Licensure and advanced voluntary school counseling credentials

Certification is the recognition that a professional has met specific qualifications to practice in a particular profession. Advanced voluntary certifications distinguish professionals as dedicated to the continued pursuit of competence. School counselors are encouraged to secure advanced voluntary credentials and actively seek out opportunities for professional development, embracing a continuous state of learning in order to provide optimal counseling services and to strengthen professional identity.

---

*ASCA Position on The School Counselor and Credentialing and Licensure*

Effective school counselor credentialing or licensing laws include a definition of the profession, minimum qualifications for entry into the profession and requirements for continuing professional development. All state education certification or licensure agencies are encouraged to adopt the ASCA School Counselor Professional Standards & Competencies for school counselor credentialing or licensing.

*Position statement adopted 1990; revised 1993, 1999, 2003, 2009, 2015, 2021*

---

The National Board for Certified Counselors (NBCC) is the national professional certification board that monitors the certification system for counselors and maintains a national register of certified counselors. NBCC examinations are used by more than 48 states to credential professional counselors on a state level. NBCC was created by the ACA. Both organizations work closely to advance the counseling profession and maintain high standards of excellence, including providing counselors with ethical codes for guiding professional practices.

NBCC administers the Uncle Sam of national general counseling credentials—the National Certified Counselor (NCC) credential. Students who are graduating from CACREP accredited programs are afforded the opportunity to waive the experience requirement and take the National Counselor Exam (NCE) that, when passed, results in acquiring the NCC credential.

NBCC also administers several national specialty counseling credentials such as the National Certified School Counselor (NCSC) credential, first awarded in 1991. School counselors who hold the NCSC have a master's degree and have demonstrated competence in areas specific to contemporary school counseling by way of training and experience. The NCC credential is a prerequisite to the NCSC credential. School counselors who earn the NCSC demonstrate a high level of professional commitment that goes beyond required state licensing. The NCSC credential is a result of a collaborative effort with professional counseling associations, counselor educator accrediting bodies, and certification organizations in counseling and is governed by a board of counselors.

Holding the NCC and the NCSC and other advanced voluntary credentials serves to inspire both school and community confidence in the school counselor's clinical ability to meet the personal, social, and emotional needs of their children. This is particularly significant in a charged climate where the public's confidence in our educational system is already wavering if not waning. Parents are questioning not only the ability of public schools to successfully educate their child, but the ability of public schools to identify and effectively intervene in situations with troubled students who threaten the safety of their progeny. NBCC certification requirements and benefits are outlined on their website at www.nbcc.org.

National Board for Professional Teaching Standards (NBPTS) also offers a national voluntary credential for school counselors (NBPTS, 2012). Like the NCSC credential, obtaining the national teacher board certification in school counseling demonstrates a high level of professional commitment that goes beyond required state licensing. Unlike the NCSC credential, the national teacher board certification does not require a master's degree, nor is it a collaborative effort with professional counseling associations, counselor education accreditation bodies, and/or certification organizations in counseling. The credential is governed by a board of primarily teachers.

## Ethical, legal, and professional considerations

Personal ethics are moral principles guiding an individual's behavior; codes of ethics and ethical behavior are values that guide an entity with which members of that entity are bound (Remley & Herlihy, 2019; Stone, 2022). Ethical codes for the counseling profession steer the professional practices of counselors to ensure the safety and well-being of clients. Counselors' ethical standards, regardless of specialty, are grounded in five ethical principles (autonomy, nonmaleficence, beneficence, justice, and fidelity), which are described as follows (Kitchener, 1984):

> *Autonomy* refers to the notion of independence, which encourages the client to exercise freedom of choice and behavior when those actions do not infringe upon the rights and beliefs of others. Autonomy is promoted versus dependence upon the counselor.
> *Nonmaleficence* is often defined as "above all do no harm" and viewed by many as the most critical of the five ethical principles. In brief, this concept promotes the idea of avoiding any actions or intentions that may place the client at risk for harm.
> *Beneficence* refers the counselor's responsibility to *do good*. Counselors contribute to the well-being of clients.
> *Justice* should be conceptualized as treating others equally, but in relation to their individual differences. When treating clients differently in order to meet their unique needs, counselors operate from a sound rationale for such actions.
> *Fidelity* refers to the trusting nature of the therapeutic relationship built upon a demonstrated reliability and authenticity toward the client. Counselors promote fidelity by honoring commitments and obligations to clients.

School counselors follow the *ASCA Ethical Standards for School Counselors* (ASCA, 2022a), which are accessible at www.schoolcounselor.org. There will likely be many times during the course of your life as a school counselor that you will encounter ethically laden situations that require tough decisions. Trust me, some will be real head scratchers and finger drummers. Fortunately, *Section F* of the *ASCA Ethical Standards for School Counselors* (ASCA, 2022a) include a decision-making model, while citing a few other models for consideration as well. One of those models is known as the STEPS (**S**olutions **T**o **E**thical **P**roblems in **S**chools) model (Stone, 2022), which is widely used in the schools. The model consists of nine steps that include applying Kitchners' moral principles noted earlier. The STEPS model is detailed in the textbook *School Counseling Principles, Ethics, and Law* (Stone, 2022).

> **THE SAME OR DIFFERENT?**
>
> The school counselor meets with a fifth-grade Caucasian female student, Rita, for issues related to social skills. The school counselor meets with a different fifth-grade student, Regina, an African American female, for issues related to social skills. The school counselor uses a different counseling approach for each student, although both are experiencing issues with social skills. The school counselor is applying which ethical principle in these two students' cases?
>
> a. Fidelity.
> b. Nonmaleficence.
> c. Justice.
> d. Autonomy.
> e. Beneficence.

The importance of a school counselor's knowledge of the laws, regulations, and policies related to counseling minors in the schools in order to protect student rights resonates throughout the ASCA *Ethical Standards for School Counselors* (ASCA, 2022a). Protecting the rights of children while those children are in our care during the school day is also emphasized in the common-law doctrine *in loco parentis*.

In addition to ethical guidelines, school counselors must be assiduously mindful of the legal issues related to the population for whom they are providing services—minors. Minors are typically those students who are under the age of 18. While school counselors follow fairly consistent national ethical standards created by our governing bodies and professional associations, a large variation exists in the law and policy from state to state, city to city, and school division to school division. Such differences necessitate that school counselors become familiar with legislation and policy as it pertains to counseling minors in their state and locality. There are times when division policy, ethical standards, and legal mandates conflict. It is necessary for school counselors to find a way to balance ethical, legal, and school policy requirements which can feel like walking a greased tightrope.

Although school counselors rely on school division policy to guide practices, school division policy does not substitute for knowing and abiding by the law and ethical guidelines for the profession. In cases where ethical guidelines and the law conflict with school division policy, school counselors should advocate for change. The simple fact is that in some cases school administrators are unaware and unfamiliar with the law as it pertains to school counseling and that which may place school counselors in an unethical situation. And, since principals are vicariously responsible for the actions or inactions of school counselors in their building, principals, more often than not, appreciate your knowing your stuff, which keeps him or her from stumbling into bad lighting. Roger that?!

## Confidentiality

Confidentiality, the hallmark of a trusting therapeutic relationship, is one of the most common areas of controversy. Perhaps, this is why the *Confidentiality* section in the *ASCA Ethical Standards for School Counselors* (ASCA, 2022a) is as long as the Mississippi River. Confidentiality is a concept grounded in ethical principles that refer to a client's right to privacy in the practice of counseling. A related construct, privileged communication, is a legal term that refers to the requirement to protect the privacy between counselor and student (Stone, 2022).

In many states, the school counselor and student relationship is not recognized by law as privileged. School counselors need to know if the state in which they practice recognizes privileged communication between the school counselor and student and under what circumstances. Perhaps privilege exists, but only with specific school counselors in the school (e.g., student assistance counselors).

### ASCA Position on The School Counselor and Confidentiality

School counselors recognize their primary obligation regarding confidentiality is to the student but balance that obligation with an understanding of the family or guardians' legal and inherent rights to be the guiding voice in their children's lives.

*Position statement adopted 1974; reviewed and reaffirmed 1980; revised 1986, 1993, 1999, 2002, 2008, 2014, 2018*

School counselors are ethically and morally obligated to maintain a minor client's confidentiality except in circumstances of harm to self/others, abuse, court order, or when the client has provided written permission to share his or her disclosures made during counseling sessions. Keep in mind that harm to others can include property. Also, there are policies in some school divisions that require school counselors to breach confidentiality such as engaging in sexual activity, alcohol use, or in cases of student pregnancy. Know your school division's policy.

When counseling minors, the law's perspective is often that counselors are obligated to the parents or guardians of their minor clients with regard to the disclosure of information shared in a counseling session. In short, school counselors have an ethical obligation to the minor client and a legal obligation to the parent or guardian.

On the other hand, if privileged communication exists between school counselors and minors in the state in which the school counselor is practicing, then it is illegal for the school counselor to disclose counseling session information without the consent of the minor student in the absence of clear and imminent danger. Also, some states have minor consent laws in place that allow minors, deemed *emancipated minors*, to enter into counseling relationships and make other decisions without the consent of an adult, which affords those students privileged communication (Remley & Herlihy, 2019; Stone, 2022).

### ORDER IN THE COURT, HERE COMES THE JUDGE

A school counselor has been subpoenaed to appear in court in a state that does not recognize privileged communication between school counselors and students. The school counselor expresses her reluctance to answer the attorneys' questions regarding the case of Donna, the 15-year-old student that the school counselor has been providing individual counseling services to for the past four weeks. When the judge requires that the school counselor answer the attorneys' questions, the school counselor responds by attempting to explain the importance of maintaining counselor–student confidentiality and requesting a withdrawal of the requirement. What are the ethical implications in this case? Are the school counselor's actions in accordance with professional ethical standards?

When confidentiality must be breached, remind the student of the conversation held during the initial session pertaining to the limits of confidentiality. Then, explain the reasoning behind the need to break confidentiality. If it is a situation where the parent needs to be contacted, empower the student to be the one to make contact with the parent in your presence. Another option is to offer to be the one to initiate the communication with the parent in the student's presence. At a minimum, let the student know that you will be contacting the parent as legally/ethically required and discussed in the initial counseling session.

If the issue requires that contact be made to social services or the local police, the school counselor should make contact and keep the student involved as much as possible or prudent. The school counselor should continue to maintain sensitive and open communication with the student throughout the process. Whether or not it is appropriate or practical to allow the student to be present during mandatory contacts should be considered on a case-by-case basis.

In situations where parent involvement may be helpful to the student's progress, but is not ethically or legally required, the student's consent should be secured. In these cases, it is recommended that school counselors discuss with the student the reasons why parent involvement is desired and let the student know what information will be shared. The school counselor might encourage the student to be present to hear what is shared and encourage the student to speak freely during the communications. It has been this school counselor's experience that even the most reluctant students come around when they understand the school counselor's reasoning and trust that the school counselor will remain involved and supportive throughout the process.

In the secret-keeping business, a primary and legitimate concern for parents is that counseling sessions will not be kept private. Parents express concern that teachers, staff, and other parents or students, may overhear or somehow find out about personal information shared in the counseling session, which may result in harm or embarrassment for their child and/or their family. Having an open discussion with the parent and the student about confidentiality and its limits at the time that counseling is initiated is paramount to helping the parent and student to understand the nature of counseling. I would also advise school counselors to post limits to confidentiality in their offices, in the student-parent handbook, and on parent-teacher counseling referral forms.

If the student will be participating in group counseling, school counselors need to let students and parents know that confidentiality cannot be guaranteed in group counseling sessions. School counselors should also let the parent and student know that there may be times when sharing information with faculty and school administrators is deemed in the best interest of the student in order to provide the student with additional support and allies during times of stress. During these times, permission will be sought from the student, and perhaps the parent as well depending upon the developmental level of the student.

The *ASCA Ethical Standards for School Counselors* (ASCA, 2022a) encourages school counselors to recognize the powerful potential alliance between teachers and students in supporting students in times of stress, while filtering confidential information so as to provide these allies only with what they "need to know" in order to advantage the student. Seek *consultation* with other school counseling professionals when in doubt as to what constitutes a need-to-know basis.

Filtered confidential information is considered that which is true and accurate and shared in a sensitive and caring manner (Remley & Herlihy, 2019; Stone, 2022). Information shared that might be construed as an invasion of privacy or defamation of character may place the school counselor in a legally troubling situation that transcends the lunacy of just another day.

> **ALLIANCES**
>
> Robert is an elementary school counselor. In an attempt to establish a partnership with parents toward the well-being of their children and to ease parents' concerns about their child having sessions with the school counselor, Robert announces during a PTA meeting that he is happy to share information discussed during counseling sessions with their children. Robert emphasizes the importance of sharing information and working together in order to help students to be successful. What do you think about Robert's approach to promoting positive school counselor–parent relations? Are there ethical concerns to be considered here?

In cases of divorce, make every attempt to provide information to both parents that is objective and respectful unless, of course, explicitly prohibited by court order. The *ASCA Ethical Guidelines for School Counselors* (ASCA, 2022a) avows that in cases of divorce or separation, school counselors make a *good-faith effort* to keep both parents informed, while not engaging in the support of one parent/guardian over the over. For ten points—what is Switzerland?

In the case of guardians and noncustodial parents, school counselors generally provide them with information that the school counselor deems helpful to the student and family with the custodial parent's knowledge. The *ASCA Ethical Standards for School Counselors* (ASCA, 2022a) cautions school counselors with regard to recognizing the diverse rights of both custodial and noncustodial parents, who have vested interest in the well-being of the minor in the eyes of the law. With this said, however, school counselors are well advised to be aware of any restraining orders that may exist to ensure information is shared only with parents and guardians legally eligible to receive such information.

## Confidentiality of counseling-related electronic communication

When using technology for counseling and counseling-related communications, and for the transmission of student records, school counselors are careful to consult the ethical guidelines to ensure confidentiality is maintained. Parents and students often request that school counselors provide services via the Internet, e-mail, texting, or other forms of electronic communication. School counselors are in no way required to provide electronic counseling to students, parents, teachers, or other school personnel.

School counselors aflame with the desire to make use of the banquet of avant-garde (you may have to look that one up—got to keep you from falling asleep on me…) modalities of communication need to be aware of the school's and the school division's policy on this issue, as well as relevant ethical and legal standards of practice. Even those school counselors who are not intending to provide technologically-based counseling services should be aware of the legal and ethical implications involved.

Unintentional electronic counseling may occur disguised simply as e-mail. Do not fall for the old e-mail disguise! E-mail has been considered in legal cases to be an educational record and therefore subject to the proviso of the Family Educational Rights and Privacy Act (FERPA) of 1974, P.L. 93-380 (United States Department of Education, 2023). See what I mean about the infamous e-mail masquerade? Using technology to communicate with parents/students has advantages; but, bring your A-game!

School counselors should gain an understanding of FERPA, also known as the Buckley Amendment. It is important for school counselors to know how this legislation applies to student records and accessing school counseling case notes. FERPA's arm extends far and wide. It is a legal and ethical mandate to safeguard the rights of students and parents in relation to educational records (ASCA, 2022a).

FERPA is a federal law that applies to all schools that receive funds from the U.S. Department of Education. FERPA protects the privacy of student records and provides parents (or students over 18 and/or postsecondary school students) with rights pertaining to record inspection, correction, copying, and general consent before release. Requests must be made in writing. Schools will provide the parent or student with access to the record within 45 days of the date of the request.

Unless a parent specifically requests that a school not disclose directory information about the student, directory information may be disclosed. Directory information may be considered to be any of the following:

- Name.
- Address.
- Telephone number.
- Grade level.
- Sports activities.
- Weight and height of members of athletic teams.
- Enrollment status.
- E-mail.
- Date and place of birth.
- Photograph.
- Major field of study and degrees obtained.
- Previous schools attended and dates of attendance.
- Honors and awards.

While disclosing information that is not considered directory information requires parental consent, like all good rules there are exceptions to this one as well. Consent is not required by the parent to disclose information contained in a student's record under the following circumstances:

- Judicial order/subpoena.
- State law (local juvenile justice authority).
- School studies/audit/evaluation.
- School safety/health emergency.

- Student's financial aid advisor.
- School officials with legitimate educational interest.
- School transfer.

School counseling case notes are not part of the educational record. For this reason, case notes are not accessible under FERPA.

The *ASCA Ethical Standards for School Counselors* (ASCA, 2022a) emphasizes the need for school counselors to take extra precautions when using electronic communications to transmit student personal information. The Standards further encourage school counselors to advocate for encryption standards and data systems that allow for maximum protection of student information in accordance with federal and state laws.

*NBCC Code of Ethics* includes a section that provides detailed guidance related to counseling and technology as well as tele-mental health and social media (NBCC, 2023). *NBCC Code of Ethics* is accessible at https://www.nbcc.org/ethics.

In situations where sharing student information meets the need-to-know ethical guidelines noted previously, school counselors are mindful of the confidential nature of student information when using technology and electronic storage devices (e.g., CD, DVD, flash drives). In these cases, be sure that what is communicated is free of any identifying information (e.g., student name, social security number, student identification number, photograph) and that it is professional and aligned with the school counselor duties and responsibility to students and parents. A good rule of thumb is to only communicate electronically that which could be shared in a public forum. So—if the National Educational Inquirer intercepted it, there would be no story.

There are also times when the electronic transfer of student information may not be appropriate (e.g., sensitive, personal information that may be linkable to a particular student). In such cases, a plan needs to be developed for the sharing of confidential information between professionals (e.g., school counselor to personal counselor). The *ASCA Ethical Standards for School Counselors* (2022a) notes that school counselors should seek to convey highly sensitive information either by phone or in person.

## Harm to self or others

School counselors have a duty to protect and a duty to warn in cases of harm to self or others (or their property), respectively. This duty requires a breach in confidentiality. When a student names an identifiable other to which they have a plan to do harm, then the school counselor needs to warn the identified victim. This may require more than parent notification, but police officer involvement as well to be sure protection can be obtained for the intended victim.

School counselors have a duty to protect in cases where students threaten harm to self. In such cases, school counselors should assess for clear and imminent danger. Most school divisions have policy, guidelines, and forms to aid school counselors in making such assessments—know your school division's policy and review assessments and guiding forms used by the school counselors to be sure they accurately reflect current federal and state legislation. If it is believed that the student is at risk for self-harm, the proper authorities must be notified and the student should remain under adult supervision until the appropriate authorities arrive.

The ASCA *Ethical Standards for School Counselors* (ASCA, 2022a) emphasizes the importance of balancing student privacy and parental rights, but does not go into details that can be a gray area, for example, when a student threatens suicide. Because the student is a minor, the immediate reaction of some may be to contact the parent when a student threatens harm to self. In fact, this may be written in school division policy. However, this may not be the appropriate action in some cases.

### ASCA Position on The School Counselor and Suicide Prevention/Awareness

School counselors work to identify behavioral and social/emotional signs of suicide risk among their students and ensure prevention methods are in place. It is the school counselor's ethical and moral responsibility to report suspected suicide risk to legal guardians and the appropriate authorities. In acknowledging suspected suicide risk, school counselors exercise reasonable care to protect students from unforeseeable harm (ASCA, 2022).

*Position statement adopted 2018*

If the parent is implicated by the student as a factor for suicidal thoughts, the parent would not be the first contact. In fact, the school counselor may not contact the parent at all in such cases. School counselors would contact Child Protective Services (CPS), a division of Social Services. The CPS personnel would make contact with the parent at their discretion based on a more detailed investigation and discussion with the student. If parents are not implicated, they should be the first contact.

School counselors should provide parents with a list of resources that provide counseling services to children, adolescents, and families. In some states, if parents indicate in any way that they will not be seeking professional counseling for their child or adolescent who is at risk of suicide or other self-injurious behaviors (e.g., cutting), this is viewed as child neglect. In such cases, generally, CPS would be contacted immediately.

In some cases, school counselors may not deem particular information shared by a student as constituting harm to self or others. In such cases, and where law or policy is not in place, school counselors may decide not to disclose particular information to a parent (e.g., risky behaviors, drug and/or alcohol use, issues related to eating/diet, sexual activity) to avoid a possible negative impact on the counseling relationship. In these situations, school counselors are assuming responsibility for the student's safety and wellbeing. Should any harm come to the student as a result of withholding such information, school counselors may be held legally responsible for those inactions.

The reverse can also be true, in cases where the school counselor shares information with the parent or guardian that should not have been disclosed even in the absence of privileged communication and in the presence of clear and imminent danger. For example, if a student threatens to commit suicide and implicates their parent or guardian as a reason for their suicidal thoughts, disclosing this information to the parent could result in serious harm to the student at the hand of him or herself or an abusive parent. In this case, the school counselor may be found negligent and held liable if the law in the state in which they practice requires that school counselors contact CPS when parents are implicated—perhaps even in the absence of such law.

School counselors are strongly encouraged and supported by the *ASCA Ethical Standards for School Counselors* (ASCA, 2022a) to consult, consult, consult. Consultation that is in the *best interest of a student* to determine the appropriate best course of action. Generally, that consultation takes place with other division school counselors and/or division school counselor supervisors.

> **THOUGHTS OF SUICIDE**
>
> Patrick, a ninth grader, was referred to you by a teacher who said Patrick expressed suicidal intentions because he is having some personal and family issues. You talk to Patrick long enough to assess that he is at imminent risk of suicide. Understanding that Patrick is a minor, the school counselor contacts the student's parent(s) and prints a resource list of community mental health counselors to give to the parent. Is this the best course of action, ethically and legally, on behalf of this student?

## Child abuse and neglect

School counselors are mandated reporters of suspected child abuse and neglect in all 50 states with legislation imposing penalties on school counselors who do not report suspected child abuse or neglect with a given timeframe, which varies by state. Generally, school counselors must make verbal contact with appropriate authorities in cases of suspected child abuse or neglect within 24–72 hours. It is essential that school counselors be intimately familiar with child abuse and neglect reporting guidelines and timeframes for the state in which he or she practices so as to know the reporting window requirement and to understand, specifically, that which constitutes child abuse or neglect in accordance with your state's law. The federal *Child Abuse Prevention and Treatment Act* (CAPTA) defines *child abuse* and *child neglect* as

> any recent act or failure to act on the part of a parent or caregiver that results in death, serious physical or emotional harm, sexual abuse, or exploitation, or an act or failure to act that presents an imminent risk of serious harm.
> 
> Child Welfare Information Gateway, 2023

## ASCA Position on The School Counselor and Child Abuse and Neglect Prevention

It is the school counselor's legal, ethical and moral responsibility to report suspected cases of child abuse and neglect to the proper authorities. School counselors work to identify the behavioral, academic and social/emotional impact of abuse and neglect on students and ensure the necessary supports for students are in place.

*Position statement adopted 1981; revised 1985, 1993, 1999, 2003, 2015, 2021*

---

Some states still allow corporal punishment in schools. Not having been accused of being a woman of few words, let me say with the greatest conviction—corporal punishment in our schools pollutes the very air that we seek to purify. ASCA, too, takes a strong stand, supporting the extermination of corporal punishment in schools. School counselors remain diligent in reporting suspected child abuse that may be occurring *within* and outside of the school—not excluding those schools that still practice this archaic form of discipline that is purposeful in its intent to humiliate and inflict physical pain upon children and adolescents.

## ASCA Position on The School Counselor and Corporal Punishment

School counselors oppose the use of corporal punishment and advocate for trauma-sensitive discipline policies and procedures.

*Position statement adopted 1995; revised 2000, 2006, 2012, 2019*

> **CHARLIE'S WORLD**
>
> Charlie is a nine-year-old student who went to the school nurse because his back was hurting. The school nurse did not see any visible signs of injury, but asked the school counselor to talk to Charlie because he said that while he was staying with his dad last weekend his dad punched him, so he called his mother crying to come and get him. The school counselor talked to Charlie and found out that his father was very angry and hit Charlie, repeatedly, in the stomach and back about a week ago. Charlie had been out of school for the past week while back with his mother, who told Charlie's teacher that he was playing and fell out of a tree. Since the school counselor knew that Charlie's parents were separated and this happened at the dad's house, the school counselor called the mother. Do you agree with the school counselor's actions in this case? Why or why not?

In most states, school counselors need only to have reasonable cause to suspect child abuse and/or neglect and do not need to see bruises, cuts, or marks of any kind in order to request CPS intervention on behalf of a child, adolescent, or the elderly (Child Welfare Information Gateway, 2023). If the school counselor suspects that the student may run or that the student is afraid to go home, this needs to be shared in the initial contact with CPS. Together, the school counselor and CPS intake specialist should determine an immediate course of action based on the information provided by the student.

Many students that school counselors serve are in foster care. Often educators and school counselors are not aware of which students are in these situations, making it difficult to provide additional services to mitigate the potential distress of a child who has been removed from their home and placed in the care of others, who are often strangers. School counselors should advocate for information that would allow the school counselor to support students in foster care and seek to meet the unique needs of each child.

---

*ASCA Position on The School Counselor and Supporting Students in Foster Care*

School counselors implement school counseling programs to meet the academic, career and social/emotional needs of all students. School counselors recognize that some students cope with situations that place them at higher risk. Youth in foster care represent an underserved and often-overlooked student population.

*Position statement adopted 2018*

---

## Scope of practice

Another area that is potentially problematic for school counselors involves the scope of practice and referrals. School counselors want to be careful not to practice outside of their areas of expertise and training. ASCA supports the use of referrals and a collaborative approach to meet the persistent and long-term needs of these students.

---

*ASCA Position on The School Counselor and Student Mental Health*

School counselors recognize and respond to the need for mental health services that promote social/emotional wellness and development for all students. School counselors advocate for the mental health needs of all students by offering instruction that enhances awareness of mental health, appraisal and advisement addressing academic, career and social/emotional development; short-term counseling interventions; and referrals to community resources for long-term support.

*Position statement adopted 1974; reviewed and reaffirmed 1980; revised 1986, 1993, 1999, 2002, 2015, 2020*

---

School counselors do not provide ongoing counseling sessions with students whose issues are so severe, frequent, and enduring that they cannot be sufficiently addressed within the scope of school counseling and within the expertise of the school counselor which is in violation of professional ethical guidelines. Section A.6 of the *ASCA Ethical Standards for School Counselors* (ASCA, 2022a) notes that school counselors provide a list of potential support resources in the community for students who need or request additional support and encourage parents/guardians to research resources as well. School counselors are careful not to endorse or give preference to any one referral source.

### MOONLIGHTING

Stuart is a school counselor and a licensed professional counselor. Since counseling students for an indefinite period of time and providing diagnoses and therapy is outside of the scope of school counseling services, Stuart has decided to offer his counseling services to students outside of the school day in his private practice setting. This will allow students in his small rural town to get the needed outside counseling services. Since he is the students' school counselor, he is offering a reduced rate. Are there ethical implications to consider here?

There are times when a school counselor and agency counselor may wish to collaborate to help the student. In such instances, all parties involved (i.e., parents, student, both counselors) should agree to the collaborative relationship, which will require the sharing of confidential information, communications, and student records. All parties will need to sign a release of information, which should include a statement that clearly defines and describes the nature of the collaborative relationship between all parties involved.

Another consideration with regard to scope of school counseling practice involves student evaluation, assessment, and interpretation. Psychological and *intelligence testing* by school counselors can be particularly problematic. Testing and assessment of this nature may be acceptable practices for school counselors in some school divisions, while unacceptable in others. *Know your school division's policy.* Yes, I realize by repeating this statement yet again I am running the risk of your having me committed for echolalia! Just so you know—I am not answering the door to anyone wearing a white coat. Although, a stint in a sanitarium does offer something of a restful appeal. In the presence or absence of school division policy on the assessment matter, familiarity with the *ASCA Ethical Standards for School Counselors* (ASCA, 2022a) is helpful. Those standards clearly state that school counselors only engage in evaluation, assessment, and interpretation when adequately trained and when those assessments are within the scope of school counseling practices.

## Informed consent

School counselors are not legally obligated to obtain parental permission prior to counseling unless there is a federal or state statute to the contrary (Remley & Herlihy, 2019; Stone, 2022). However, many school division policies require that school counselors obtain parental consent, particularly if counseling will extend beyond one or two sessions, as a matter of best practice (Stone, 2022).

School administrators, intent on promoting positive relations and support for the school counseling program, are aware that judicial rulings have historically favored parental rights (Remley & Herlihy, 2019). For this reason, school systems generally have a policy in place with regard to parental consent for individual and small group counseling. Classroom instruction provided by the school counselor, unless the topic is of a sensitive nature (e.g., sexual abuse), is viewed as part of the curriculum afforded to all students.

Many school systems include an "opt out" of counseling form in the student handbook. In this case, if a parent does not specifically opt a student out of counseling services, then school counselors are free to provide counseling services to students as needed. Still, if two or more sessions are deemed appropriate, the school counselor should reach out to parents/guardians to make them aware of ongoing counseling services.

### SENSITIVE TOPICS

In an effort to be proactive in promoting child safety, an elementary school counselor delivered classroom instruction for all fourth- and fifth-grade students on Internet safety. The school counselor invited a community police officer to talk about a particular case where a

> boy was lured by a stranger over the Internet, abducted, and killed. The next day, a very upset parent called because their fifth grader, Kirbi, came home in tears as the program reminded her of what had happened to her brother, who had been abducted and killed. The parent said she had not been informed that this program would take place, or she would not have allowed her child to participate. Are school counselors required to inform parents about the topics of the school counseling curriculum presented in the classroom and/or school-wide? Should the parent have been informed about this specific curriculum?

Informed consent from parents and guardians should be in writing. It is not necessary to get informed consent in writing from the minor, although it is necessary to obtain agreement, or assent, from minor clients. School counselors use developmentally appropriate language to discuss counseling services so that students can make informed decisions about whether or not they wish to engage in a counseling relationship with the school counselor.

## Student records and counseling case notes

Documenting counseling session information and storing such information in the form of formal professional case notes is another consideration with regard to maintaining confidentiality. School counselor formal case notes should be kept as a critical part of professional and accountable practices. These notes are not a part of the student's academic record. These case notes are objective in nature and discussed in more detail below. In some states, general counseling case notes may be considered part of the educational record. In those states, school counselors are well advised to have a specific understanding of exactly what is required to be placed in the student's education records. Likely, it is no more than dates that the student visited the school counselor and whether the topic was personal, social, emotional, academic, or career related.

School counselors may also consider creating sole possession records written as a memory aid. Unlike the more objective nature of the official case notes, sole possession records are more subjective in nature, documenting professional opinion and observations. These notes are not accessible or shared verbally or in writing with any other party. Like case notes, the school counselor's sole possession notes are not to be kept in the student's school record, which is accessible to many other educators and could constitute a breach of confidentiality. My best advice is to keep two sets of counseling notes: sole possession records and formal counseling records. This will allow you to capture both objective information and your valuable perceptions/interpretations during counseling sessions.

The advanced voluntary credentialing of school counselors (e.g., NCC, NCSC, LPC) require that they abide by the standards of practice of the credentialing agency. Many advanced voluntary credentials earned by school counselors have placed them in the category of mental health provider. Mental health providers are subject to compliance with HIPAA.

In brief, the Health Insurance Portability and Accountability Act (HIPAA) established national standards related to the confidentiality and security of health information. Health records in the school setting are exempt from HIPAA because those are covered under FERPA. However, it is not entirely clear how school counseling related communications, apart from case notes, which are not accessible under FERPA, would be viewed in the event of litigation when the school counselor holds advanced credentials should there be a mighty clash of the titans—HIPAA versus FERPA. So, as the adage goes, better safe than sorry. Since FERPA has no requirements for, nor jurisdiction over, school counseling case notes, why not use what HIPAA requires of mental health providers? As a school counselor with advanced counseling credentials, not only will you be prepared for a curve ball from HIPAA, but you will also have an outline for keeping formal case notes, which is generally not provided in school divisions and would serve double-duty by also meeting the accountability demands of today's society. Formal counseling case notes should include the following factual information:

- Dates of sessions.
- Number of sessions.
- Assessment data.
- Presenting problem.
- Treatment/counseling plan.
- Information related to collaboration and consultation with others.
- Session notes.
- Associated documents (e.g., informed consent, drawings, letters, referrals).

Case notes and sole possession records need to be stored in a secure location (e.g., locked in the school counseling office file cabinet) and maintained for several years and perhaps indefinitely in some cases (Remley & Herlihy, 2019; Stone, 2022). The *ASCA Ethical Standards for School Counselors* (ASCA, 2022a) suggests shredding sole possession records or deleting electronic sole possession records once the student transitions to the next level, transfers to another school, or graduates.

Case notes can be quite valuable, confirming meeting dates and times, dates of conversations with relevant others, and actions taken. Case notes may demonstrate a school counselor's professional, ethical, and legal actions in a given situation. Therefore, school counselors are encouraged to hang on to records that may be needed in a court of law, such as notes related to child abuse, suicide, sexual violence.

Case notes and sole possession records are accessible under a subpoena or court order in the absence of privileged communication statutes (ASCA, 2022a). If (I should say when) you are subpoenaed to appear in court regarding one of your students and you are uncertain about what to say or what information to provide, seek advice from your school division's attorney. In fact, it is good practice to touch base with your division's attorney when subpoenaed to court for school-related matters.

There may be times when a parent or guardian demands access to case notes or wants to know exactly what has been communicated in a counseling session. In these cases, first try to persuade the adult by expressing that it would not be in the best interest of their child to reveal such information without their child's knowledge—even better their permission. Explain your ethical obligation to the student as well as your desire to collaborate with the parent on their child's behalf. Reassure the parent that had anything been shared by the student that the parent should know in order to help the student you would have requested permission from the student to share that information. Encourage the parent to ask their child about the counseling sessions.

If the parent is still insistent, let the parent know that you would like to request the student's permission to share the session content in order to preserve not just the counselor–student relationship, but the parent–child relationship. If the student would like to maintain confidentiality, then encourage a meeting with the student and the parent to mediate a solution. If the meeting is not productive and you decide not to disclose the information to the parent, ensure that you have the support of your administrator. The parent may decide to legally pursue the matter and may have a legal right to the information.

> **WHEN TO SAY NO**
>
> Shirley is a school counselor in a very large inner-city school. Her principal has asked her to include a copy of her counseling notes in the student's educational record in the file room to ensure they are made available under FERPA, if requested. The principal believes this is the only place those case notes will really be secure and made available to teachers, who may wish to know more about the students' issues to better provide assistance. Shirley politely says "no," sharing that these are official counseling case notes that are not intended to be part of the student's educational record in accordance with ethical guidelines and the law. And, because the case notes are not part of the educational record, they are not accessible under FERPA. Shirley further explains that should the counseling notes be included in the educational records of students, then parents may have grounds for legal action based on a breach of confidentiality in the school counselor–student relationship. Do you agree with the school counselor's actions in this case? Why or why not?

## IDEA and Section 504

The Individuals with Disability Education Act (IDEA) is civil rights legislation created to ensure equality in education for students with an identified *disability* under three major types of disorders: physical and neurological disabilities, sensory disabilities, and developmental disabilities (United States Department of Education, 2023). Students who are found eligible for services under IDEA will receive an individualized education plan (IEP), which entitles the student to accommodations and specialized services as decided upon by the IEP team and included in the student's IEP.

A civil rights law, the Rehabilitation Act of 1973 (*Section 504*), as amended (United States Department of Education, 2023), includes information about the *Americans with Disabilities Act of 1990* (ADA) and protects the rights of students with disabling conditions that limit one or more major life activities (e.g., vision, hearing, speaking, walking, learning). Students who do not qualify for special education services under IDEA are often eligible for services under Section 504. Students who are found eligible under Section 504 will receive a *504 plan*, which entitles the student to accommodations and specialized services as decided upon by the 504 team and included in the 504 plan.

Together, IDEA and Section 504 of the Rehabilitation Act are powerful tools that school counselors use to advocate for *equity and access* to rigorous and appropriate educational programming and services in the schools for all students. School counselors are often the first person parents, teachers, and administrators involve when a student is struggling. Early intervention coupled with resources is key to ensuring that students' needs are met.

Parents, teachers, administrators, school counselors, and just about anyone can refer a student to the *child study* team or to the 504 committee, if a disabling condition and/or learning disability is suspected. Most schools have an early intervention team that assumes many different names but have a similar purpose, which is to begin a plan of action to help students who are struggling academically, personally, emotionally, socially, physically, and/or behaviorally. School counselors are generally members, even chairs, of these teams that also include the parent, classroom teacher(s), a special education teacher, and upon invitation, the school psychologist, social worker, and/or educational diagnostician.

The early intervention team develops and monitors an intervention plan. The intervention plan is distributed to all who work with the student and a copy is included in the student's educational record. An early intervention plan may be all a student needs to get back on track or to stay on track. If not, the team refers the student to the child study team or the 504 committee for possible *diagnostic testing* and/or additional intervention assistance.

Many schools are now requiring that teachers refer students to the early intervention team before a referral can be made to the child study team. This helps to reduce the number of students in special education because of an overreliance on IEPs versus other less restrictive forms of intervention. However, a parent who wishes to take their child directly to the child study team has a legal right to do so and is not required to go through the early intervention team first.

> **THE 504 PLAN**
>
> Kenneth is a third-grade student with a 504 plan. The plan allows Kenneth to have extended time, frequent breaks, and small group instruction and testing. The school counselor is creating a standardized testing schedule for their school for special needs students. Kenneth's teacher tells the school counselor not to worry about pulling Kenneth out of the classroom since she has not really been doing this throughout the school year and Kenneth is doing just fine without those accommodations. The school counselor pulls the student out of the class on the day of statewide standardized testing to adhere to the accommodations listed on the student's 504 plan. What issues do you view as problematic in this case? Do you agree with the school counselor's actions in this case? Do you agree with the teacher's actions in this case? What are the implications for Kenneth?

## Homelessness

The 2022 Annual Assessment Report to Congress revealed that chronic homelessness in the United States is up from the previous year(s). Of the 582,462 people experiencing homelessness in 2022, 98,244 were under the age of 18 and 30,090 were unaccompanied youth (United States Department of Housing and Urban Development, 2023). Homeless school-age children have a higher incidence of depression and developmental issues, behavioral problems, and poor academic performance, which makes poverty a pervasive risk factor (Murran & Brady, 2023). Studies have confirmed that youth who experience homelessness count on informal support systems to enhance reliance; and, enhanced coping skills are associated with spirituality, mental health, and creativity (Cronley & Evans, 2017).

> *ASCA Position on The School Counselor and Children Experiencing Homelessness*
>
> School counselors recognize that homelessness/displacement may greatly affect the whole child, encompassing mental, physical, social/emotional and academic

development. School counselors help to identify students who are experiencing homelessness. As social justice advocates, it is school counselors' duty to recognize and work with students around their specific strengths. School counselors collaborate with community stakeholders to connect students and their families who are experiencing homelessness to community supports, work to remove barriers to academic success and implement responsive prevention and intervention programs for children experiencing homelessness.

*Position statement adopted 2010; revised 2018*

School counselors collaborate with stakeholders to remove the barriers to school success perpetuated by homelessness. School counselors need to be aware of the McKinney-Vento Act of 1987 (United States Department of Education, 2023), which defines homelessness as lacking a fixed, regular, and adequate nighttime residence, and provides federal money for homeless shelters.

## Research

Conducting research that results in information that can improve the school counseling program and better meet the needs of specific populations, as well as the general school community is an admirable goal. Sections *A.3* and *B.2* of the *ASCA Ethical Standards* (2022a) specifically address pertinent areas related to conducting research in the school. When conducting research in the schools it is important to use and share data and related findings in a manner consistent with acceptable educational and psychological research practices, which advocate for the protection of individual students' identities, adhering to the construct of confidentiality, obtaining parental and student informed consent, and selecting measures that are free of culture and gender bias. Policy/law to consider include:

- Federal Education Rights and Privacy Act (FERPA).
- U.S. Department of Education Protection of Pupil Rights Amendment (PPRA).

- U.S. Department of Education Privacy Technical Assistance Center (PTAC).
- School District Research Department and/or Research Policy.

## *Dual relationships*

Maintaining professional distance is sometimes more difficult for the school counselor, as opposed to a private practitioner or community counselor. School counselors are often asked by administrators to take on any number of extracurricular program sponsorship roles, making dual relationships in the world of school counseling inevitable.

When dual relationships are unavoidable, it is important that school counselors continuously examine their professional and ethical behaviors by reflectively considering whose needs will be met by a specific action or inaction. If you find that the need being met is your own, then, in the words of our former first lady, Nancy Reagan—*just say no*!

The *ASCA Ethical Standards for School Counselors* (ASCA, 2022a) caution school counselors to avoid relationships that might impair objectivity and potentially increase the risk of harm to students (e.g., counseling one's family members or the children of close friends or associates). *ASCA* defines a dual relationship as one in which the school counselor participates in two or more roles with a student concurrently (2022a). With this said, if a dual relationship is unavoidable, the school counselor is responsible for taking action to eliminate or reduce the potential for harm to the student through use of safeguards, which might include informed consent, consultation, supervision, and documentation.

## *Supervision*

Ideally, school counselors will be provided two types of supervision: administrative and clinical supervision. Administrative supervision is generally provided at the building level by the school counseling director or principal. The director or principal provides the school counselor with general guidance pertaining to the daily operations of the school counseling program and evaluates the school counselor's professional performance. Often, there is a division level school counselor supervisor as well, who generally provides administrative support and opportunities for ongoing school counseling specific professional development.

Clinical supervision provides school counselors with consultation and supervision as it pertains to improving counseling skills and providing needed personal counseling support. As important as this is, clinical supervision is the least received type of supervision for school counselors. ASCA (2022a) calls upon school counselors to monitor our emotional and mental health and attend to our wellness so that we can provide optimal effective counseling services and prevent burnout.

Although school counselors may obtain clinical supervision from community counseling agencies and local counselor educators who are licensed professional counselors, individual and group peer supervision or consultation by fellow practicing school counselors are the most commonly used methods of school counselor clinical supervision and endorsed by way of the *ASCA Ethical Standards for School Counselors* (2022a).

Developmental models of supervision allow school counselors to meet peers where they are in their developmental process as a practicing counselor. Developmental models posit that counselors move through qualitatively different stages that require qualitatively different levels of supervisor involvement (e.g., less, moderate, or highly structured) and roles (e.g., teacher, trainer, colleague, consultant) to meet the unique needs of the supervisee (Bernard & Luke, 2015; Bernard & Goodyear, 2018).

Peer supervision or consultation as a type of clinical supervision aids school counselors in case conceptualization and working through complex ethical and legal issues that often arise when counseling minors, while also providing a medium for shared feedback, exploration of thoughts and emotions, and the validation and support critical to self-care (Page, Pietrzak, & Sutton, 2001).

## *ASCA Position on The School Counselor and School Counselor Supervision*

School counselors engage in quality school counseling supervision during their training and professional practice to enhance the implementation of their school counseling program. Supervision by individuals who have a background in school counseling or certification in supervision enhances school counselors' professional growth and leadership development in their roles as practitioners and potential supervisors.

*Position statement adopted 2021*

We do not need Nostradamus to tell us what the future holds for school counselors who do not find ways to destress, reenergize, and maintain well-being. How can we effectively meet the needs of others in the lingering presence of our own unmet needs? School counselors are like the cobbler with no shoes. We get so busy fashioning shoes for all of our students, teachers, and parents, that we do not make time to create a pair for ourselves. School counselors must take the time to design shoes for themselves as well.

It is the school counselor's personal, professional, and ethical responsibility to prevent our own impairment that is often the result of professional burnout and/or lack of self-care. Peer supervision/personal counseling are not the only ways to reduce burnout and address self-care. School counselors may wish to engage in yoga, meditation, bibliotherapy, and/or social activities that promote relaxation. Building strong support systems and making lifestyle changes that include a healthy diet and regular exercise are proven to aid in health and well-being. Just plainly setting aside time for good old-fashioned fun can make a world of difference!

## Human development, learning, and motivation

Human development is simply the change that occurs in human beings over the course of their lifespan. The process of growth from *cradle to grave*, however, is not so simple. Human development is multidimensional and complex. For these reasons, it is not appropriate to generalize developmental processes and stages across cultures or ethnicities because some developmental characteristics are socially engineered or thwarted by culturally engendered developmental processes. This section will look at key developmental theories and general developmental characteristics of elementary-, middle-, and high-school students.

Understanding the characteristics and processes of a student's psychological, social, cognitive (including learning, motor skills, and language development), spiritual, and moral development during the school-age years is necessary to distinguishing between what may be considered normal developmental characteristics and minor to serious developmental impediments. Knowledge of the multifaceted aspects of human development is also essential to designing developmentally appropriate strategies for successful intervention with specific populations such as students with physical, mental, and emotional disabilities and/or advanced functioning students.

An understanding of human development across the lifespan enables school counselors to adjust language, approaches, and techniques to meet the unique needs of school-age children. It is also important that school counselors consider those biological and environmental forces that impact human development.

Theorists continue to ponder the impact of nature versus nurture on human development. That is, to what extent do genetic factors (i.e., nature) and environmental factors (i.e., nurture) and their interactions influence human development? To date, the topic has been widely researched, and data indicates that both play a significant role in determining our attitudes, beliefs, and behaviors. For this reason, school counselors are encouraged to consider both nature and nurture when working with children, adolescents, and adults.

The fundamental nature of counseling, thus school counseling, and human development is change. Meeting students where they are when prevention and intervention is needed is critical. School counselors achieve this with an understanding of human development theories. The human development theories discussed in this section are categorized as follows: psycho-social development, cognitive development and learning theories, and moral and spiritual development. Figure 1.1 presents this information in a fashion that aids learning and recall.

## *Psychosocial Development*

Psychosocial development theories seek to explain personality development and the acquisition of social skills and social attitudes. The three primary psychosocial theorists discussed in this chapter are Erik Erikson, Robert Havighurst, and Sigmund Freud. However, Eric Berne's theory of personality development, *transactional analysis*, is also discussed because it is often applied in the school setting.

Erik Erikson (1950, 1959) is best known for his eight stages of psychosocial development. Erikson postulates that each stage held a developmental

Foundations of school counseling ■ 41

## Psychosocial Development
Explains personality development and the acquisition of social skills and social attitudes

**Erik Erikson**
Development driven by stage-related tasks resolve Eight stages of psychosocial development: Trust vs. Mistrust; Autonomy vs. Shame and Doubt; Initiative vs. guilt; Industry vs. Inferiority; Identity vs. Confusion; Intimacy vs. Isolation; Generativity vs. Stagnation; Integrity vs. Despair Key Constructs: identity crisis; virtues

**Robert Havighurst**
Development driven by stage-related tasks resolve Six stages of personality development: infancy; early childhood; middle childhood; adolescence; early adulthood; middle adulthood; later maturity Key constructs: developmental tasks (physical maturation, personal values, societal pressures)

**Sigmund Freud**
Development driven by sexual pleasures and interactions of the id, ego, and superego Five psychosexual stages: oral, anal, phallic, latent period, and genital stage Key constructs: conscious, unconscious; Oedipus and Electra complexes; libido; fixation; erogenous zones; pleasure principle

**Eric Berne**
Development driven by interactions Key constructs: strokes, ego states, transactional stimulus, transactional response

## Cognitive Development and Learning Theories
Explains the development of thought, intelligence, and problem solving abilities

**Jean Piaget**
Development is a continuous process of achieving balance between assimilation and accommodation (i.e., equilibrium) and the resulting modification of schemas. Four stages of cognitive development: sensorimotor; preoperational; concrete operational; formal operational Key constructs: egocentrism; sociocentrism

**B. F. Skinner**
Learning driven by operant conditioning Key constructs: behavior modification; stimulus; response; positive and negative reinforcement and punishment; schedules of reinforcement

**Lev Vygotsky**
Learning is contextual and driven by culture, environment, and social interactions. Key constructs: guided participation; zone of proximal development; scaffolding; cultural mediation; internalization

**Albert Bandura**
Learning driven by modeling Key constructs: motivation; observational learning; reciprocal determinism

## Moral and Spiritual Development
Explains the development of attitudes and behaviors toward others, and the meaning and nature of our existence

**Jean Piaget**
Moral reasoning develops from cognitive structure and social relationships in two stages. Individuals construct/reconstruct their perceptions of the world based on their interactions with environment and others. Key constructs: heteronomy; autonomy; goodness; evil

**Lawrence Kohlberg**
Moral thinking is developed through an understanding and exposure to concepts such as justice, human rights and welfare, and equality. Three levels containing six stages of moral reasoning: Level 1 (pre-conventional), Level 2 (conventional), Level 3 (post-conventional). Key constructs: justice operation; moral universalism; formalism; relativism

**James Fowler**
Faith development occurs in six stages and involves cognition, emotion, and imagination: intuitive-projective; mythic-literal; synthetic-conventional; individuative-reflective; conjunctive faith; universalizing (or enlightenment) Key constructs: transcendence

**Figure 1.1 Human development theories.**

task that needed to be successfully resolved in order to experience healthy personality development. When the task was successfully resolved, a *psychosocial strength*, or *virtue*, would emerge. Table 1.1 presents Erikson's eight stages, corresponding ages, the conflict to be resolved, and the resulting virtue in a manner that will aid in learning and recall.

Erikson is credited for coining the term *identity crisis*, which he suggests occurs during adolescence. Identity crisis is used to describe a period of role confusion, or *role diffusion*, whereby the individual explores roles, questions authority, strives to find his or her own unique self or identity, and struggles with social relationships and social and moral issues. When the individual commits to an identity, role confusion/diffusion ends and role achievement is reached.

**Table 1.1 Erikson's Eight Stages of Psychosocial Development**

| Stage/Age | Task to be Resolved | Characteristics | Virtue |
| --- | --- | --- | --- |
| Infancy Ages 0-1 | Trust vs. Mistrust | Need for reliable care (e.g., feeding) from caregiver. | Hope |
| Toddler Ages 2-3 | Autonomy vs. Shame and Doubt | Need for sense of control over physical tasks (e.g., toilette training). | Determinism/ Will |
| Preschool Ages 3-5 | Initiative vs. Guilt | Need for control over environment (e.g., exploration). | Courage/ Purpose |
| School Age Ages 6-11 | Industry vs. Inferiority | Need to successfully navigate social and educational demands (e.g., school). | Competence |
| Adolescence Ages 12-18 | Identity vs. Role Confusion | Need to develop a personal identity and sense of self (e.g., peer relationships). | Loyalty/ Fidelity |
| Early Adulthood Ages 19-40 | Intimacy vs. Isolation | Need for intimacy and love (e.g., social relationships). | Love |
| Middle Adulthood Ages 40-65 | Generativity vs. Stagnation | Need to create and nurture (e.g., work/parenthood). | Caring |
| Late Adulthood Ages 65 > | Ego Integrity vs. Despair | Need for a sense of fulfillment (e.g., reflection on life). | Wisdom |

> **DEFIANCE**
>
> Kelly is in middle school, and his parents are worried that he is exhibiting defiance that could lead to more serious behaviors. His parents say that he just does not listen to a thing they say or comply with what they ask him to do. His grades are good as well as his relationships with peers. His teachers report that he is respectful but questions everything they ask him to do. Developmentally, what might Kelly be experiencing?

Robert Havighurst (1972) applied Erikson's concept of stages of psychosocial development, postulating six different stages and an emphasis on the successful achievement of each task at each stage, which derive from three sources: physical maturation (e.g., motor skills, walking and talking, adjusting to menses and menopause), personal values (e.g., spirituality/philosophical beliefs, selecting an occupation), and societal pressures (e.g., learning to be responsible, citizenship). Table 1.2 presents Havighurst's six stages of personality development along with the developmental tasks associated with each stage. Havighurst believed that introducing students to these developmental tasks at the *ripe time* creates a teachable moment.

Sigmund Freud believed that personality development was driven by sexual interests or pleasures that focused on specific *erogenous zones* (i.e., mouth, anus, and genital area) at particular stages of development (Nye, 1975). Like other stage theorists, Freud emphasized the importance of resolving developmental conflicts at each stage. Freud proposes that unresolved conflicts at each stage results in *fixation*, thereby leaving a part of the child's *libido* (i.e., psychic energy of the mind) fixed at that stage, impacting personality into adulthood. One wonders at which stage Freud developed his rumored fear of ferns—things that make you go hmmm? Nonetheless, Freud's brilliant mind conceptualized five stages of psychosexual development which are still quite influential to this day. Each stage and the characteristics of each stage are listed in Table 1.3.

Freud further believed that personality was driven by the interactions of the mind, or psyche made up of the id (i.e., primal instinct), ego (i.e., realistic, organized part of the mind), and superego (i.e., moralistic part of the mind). The id is our unconscious and driven by the *pleasure*

**Table 1.2 Havighurst's Stages of Personality Development**

| Stage/Age | Developmental Tasks |
|---|---|
| Infancy and early childhood/ages 0–6 | Learning to talk, crawl, and walk; learning to control bowels; learning concepts, learning gender differences |
| Middle childhood/ages 6–12 | Learning interpersonal skills and daily living concepts; developing attitudes about self, others, social groups, institutions, and society; developing a conscience, values, and morality; learning masculine or feminine social roles; achieving independence/autonomy |
| Adolescence/ages 13–18 | Continued development of independence and relationships with males and females; adjusting to one's physique; securing a job; adjusting to physiological changes |
| Early adulthood/ages 19–30 | Selecting a mate; starting a family; becoming a caregiver; achieving social responsibility, values, and morality; selecting an occupation |
| Middle age/ages 30–60 | Achieving occupational satisfaction; developing leisure activities; adjusting to physiological changes; assisting aging parents |
| Later maturity/ages >60 | Adapting to living arrangements and declining physical strength/health; adjusting to retirement and reduced income |

*principle*—if it feels good do it, if it doesn't don't do it! The ego, mainly but not entirely conscious, operates on the *reality principle*, which has us delay gratification and endure necessary pain when needed, meeting the needs of the id in a realistic way. The superego mainly but not entirely unconscious, seeks perfection, discerns right from wrong, and acts as the conscience.

To illustrate, imagine you are sitting in class and your belly begins to grumble and rumble with hunger. Your immediate instinct is to "go now seek sustenance" (id). But, before you can stand up, you hear, "Dude, you can't just get up and leave right in the middle of the professor's lecture, but we may be able to leave early and go get three or four tacos and a couple of burrito supremes" (ego). Now, at this point, superego would be the cloaked voice from deep within that chimes in now and says (depending upon our individually developed conscience), "For crying out loud, you can wait until the end of class and then go to Taco Bell."

**Table 1.3 Freud's Stages of Psychosexual Development**

| Stage/Age | Characteristics |
|---|---|
| Oral stage/ages 0–1 | The mouth is the child's primary interaction with the world and derives pleasure from oral stimulation (e.g., sucking and tasting). If gratification is not achieved, fixation on oral stimulus is the result into adulthood (e.g., nail biting, thumb-sucking, overeating, smoking) |
| Anal stage/ages 1–3 | The primary focus is on bowel control. Too much emphasis can result in excessive need for organization or order and cleanliness into adulthood, whereas too little emphasis can result in sloppiness and destructive behavior into adulthood |
| Phallic stage/ages 3–6 | The genitals are the child's primary focus. Children develop an attraction to the opposite sex parent. Freud termed this the - (boy's attraction to mother) and *Electra complex* (girl's attraction to father) |
| Latent stage/ages 6–11 | The primary focus is on the development of social skills, peer relationships, and values. The superego continues to develop while the id is suppressed |
| Genital stage/ages 11–18 | Physiological changes due to puberty, again create a focus on the genitals, and an interest in the opposite sex develops. Individual continues healthy development if progression through the stages have been successful to this point |

Eric Berne (1961), largely influenced by the work of Freud, is best known for his theory of personality development known as TA. According to TA, to understand personality we must analyze the interpersonal interactions. During a personal encounter, one individual will act toward the other in some fashion (*transactional stimulus*) and the other will respond in some manner (*transactional response*). TA holds that individuals take on one of three ego states: parent, adult, and child. In the parent ego state, individuals are either critical or nurturing, acting in a manner consistent with that of their parents. In the adult ego state, individuals act in a manner that illustrates self-discovered thinking and behavior. In the child individuals act as their true, unencumbered self for better (e.g., endearing) or worse (e.g., disobedient). TA also emphasizes the importance of attention in shaping our personalities and interactional patterns. Attention, or *strokes*, which can be nonexistent (i.e., no strokes, ignoring), negative (i.e., strokes that feel bad), or positive (i.e., strokes that feel good) impact our thoughts, feelings, and behaviors.

> **EDDIE'S EGO STATE**
>
> You are the middle-school counselor meeting with a group of four seventh-grade males. The students were referred to you because of behavioral problems. Eddie, one of the group members, continued during the first group session to do just as the teacher described observing during class—he put others in the group down with hurtful and unsolicited remarks. Together, the school counselor and the other group members helped Eddie to explore his motivation for those behaviors. Eddie realized that this is how his father interacted with him. According to TA, what ego state is Eddie incorporating when he interacts with others?

## Moral and spiritual development

Moral and spiritual development theories seek to explain the development of attitudes and behaviors toward the self and others and the meaning and nature of our existence. Morality and spirituality are largely determined by cultural and societal norms and laws and form the foundation of ethical behavior (Matsumoto & Juang, 2016). Three theorists, Jean Piaget, Lawrence Kohlberg, and James Fowler, have made lasting impacts on our understanding of moral and spiritual development.

Jean Piaget (1932), most widely known for his theory of cognitive development, discussed in the next section, suggested that moral thinking develops from cognitive structure and social relationships. Piaget studied the moral development of children using exercises of judgment based on the goodness or evil of storybook characters. Piaget's theory of moral development involves two stages: *heteronomy* and *autonomy*. Piaget's stages, ages, and primary characteristics for each stage of moral development are described in Table 1.4.

Lawrence Kohlberg (1967, 1969), inspired by Piaget's work and agreeing with his contention that moral development is a reflection of cognitive development, expanded on Piaget's stage model of moral development. Kohlberg contended that advanced cognitive functioning was necessary, but not sufficient for advanced moral reasoning.

Kohlberg proposed three sequential levels and six stages of moral reasoning, emphasizing the need to experience each stage—no stage

**Table 1.4 Piaget's Stages of Moral Development**

| Stage/Age | Characteristics |
|---|---|
| Heteronomy/birth to ages 9 or 10 | Children do not understand rules or morality. Children at this stage depend on those in authority to reinforce or punish what is considered to be right (goodness) or wrong (evil) |
| Autonomy/ages 9 or 10+ | Children begin to understand behaviors of right and wrong and allow principles and ideals to guide behavior, which are largely determined by that which was reinforced during the heteronomy stage and by their own maturing perspectives |

skipping—in order to advance to the subsequent higher level of moral reasoning. The *preconventional* level (level one) consists of stage one, *obedience and punishment* (ages 5–7), and stage two, *instrumental relativist*. The *conventional level* (level two) consists of stage three, *interpersonal relationships* or *good boy, nice girl orientation*, and stage four, *law and order*. The postconventional level (level three) consists of stage five, *social contract and individual rights*, and stage six, *universal principles*. Kohlberg's levels, stages, ages, and characteristics at each stage of moral reasoning are illustrated in Table 1.5.

James Fowler (1981) is credited for his significant contributions toward our understanding of the development of faith. In his model, Fowler views faith not as a particular religion but in terms of one's relationship to the universe and to a transcendent power. Fowler's model, illustrated in Figure 1.2, is hierarchical, with each stage building upon the other. The stages of Fowler's model include undifferentiated, intuitive–projective, mythic–literal, synthetic–conventional, individuative–reflective, conjunctive, and universalizing. Although Fowler believes that all individuals have the capacity for faith development, he points out that not all individuals make it to all stages of the developmental model.

School counselors use a variety of clever strategies to promote the development of morality including character education (discussed in Chapter 3), bibliotherapy, ethical case discussions, current and past events to help students understand the impact of our actions and inactions on others. School counselors foster moral development by encouraging reflection, reasoning, self-esteem, positive social interactions, peaceable schools, respect for others, and appreciation for differences. And, don't forget the significant impact of *positive role models!*

## Table 1.5 Kohlberg's Levels and Stages of Moral Reasoning

| Level | Stage (Age) | Characteristics |
|---|---|---|
| Level I, Preconventional | Stage one (ages 5–7), *obedience and punishment*<br>Stage two (ages 8–12), *instrumental relativist* | Obey rules to avoid punishment/gain reward<br>Can break rule for reciprocal gain or to meet needs |
| Level II, Conventional | Stage three (ages 13–16), *interpersonal relationships* or *good boy, nice girl*<br>Stage four (ages >16), *law and order* | Actions intended to gain approval of others (be nice)<br>Actions intended to please society; follow rules and obey the law; respect authority |
| Level III, postconventional | Stage five (adult), *social contract and individual rights*<br>Stage six (adult), *universal principles* | Rules important for an orderly society but should be decided on by all based on differing values/beliefs<br>Actions begin to reflect internalized morality even if it conflicts with rules and the law |

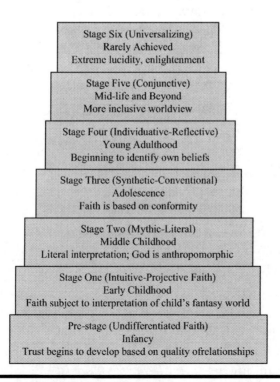

Figure 1.2 Fowler's stages of faith development.

## Cognitive development and learning theories

Cognitive development theories seek to explain the development of thought, intelligence, and problem-solving abilities. The most prominent cognitive development theorists include Jean Piaget, B. F. Skinner, Albert Bandura, and Lev Vygotsky. Each of these theorists has contributed significantly to our understanding of learning, information processing, and the development of language and reasoning skills.

Considered to be educators, moreover theorists, Benjamin Bloom and Robert Marzano have also contributed significantly to our understanding of student learning. For this reason, their educational philosophies and instructional strategies widely used in today's educational environments are covered in this section as well.

Piaget (1963) proposed four stages of cognitive development: sensorimotor, preoperational, concrete operational, and formal operational. Piaget's stages encompass birth to adolescence, describing a child's cognitive evolution from egocentrism (i.e., orientation to self) to sociocentrism (i.e., orientation to society). Table 1.6 presents Piaget's stages and the thinking and reasoning characteristics associated with each stage of a child and adolescent's development.

As school counselors, understanding the importance of Piaget's stages of cognitive development is critical. School counselors must design lessons and counseling interventions that are developmentally appropriate for the intelligence/cognitive level of a diverse student body. Meeting students where they are cognitively is imperative to the success of a given program, lesson, session, and/or intervention, and to the understanding of a student's thought processes at a given point in time.

### GRANDMA WILL BE BACK

Caryn is an elementary school student whose grandmother just passed away. Caryn is not upset because she said that grandmother will wake up and come back over to play with her soon. Which of Piaget's stages of cognitive development is representative of Caryn's thought processes in this situation?

As one of the most influential psychologists of the twentieth century, Skinner's behavioral concepts are still widely used by school counselors

### Table 1.6 Piaget's Stages of Cognitive Development

| Stage/Age | Thinking and Reasoning Characteristics |
|---|---|
| Sensorimotor/ages birth to 2 | Primarily motor and reflex actions; sucking; grasping; kicking; understands the world through senses; speech is single utterances |
| Preoperational/ages 2–7 | Personifies objects; play important for exploring self and world; present orientation; little perception of time; judgment based on perceptions; egocentric thinking (self the center of all things); egocentric speech (speech said aloud, but to self) to more socialized speech (speech that depicts thought and language as separate functions) |
| Concrete operational/ages 7–12 | More organized, logical thought; good inductive logic (specific to general); sequencing and categorizing; problem solving; understands concept of reversibility; thinking less egocentric and more sociocentric (orientation toward society); socialized speech |
| Formal operational/ages >12 | Ability to understand abstract and hypothetical concepts; good deductive logic (general to specific); socialized speech and vocabulary continue to develop |

in the twenty-first century. This study guide highlights the most salient concepts of Skinner's behavior modification and learning theory. Skinner contended that our behavior is determined by environmental factors, dismissing the notion of individual freedom (Skinner, 1971; Nye, 1975).

Skinner introduced the process of *operant conditioning*, which is grounded in the belief that behavior is learned. Voluntary behaviors, also referred to as responses, that are followed by a reinforcing stimulus are repeated as the result of desirable consequences and behaviors that are followed by a punishing stimulus and are not repeated as the result of undesirable consequences. The behavior reinforcements or punishments may be *positive* (e.g., applied after the response) or *negative* (i.e., removed after the response). Skinner promoted the use of *schedules of reinforcement* (i.e., multiple reinforcements over time) to modify, or shape, behavior.

School counselors most often use schedules of reinforcement to either increase or decrease the frequency of specific child and adolescent behaviors. This often takes on the form of a *behavior contract* or classroom management strategies in which the school counselor identifies expected behaviors (responses) and consequences based on the removal or application of a punishment or reinforcement (stimulus). Skinner advocated for reinforcement over punishment unless repeated attempts using schedules of reinforcement were unsuccessful.

Behavioral counseling is the approach most often used with the growing number of children and adolescents diagnosed with Attention-Deficit/Hyperactivity Disorder (ADHD) during the school years. Although ADHD is often diagnosed during the early school years, school counselors *do not diagnose* students. Instead of a diagnosis, school counselors may wish to share observations as being "consistent with symptoms that are associated with_____" and provide parents with a list of pertinent resources.

The Connors Scale, also referred to as the Connors Test or the Connors Checklist, is completed by parents/caregivers and those who work closely with the student, documenting observations of student functioning with the purpose of aiding clinicians in making a diagnosis. Clinicians from outside the school system will often request a release of student records and call upon teachers, school nurses, school psychologists, and school counselors to complete the Connors Scale. The Connors Scale is generally associated with the diagnosis of disorders such as ADHD.

## DR. CANTHOLDEM

A teacher, Dr. Cantholdem, comes to you, the school counselor, to ask for guidance. She is having a problem with attendance in her class. She is considering exempting students from the final exam if they have perfect attendance. This is an example of:

a. Negative reinforcement.
b. Positive reinforcement.
c. Positive punishment.
d. Negative punishment.

Vygotsky (1934, 1978) suggests a sociocultural approach to human development, or social development theory, which holds thought, language, and reasoning development as contextual and driven by culture, environment, and social interactions. Vygotsky's key premise is *cultural mediation* (i.e., interactions between a child and the cultural group as well as individuals of the culture that develops cognitive constructs such as speech patterns, written language, and symbolic knowledge), which occurs during the process of *internalization* (e.g., the acquisition of specific and shared knowledge of a culture).

Vygotsky believed that cognitive development occurs within the *zone of proximal development*, which he defines as the difference between what a child can do without assistance (i.e., actual development) and what a child can do with assistance (i.e., potential development). In the process of assisting the child in mastering new skills, the adult adjusts to the child's level of development, which Vygotsky termed *scaffolding*. *Guided participation* may be used, whereby students help each other (e.g., peer tutoring) under the general guidance of a teacher.

Bandura (1969, 1977), the originator of social learning theory, believed that behavior was the result of a reciprocal relationship between the world and the person, which he termed *reciprocal determinism*. Bandura postulated that individuals learn through *modeling* (i.e., imitating another), or *observational learning*, driven by a rationalization or perceived reward (e.g., motivation).

Benjamin Bloom (1953) introduced six classifications of learning levels progressing from the most basic to the most complex in the following hierarchical order: knowledge, comprehension, application, analysis, synthesis, and evaluation. Bloom's taxonomy has been revised (Anderson & Krathwohl, 2001) to associate specific verbs that represent ways to promote the development of higher-level thinking skills at each level illustrated in Figure 1.3.

Robert Marzano introduced instructional strategies that have been empirically validated as approaches that build background knowledge and improve student achievement across grade levels (Marzano, 2004). These strategies are listed in Table 1.7.

The theory of learning style suggests that individuals have a propensity toward receiving and storing information using one or more of the three sensory modalities: visual (e.g., pictures, written word), kinesthetic (e.g., body movement, tactile), and auditory (e.g., spoken word). It is not only important for school counselors to gain an understanding of learning

Foundations of school counseling ■ 53

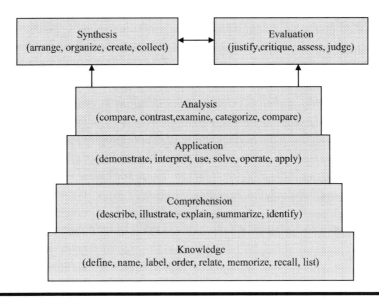

**Figure 1.3** Bloom's taxonomy and associated verbs.

**Table 1.7 Marzano's Nine Instructional Strategies**

| Instructional Strategy | Characteristics |
|---|---|
| Identifying similarities and differences | Breaking concepts into similar and dissimilar pieces; representing concepts in graphic forms (e.g., Venn diagrams, charts, analogies). |
| Summarizing and note taking | Conceptualizing presented material then restating it in one's own words; when note taking, more notes are better and allow time to process. |
| Reinforcing effort and providing recognition | Show the connection between effort and achievement (e.g., share success stories, underscore student's achievements); recognize individual accomplishments and personalize recognitions. |
| Homework and practice | Amount of homework should vary by grade level; homework schedule and setting should be consistent; homework provides practice; provide feedback on homework in a variety of ways. |
| Nonlinguistic representations | Use with linguistic representations; nonlinguistic representations stimulate and increase brain activity; use tangible models, physical movement, and apply symbols to represent words/images. |
| Cooperative learning | Positive impact on learning; vary group sizes and objectives. |

*(Continued)*

**Table 1.7 Continued**

| Instructional Strategy | Characteristics |
|---|---|
| Setting objectives and providing feedback | Provides direction for learning, students should personalize goals; use contracts; feedback should be timely, specific, and rubric based. |
| Generating and testing hypothesis | Use general rules to make a prediction; student should explain their predictions. |
| Cues, questions, advanced organizers | Students use background knowledge to enhance learning; expose students to material prior to their learning it (e.g., create a graphic image, tell a story). |

styles and teach to all learning styles but also important for students to help students identify their learning styles—students learning how to learn.

Generally speaking, individuals also have a preference for particular learning environments and times of day where conditions are optimal for learning. School counselors help students to understand their individual learning preferences and how those preferences can change over time. This self-knowledge enables students to adapt to a variety of teaching environments, selecting a preferred approach to the assigned task.

## *Motivation*

Theories of motivation are often categorized under three broad schools of thought: behavioral, cognitive, and humanistic. In addition to understanding the behavioral, cognitive, and humanistic interpretations of motivation, it is important for school counselors to be familiar with a fourth force—achievement motivation theory and its implications for motivating student learning.

Albert Bandura and B. F. Skinner are considered to be two of the most influential behavioral theorists on the topic of motivation. Both Bandura and Skinner were discussed earlier in some detail. To recap, Bandura holds modeling as having a considerable impact on student learning and motivation. In light of Bandura's suppositions, it is paramount that parents, educators, and important others in a student's life serve as positive role models, illustrating the significance of education and learning. Skinner's behavioral learning theory interprets motivation toward learning as a result of reinforcement. That is motivation occurs on the basis of extrinsic rewards and punishments.

The cognitive view of motivation, significantly influenced by Jean Piaget, also discussed earlier in this chapter, contends that learning is motivated when dissonance occurs. That is, when students recognize a gap in their knowledge (e.g., inconsistency between newly presented information and what is already known), they experience cognitive discomfort, or disequilibrium, thus motivating them toward learning in order to regain balance, or equilibrium. Sort of like the impact that this study guide may be having on some of you—hey, just keeping it real.

Human *motivation* is believed to be both intrinsic and extrinsic. Piaget emphasized the importance of intrinsic motivation. *Intrinsic motivation* rests within the individual, who derives pleasure from accomplishment of the task itself and an interest in the content. Intrinsic motivation is considered to be the highest level of self-regulated behavior often centered in curiosity that drives individuals to pursue higher learning and new challenges, even when it is not required (Moldovan, 2014). For example, connecting life to academics often piques students' inquisitiveness and interest in learning, perhaps even unearthing a deeply buried and now unremitting passion that takes up permanent residence in the student.

*Extrinsic motivation* rests outside of the individual, driven by reward or threat of punishment. School counselors are careful not to overuse extrinsic rewards (e.g., money, treats, praise), which have often been associated with temporary change and may result in the reduction of intrinsic motivation. School counselors promote learning and holistic student development by applying intrinsic/extrinsic motivation tools and strategies. Research demonstrates that students who view academics as personally relevant to their future are generally more motivated (Moldovan, 2014).

Although research to date demonstrates the superiority of intrinsic motivation on student success, extrinsic rewards such as praise have been shown to produce lasting change when provided in an explicit manner. For example, there is sound research to support the positive impact of praise when the praise is specific and spontaneous and attributes accomplishment to effort. Under these conditions, praise has been found to increase motivation and self-esteem in students. Praise matters—even to adults!

**56** ■ *Foundations of school counseling*

> **INTRINSIC MOTIVATION**
>
> You are a school counselor conducting classroom instruction in a second-grade classroom. One of the activities is to draw a picture. While the students are sharing their completed pictures, you are providing praise as a means of recognition. When you get to Ronnie's picture, which of the following statements would be considered specific praise that attributes success to effort?
>
> ■ Ronnie, what a beautiful picture; you worked really hard!
> ■ Ronnie, you finished your picture so quickly and it is very nice!
> ■ Ronnie, your picture is so beautiful!
> ■ Ronnie, your picture has such a beautiful, yellow, smiling sun, your hard work really shows!

Abraham Maslow's theory of motivation (1970), a humanistic view of motivation, may well be the single most influential theory of motivation to date. Maslow suggests that the most basic human needs must be met before an individual will actively seek out, or be motivated toward, higher levels of need. The simplicity of Maslow's brilliance is undeniable.

Maslow's hierarchy of needs consists of five levels and is illustrated in Figure 1.4. The most fundamental needs are portrayed at the bottom

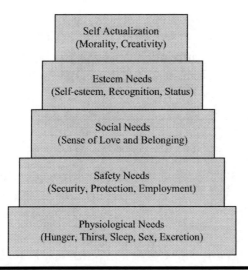

**Figure 1.4 Maslow's hierarchy of needs: A theory of motivation.**

level with progression up the hierarchy to the top level, which depicts an individual's need to reach his or her full potential. Maslow's levels in order from bottom to top include physiological needs, safety needs, social needs, esteem needs, and self-actualization. Maslow theorizes that a needs deprivation at any level can result in grave consequences. For example, an imbalance of physiological needs can obviously result in death. An imbalance at the safety level may result in a sense of insecurity that will interfere with motivation toward the next level of need. When social needs and/or esteem needs are not met, the intensity can be so overwhelming as to ignore more basic physiological and safety needs. In the absence of feelings of acceptance, intimacy, and belonging, individuals may experience extreme loneliness, anxiety, distress, crippling esteem issues, and feelings of inferiority, resulting in clinical depression, anorexia, and a number of other disorders.

We can understand, then, how the development of disorders at these levels prevents further progression on the hierarchy. We can understand, too, how death can be the ultimate result of imbalances at the higher levels when physiological and safety needs are disregarded. The journey to self-actualization, which might be viewed as meeting one's full potential, is an internally driven human development process. Needs at all the levels must be mastered in order to achieve the upper most level of self-actualization.

The implications of Maslow's work are clear with regard to student learning. As educators, we must help to ensure through school and community collaboration, advocacy, counseling, and the promotion of safe and equitable environments, that a student's basic needs are met in order for the student to be available to learn and so that students are motivated to achieve to their full potential.

There are a multitude of family and community issues that may negatively impact a student's need for achievement and their development and functioning, such as abuse, neglect, poor peer relations, divorce, parenting styles, crime, homelessness, and poverty, to name a few. Later chapters focus on counseling theories and school counseling prevention and intervention services delivered by school counselors to mitigate issues related to student development and well-being.

Last, achievement motivation theory (McClelland, 1961, 1985) is grounded in the belief that individuals are driven toward success, or avoidance of failure, which is influenced by varying levels of need for achievement and values. Thus, once success is experienced, more success is desired, much like a snowball effect, resulting in self-sustaining desires toward continued achievement (while enhancing self-esteem). More recent research suggests that the following are powerful predictors for enhancing student achievement with ability self-concept leading the charge (Steinmayr et al., 2019):

- Ability self concept.
- Task value.
- Learning goals.
- Motives.

### MOTIVATING JOHN

John is an academically average eighth-grade student who has not generally demonstrated motivation toward school and learning. John's parents, recognizing their son's ability in graphic design, encourage him to enter his work in a school competition. John received first place among 100 entries. For the first time that John's parents can recall, John was excited about learning more in the specific domain. According to achievement motivation theory and recent findings related to ability self-concept, what would be John's parents' next-best course of action if they wish to keep him motivated?

a. Celebrate with John.
b. Work with John's school counselor to get him involved in domain-specific opportunities that will heighten his skills and perceptions of his own competencies.
c. Investigate why John does not apply himself in other academic domains.
d. Do not get overly excited about John's accomplishment and encourage him to submit his work to local and state competitions, which may set him up for future disappointment.
e. a, b, and d.
f. a and b.

# Chapter 1 Case conceptualization responses

## Foundations of school counseling

### *The same or different?*

The correct response is "c." The school counselor is applying the ethical principle of justice, meeting the unique needs of each student in relation to individual differences.

### *Order in the court, here comes the judge*

The school counselor is supported by the ASCA *Ethical Standards for School Counselors* (2022a), when requesting that the court withdraw the requirement to divulge counseling session information without the consent of Donna, the 15-year-old minor client. Respecting the confidential nature of the school counselor and minor client relationship and the information disclosed by the student in counseling sessions adheres to a critical ethical principle—nonmaleficence. Should the judge order disclosure despite the school counselor's request, she should submit to the court order.

### *Alliances*

Although school counselors are diligent toward establishing alliances and partnerships with parents and make it clear that they understand and respect parental rights, school counselors do not divulge the content of counseling sessions to parents. Instead, school counselors explain to parents the need for confidentiality in counseling sessions for establishing a trusting relationship with their children, reassuring parents that confidentiality will be breached if needed in order to protect the child or others. Also, sharing with parents that you encourage students during counseling sessions to talk to parents about the issues shared in order to promote family communications and to help students to identify and make use of their support systems.

## Thoughts of suicide

Patrick's reason for suicidal intentions included his "family," which may indicate that his parent(s) are implicated. The school counselor should explore this area more deeply. If Patrick's parents are implicated, many, if not all, state guidelines would warrant a call to social services instead of a call to Patrick's parents. It would also be important to find out if Patrick was afraid to go home, in which case social services would likely come to the school before the end of the school day to talk with Patrick.

## Charlie's world

Since it appears that Charlie's mother knew the truth about what happened to Charlie even though the incident occurred at his father's home, CPS should have been contacted. The school counselor would be wise to directly ask Charlie if he told his mother that his father struck him. If Charlie had said "no" that he did not tell his mother, then asking the student what stopped him from sharing this important information with his mother would be important and could lead to additional critical information (e.g., perhaps both parents are striking the child). Or, perhaps, the child dislikes dad and is not telling the truth in order to stay with mom all the time? In either case, however, contacting CPS based on the existing information provided by the child is warranted and essential—err on the side of child safety. Another important piece of information here is that school counselors and school nurses do not have to see scars, bruises, or cuts in order to report suspected child abuse.

## Moonlighting

The ASCA *Ethical Standards for School Counselors* (2022a) make it clear that school counselors do not recruit or gain clients for his or her private practice to gain goods or services. School counselors "ensure there is not a conflict of interest in providing referral resources. School counselors do not refer or accept a referral to counsel a student from their school if they also work in private counseling practice."

## Sensitive topics

The nature of the school counselor's classroom lesson, while seemingly not so sensitive based on the title of "Internet safety" contained graphic content that is considered to be sensitive in nature, particularly for some students, depending on past experiences. Although school counselors do not generally need to seek parental consent for school counseling curriculum that is intended to be educational in nature and afforded to all students via classroom instruction and/or school-wide presentations, the curriculum content warranted informed consent from parents, or at the very least, the opportunity for the parent to opt the student out of this particular curriculum by providing information about the program and when it was to occur.

## When to say no

The school counselor's actions are appropriate.

## The 504 plan

The school counselor's actions are appropriate and in compliance with the student's 504 plan—a legal document entitling the student to these *accommodations* as agreed upon by a 504 committee that included the parent/legal guardian. The school counselor would want to discuss their intended actions in advance of testing day, to ensure that the teacher and others involved in testing understand the process and testing arrangements for students with special needs. The school counselor should consult with the teacher to understand why the accommodations are not being followed in the classroom and to encourage either going back to the 504 committee if the teacher believes accommodations are no longer needed or to begin compliance immediately. Another point is to be made here: if a student is not being given the small group testing accommodation outlined in a 504 plan or IEP and is given this accommodation on the day of standardized testing, this could adversely impact the student's performance on the test. Nonetheless, the school counselor is acting in the best interest of the student by following the currently active and legally binding 504 plan.

## Defiance

Kelly is experiencing the developmental stage of adolescence, possibly struggling with identity crisis by resisting authority and questioning adults in an effort to explore and discover his individual self, thoughts, ideas, and behaviors. School counselors can help Kelly's parents to understand this sensitive developmental stage and encourage Kelly's self-development by providing answers to Kelly's questions, which helps to reassure Kelly's sense of self and self-worth. Planned family activities and mealtimes are great mediums for encouraging exploration of Kelly's own thoughts, ideas, and communications.

## Eddie's ego state

According to TA, Eddie is acting in the parent ego state when he says hurtful things to others. Eddie has discovered during the group process that he is treating others in the same critical manner that his father treats him while also realizing how he has internalized those influential communications.

## Grandma will be back

Caryn is likely between the ages of 2 and 7 years old. According to Piaget's stages of cognitive development for this age, Piaget would consider Caryn to be in the preoperational stage of development since she views death as reversible.

## Dr. Cantholdem

The correct response is "a." The school counselor is attempting to apply negative reinforcement in Dr. Cantholdem's class, that is, removal (negative) of the final exam (stimulus) in an effort to increase attendance (desired behavior/response).

## Intrinsic motivation

The correct response is "d." The school counselor's praise is attached to a very specific part of the picture. The school counselor also makes it very clear to Ronnie that his success is due to his hard work or effort.

## Motivating John

The correct response is "f." It is important to celebrate the accomplishments of others, particularly those of your children. John's parents should continue to fuel this flame ignited in John by encouraging him in this specific domain and working with the school counselor to establish an academic plan that supports John's talent and interest (e.g., digital photography, graphic art, computer science, multimedia, and web technologies) potentially enhancing his ability self-concept. Encouraging John to continue to showcase his talent and enter competitions, whether his work places or not, will provide John with additional opportunities to experience successes and to grow from valuable feedback and exposure to others' work. Pushing to understand why John is not doing as well in other personal or academic areas of his life may negatively impact his ability self-concept in this particular domain where he is experiencing motivation. Motivation can breed motivation, so ride this particular motivational wave and see where it leads!

# Chapter 1 Simulation: Ernesto

## Brief case description

You, the school counselor, are the chair of the elementary school's early intervention team. The team is meeting today with the parent (biological mother) of a fifth-grade student, Ernesto, who is failing multiple subjects. The teacher also reports a lack of motivation on the part of the student toward school and learning over the past few months. The teacher has not observed any issues socially, that is, the student appears to get along well with peers.

## *Section A: Ernesto*

What information would be important to obtain at the beginning of the first meeting of the intervention team to help the committee to gain a greater understanding of Ernesto's case?
   (Select as many as you consider indicated in this section.)

| | | |
|---|---|---|
| _____ | A—1.  | Relationship with peers |
| _____ | A—2.  | Interventions applied previously |
| _____ | A—3.  | Academic history |
| _____ | A—4.  | Psychological history |
| _____ | A—5.  | Subject areas of struggle |
| _____ | A—6.  | Amount of time spent watching television |
| _____ | A—7.  | Interests and hobbies |
| _____ | A—8.  | Information Ernesto has shared with teacher and parent |
| _____ | A—9.  | Amount of time spent on the computer |
| _____ | A—10. | Recent changes in Ernesto's life |

## *Section B: Ernesto*

After sharing a variety of information and gaining some insight into Ernesto's situation, the parent reveals that Ernesto has been crying at home for the past two to three months while doing his homework. When she asks him what is wrong, he says that the math is just too hard and he does not understand it. Ernesto's mother expressed her concern because although Ernesto has experienced many transitions in his young life and struggled with schoolwork before, she has never seen him cry, which was why she was very happy about this academic intervention meeting at school. Which of the following questions might yield the most beneficial information at this time?

(Select as many as you consider indicated in this section.)

| _____B—1. | Has Ernesto reported feeling poorly lately? |
|---|---|
| _____B—2. | What else did Ernesto name as the reason for crying? |
| _____B—3. | What other behaviors have the teacher and parent noticed in the past three months? |
| _____B—4. | What has changed in the past three months? |
| _____B—5. | How is Ernesto's relationship with his father? |
| _____B—6. | Does Ernesto currently receive tutoring? |

## Section C: Ernesto

Further communication during the intervention meeting reveals that Ernesto has a good relationship with his father, who has been deployed for the past year. Ernesto's father is very involved in Ernesto's life and, generally, is the parent who attends the school functions and helps in the classroom when he is not deployed. Ernesto has shared with his mother that he misses his father very much, although they write to each other often. At this point in the meeting, what would be the best course of action by the committee?

(Select as many as you consider indicated in this section.)

| _____C—1. | Have the teacher and parent talk alone |
|---|---|
| _____C—2. | Request the assistance of an administrator |
| _____C—3. | Develop an academic intervention plan |
| _____C—4. | Come up with rewards for Ernesto when he completes his classwork and homework |
| _____C—5. | Request that Ernesto join the school counseling small group for students with parents/guardians who are deployed |
| _____C—6. | Table the meeting until Ernesto's father can be present |

## Section D: Ernesto

Over the next week, the teacher reports to the parent that Ernesto is beginning to push and yell at fellow students, and he gets angry very easily. The parent and teacher agree to send Ernesto to you for individual counseling sessions. During the first session, Ernesto becomes very emotional and shares that he overheard his mother telling his grandmother that she was planning to divorce his father when he returned to the States. Your most immediate courses of action with Ernesto should be:
   (Select as many as you consider indicated in this section.)

| | | |
|---|---|---|
| _____ | D—1. | Discuss divorce |
| _____ | D—2. | Discuss deployment |
| _____ | D—3. | Work on securing a support system |
| _____ | D—4. | Discuss involving his mother |
| _____ | D—5. | Discuss feelings |
| _____ | D—6. | Work on strategies for managing emotions |
| _____ | D—7. | Work on strategies for reducing stress |

## Section E: Ernesto

Ernesto comes to your office first thing in the morning immediately after getting off the bus. He is shaking and crying. As you calm Ernesto and sit down to talk, he reveals that his mother has a boyfriend who has been touching him when mom is not around. He has been telling Ernesto that they are just "wrestling." He said that last night, mom's boyfriend came into his bedroom. Ernesto describes the sexual acts, but says he is not in any pain right now. He said he yelled for his mother, but she did not come into the room. What is the most essential course of action?
   (Choose ONLY ONE in this section.)

| | | |
|---|---|---|
| _____ | E—1. | Ask questions to determine the mother's knowledge and involvement |
| _____ | E—2. | Contact the local police |
| _____ | E—3. | Call the mother |

| _____E—4. | Contact CPS |
|---|---|
| _____E—5. | Request that the school nurse examine Ernesto |
| _____E—6. | Make contact with the father |

## Section F: Ernesto

Two weeks later, you receive a letter in the mail that says the case is "unfounded." The following week, Ernesto comes to your office, again, right off the bus, shaking and crying, saying that his mother's boyfriend did it again. Ernesto's mother shows up at your door with the principal while Ernesto is in your office. Ernesto's mother very calmly taps on your door and walks in. She said she is there to take Ernesto to a doctor's appointment and that he was not supposed to get on the bus this morning. You express your concern and ask Ernesto if he would like to tell his mother what he just told me. Crying, he nods his head and tells his mother. Calmly, she said, "Ernesto, you know this is a lie, and this is why the social services people dismissed it." What is the best course of action?

(Select as many as you consider indicated in this section.)

| _____F—1. | Call CPS |
|---|---|
| _____F—2. | Contact the local police department |
| _____F—3. | Make contact with the father |
| _____F—4. | Tell the parent that she cannot take Ernesto |
| _____F—5. | Call in the boyfriend and talk with all three (i.e., mother, boyfriend, and Ernesto) |
| _____F—6. | Be stern with Ernesto and ask him for the truth |

# Chapter 1 Simulation responses: Ernesto

## Brief case description

You, the school counselor, are the chair of the elementary school's early intervention team. The team is meeting today with the parent (biological mother) of a fifth-grade student, Ernesto, who is failing multiple subjects. The teacher also reports a lack of motivation on the part of the student toward school and learning over the past few months. The teacher has not observed any issues socially, that is, the student appears to get along well with peers.

## *Section A: Ernesto*

What information would be important to obtain at the beginning of the first meeting of the intervention team to help the committee to gain a greater understanding of Ernesto's case?

(Select as many as you consider indicated in this section.)

| A—1. | Relationship with peers <br> No <br> Peer relations have already been addressed by the teacher sufficiently at this time |
|---|---|
| A—2. | Interventions applied previously <br> Yes <br> Knowing what has been done in the past and what has or has not been effective is helpful toward understanding Ernesto's case better. It can also assist in identifying present and future interventions |
| A—3. | Academic history <br> Yes <br> Gaining a better understanding of past and present academic functioning provides insight into academic change and patterns over time, specific subjects of challenge and strength, and the scope and magnitude of academic problems |
| A—4. | Psychological history <br> Yes <br> It is a good idea to find out what psychological issues, if any, may be a contributing factor when conceptualizing the student's case |

| | |
|---|---|
| A—5. | Subject areas of struggle<br>Yes<br>Difficulties across subject areas may be indicators of broader issues related to learning disabilities or other special needs (e.g., attention-deficit/hyperactivity disorder). Difficulty in isolated subjects may simply indicate an area of challenge that can be remediated with interventions such as additional study |
| A—6. | Amount of time spent watching television<br>No<br>The student's struggles are not limited to home. This may be warranted later depending on other information shared |
| A—7. | Interests and hobbies<br>No<br>This information would not be helpful, at this time, in gaining an insight into Ernesto's struggles |
| A—8. | Information Ernesto has shared with teacher and parent<br>Yes<br>It is very important to hear what the student identifies as the struggle |
| A—9. | Amount of time spent on the computer<br>No<br>The student's struggles are not limited to home. This may be warranted later depending on other information shared |
| A—10. | Recent changes in Ernesto's life<br>Yes<br>This is particularly important considering the teacher's referral to the intervention team is based on changes in the student's academic-related behavior over the past few months |

## Section B: Ernesto

After sharing a variety of information and gaining some insight into Ernesto's situation, the parent reveals that Ernesto has been crying at home for the past two to three months while doing his homework. When she asks him what is wrong, he says that the math is just too hard and he does not understand it. Ernesto's mother expressed her concern because although Ernesto has experienced many transitions in his young life and struggled with schoolwork before, she has never seen him cry, which was why she was very happy about this academic intervention meeting at school. Which of the following questions might yield the most beneficial information at this time?

(Select as many as you consider indicated in this section.)

| B—1. | Has Ernesto reported feeling poorly lately? |
| | Yes |
| | It is a good idea to rule out possible medical reasons for Ernesto's lack of motivation toward school and learning |
| B—2. | What else did Ernesto name as the reason for crying? |
| | Yes |
| | Exploring the conversation between Ernesto and his mother may lead to more information about what is particularly related to the student's struggle |
| B—3. | What other behaviors have the teacher and parent noticed in the past three months? |
| | Yes |
| | This is particularly important since the teacher indicates the onset of the academic difficulties as beginning a few months ago |
| B—4. | What has changed in the past three months? |
| | Yes |
| | It is important to fully explore this area, particularly since the teacher indicates the onset of the academic difficulties as beginning a few months ago |
| B—5. | How is Ernesto's relationship with his father? |
| | Yes |
| | Exploring Ernesto's relationship with others in the family is important, particularly since his father has not been brought up as of yet, and there is much research on the correlation between family interpersonal relations and academic performance |
| B—6. | Does Ernesto currently receive tutoring? |
| | No |
| | Asking about what interventions may have been successful or unsuccessful in the past is appropriate. However, it is not warranted to specifically target tutoring to elicit information that may provide insight into Ernesto's lack of motivation toward school and learning |

## Section C: Ernesto

Further communication during the intervention meeting reveals that Ernesto has a good relationship with his father, who has been deployed for the past year. Ernesto's father is quite involved in Ernesto's life and, generally, is the parent who attends the school functions and helps in the classroom when he is not deployed. Ernesto has shared with his mother that he misses his father very much, although they write to each other often. At this point in the meeting, what would be the best course of action by the committee?

(Select as many as you consider indicated in this section.)

| C—1. | Have the teacher and parent talk alone |
| --- | --- |
| | No |
| | This is a committee meeting where the parent and teacher are encouraged to talk openly with the committee so that a plan of action can be created with the team's input in the best interest of the student. If the parent and teacher wish to talk after the meeting, this is encouraged |
| C—2. | Request the assistance of an administrator |
| | No |
| | Administrators hire licensed professionals, who they appoint to interdisciplinary intervention teams to make good informed decisions about the educational needs of students in their absence and, often, outside of their area of expertise (e.g., school counselor, school psychologist, nurse) |
| C—3. | Develop an academic intervention plan |
| | Yes |
| | Now is a good time to establish an intervention plan based on current information. The plan will have progress review dates and be redesigned if it is not being effective or if new information is presented and new developments occur |
| C—4. | Come up with rewards for Ernesto when he completes his classwork and homework |
| | No |
| | Ernesto's academic struggles require more than rewards for work completion. A comprehensive action plan with multiple strategies is warranted. Also, extrinsic motivation has been linked to reducing intrinsic motivation and must be used sparingly and carefully and not in the absence of more concrete, research-supported, individualized academic supports |
| C—5. | Request that Ernesto join the school counseling small group for students with parents/guardians who are deployed |
| | Yes |
| | In addition to an academic intervention plan, Ernesto has clearly indicated a need for involvement in small group counseling with other students who experience issues related to parent deployment |

| | |
|---|---|
| C—6. | Table the meeting until Ernesto's father can be present<br>No<br>School counselors and other educators meet students' needs in the presence and/or absence of parents. Although parental permission and informed consent are required in some circumstances, this is not the case here. |

## Section D: Ernesto

Over the next week, the teacher reports to the parent that Ernesto is beginning to push and yell at fellow students, and he gets angry very easily. The parent and teacher agree to send Ernesto to you for individual counseling sessions. During the first session, Ernesto becomes very emotional and shares that he overheard his mother telling his grandmother that she was planning to divorce his father when he returned to the States. Your most immediate courses of action with Ernesto should be:

(Select as many as you consider indicated in this section.)

| | |
|---|---|
| D—1. | Discuss divorce<br>No<br>There is no substantial evidence to support the notion that Ernesto's parents are divorcing. Also, if a school counselor wants to meet with elementary students to discuss parental divorce, parental permission is warranted. This is not to say that the counselor should not listen and validate Ernesto's concern about his belief |
| D—2. | Discuss deployment<br>No<br>This is not the topic Ernesto has indicated. Not warranted at this time |
| D—3. | Work on securing a support system<br>Yes<br>It is important to help Ernesto to identify important others, particularly adults that he can talk to about what he overheard and his beliefs |
| D—4. | Discuss involving his mother<br>Yes<br>It is important to help Ernesto to understand the importance of involving his mother, who can talk to him about what he overheard her say to his grandmother |
| D—5. | Discuss feelings<br>Yes<br>Allow Ernesto to express his thoughts and emotions, and offer validation |

| D—6. | Work on strategies for managing emotions |
| --- | --- |
| | Yes |
| | Helping Ernesto to express his emotions appropriately and to develop an understanding that he does not have to be a puppet to his emotions is an important life skill |
| D—7. | Work on strategies for reducing stress |
| | Yes |
| | Helping Ernesto to understand what he is feeling and to teach him strategies for managing the stress he is experiencing |

## Section E: Ernesto

Ernesto comes to your office first thing in the morning immediately after getting off the bus. He is shaking and crying. As you calm Ernesto and sit down to talk, he reveals that his mother has a boyfriend who has been touching him when mom is not around. He has been telling Ernesto that they are just "wrestling." He said that last night, mom's boyfriend came into his bedroom. Ernesto describes the sexual acts. He said he yelled for his mother, but she did not come into the room. What is the most essential course of action?

(Choose ONLY ONE in this section.)

| E—1. | Ask questions to determine the mother's knowledge and involvement |
| --- | --- |
| | No |
| | At this time, it is in the best interest of Ernesto to assume the mother had knowledge of the incident and seek immediate safety for Ernesto |
| E—2. | Contact the local police |
| | No |
| | The local police will likely request that you contact CPS, or they will contact CPS |
| E—3. | Call the mother |
| | No |
| | The mother may be involved |
| E—4. | Contact CPS |
| | Yes |
| | You are suspecting child abuse. Although the suspected sexual abuse is not by a family member, a family member (i.e., the mother) may be involved. The best course of action to protect Ernesto is to call CPS, and they can assess the mother's involvement |

| E—5. | Request that the school nurse examine Ernesto |
| --- | --- |
| | No |
| | This can be humiliating for a child or adolescent (even adults), particularly when care is not taken in the manner in which this may be accomplished. You can report suspected abuse without personally seeing any physical signs or in the absence of physical signs. *If*, however, the student was in pain, asking for school nurse involvement may be essential |
| E—6. | Make contact with father |
| | No |
| | The father is deployed. Contact CPS |

## Section F: Ernesto

Two weeks later, you receive a letter in the mail that says the case is "unfounded." The following week, Ernesto comes to your office, again, right off the bus, shaking and crying, saying that his mother's boyfriend did it again. Ernesto's mother shows up at your door with the principal while Ernesto is in your office. Ernesto's mother very calmly taps on your door and walks in. She said she is there to take Ernesto to a doctor's appointment and that he was not supposed to get on the bus this morning. You express your concern and ask Ernesto if he would like to tell his mother what he just told me. Crying, he nods his head and tells his mother. Calmly, she said, "Ernesto, you know this is a lie, and this is why the social services people dismissed it." What is the best course of action?

(Select as many as you consider indicated in this section.)

| F—1. | Call CPS |
| --- | --- |
| | Yes |
| | Again, call CPS with an additional report |
| F—2. | Contact the local police department |
| | No |
| | The mother has every legal right at this point to take Ernesto unless she is intoxicated. If so, you may contact the police so that the student is not put in harm's way (e.g., driving under the influence). Police involvement may be warranted, too, if the parent is behaving in a manner that is disruptive in the school |
| F—3. | Make contact with the father |
| | No |
| | The father is deployed. The mother, too, is custodial parent and, so, can pick up her child for a doctor's appointment |

| F—4. | Tell the parent that she cannot take Ernesto |
| --- | --- |
| | No |
| | The parent has a legal right to take Ernesto under the current circumstances |
| F—5. | Call in the boyfriend and talk with all three (i.e., mother, boyfriend, and Ernesto) |
| | No |
| | Do not involve the boyfriend, who has no legal rights in the case of Ernesto and is the alleged perpetrator |
| F—6. | Be stern with Ernesto and ask him for the truth |
| | No |
| | Assume Ernesto is giving you the truth |

# Chapter 1 Guided reflection

Identify key events, people, associations, trends, and movements, and discuss their significance in the history of the school counseling profession.

Describe and support the importance of CACREP and CAEP for a school counselor education program.

Explain the purpose of ASCA with regard to the school counseling profession.

Identify the dual roles of the school counselor. Then, summarize the functions inherent in each role.

List critical ethical and legal considerations associated with each construct:

Confidentiality

Confidentiality of counseling-related electronic communication

Harm to self or others

Child abuse and neglect

Scope of practice

Informed consent

Student records and counseling case notes

78 ■ *Foundations of school counseling*

IDEA and Section 504

Homelessness

Research

Supervision

Match the following theorists to one of the primary categories of human development. It is possible that one theorist could be connected to multiple theories. Then, identify key constructs of the theory, and summarize the theory.

Jean Piaget

Erik Erikson

Lev Vygotsky


Fowler


Freud


Kohlberg


Skinner


Havighurst


Bandura

Support the use of Bloom's taxonomy in school counseling.

Discuss the importance of Marzano's nine instructional strategies, and explain how an understanding of those strategies would be useful in school counseling.

Compare and contrast intrinsic and extrinsic motivation. Consider the pros and cons of the application of extrinsic motivators.

What is the importance of Maslow's theory in relation to student learning and motivation. Provide an example.

# Chapter 2

# Comprehensive school counseling programs

A comprehensive developmental school counseling program (CDSCP) provides developmentally appropriate prevention and intervention services that support the academic achievement mission of schools. The hallmark of a CDSCP is its focus on providing career, academic, social, and emotional development to all students. Additionally, CDSCPs include support services for teachers, parents, administrators, and the community as an integral part of the educational system.

As stated previously, the ASCA National Model is the only officially organized and recognized national CDSCP model that defines and seeks to unify our profession. Some states have their own comprehensive, developmental school counseling models that share elements of the ASCA National Model and have merit.

## The ASCA national model and a comprehensive school counseling program

This chapter, while covering the ASCA National Model to the extent that a study guide should for the profession of school counseling, goes beyond the components of the ASCA National Model and/or provides more detail with constructs and concepts school counselors need to know to effectively provide counseling services to students in K-12 schools and to promote a passing score on all exams in school counseling. The Council for Accreditation of Counseling and Related Educational Programs (CACREP) and the Board of Education recognizes general counseling knowledge, skills, and abilities as foundational to the specialty of school counseling. Finally, as noted in Chapter 1, the National Board for Certified Counselors (NBCC) requires that school counselors pass the National Certified Counselor exam (NCE) as a prerequisite to earning the National Certified School Counselor (NCSC) credential, which is another reason for including information that school counselors will see on prerequisite exams in order to secure advanced voluntary school counseling credentials.

ASCA advocates for both prevention and intervention services that promote academic success, postsecondary readiness, and social emotional learning to the extent reflected in the ASCA National Model.

### ASCA Position on The School Counselor and School Counseling Programs

School counselors design and implement school counseling programs that improve a range of student learning and behavioral outcomes. "The ASCA National Model: A Framework for School Counseling Programs" outlines the components of a school counseling program and brings school counselors together with one vision and one voice, creating unity and focus toward improving student achievement and supporting student development.

*Position statement adopted 1988; revised 1993, 1997, 2005, 2012, 2017, 2023*

ASCA recognizes the unique qualifications of school counselors, who are credentialed/licensed and hold a minimum of a master's degree. As such, ASCA has provided a clear statement about who is eligible to be creating, planning, and implementing school counseling programs.

### ASCA Position on The School Counselor and the Use of Non-School Counseling Credentialed Personnel In Implementing School Counseling Programs

School counselors and the school counseling programs they design and implement serve a vital role in maximizing student success (Dimmit & Wilkerson, 2012; Olsen, Parikh-Foxx, Flowers, & Algozzine, 2017; Wilkerson, Perusse, & Hughes, 2013). School counselors are uniquely qualified and solely eligible to meet the requirements of designing and implementing these programs. School counselors recognize that personnel who do not hold a master's degree in school counseling are not qualified to deliver a school counseling program that supports academic, career and social/emotional development and positively affects achievement for all students.

*Position statement adopted 1994;
revised 2000, 2006, 2012, 2018*

---

ASCA recommends an ideal student-to-school counselor ratio of 250:1. However, the most recent data (2021–2022) depicts a national average of 408:1 (ASCA, 2023b), which is clearly not meeting ASCA's recommended caseload. For this reason, school counselors are encouraged to make use of the manpower that is available and willing to assist with program support related tasks that will allow the school counselor to provide effective student services more efficiently.

## *ASCA Position on The School Counselor and the Use of Support Staff in School Counseling Programs*

The school counselor understands the value added to a comprehensive school counseling program through the effective use of support staff. Assistance from school counseling program support staff members allows school counselors to use their time more efficiently and use their professional expertise and leadership skills more effectively to meet student needs.

*Position statement adopted 1974;
reviewed and reaffirmed 1980;
revised 1986, 1993, 1999, 2001, 2008, 2013, 2019*

---

The ASCA National Model has had an epic impact on the profession of school counseling. In fact, ASCA established the School Counseling Analysis, Leadership, and Evaluation (SCALE) Research Center to aid school counselors in identifying best practices that demonstrate how a comprehensive school counseling program is connected to student success. The SCALE Research Center helps to connect school counselors with counselor educators for collaborative research design, implementation, evaluation, and publication. The center also provides school counselors with professional development opportunities grounded in accountable research-supported programming and practices as well as training related to data collection and analysis. To access the SCALE Research Center go to http://scale.schoolcounselor.org.

The ASCA National Model consists of four fundamental components: (1) define, (2) manage, (3) deliver, and (4) assess. Integral to the implementation of each component of the ASCA National Model, and weaved throughout, are attributes of leadership, advocacy, and collaboration that focus on promoting positive systemic change outcomes.

## Define: student standards and professional standards

Foundational to the first operational level of ASCA's National Model are three sets of standards that define school counseling as a profession (ASCA, 2019a). The standards upon which the foundation of your school counseling program is built must be strong since it is sitting on the San Andreas Fault scrutiny of our educational climate of accountability, and ASCA has risen to the challenge. The *define* component standards include ASCA Student Standards: Mindsets and Behaviors for Student Success, ASCA Ethical Standards for School Counselors, and ASCA School Counselor Professional Standards and Competencies. These three sets of standards can be found in *The ASCA National Model: A Framework for School Counseling Programs* (2019a).

### Student standards and domains
The research-based Mindsets & Behaviors for Student Success address three broad developmental domains (i.e., academic, career, and social/emotional). Primary developmental domains are discussed in detail in the next chapter. The 36 ASCA Mindsets & Behaviors guide programming, service delivery, and assessment identifying what a student should know and be able to do as a result of the school counseling program (ASCA, 2021).

### School counselor professional standards and competencies
Unifying our roles and functions, ASCA developed the School Counselor Professional Standards and Competencies, which underscore the mindsets

and behaviors that a school counselor should possess in order to be well equipped to meet the needs of students and the complexities of a comprehensive school counseling program. These standards may be used for self-assessment, administrator assessment of school counselors, and as a tool for counselors.

Like other counseling professions, ASCA has established a set of ethical principles intended to establish and maintain the highest level of integrity, professionalism, and leadership. A wise person once said that ethics are what we do when others aren't looking. I say *amen* to that brilliant summary. Together with school policy and the law, ethical principles aid school counselors in making sound decisions that are in the best interest of all involved. ASCA's Ethical Standards help to guide school counselors through the murky waters of complicated situations often encountered in the school setting (ASCA, 2022a).

## Manage: program focus and planning

Managing a school counseling program is an involved process whereby school counselors design a multi-faceted program in such a way that it can be measured and gets results. Key aspects of the *manage* component of the ASCA National Model are: 1) beliefs, vision, and mission statements, 2) data-informed practices, 3) annual data review and student outcome goals, 4) classroom-group and closing-the-gap action plans, 5) lesson plans, 6) annual administrative conference, 7) use of time and calendars, and 8) advisory council (2019a).

### Beliefs, vision, and mission statements

School counselors are called to examine their personal and professional belief systems as well as those of the school, district, and state to integrate those beliefs with the ASCA Professional Standards and Competencies. Understanding all these beliefs in relation to students, education, counseling, fellow educators, and the philosophies that drive us and our work is essential to program focus and to developing school counseling program beliefs that align with the school, district, and state. These school counseling program beliefs inform the vision statement that articulates desired outcomes for students now and into the future while the mission statement that follows summarizes a clear program focus for achieving that vision.

Vision statements provide sufficient detail but are not meant to be dissertations. Literary buffs may be tempted to create the next unabridged, complete, deluxe edition of John Dewey's works. I do not mean to blow the mood because hey, I get it. The printed word is my ambrosia. Similar to the stirrings that consume my soul when I walk into a basilica, a euphoric virus invades my mind at the mere scent of books when I walk into a library. I suspect that my true birthplace was in the self-help stacks in a *biblioteca pubblica* in south-central Europe. I can only hope that *Kindle* and *Nook* do not kill the printed text. After all, *video did kill the radio star*.

Okay, if I am not careful, we could be on that subject for the remainder of this chapter. The point is that the school counseling program vision statement is meant to be an inspiring futuristic description of optimistic outcomes for students that reflect the mutually agreed upon beliefs and worldviews of all stakeholders. With this said, unearthing the appropriate optimistic words while writing a vision statement can be like locating a rental car in Bermuda. For this reason, ASCA offers guidance in writing superb mission and vision statements (ASCA, 2019c), although you may still have to explore Bermuda by horse, taxi, bicycle, or carriage.

---

**VISION OR MISSION STATEMENT?**

Is the following an example of an excerpt from a vision or mission statement?

"After participating in the school counseling program, all students of Overthetop Middle School use their strengths and talents to achieve desired goals."

---

*Data-informed and data producing school counseling practices*

An essential part of school counseling leadership is data management. School counseling programs are data-driven and data-producing. That is, school counselors make use of data to identify *why* a particular program, approach, or activity was selected for implementation and data is collected post services/interventions to determine how, and to what extent, students are different as a result of the school counseling program (ASCA, 2019a, 2019b, 2022b).

In some circles, just the mention of the word *data* elicits a stomach-knotting panic response that is transparent on anguish-stricken faces. You'd think I just tried to pickpocket their superhero powers. My compassion runs deep for those terrified of data since I had been one of those folks myself at one time. Please let me say in the sincerest tone that

I can muster—*relax Superman, it's not kryptonite*. It is time to square with both the constructs and processes related to data and accountability.

Although the term accountability can bring about internal thunder as well, it is a reality to be embraced. Where there is data there can be accountability and where there is accountability there is likely data—the marriage is strong. Best practices necessitate that school counselors use data to create needs-driven school counseling programs and to assess the effectiveness of school counseling programs and practices. In this regard, school counseling programs are both data-driven and data-producing.

> **DROPOUT PREVENTION**
>
> A high-school counselor designed a program using attendance and graduation reports to identify specific populations of students, who for a variety of reasons are not coming to school. He designed a program to meet the needs of these students with the goal of reducing truancy and school dropout rates and improving school attendance. The school counselor just evaluated the program to find that the program has been effective in meeting the established goals. Which of the following would best describe the practices used by this school counselor?
>
> a. Data-producing program.
> b. Data-driven and data-producing program.
> c. Research-based programming.
> d. None of the above.

*Participation, mindsets & behaviors, and outcome data*
When planning for program activities and the assessment of those activities ASCA (2019a, 2019d) calls upon school counselors to make use of three types of data: 1) participation data (who), 2) Mindsets & Behaviors data (what), and 3) outcome data (why). Participation data is simply the number of students engaging in a specific school counseling service and the frequency and duration of participation. Thus, participation data defines *who* is being served. Mindsets & Behaviors (discussed earlier) data identifies *what* attitudes, knowledge, and skills are being addressed. Outcome data demonstrates how school counselors impact student attendance, achievement, and discipline by way of

advising, instruction, appraisal, and counseling, thus answering *why* school counselors and school counseling programs are needed.

In order to better understand the importance and use of outcome data, school counselors need to understand what is meant by baseline data. Baseline data is the data with which school counselors compare any subsequent data collected. For example, pre-assessment responses will become the baseline data for comparing the post-assessment response data. Also, outcome data such as attendance rates, disciplinary data, graduation rates (listed below), reviewed at any point in time is the baseline data upon which any subsequent data reviews are compared. For example, the school counselor may review attendance data two months into school to find an overall attendance issue in the school or an attendance issue with a specific group of students. After targeting the attendance concern with the targeted population by way of a school counseling program service, or multiple services, the school counselor would again view the attendance data to assess for change. The school counselor would likely review the data multiple times during or post school counseling program intervention to determine intervention effectiveness with regard to positive student outcomes. In this case, improved school attendance.

School counselors, who make use of the robust sources of outcome data on hand, have a foundation for accountable program construction. Understanding where to find the right sources of data to target school counseling programming and specific populations is an essential first step to being inducted into the accountability ranks of the *data-informed* school counselors. The following list is not exhaustive but includes some possible data sources generally available to school counselors within the school in which they practice.

- Attendance rates.
- Career assessments.
- Classroom performance data.
- College acceptance rates.
- Course enrollment.
- Demographic data.
- Department of Education website.
- Discipline records.
- Dropout rates.
- Expulsion records.

- GED-track records.
- Gifted education placement records.
- Grade point average.
- Grade reports.
- Graduation rates.
- Program placement.
- Promotion and retention rates.
- Scholarship records.
- School data reports/report cards.
- School improvement plan.
- Special education placement records.
- Standardized assessment data.
- Suspensions (in school).
- Suspensions (out of school).

### Needs assessments and supplemental information gathering

Let's consider the attendance example used the previous section to better understand how other approaches to gather data may be useful. If, after a review of attendance data, the school counselor identified an attendance problem it could be difficult to design a program that would improve attendance without understanding the reason why students are not coming to school. Supplemental data collected by way of needs assessments and other approaches may offer insights that will shed light on the *why*.

This supplemental data may be collected by way of formal and informal conversations, interviews, opinions, and surveys. While needs assessment surveys are generally used to systematically identify the needs of the broader population (e.g., student body, teachers, parents, community agencies) and subpopulations (e.g., special education students, fifth-grade teachers, parents of gifted students, mental health agencies), it can be used for smaller groups. Information obtained from needs assessments aids school counselors in designing or redesigning programs for targeted populations and topics and continuous program improvement.

Needs assessment surveys gather data in the form of participant perceptions. Assessing needs based on participant perceptions is not generally considered standardized (discussed later in the chapter) but can take a more formal tone versus an informal tone. Needs assessment surveys may be written (e.g., survey, questionnaire) or oral (e.g., interview) and conducted in person, on the telephone, via video conferencing, by way of snail mail, or by some other creative approach. School counselors examine survey results looking for patterns and inconsistencies.

A school counselor might elect to use focus groups and/or key informants as supplemental means of data collection. These types of data collection approaches, unlike the one-way needs assessment survey, allow for an interactive and potentially more in-depth discussion. School counselors who elect to use focus groups select several individuals who are representative of the population to be served—like cherry picking. Collectively, in a structured or semi-structured format, differing needs are discussed along with potential reasons for those needs, and together the group prioritize needs. If you picked ripe cherries, the data will be sweet! Like focus groups, key informants are individually selected by the school counselor. However, these participants may not necessarily be a member of the target population. The school counselor picks key informants based on their vast knowledge of the population to be served. Key informants are generally surveyed individually, in pairs, or in small groups.

Another solid method for collecting data is the use of community forums. Community forums offer comprehensive data from diverse participants since this approach invites the participation of any stakeholder wishing to be involved. School counselors announce the community forum meeting and the topic of discussion, and those interested participate in much the same fashion as the focus group.

### DR. DATARULES

Dr. Datarules, your school principal, has asked you, the school counselor, to provide him with data other than what is already available to him (e.g., school report cards, standardized testing results, classroom assessment results) that identifies instructional strategies that are both enjoyed by students and effective in producing higher levels of academic achievement. You decide to administer a needs assessment. Who would be the target of your assessment?

### Annual data review and student outcome goals

The persistent review of data over time allows school counselors to observe trends, changes, and gaps to be addressed. After a while, data review and collection will become second nature and you will rely on data as an ally useful in edifying school counseling programming and school counselor services.

School personnel engage in annual data reviews that generally result in school improvement plans. It is critical that school counselors be a part of these communications and processes in order to get a sound understanding of the data-driven priorities established by the school and division administrators, educators, and other specialty personnel (e.g., school psychologist, school social worker, educational diagnostician, nurse). ASCA specifically calls upon school counselors to fully understand student needs related to achievement, attendance, and discipline, uncovering areas of concern or areas whereby gaps exist.

Skills considered essential to effectively managing data in order to identify student and school community needs and prioritize those needs are noted in Table 2.1 (Erford, 2019; ASCA, 2019a, 2019d, 2022b; Schellenberg, 2019).

Once the student and school community needs are identified and prioritized, those needs are converted to *outcome goals* that are stated as measurable impacts that the school counseling program will have on student achievement, attendance, and discipline, particularly related to closing any identified gaps in these areas. These are tied

**Table 2.1 Essential Data Skills for School Counselors**

- Ability to identify existing data sources within and outside of the school
- Ability to collect data related to individuals, groups, and programs
- Ability to disaggregate data and identify inequities and barriers to student success
- Ability to analyze and interpret data to identify and prioritize needs and develop appropriate programming
- Ability to establish baselines and create measurable goals and action plans based on data
- Ability to assess counseling progress and evaluate programs to determine effectiveness of practices
- Ability to use data to create a continuous cycle of program improvement
- Ability to create results reports from program outcome data

**92** ■ *Comprehensivs school counseling programs*

into the school counseling vision and mission statements as well as the school improvement plan. ASCA provides significant guidance for creating *student outcome goals* that are specific, and as the name implies, focused on *student outcomes*. ASCA's *Student Outcome Goal Plan Template* steps school counselors through the process of creating a systemic-focused, data-supported goal statement that identifies the Mindsets & Behaviors, student learning objectives with pre-post assessment items, and the interventions/activities to be carried out (ASCA, 2019a, 2019d). The *ASCA National Model Implementation Guide: Manage and Assess* (2019d), provides a multitude of outcome goal examples and *do's and don'ts* when summarizing data to create outcome goals. ASCA recommends that outcome goals include three primary components: baseline data, target data, and percent change. It is important to establish realistic percentages of change that take into consideration the population targeted for change. For example, if targeting the entire school, a one percent to two percent change is significant, however if targeting a smaller sub-group of at-risk students, a change of 15 percent to 20 percent would be realistic. Seek to establish goals that are not overly challenging but are not too easy either—find the significance sweet spot! ASCA's *Annual Student Outcome Goal Plan* requires the creation of an outcome goal statement that includes the three components noted above as well as several others, which are outlined in Table 2.2 below.

**Table 2.2 Components of Annual Student Outcome Goal Statement**

| End Date |
|---|
| End date examples: |
| By March 2027… <br> By the conclusion of the six-week group session … <br> By the end of the sixth week of school … |
| Targeted Students |
| Targeted student examples: |
| …eighth grade students will … <br> …the number of students who accrued more than ten absences … <br> …the number of school-wide office referrals for aggressive behavior … |

(Continued)

**Table 2.2 (Continued)**

| |
|---|
| Increase/Decrease |
|    Increase and/or decrease examples: |
|       *…will increase by …*<br>      *…will be less than …*<br>      *…will be reduced by …* |
| Outcome to be Changed |
|    Outcome to be changed examples: |
|       *…failed math …*<br>      *…at risk of school drop out …*<br>      *…twenty or more absences …* |
| Percentage of Change |
|    Percentage of change examples: |
|       *…school-wide attendance will increase by 2% …*<br>      *…first grade math scores will increase by 10% …* |
| Baseline Data (*numbers only*) |
| Target Data (*numbers only*) |

The following is an example of a student outcome goal statement created after examining the school's annual discipline report. The report confirmed the highest number of incidences were in the category of "threaten, intimidate and/or physical contact with another student" (ASCA, 2019d, p. 50):

- By 20 May 2022, the number of discipline referrals involving "threaten, intimidate and/or physical contact with another student" will decrease by 20 percent from 137 (previous school year) to 110 (current school year).

**CAN THIS BE MEASURED?**

You are a school counselor facilitating a small group on the topic of anger management based on school discipline data. The outcome goal of the group is to learn how to express anger in a healthy way. This is a fine goal; however, it is not measurable as it is. Which of the following outcome goals would be considered exemplary in the eyes of ASCA?

> a. By October 2026, students will learn healthy ways to express anger.
> b. Students will express anger in ways that are not hurtful to others.
> c. By the conclusion of the anger management group, students will complete an anger management worksheet.
> d. At the conclusion of the anger management group, students will demonstrate a decrease in discipline referrals by 30 percent from ten referrals each month to seven referrals each month.

In addition to the ASCA National Model's Outcome Goals, it is important that school counselors be aware of *SMART Goals* (Doran, 1981). Although, not considered part of the ASCA National Model, SMART (**S**pecific, **M**easurable, **A**ttainable, **R**esults-oriented, **T**ime-bound) goals have been widely adopted in educational settings, including schools that follow the ASCA National Model as well as those following their own CDSCP model. The SMART goal format is well-documented as being helpful for conceptualizing the process of goal attainment.

## Classroom-group and closing-the-gap action plans

Action plans aid school counselors in effectively delivering curriculum that is aligned with the ASCA Mindsets & Behaviors in: (1) classrooms, (2) small groups, (3) large groups, and (4) individual settings. The *Classroom and Group Mindsets & Behaviors Action Plan* and the *Closing-the-Gap Action Plan* are similar in that both delineate scope, focus, timing, and setting of planned instruction (ASCA, 2019a, 2019d). The Closing-the-Gap Action Plan specifically addresses academic, disciplinary, and attendance gaps identified during a review of disaggregated data. The *ASCA National Model Implementation Guide: Manage and Assess* (2019d) provides blank templates and examples of completed templates for both types of action plans to serve as a guide for school counselors. Keep in mind that action plans are living documents that should be changed annually and may be changed throughout the school year as warranted. Classroom and Group Mindsets & Behaviors Action Plans include a minimum of the following components (ASCA, 2019a, 2019c):

- Date created/revised.
- Identification of service delivered (Classroom Lesson, Unit, or Small Group).

- Grade level.
- Topic/Focus/Purpose.
- Targeted ASCA student standards (Mindsets & Behaviors).

The Closing-the-Gap Action Plan includes the following components (ASCA, 2019a, 2019c):

- Annual student outcome goal.
- ASCA Mindsets & Behaviors with pre-post assessment items for each.
- Interventions supporting achievement of the annual student outcome goal.
- Systemic focus.
- Baseline and results data (anticipated and actual).
- Mindsets & Behaviors pre-post assessment results.
- Outcome data plan and results (baseline and final data).
- Reflection.

### Lesson plans

Lesson plans are specific to the delivery of classroom instruction that is built upon the school counseling curriculum. The lesson plan requires the creation of pre-post lesson/session items (discussed later in this chapter) essential to measuring outcomes and the achievement of targeted Mindsets & Behaviors. Like action plans, ASCA provides a lesson plan template and examples of completed lesson plans (2019c) to aid school counselors in including what ASCA considers to be the seven essential components of a lesson plan:

- Mindsets & Behaviors for Student Success.
- Learning Objectives.
- Materials.
- Evidence Base.
- Procedure.
- Assessment Plan.
- Follow Up.

The *evidence base* component of the lesson plan necessitates that school counselors stay current on trends and developments in counseling, which includes empirically validated methods, theories, techniques, programs— *what works or has worked with which populations*. School counselors are research-informed practitioners, which increases their knowledge of best practices (i.e., commonly used quality practices), research-informed practices (i.e., research-supported foundation), and evidence-based practices (i.e., highest caliber published in peer-reviewed journals) (ASCA, 2019a). Action research (i.e., school counselor's own examination of practices/interventions) is also a viable evidence base for the school counselor's lesson plan.

School counselors are savvy consumers of professional literature and research. Unlike the murmurs of idle gossip or scratching's of graffiti, research communicates factual information. Information shared through published, peer-reviewed research in education, counseling, psychology, and related journals identifies evidence-based techniques, models, and approaches that describe what works and with whom. The fundamental fact is that a tried-and-true school counseling intervention can forever change the direction of a student's life.

Having a sound evidence base requires the ability to identify and critically evaluate important components of relevant studies such as (1) theoretical orientation, (2) target population, (3) setting, (4) intervention used, (5) method of data collection and analysis, and (6) results. The ACA has a list of counseling-related peer-reviewed journals on their website at www.counselor.com. Although there are hundreds of journals that could prove to be useful resources, there are two primary professional school counseling journals available that identify innovative methods and research for promoting effective practices in school counseling. *Professional School Counseling* (PSC) ASCA's award-winning, peer-reviewed journal is available in print or online and free of charge to ASCA members. The peer-reviewed *Journal of School Counseling* (JSC) sponsored by the College of Education, Health, and Human Development at Montana State University is an online journal dedicated to the practice of school counseling (www.jsc.montana.edu/index.html). Peer reviewed journals provide results for empirically validated, evidence-based practices that are considered to be the highest caliber.

School counselors are encouraged to check out The National Technology Institute for School Counselors at www.techcounselor.org, which houses research-supported information and resources specific to the practice of school counseling. Also, *ASCA Scene* at www.schoolcounselor.org/SCENE is loaded with research-supported programs and interventions.

The Center for School Counseling Outcome Research and Evaluation (CSCORE), established by a diverse group of counselor educators, aids school counselors in identifying school counseling practices that result in positive student outcomes. CSCORE provides international leadership that focuses on research-supported systemic programming and assessment to support families and communities and to aid students in achieving academically. To access CSCORE go to www.umass.edu/schoolcounseling.

## Annual administrative conference

School counselors and administrators are called to meet at least annually to engage in an interactive discussion about the school counseling program. This is an opportunity for the school counselor to explain how the school counseling program aligns with the school's mission and improvement plan. It's an opportunity for administrators to better understand the roles and functions of the school counselor and provide input into program priorities. ASCA recommends that the meeting take place within the first two months of school and that the *Annual Administrative Conference Template* created by ASCA (2019a) be used as a conversation road map during the conference.

## Use of time and calendars

If school counselors do not plan their time, others will and historically *have* assigned inappropriate duties to fill those gaps. ASCA recommends that 80 percent of a school counselors time be used providing direct and indirect services to students with the remaining 20 percent dedicated to program planning and school support services. This is a general guideline, since schools differ and therefore percentages of time in the delivery of direct and indirect student services may vary from school-to-school. ASCA provides school counselors with guidance regarding that which constitutes appropriate and inappropriate duties for the school counselor in accordance with the *ASCA National Model* (ASCA, 2019a).

ASCA created the *Use of Time Calculator* (2019a) to track time spent daily engaging in school counseling and non-school counseling tasks. This form could prove to be helpful during the annual conference with administrators to illustrate how the school counselor's time is being utilized. Essentially, the *Use of Time Calculator* has replaced what was historically known as service logs, which were used to document time on task and illustrate the numerous and diverse duties and levels of responsibilities of the school counselor. The *Use of Time Calculator* allows school counselors to track time spent in the following areas:

- Instruction (classroom; small group; large group).
- Counseling (individual; small group).
- Appraisal and Advisement.
- Consultation, Collaboration, and Referral.
- Defining, Managing, and Assessing Activities.
- Fair Share Responsibility Activities.
- Non-School Counseling Tasks.

Calendars, too, document the activities, services, and programs of a school counselor, which can aid in justifying school counseling programming and protect the school counselor's time spent delivering direct and indirect student services. ASCA recommends that school counselors post, in a timely manner, complete and visually appealing calendars so all stakeholders know when and where school-wide and community activities will take place, and to enhance accountability in a climate that continues to ask, *what does the school counselor do?* Annual and weekly calendar templates are provided by ASCA (2019a), which can be used as they are, or you can get creative in personalizing the template and perhaps even improving the design. As the adage goes—*there's always room for improvement*!

Although services delivered as illustrated by the *Use of Time Calculator* and weekly and annual calendars have their value in identifying *what* it is that school counselors do from day to day, it does not take the place of assessing for the outcomes of what school counselors do on a daily basis. Assessment, discussed at the end of this chapter, demonstrates *how* we make a difference in the lives of our students and establishes *why* school counseling programs, and the very existence of school counselors in K-12 settings, are needed.

### Advisory council

While school administrators generally establish school leadership teams, school counselors establish advisory councils as an important component of a CDSCP. This is another area of the manage component that cannot be overemphasized. This is a school counseling program brain trust who takes pride in helping the school counselor to create an optimal school counseling program that meets the needs of the many. How can you make a delicious cake without representative ingredients essential to making that cake taste good? Would you skip a sweetener? How about an egg that tends to hold everything together? Flour? Would you include milk or some kind of liquid to moisten the batter? A strained analogy I know, but I think you get my point.

ASCA recommends that the council meet at least twice a year, while some meet more times during the school year (and sometimes in the summer) based on time constraints and level of desire for involvement. Meetings may involve recommendations for specific goals and programs, review of programming outcomes, assignment of roles for non-counseling related activities such as the logistics of coordinating programs such as career week, funding/resource advocacy, and program advocacy/public relations. Meeting minutes and agendas are advised and ASCA has created a template for both (2019a) with all council members having input as to what will be discussed. ASCA recommends the following be considered when creating an Advisory Council and outlines each in detail in the *ASCA National Model: A Framework for School Counseling Programs* (ASCA, 2019a):

- Purpose.
- Representation.
- Size.
- Appropriate Candidates.
- Chairperson.
- Membership Terms.
- Agenda and Minutes.

## *Deliver: direct and indirect student services*

Program delivery describes how the school counseling program is implemented, consisting of both direct and indirect student services (ASCA, 2019a). As noted earlier, ASCA recommends that 80 percent of a school counselors time be used providing a combination of both direct and indirect services. School counselors blend both methods for a balanced approach to service delivery to meet the needs of all students.

Both direct and indirect student services are useful when engaging in prevention and intervention activities for a variety of purposes related to personal, social, emotional, academic, and career development. Prevention is aimed at stopping a problem or problematic situation before it starts, while intervention, sometimes referred to as responsive services, occurs post-onset or after a particular problem or disorder has been identified.

### ASCA Position on Identification, Prevention and Intervention of Harmful or Disadvantageous Behaviors

School counselors design and implement comprehensive school counseling programs that include processes for identifying students who may be engaging in harmful or disadvantageous behaviors. As part of that program, school counselors provide developmentally appropriate, culturally sensitive interventions and supports to assess the unmet need or lagging skill behind those behaviors and to promote the mindsets and behaviors all students need for success now and in the future.

*Position statement adopted 1989–1990; revised 1993, 1999, 2004, 2011, 2017, 2023*

School counselors embrace the proverb that *an ounce of prevention is worth a pound of cure* providing students with primary and secondary prevention programs. The school counselor also provides resources and conducts workshops that spotlight at-risk behaviors and teach parents, teachers, and the community what to look for when identifying students who may be contemplating suicide or homicide or both and who are experiencing depression, severe anxiety, or other debilitating conditions. However, we must be realistic about what we are dealing with here—complex human beings. So, no matter how diligent we are as school counselors, we cannot always head off all problems before onset. For this reason, most if not all schools with a CDSCP have *Response to Intervention* (RTI) programs as part of a *Multitiered System of Supports* (MTSS).

## ASCA Position on The School Counselor and Multitiered System of Supports

School counselors are stakeholders in the development and implementation of multitiered system of supports (MTSS), including, but not limited to, response to intervention and responsive positive behavioral interventions and supports. School counselors align their work with MTSS through the implementation of a school counseling program designed to affect student development in the academic (achievement), career (career exploration and development) and social/emotional (behavior) domains.

*Position statement adopted 2008; revised 2014, 2018, 2021*

School counselors collaborate with administrators, community agencies, families, the advisory council (discussed later in this chapter), and other school professionals when designing and implementing MTSS. Table 2.3 demonstrates the relationship between MTSS and school counseling direct and indirect student services (ASCA Position Statement, MTSS, 2021).

Response to intervention helps struggling students to improve behavior, achieve academically, and stay in school. RTI relies on educator referrals and data to identify struggling students so that individualized services can

**Table 2.3 MTSS Alignment with ASCA Model Direct and Indirect Student Services**

| TIER | ASCA National Model Direct & Indirect Student Services |
| --- | --- |
| Tier one: | Classroom instruction and school wide programming/initiatives that emphasize use of data, collaboration, and evidence-based prevention work |
| Tier two: | Small group and individual counseling, consultation and collaboration with families and community and school stakeholders |
| Tier three: | Indirect student support services through consultation, collaboration, and referral |

*Source*: Adapted from *ASCA Position Statement, Multi-tiered System of Supports* (2021).

be designed to meet their unique, multifaceted, and sometimes complex needs. Interventions are put into place, and students are monitored to ensure progress toward established goals.

Primary prevention, secondary prevention, and tertiary prevention are used by school counselors to promote a safe and preventative school climate that meets the developmental needs of students (Goodman-Scott, Betters-Bubon, & Donohue, 2015). *Primary prevention* focuses on programming for the entire student body using education to ward off any potentially at-risk behavior or problematic situations. *Secondary prevention* is aimed at mediating a specific behavior or problem identified as a potential threat for a specific population deemed at risk. *Tertiary prevention* targets a specific population to reduce or eliminate a problem or behavior that is already occurring.

> **WHITNEY'S BEHAVIOR**
>
> A school counselor has been working with Whitney, a middle-school student, for several months. Whitney is having many behavioral problems. The school counselor began working with Whitney when she was referred to the school's early intervention team. The intervention plan was not successful in creating behavioral change. The school counselor continued to consult and collaborate with the school psychologist and school social worker but the strategies designed to help Whitney continued to be unsuccessful. The school counselor is now strongly encouraging Whitney's parents to seek outside mental health counseling services and has provided the family with a resource list from which to select an individual and family counselor. When considering ASCA's tiers of the RTI process, which tier represents the current role of the school counseling in helping Whitney?
>
> a. Tier two.
> b. Tier three.
> c. Tier one.
> d. None of the above.

RTI teams are a specialty blend of expertise (e.g., school counselor, school psychologist, teacher, school social worker, reading specialist). The union of disciplines allow for a deeper conceptualization of student needs and a holistic and integrated perspective from which to identify promising interventions and tools. RTI services may be delivered by collaborating with select professionals within and outside of the school based on student needs.

RTI services are as unique as the students, varying in type, intensity, and duration. RTI services are based on student needs and established educational, career, and personal–social goals. A sampling of services may include:

- Dropout prevention.
- Decision making.
- Behavioral support.
- Referral.
- Counseling.
- Career planning.
- Assessment.
- Goal setting.
- Parenting skills.
- Transitioning.

Working within the MTSS/RTI framework, data from universal screenings (e.g., existing data, input from teachers), too, help school counselors to identify areas to be targeted. Data collected in this manner requires only passive consent, meaning parents only need notification via postal mail or email and given the chance to opt out of the survey.

## ASCA Position on The School Counselor and Universal Screening

Universal screening provides invaluable data to multidisciplinary teams, including school counselors, as they identify student needs and match them to interventions within a multitiered, multidisciplinary system of supports (MTSS). Universal screening must be carried out in an ethical manner that complies with federal and state laws and school district policies.

*Position statement adopted 2023*

*Direct student services*

Direct services are in-person interactions with students delivered by way of instruction, counseling, and appraisal and advisement. Hours spent providing direct student services vary from school-to-school, depending on the needs of the student population.

**Instruction**

School counselors teach the school counseling curriculum by way of instruction in the classroom, in large and small groups, and with individuals to promote academic, career, and social/emotional development. The curriculum for *classroom lessons/units* and *groups* is structured and meets the components of action plans and lesson plans discussed earlier in this chapter. *Individual* instruction creatively meets the specific needs of a given student.

The school counseling core curriculum includes both group activities—not to be confused with group counseling—and classroom lessons. Group activities as part of the core school counseling curriculum may include peer helping programs, transitioning programs, educational groups, and any number of group activities offered directly to students by the school counselor.

Classroom instruction is the mainstay of school counseling, deeply rooted in the teaching profession during the vocational guidance movement. Delivery of the school counseling curriculum may cover a single topic in one lesson or in multiple lessons *as a unit* over a specified period of time. At times, classroom instruction delivered by the school counselor is at the request of the teacher to supplement specific course material and/or to address pressing sensitive issues or issues that have surfaced unique to the needs of their classroom and interfering with classroom instruction.

School counseling lesson delivery may be 20–90 minutes, depending on the developmental level of the students. Kindergarten and first grade lessons are likely to be about 20–25 minutes to accommodate the shorter attention spans of young children. Lessons for the upper elementary level students and middle-school students (i.e., grades 3–8) are generally 30 minutes to an hour. Delivery of the school counseling curriculum for high-school students can take an entire class period, including 90-minute block schedules, as long as teachers' schedules permit.

School counselors make use of differentiated instruction and provide teacher support in the use of differentiated instruction to meet the learning needs of diverse students. Differentiated instructional strategies are empirically supported as equitable and effective methods that result in positive student outcomes (Lopez & Mason, 2018).

It is important to note that no amount of differentiated instruction will likely make a difference if the curriculum is delivered in an unstructured, unruly environment. For this reason, classroom management is a skill specialty that should be learned, practiced, and honed by school counselors in order to provide efficient and effective instruction. School counselors draw upon training in counseling, school counseling, and education to create effective classroom management strategies. Teachers, too, may look to school counselors for help in identifying classroom management strategies that meet the needs of varied student learning styles, developmental needs, and personalities.

While some students stroll through the school years with no greater ambition than to please the teacher, others plow through school with seemingly no greater purpose than to make us nuts—a phenomena that is tough to become accustomed to no matter how seasoned the school counselor. There are times when school counselors enter classrooms where chaos blows as strong as Chicago winds capable of ripping royal fascinators off your head—*for you Kate Middleton fans*. Predetermined, well-tuned classroom management strategies help us to avoid flying by the seat of our proper toppers!

Well-executed classroom management strategies help students understand the power of good choices and to understand how our lives are the cumulative consequences of those choices. Thus, foundational to classroom management are classroom rules, which need to be easily understood, unbiased, and realistic. Rules need to be clearly communicated along with the consequences for breaking those rules. Consequences need to be reasonable and respectful. Students need to understand that there are two types of consequences to misbehavior—natural and logical. For example, *if you grab another student's crayon, they may smack you* (natural consequence); *if you grab another student's crayon, one minute will be taken off of your recess* (logical consequence). The consistent application of rules and consequences is critical to continued behavioral management and for reducing behavioral backsliding. If a student gets away with texting even once during the lesson, the student will likely do it again.

In addition to rules and consequences, it is important to catch students engaging in desired behaviors and reinforce those behaviors. Chapter 1 and Chapter 4 discuss behavior modification and the appropriate use of both extrinsic and intrinsic motivation to shape student behavior.

Also important to classroom management is the physical structure of the learning environment. School counselors who have good grasp on these nuances will be able to offer guidance to teachers while also manipulating the physical structure of the classroom for the delivery of the school counseling curriculum. Classroom structure is largely determined by targeted instructional goals. For example, some teachers and/or school counselors may prefer a formal tone to the classroom, and an environment that promotes individual work versus group work. In this case, desks or tables in the classroom might be physically arranged in a U-shape, V-shape, or lecture hall style. Those who desire a more relaxed tone and an environment that promotes cooperative learning may desire a physical arrangement that places the desks or tables in a square, circle, or small groupings.

There are both interior and exterior facets to consider when seeking to effectively manage a classroom. Think about who is coming and going, processes, and situations that may be going on outside the classroom that impact the classroom environment. Additional areas to consider for effective classroom management include:

- Noise levels.
- Resources.
- Volunteers.
- Breaks.
- Bathroom visits.
- Homework and classwork submission.
- Procedures for visiting the school nurse or school counselor.

Classrooms do not need to resemble holding cells where the sound of the bell is the signal for escape with students firing off vows of freedom while fleeing with inmates. An effective system of classroom management maintains a student-friendly focus and air of nurturing—interrogation is optional and called *Socratic dialogue*.

## Counseling

Counseling services are direct student services delivered by way of individual counseling and small group counseling. Often referred to as responsive services, these direct school counseling services meet students' pressing developmental or situational needs, including situations whereby school counselors aid students in working through grief and trauma in a brief, solution-focused manner within the scope of school counseling. Students in need of responsive counseling services are generally self-identified or identified by way of a referral from a concerned teacher, parent, and/or school administrator.

ASCA recognizes both individual and small group counseling as direct methods of service delivery to K-12 students (2019a). Whether school counselors elect to meet students' counseling needs individually or in a small group setting is determined on a case-by-case basis, to include an understanding of the student's current level of functioning, the nature of the presenting issue (include assessing severity, frequency, and immediacy), and the student's desired level of privacy.

School counseling services, whether individual counseling or small group counseling, are short-term. *Short-term* should be emphasized because school counseling alone is not in the best interest of children and adolescents experiencing severe, persistent, and progressive issues. Additionally, to provide ongoing counseling sessions with students whose issues cannot be sufficiently addressed within the scope of school counseling and within the expertise of the school counselor is in violation of professional ethical guidelines (ASCA, 2022a). School counselors can best meet the more severe (e.g., eating disorders, substance abuse, suicide ideation) personal, social, and emotional needs of students by making use of a collaborative model that involves referral services.

## Individual counseling

Individual counseling in the schools requires that the school counselor draw upon the counseling theories and techniques discussed in Chapter 4. School counselors understand the importance of establishing and maintaining effective counseling relationships throughout the counseling process, from goal setting to termination.

Although many secondary schools have student assistance counselors with advanced level credentials (e.g., LPC) and/or student assistance programs (SAPs), school counselors are trained in working with students who have experienced trauma and/or experiencing heightened levels of personal, social, and emotional distress and behavioral issues. School counselors are mindful to address such issues to the extent possible within the scope of school counseling, offering referral resources when needed.

School counselors often work with students who are grieving the loss of a friend or loved one as well as students who have experienced trauma. School counselors aid students in identifying copying strategies by exploring past coping successes and promising support systems.

---

### ASCA Position on The School Counselor and Trauma Informed Practices

School counselors understand the impact adverse childhood experiences have on students' academic achievement and social/emotional development. Through the implementation of a school counseling program, school counselors strive to identify, support and promote the success of students who have experienced trauma.

*Position statement adopted 2016; revised 2022*

---

When working with grieving children and adolescents, it is important to understand (1) the child's developmental level, (2) the child's level of maturity, (3) the family's values, perceptions, and rituals related to death and burial, (4) the factors surrounding the death (sudden, anticipated, relationship). School counselors need to be in the moment with the student, helping the student at their own pace, identify feelings and work through those feelings. Students can be taught appropriate ways to express those feelings as a part of the counseling goal.

School counselors also look for behaviors that are out of the ordinary and impact on academic, social, and emotional functioning. It is also important to be familiar with the stages of grieving (i.e., denial/isolation, anger, bargaining, depression, acceptance) to identify the difference between the normal grieving process and possible post-traumatic stress (Kubler-Ross & Kessler, 2014).

Often, parents consult with the school counselor about whether or not to allow their child to participate in a funeral. After fully explaining to a child what a funeral entails, allowing the child to attend based on his or her level of maturity and desire to attend provides the child with an understanding of a customary practice and the opportunity to grieve, say good-bye, and experience closure.

> **KYLEIGH'S MOTHER**
>
> Kyleigh, a second grader, is meeting with the school counselor due to the death of her mother, which occurred during a natural catastrophe one week ago. Kyleigh has been uncharacteristically quiet since the tragedy. What might be your primary focus during this first session with Kyleigh?
>
> a. Reassuring Kyleigh that everything will be okay.
> b. Assisting Kyleigh in identifying and expressing her feelings appropriately.
> c. Sharing your own experience with death.
> d. Having Kyleigh recall the experience.

## Group counseling

Group counseling is considered both educational and therapeutic. A school counselor may decide that group counseling may be the best fit for a student and his or her particular presenting issues and situation. At times, the school counselor may decide a combination of both small group and individual counseling would be most effective. Psychoeducational groups are the most widely used type of group counseling in the schools and are time limited, imparting information and offering opportunities for self-development.

---

### *ASCA Position on The School Counselor and Group Counseling*

Group counseling is a vital direct service to students and is an effective part of a school counseling program. It has a positive effect on academic, career and social/emotional development and should be supported by school administration and school districts.

*Position statement adopted 1989; revised 1993, 2002, 2008; reviewed 1999, 2008, 2014, 2020*

Psychoeducational groups in the K-12 school may include study skills, social skills, test-taking strategies, conflict resolution, organization, time management, problem solving, and anger management. Psychoeducational groups are also used to respond to the needs of students who are experiencing difficult life situations such as the deployment of a military family member, adoption, divorce, and family transitions (e.g., leaving for college, moving, remarriage, and blending families).

## ASCA Position on The School Counselor and Military-Connected Students

School counselors recognize military-connected students' unique and diverse needs. To support military-connected students, school counselors design and implement school counseling programs that promote an inclusive school climate, include activities and services supporting their distinct challenges and build school-family-community partnerships that create a sense of connectedness and belonging.

*Position statement adopted 2023*

Group counseling unites students with shared issues; promotes supportive relationships, healthy personal development, team problem solving, and cooperative behaviors; and provides opportunities for building communication, knowledge, and coping skills. The group experience may also enhance students' ability to empathize with others, to more fully understand the behavior of others, and to develop insight into themselves and into the unique and common aspects of their problems. For example, *dyadic counseling*, a form of group counseling that is popular in the schools, involves pairing two children in a relationship that revolves around play. In dyadic counseling, these children are paired based on opposing interpersonal orientations and guided by the school counselor toward more developmentally mature social interactions.

The Association for Specialists in Group Work (ASGW), a division of the ACA, as well as ASCA, promotes the value of group work in the school setting at the elementary, middle, and high school levels. The Council for Accreditation of Counseling and Related Education Programs (CACREP) and ASCA underscore the need for school counselors to develop professional competencies in group work (ASCA, 2022a).

Consider the follow process when coordinating and facilitating small group counseling in K-12 schools: (1) selecting/screening group members, (2) defining the group's purpose based on student need, (3) securing parent, teacher, and student permissions, (4) identifying meeting space, (5) determining length and number and days and times of meetings, (6) developing group activities, (7) facilitating group movement through the four stages of the process (i.e., initial stage, transition stage, working stage, and termination), (8) evaluating the effectiveness of the group intervention, and (9) providing for group follow-up. While planning small groups, the school counselor also considers whether or not the group will be an *open group* (i.e., new members are accepted after the group facilitation process in underway) or a *closed group* (i.e., new members are not accepted after the initial group meeting).

When screening, group members look for appropriate fit and aligned goals in relation to the group's purpose and focus. School counselors may elect to create small groups that are homogeneous (i.e., members share a variety of common characteristics), heterogeneous (i.e., diverse membership), or a combination of the two.

An example of a homogeneous group would be a self-esteem group for sixth-grade African American male students with similar backgrounds, experiencing low self-esteem. An example of a heterogeneous group would be a study skills group for grades 3–6 students, who may or may not be experiencing study skills issues, who represent a mix of race, gender, age, backgrounds, ethnicity—a microcosm of society. An example of group members that may be both heterogeneous and homogeneous is a social skills group at the elementary level which may be homogeneous in that all members are having some issues with social skills and that they are all in third grade. However, the group may be heterogeneous in that the group is cross-cultural and includes both male and female students.

The number of group sessions and the length of the group sessions generally vary by school, often dependent upon teacher and administrator support because students will miss class time to take part in counseling. ASCA recommends that groups be brief and solution-focused. Generally speaking, small groups in the school setting meet once or twice a week for a total of four to eight sessions. Groups are typically 30 minutes in length for students at the elementary level and 40–60 minutes for students at the secondary level.

One of the most significant concerns with group work is that despite the school counselor's vigilance in protecting the psychological and physical well-being of group participants during member interactions within the group, confidentiality cannot be guaranteed—that is the nature of group work. Thus, school counselors are vigilant in ensuring that parents and students understand these limits to confidentiality in a group counseling setting.

## Appraisal and advisement

The legacy of student *appraisal* and *advising* is rooted in the vocational guidance movement whereby school counselors used standardized tests to assess student knowledge, skills, abilities, and aptitudes in order to make the most advantageous occupational choices. The movement gained popularity with school counselors broadening their scope and coordinating and administering assessments to make school placement decisions and to monitor student achievement.

Relating learning to students' career aspirations and providing students with opportunities for success and involvement in courses which they perceive as interesting have been linked to enhanced academic motivation and problem-solving skills that transfers to real life well into adulthood (Whiston et al., 2011). As such, appraisal performed by school counselors in the K-12 school setting is still primarily focused on interests, abilities, skills, aptitudes, and achievement often going hand-in-hand with advisement that is based on appraisal findings to promote academic and career development and planning. School counselors also conduct appraisals geared toward assessing levels of social/emotional distress for a better understanding of student intervention needs and levels of progress toward the attainment of individual counseling and small group counseling goals. Appraisal may aid in doing the following:

- Identify student strengths and challenges.
- Develop targeted interventions.
- Provide optimal learning environments.
- Provide important information to parents, students, and school personnel.

School counselors are careful to consider context, developmental level, and students' cultures and worldviews when using both formal and informal appraisal. As such, school counselors are vigilant in evaluating appraisal instruments for cultural bias (no one instrument is entirely bias-free). The ASCA *Ethical Standards for School Counselors* (ASCA, 2022a) underscores the importance of applying basic principles for scoring, interpreting, and relaying appraisal results to students, parents, and important others. Table 2.4 describes specific measurement concepts

**Table 2.4 Measurement Concepts**

| |
|---|
| *Correlations* are the degree to which two measures/constructs are related (e.g., the examination between a class of students' test scores in mathematics and their level of self-esteem) |
| *Criterion-referenced assessments* are those that compare an individual's score to a preestablished standard |
| *Derived scores* are scores that are drawn from raw scores by comparing the raw score to those of a norm group; sometimes referred to as norm-referenced scores |
| *Grade/age equivalents* are a type of developmental score that compares an individual student's raw score with that of others of a certain grade/age level |
| *Measures of central tendency*, known as *mean, median,* and *mode,* are representative of averages. The mean is the mathematical average of a set of scores; the median is the middle score below which, and above which, half of the scores of a set of scores will fall; the mode is the score that appears the most frequently in a set of scores |
| *Norm-referenced assessments* are those that compare an individual's score to that of a norm group |
| *Norms* are representative of a distribution of scores obtained through the administration of an instrument to a standardized sample against which all other scores are assessed |
| *Percentile rank* is the percentage of scores that are at or below a named score |
| *Rank* is the relative position, standing, or degree of a specific grouping, often used at the secondary and postsecondary levels of education to describe a student's standing in relation to others based on GPA |
| *Raw scores* are original scores that have not yet been converted into a meaningful score |
| *Reliability* refers to the consistency with which an instrument measures that which it purports to measure (i.e., does the instrument yield the same or similar results at each administration for the same individual?) |
| *Standard deviation* is a measure of variability in a given set of data |

(*Continued*)

## Table 2.4 Continued

| |
|---|
| *Standard scores* represent the distance between a given score and the mean and are used in norm-referenced (see norms above) assessments to compare a student's performance to that of his or her peers. |
| *Validity* refers to the extent to which an instrument measures that which it purports to measure (i.e., can meaningful inferences be made based on the instrument's results?) |

with which school counselors need to be familiar in order to adequately interpret assessment outcomes: measures of central tendency, norms, rank, percentile rank, grade equivalents, standard deviation, standards scores, raw scores, derived scores, criterion-referenced scores, correlation, reliability, validity, and norm-referenced assessments.

Appraisal activities may take place with individual students, small groups of students, or within the classroom. Interventions and plans that are developed as a result of appraisal may be immediate, short-term, and/or long-term.

### JENNIFER'S SCORE

Jennifer is a high-school student who obtained a raw score of 73 on her mathematics exam. Her score was compared to a norm group in order to obtain a derived score. Jennifer must have taken:

a. A nonstandardized assessment.
b. A norm-referenced assessment.
c. A criterion-referenced assessment.
d. None of the above.

While engaging in formal or informal student appraisal, school counselors carefully consider appropriate procedures for conducting verbal and/or written assessments in a variety of situations with diverse populations (e.g., language proficiency, special needs). A combination of both formal and informal approaches are recommended as best practices for school counselors appraising individual needs and academic and counseling progress. Together, informal and formal appraisal ensnare all the senses and sensibilities, capturing the whole essence of the individual. Each has value in providing useful information that can result in a deeper understanding of students' issues in relation to their personal, social, emotional, environmental, developmental, and cultural worlds.

## Formal and informal appraisal

Standardized tests, or standardized appraisal instruments, are objective, often norm-referenced (e.g., compare scores against an average), generally quantitative in nature, and ensure consistency in content, administration, scoring, and interpretation. Standardized tests are frequently referred to as formal assessments or formal appraisals.

It is essential that school counselors be able to identify a variety of formal appraisal instruments based on type or purpose. There are generally five categories: achievement, aptitude, intelligence, interests, and personality. Appraisal instruments most often used in the schools within each category are summarized in Table 2.5. School counselors become familiar with the validity, reliability, limitations, bias, and characteristics of the appraisal instruments they plan to administer. It is important for

**Table 2.5 Summary of Key Appraisal Instruments Used in Schools**

| *Appraisal Category* | *Appraisal Instrument* |
| --- | --- |
| *Achievement* evaluates general knowledge/performance in a variety of subject areas | Woodcock–Johnson Test of Achievement (Woodcock–Johnson) <br> PIAT <br> Stanford Achievement Test Series ACT— college entrance |
| *Aptitude* evaluates potential or ability to learn, assessing a variety of specific areas | ASVAB <br> GATB <br> Kaufman Assessment Battery for Children <br> PSAT—practice for SAT <br> SAT—college entrance |
| *Intelligence* evaluates general cognitive ability | WISC <br> WAIS <br> Stanford–Binet Intelligence Scales (Stanford–Binet) |
| *Interests* identify preferences for specific activities, matching personality type with six workplace environments | SDS <br> SII <br> KOIS |
| Personality identifies attitudinal, emotional, interpersonal, and motivational characteristics | Vineland Adaptive Behavior Scales (Vineland) <br> MBTI |

school counselors to understand the appropriate uses of each specific appraisal instrument as it relates to each category and as it pertains to a given situation with a specific population and possess the ability to identify specific assessments and the category to which they belong.

School counselors are aware of the options available to students with special needs (e.g., Braille print, large print, tape-recorded tests). Also, students whose primary language is not English may need bilingual test administration, test administration by a translator or interpreter, and/or a version of the test written in the students' primary language.

The most well-known and controversial formal appraisals are standardized academic achievement tests. These tests are designed to measure a student's knowledge of subject content based on core academic standards up to the date of test administration. Achievement tests vary by name across states but are often referred to as *high stakes testing*. They are high stakes because in most states, students cannot graduate without passing scores on these tests, and school and teacher performance is often measured by student performance on these tests.

## ASCA Position on The School Counselor and High-Stakes Testing

School counselors recognize that standardized test results are one of many measures that can be used to assess student learning and performance across standards. School counselors advocate for the use of multiple criteria when educational decisions such as course enrollment and admissions are made about student performance and oppose the use of a single test to make important educational decisions affecting students, teachers and schools.

*Position statement adopted 2002; revised 2007, 2014, 2017*

While serving as an elementary school counselor, I coordinated school-wide standardized achievement testing for eight years—SOL in Virginia. Over the years, I became consumed with admiration and respect for classroom teachers who instead of kicking and screaming gazed fearlessly into the eyes of achievement tests as Ahab into the eyes of the massive Moby Dick.

In addition to academic standards-driven achievement tests, other achievement tests, often used in the schools to assess students in kindergarten to grade 12 for gifted or special education, include the Woodcock–Johnson Test of Achievement (Woodcock–Johnson) and the PIAT. The Woodcock–Johnson and the PIAT reveal present levels of performance compared to peers and identify students' academic areas of strengths and weaknesses.

The Stanford Achievement Test Series is often used in the schools as a measure of achievement from kindergarten to grade 12. It is a general test of knowledge in a variety of subjects including math, English, science, and writing for each grade level. The test yields national percentile bands that illustrate how a student scores in relation to others students at that grade level.

The ACT is one of the most widely used achievement tests taken by high-school students to satisfy college entrance requirements. Total composite scores for all core subject areas covered (English, math, reading, science) by the test range from 1 to 36. The ACT writing test is optional.

> **MY STUDENT MAY HAVE A DISABILITY**
>
> A third-grade teacher comes to you, the elementary school counselor and child study chair, to arrange for a child study meeting because she suspects that one of her students may have a learning disability based on low academic functioning in math and writing. Which of the following would be useful in assessing the student?
>
> a. Peabody.
> b. Standardized grade-level tests in math and writing.
> c. Classroom and homework assignments.
> d. All of the above.

Aptitude assessments are designed to evaluate an individual's potential or ability to learn. Aptitude tests measure a variety of specific areas such as art, music, mechanical, verbal, spatial, reasoning, critical reading, writing, and coding. Aptitude tests are primarily used in schools for the purpose of career decision making, special education screening, and entrance into the military. The most widely used aptitude tests in the schools are the ASVAB, the GATB, and the Kaufman Assessment Battery for Children. The ASVAB and GATB assessments are intended for students at the high-school level. The Kaufman is used for children ages 3–18.

The SAT is the most widely used college entrance test and is often used with the ACT test to assess academic readiness for college. The test yields scores in three subject areas (critical reading, writing, and mathematics), with 800 being the highest possible score for each section for a total score of 2400. The average score is 1500. The SAT is most often taken during the spring of the junior year of high school and again in the fall of the senior year of high school. Many students take the PSAT as a practice test to the SAT during the ninth and tenth grade years, although some students take it during the fall of their junior year of high school. The PSAT is also used to make scholarship awards.

Intelligence tests are used in the schools to determine a student's general cognitive ability. Intelligence tests yield a single *intelligence quotient* (IQ) score. The majority of individuals have an IQ score between 85 and 115, with 100 being the average. IQ scores above 115 are considered to depict superior intelligence, whereas IQ scores below 85 indicate borderline deficiency with a score of 70 or less signifying retardation. IQ scores are often used to determine student placement in gifted and special education programs and aid educators in identifying a variety of cognitive challenges.

### THE COLLEGE DREAM

The mother of Carolyn, one of your 11th-grade high-school students, is in your office expressing concern about Carolyn's ability to be successful in college. She shares that they do not have the money to pay for Carolyn's college just for Carolyn to "flunk out." She said that Carolyn told her that she does not qualify for any scholarships that are listed in the scholarship binder at school. You notice in the student information system that Carolyn has a GPA of 3.9 and is not showing any scores for college entrance testing. You ask the parent if Carolyn has taken any college entrance assessments as of yet. The parent said no because those, too, are expensive and she just is not sure about the whole college thing. The parent begins to cry, stating that it is just she and Carolyn, and the only income is her disability check. She said she feels lost because she nor anybody else in her family has ever gone to college. What other information might you want to find out in this case? How would you help this parent and Carolyn?

The most widely used intelligence tests in the schools are the WISC, ages 6–16, and the WAIS, ages 16–19. Individuals who are 16 can take either the WAIS or the WISC. Each assessment yields a verbal IQ, performance IQ, and full IQ (total cognitive development) score with a standard deviation of 15 and a 95% confidence level. Also widely used in schools is the Stanford–Binet Intelligence Scales (Stanford–Binet). The assessment can be administered on individuals ages 2 to 90 and yields a verbal IQ, a nonverbal IQ, and a full-scale IQ with a standard deviation of 15 and a 95% confidence level.

Interest assessments, often referred to as interest inventories (discussed in the next chapter), are primarily used for career development purposes. Generally, results obtained from interest inventories are derived by comparing student responses with individuals who have been successful in specific occupations or by comparing student responses to those of their peers. The most widely used interest inventories in the schools include the SDS, the SII, and the KOIS.

Standardized personality assessments provide information about a student's attitudinal, emotional, interpersonal, and motivational characteristics. Personality assessment may be used for (1) gaining insight into students' thoughts and behaviors, (2) placement into specialized programs (e.g., gifted, special education), and (3) career decision making. The most widely used personality assessments in the schools include the Vineland Adaptive Behavior Scales (Vineland), which measures levels of personal and social functioning, and the MBTI, which identifies patterns of behavior and preferences for relating to ideas, others, and the environment.

### MEETING ANDRE'S NEEDS

Andre is a third-grade student whose misbehavior at school has become increasingly persistent. Andre has been consistently achieving academically at higher grade levels than third grade in all subject areas. Andre scored 5.3 (grade equivalent score) on his mathematics achievement test. How would you interpret this score for Andre's parents? What programs might you want to recommend that would help to further develop Andre's academic knowledge and skills and ensure that Andre remains challenged with a rigorous program to meet his special needs? How might you address Andre's misbehavior at this time?

Non-standardized assessments are subjective, are not norm-referenced, can be either qualitative or quantitative in nature, and may vary widely in their content, process, administration, scoring, and interpretation procedures. Non-standardized tests are often referred to as informal assessments or informal appraisals. The most widely used informal appraisal used by school counselors is communication during the counseling session.

Counseling session notes may be the most helpful form of informal student appraisal the school counselor has in the appraisal toolbox. Hearing from students themselves helps the school counselor to understand the students' perceptions, which are students' realities. In addition to fully exploring the issues that brought a student to counseling, it is important that school counselors explore the student's attitude, emotionality, thought processes, academic progress, school attendance and experiences, views of homelife, and relationships at home and at school as well as virtual friends and acquaintances. In other words, gathering as much information about the student as the student is willing to share helps to provide targeted interventions and can serve to establish a positive therapeutic relationship.

School counselors understand the subjective nature of informal assessment, exercising caution during completion/implementation and interpretation. Additionally, school counselors do not rely on any single appraisal but use a variety of informal appraisal instruments or approaches when appraising student functioning, which may include:

- Records review.
- Observation.
- Case study.
- Role play.
- Checklists.
- Storytelling and story completion.
- Student self-assessment and self-monitoring.
- Portfolio.
- Work samples and writings.
- Consultation with teachers, parents, and other school personnel.
- Counseling session notes.

A commonly used method for informal student appraisals was developed by Lazarus (1976) and referred to as the BASIC ID approach (see Table 2.6). The acronym represents seven interdependent categories, or modalities, (behavior, affect, sensation, imagery, cognition, interpersonal relationships, and drugs/diet) that aid school counselors in organizing case notes,

## Table 2.6 BASIC ID

| |
|---|
| (B)ehavior<br>Fine and gross motor skills and activities |
| (A)ffect<br>Observed or client self-reported emotions |
| (S)ensation<br>Sensory experiencing: taste (gustatory), touch (kinesthetic), sight (visual), smell (olfactory), hearing (auditory) |
| (I)magery<br>Mental pictures that have an impact on the client |
| (C)ognition<br>Client thoughts and beliefs |
| (I)nterpersonal relationships<br>Observed or self-reported interactions with others |
| (D)rugs/diet<br>Biochemical and/or nutritional impact on the client |

identifying the individual's preferred modalities, clarifying problems, creating counseling interventions, and assessing the effectiveness of interventions and the progress of treatment.

SOAP notes (Cameron & Turtle-Song, 2002), too, are used by school counselors to organize case notes and develop case conceptualizations. Table 2.7 describes the characteristics of each of the four components of SOAP notes: (1) subjective observations, (2) objective observations, (3) assessment, and (4) plan.

### AYMEE'S BASIC ID

Aymee is a middle-school student who is seeing you, her school counselor, because of social issues that she is experiencing in school. You are assessing Aymee's progress and determine interventions using BASIC ID, which is considered to be which type of assessment?

 a. Standardized.
 b. Objective.
 c. Formal.
 d. Informal.

**Table 2.7 SOAP Notes**

| |
|---|
| (S)ubjective observations<br>Counselor perceptions of client thoughts, attitudes, emotions, and dispositions during sessions and the client's self-reported experiencing/observations (e.g., hopelessness, depression, client perceptions, anger) |
| (O)bjective observations<br>Directly observed behaviors and emotional experiencing during the counseling sessions (e.g., crying, posture, hygiene, orientation to time/place, physical appearance) |
| (A)ssessment<br>Appraisal based on counselor's general impressions of the client's psychological, social, and emotional functioning |
| (P)lan<br>Treatment strategies to mediate presenting client concerns, which may include individual, small group counseling, and/or family counseling and a variety of theoretical approaches and counseling techniques. The plan might also include referral and further information gathering strategies |

## Life-saving appraisal

Shamelessly pilfering a line from *Top Gun*, school counselors must go *Mach 2 with our hair on fire* just to keep up with children and adolescents who live at the maximum pace of *wide open*. At this speed, things can get very real very fast. Timely and appropriate individual student appraisal will not only identify barriers to academic achievement, post–high-school career paths, and positive, fruitful social/emotional functioning, but can literally save the life of a child who may be a victim of child abuse, neglect and/or violence. Perhaps, the student is suffering from addiction, substance abuse, eating disorders, and/or depression.

Changes in behavioral, emotional, and attitudinal patterns are often clues alerting school counselors to the possibility of problematic issues in the student's life. One or more changes, unexplained by developmental stages, and the frequency, duration, and magnitude of behaviors noted as follows should be explored (Morrison, 2016):

- Periods of disinterest.
- Flat affect.
- Interpersonal conflicts.
- Sense of worthlessness or guilt.
- Passivity.

- Agitation or irritability.
- Significant weight loss or weight gain.
- Fatigue.
- Changes in sleeping patterns (e.g., hardly sleeping, wanting to stay in bed).
- Trouble concentrating and following directions.
- Inattentive.
- Decline in academic performance.
- Excessive absences.
- Frequent/unexplained injuries.
- Flinching.
- Withdrawn.
- Unattended medical conditions.
- Emotionality.
- Does not care to (or want to) go home.

In addition to being attentive and exploring more deeply something a student has shared with you (or with the classroom or peers in a small group), conversations with parents and observations of parent–child interactions may expose signs of possible child abuse or neglect, or other problems related to family functioning. The following signs portrayed by a parent or guardian may signal child abuse or neglect (Child Welfare Information Gateway, 2023):

- Showing little concern for the child.
- Indifference toward the child.
- Apathy or depression.
- Abusing alcohol or other drugs.
- Irrational or bizarre behavior.
- Being secretive or isolated.
- Being overly protective, severely limiting child's contact, especially with opposite gender.
- Being jealous or controlling.
- Denying the existence of, or blaming the child for, problems at home or school.
- Asking the teacher to use harsh punishment on the child for misbehavior.
- Viewing the child as entirely bad, burdensome, or worthless.
- Demanding a level of physical or academic performance that the child cannot achieve.

- Looking primarily to the child for care, attention, and satisfaction of emotional needs.
- Parent and child rarely touch or look at each other.
- Parent and child view their relationship as entirely negative.
- Parent and child state that they do not like each other.

There are additional signs that warrant further exploration as potential indicators of sexual abuse. Students who are being sexually abused may exhibit one or more of the following as well as any of the signs and symptoms noted above (Bauman, 2008; Child Welfare Information Gateway, 2023):

- Nightmares.
- Bed wetting.
- Difficulty sitting or walking.
- Sophisticated sexual knowledge or bizarre sexual behaviors.
- High-risk behaviors.
- Running away.
- Early pregnancy.
- Change in appetite.
- Refusal to change for gym class.
- Thoughts of suicide.
- Substance abuse.
- Frequent medical conditions.
- Anxiety/stress.
- Depression.
- Interpersonal relationship difficulties.

School counselors are mandated reporters of suspected child abuse and neglect (discussed in Chapter 1). Additional information on violence prevention and child abuse and neglect along with mandated reporting requirements and Child Abuse and Neglect Training Modules are available at www.childwelfare.gov/preventing/developing/training.cfm.

Addiction and/or substance abuse, too, involves specific signs and symptoms of which the school counselor needs to be aware. For example, children and adolescents who are using or abusing substances may exhibit one or more of the following behaviors (Capuzzi & Stauffer, 2019):

- Withdrawal from responsibility.
- Increased secretiveness.

- Wearing sunglasses inappropriately.
- Wearing long sleeves in hot weather.
- Stealing money.
- Having associations with known substance abusers.
- Taking risks.
- Avoiding family members.
- Talking excessively about drug/alcohol use.
- Getting into legal trouble.

Duration, frequency, and intensity are important factors to take into account when considering whether a student may have an addiction or is abusing substances. When in doubt *consult, consult, consult,* and err on the side of student safety. That is, make the call to the parent, legal system, or child protective services, as deemed appropriate. School counselors balance students' rights to privacy and confidentiality with duty to warn and duty to protect while also considering parental rights in the cases of minors, discussed in Chapter 1.

Intervening in cases of suicide ideation is critical. Assessment is warranted when a student is experiencing an intense affective disturbance (e.g., rage, guilt, hopelessness, fear, depression, abandonment, anxiety), particularly when the precipitating event/issue is vague. Indicators of potential suicide are not limited to merely having *thoughts of suicide.* Indicators may include writing about suicide, drawing figures in the act of committing suicide, comments about wanting to die, and making comments or implying that others would be better off as a result of his or her death. Risk factors for suicidality in children and adolescents include (McWhirter & McWhirter, 2012):

- Negative family and/or peer interactions.
- Loneliness/isolation.
- Impulsivity.
- Low tolerance for frustration.
- Poor self-esteem.
- Lack of problem-solving skills.
- Faulty cognitions/negative beliefs.
- Substance use.
- A tendency toward risk-taking reactions to distress.

When appraising for potential suicide ideation, ask the student plainly, "are you having thoughts about committing suicide now, recently, or ever?" Depending on the developmental level of the child, the question may need to be, "are you thinking about hurting yourself on purpose?" or more plainly stating "are you thinking about killing yourself?" School counselors should assess for a plan and a means for following through on the plan. However, as noted above, err on the side of caution—above all else protect the child/adolescent. In this case, the protection would be from self.

While safeguarding the student until the appropriate contact arrives, which may not be the parent/guardian (see Chapter 1), school counselors should consider creating a no-suicide contract with the student, which can be verbal (with a handshake) or written (a document with a signature) affirming that the student will not harm himself or herself intentionally. Additionally, school counselors can help students by

- Establishing a positive relationship (the crux of counseling).
- Assisting the student in identifying support systems and internal strengths to build protective factors.
- Exploring and validating emotions.
- Identifying problems; teaching and engaging the student in problem-solving strategies.

School counselors provide teachers and staff with suicide awareness training as a part of a comprehensive approach to preventing student suicide. Elements of the training include recognizing the suicide risk factors noted previously and identifying behavioral and verbal warning signs and steps for intervention.

Behavioral warning signs may include giving possessions away, declining academic performance, a change in social interactions, and an increase in school absences. Verbal warning signs may also be present to include statements such as "life has no meaning," "nobody would miss me," and "my life is meaningless." Steps for intervention may include a formal written policy that outlines the process for referring students who may be at risk of suicide to the school counselor.

There are mixed views among school administrators and school counselors with regard to screening students for suicide ideation and implementing student programs aimed at suicide prevention education. Those who are against the screenings and prevention education believe that these strategies draw attention to suicide and may result in increased suicide attempts. Those who are in favor of these strategies believe that education will reduce the incidence of suicide. Because of this confluence of conflicting views, school counselors work closely with school administrators when planning suicide prevention programming.

---

## ASCA Position on The School Counselor and Suicide Risk Assessment

School counselors support best practice in suicide prevention to reduce suicide risk in children and adolescents and are part of a collaborative team who respond when students are identified as at-risk for suicide. When becoming aware of a student considering suicide, school counselors assert their ethical and legal responsibility to report suspected suicide risk to parents/ guardians and the appropriate authorities.

*Position statement adopted 2020*

---

Students at risk of suicide need mental health counseling and possibly hospitalization. Some schools will not allow students to return to school until parents or guardians have secured such counseling because students experiencing this level of emotional disturbance are deemed to be at risk for harm to themselves and possibly others.

---

**THE DIVORCE OF GEOFFREY'S PARENTS**

Geoffrey, a 13-year-old student, expressed to you, his middle-school counselor, that he is angry because of his parents' recent divorce. This was the second time Geoffrey came to you, but this time he seemed much more unkempt and upset. His hair was disheveled, and his clothes were dirty. During this second session, Geoffrey sat slumped over with his hands clinched and began to cry, saying that his mother must now work so he never sees her, and his dad does not care enough to even visit on the days he has visitation. Geoffrey said that sometimes he just feels numb and other times he is so angry he could explode. He went on to say that he feels all alone and just wants to quit school because he does not understand the point of it all.

Use SOAP notes to conceptualize this case.

Self-mutilation (e.g., cutting, burning, interfering with wound healing, biting, scratching) has been identified as a reaction and coping mechanism associated with feelings of depression, anger, frustration, and hopelessness and resulting in feelings of guilt, shame, and regret (Moyer & Nelson, 2007). More recent studies underscore important risk factors as self-punishment and anti-dissociation, recommending treatments that target negative self-cognition and dissociation such as mindfulness, cognitive behavioral therapy, and behavioral activation (i.e., using behavior to activate emotion vs. waiting to feel the emotion) (Ying et al., 2023).

Self-injurious behaviors such as self-mutilation is viewed by the school counselor as an imminent risk and treated in the same fashion as suicide ideation with regard to involving parents or child protective services and providing referral resources. Some students try to convince school counselors that their self-mutilating behaviors are self-decoration. Avoid succumbing to deception by staying abreast of current developments in these areas of high-risk behavior. Training oneself, as well as teachers, parents, and administrators, in understanding the difference between self-mutilation and self-decoration is critical. In the end, when in doubt, err on the side of protecting the student from his or herself. Bottom line—although self-mutilation may not be considered an indicator of a desire to commit suicide, it can lead to death.

Symptoms consistent with *anorexia* and *bulimia* are also viewed by the school counselor as imminent risk and should be brought to the attention of parents or child protective services. School counselors will also have resources ready to share as a part of their ever-evolving resource listing for parents. The growing number of adolescents with eating disorders is alarming, calling for systemic prevention efforts on topics related to body image and the all-too-real natural consequences of eating disorders and use of anabolic steroids.

To promote a continued trusting relationship with students for whom you must break confidentiality, remind the student of your legal and ethical responsibility to protect. You will have covered the limits of confidentiality earlier in the session or in your initial session with the student.

Regardless of appraisal outcomes, school counselors are careful not to offer diagnoses. Even those school counselors who hold advanced licensure and national credentialing are discouraged from diagnosing students' mental health issues in the school setting. Clinical diagnosis is more often than not considered to be outside the scope of the practice of school counseling. Instead, when deeper issues are present that are outside of the expertise of the school counselor or scope of school counseling practices, school counselors *strongly encourage* parents/guardians to seek the assistance of a mental health counselor, psychologist, psychiatrist, physician, or family therapist, providing the parent with resources as discussed in the next section of this chapter.

*Indirect student services*

Indirect services are activities that involve interactions with important others on behalf of a student or group of students resulting in individual or systemic change, respectively. School counselors broaden and strengthen their ability to provide a time-efficient and cost-effective comprehensive school counseling program using indirect student services identified by ASCA (2019a) as collaboration, consultation, and referral.

## Collaboration

School counselors work as part of a professional collective within and outside of the school community to provide optimal services that place the well-being of children first, supporting academic, career, and social/emotional development within a climate of safety. Such a gargantuan task is best accomplished with the help of others. Collaboration is a process that involves multiple individuals working together toward a common goal with shared expertise, decision-making authority, and responsibility, including responsibility for the outcome (ASCA, 2019a; Dougherty, 2013). School counselors generally collaborate with parents, teachers, administrators, school psychologists, school social workers, school nurses, special education teachers, resource teachers, community members, and any number of stakeholders to effectively meet the needs of students. School counselors may also be involved in, or a part of, 504 committees, early intervention teams, and child study teams.

Why collaboration? Strange though it may seem, we can look to nature for that answer. I am not saying that we need to be tree-huggers although I do find the concept appealing. What I am saying is that animals have collaborative instincts that guide their behavior in the most productive ways. Take ants, for example, which our airlines have studied to fashion more effective passenger seating processes. Singularly, ants have little or no ability to make an impact (other than annoying *Homo sapiens*), but altogether ants accomplish amazing feats in the most simplistic of ways with no leadership. Each ant is born with specific traits and applies their expertise as needed to ensure the survival of the species.

Also, consider the flight patterns of geese, which have been adopted by our nation's fighter pilots. By flying in a V-formation, geese conserve energy and maximize coordination and communication while attending to the wellbeing of each member. Using collaborative efforts, school counselors, like geese, harness the amplified power, energy, intellect, resources, and spirit by engaging the collective. Now, if we only had wings, we could really soar!

Collaboration, a fundamental concept, creates an intense life force through the interdependent nature and the shared resources and expertise of each member. It is this interdependence and sharing of specialties that allows us to provide optimal services to students, families, and school communities. The ASCA *Ethical Standards for School Counselors* (ASCA, 2022a) encourages the involvement of others to help identify specialized teams, support networks, and wraparound services to assist students in combating unhealthy levels of stress, reduce feelings of isolation, and remove barriers that impede personal and academic development and prevent wellness. Collaboration may include:

- Teaming with teachers to develop classroom lessons that blend academic standards with the ASCA Mindsets & Behaviors.
- Partnering with the school nurse to develop a school-wide primary prevention program to address teen pregnancy and positive body image.
- Working with the school administrator to design system-wide programs that use a combination of primary, secondary, and tertiary prevention interventions to help close the achievement gap, reduce dropout rates, improve attendance, promote positive attitudes toward school, and improve school climate.
- Connecting with community mental health agencies to provide resources and school-community programs that enhances and broadens the services for students and families.
- Joining specialized committees (e.g., 504 team, IEP team, crisis management team, intervention team) that bring specialists together to come up with the best possible prevention and intervention strategies for both individual and systemic support.
- Uniting with parents to provide individualized strategies for implementation at home in an effort to provide consistency and enhanced, unencumbered communications.

### APRIL'S IEP

You are a middle-school counselor who just participated in an IEP meeting for April, one of the students at your school. The individuals present at the meeting included the principal, special education teacher, one general education teacher, and the parents. You collaborated with these individuals to identify strategies to include in the student's IEP. Participating in the IEP meeting in this manner is an example of providing what type of services to April?

a. Direct.
b. Indirect.
c. a and b.
d. None of the above.

Collaborative partnerships heighten the likelihood of identifying creative solutions to problems or services for the client system that might otherwise go unrecognized by any one individual. Figure 2.1 illustrates the collaboration process. The thick arrows indicate the primary structure of the collaboration process (Dougherty, 2013), while the thin arrows indicate interactions that may take place in collaborative situations in the schools between either the collaborator and the client system at a given time for assessing needs, clarifying information, asking questions.

Partnerships with other professionals in the school allow school counselors to provide optimal services to all students and to better identify and tackle obscured obstacles to student performance. School counselors build collaborative, internal multidisciplinary teams that may include the school nurse, school psychologist, school social worker, *educational diagnostician*, principal, teachers, and other school personnel.

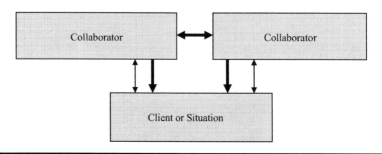

**Figure 2.1** The process of collaboration.

One of a school counselor's most valuable resources for helping students are students. There is much research to support the positive outcomes of peer-to-peer helping programs (Whiston et al., 2011). The ASCA *Ethical Standards for School Counselors* (ASCA, 2022a) addresses the importance of ensuring that student welfare is safeguarded by emphasizing the importance of proper training and supervision of peer helpers by school counselors. Peer-helping programs are instrumental in a variety of ways (e.g., mediation, tutoring, speakers, aids, mentors) and students gain a sense of empowerment and confidence by working with school counselors and other adults in the school toward the goal of helping fellow students. Students serving as peer helpers, too, are generally more in tune to the needs of other students and the school community, making them an invaluable extension to the comprehensive school counseling program.

## ASCA Position on The School Counselor and Peer-Support Programs

Peer support programs help students develop an improved sense of well-being, social confidence and health behaviors (Curren & Wexler, 2016). The informed implementation of peer support programs enhances the effectiveness of school counseling programs and provides increased outreach and expansion of services.

*Position statement adopted 1978; revised 1984, 1993, 1999, 2002, 2008, 2015, 2021*

Peer-to-peer programs might include transition/orientation programs, whereby a more senior student serves as an escort and friend to new individual students and groups of students (i.e., elementary students transitioning to middle school and middle-school students transitioning to high school) to promote a successful transition. Another type of peer-helping program would include peer tutoring, whereby a student who is adept in a particular subject coaches a student who is struggling in that subject.

The importance of collaborative relationships within and outside of the school is most apparent during times of crisis. Collaboration during crisis response and post crisis response heightens the school counselor's ability to coordinate integrated, multidisciplinary services in an efficient, unified, and timely manner.

Crisis response begins prior to a crisis by planning for crisis and creating a safe school environment that includes the programming named below in the *ASCA Position Statement on Safe Schools and Crisis Response.* School divisions generally have established crisis-management plans that are mandated by state/local policy that clearly defines the chain of command, school personnel roles, collaboration with community services (e.g., fire, police, medical), media and community responding guidelines, and follow-up procedures. Schools also have crisis-management teams that should involve the school counselor. As critical members of this collaborative committee, school counselors lend a voice to the emotional needs of students, faculty, and parents during a crisis. Crisis plans will define and document the school counselor's role during student, family, and school-wide crisis situations. As part of, or in addition to the crisis management plan, school counselors might proactively provide information and conduct workshops for faculty addressing appropriate responses and intervention during a human crisis (e.g., accidental death, suicide and homicide, terrorism) and natural disaster (e.g., hurricane, earthquake, tornado).

## ASCA Position on The School Counselor and Safe Schools and Crisis Response

School counselors serves as leaders (ASCA, 2022; Oliver, Fleck, & Money-Brady, 2016) in safe-school initiatives. ASCA seeks to promote safe schools as can be noted in its many position statements, including Gun Safety, Promotion of Safe Schools through Conflict Resolution and Bullying/Harassment Prevention, Safe Schools and Crisis Response, and School Safety and the Use of Technology. Positive perceptions, school climate and overall school health are increased with schoolwide safety programming (Goodman-Scott & Grothaus, 2018).

*Position statement adopted 2000; revised 2007, 2013, 2019*

ASCA recently reclassified crisis response as an indirect student service, loosely defining it as the collaboration of adults in the provision of support post crisis (2019a). As such, school counselors provide *crisis management* as part of indirect student services. ASCA's reclassifying crisis from a direct to an indirect student service does not mean that school counselors do not provide the direct responsive services of individual counseling and small group counseling to students in the aftermath of crisis. School counselors' response to students who come to them in crisis can be summarized in three significant, systematic steps: (1) assess students' level of risk, (2) stabilize the situation with counseling intervention, and (3) follow-up to assess well-being and determine the need for further intervention (Kerr, 2016), which may involve referral.

Post crisis follow-up and the provision of resources are critical because stress reactions are not always immediate (Kerr, 2016). Follow-up is recommended at intervals (e.g., one month, four months, crisis anniversaries). Follow-up after a crisis will help to identify those students who are experiencing symptoms of post-traumatic stress, prolonged grief-loss reactions, and/or unresolved issues that require more intense counseling services.

## Consultation

Collaborative approaches to consultation are the most widely used method of consultation in the schools. The collaborative approach to consultation broadens the traditional process to include the expertise of the consultee. That is, the consultee is recognized for his or her expertise on the clients and the system and shares this expertise in a partnership with the consultant. Together, they define the problem; establish goals; and create, implement, and evaluate a plan of action (Erford, 2019).

Consultation involves three parties: consultant, consultee, and a client or situation to be addressed (Dougherty, 2013). Consultation differs from collaboration in that the consultant (e.g., school counselor) shares a specific area of expertise and directs the consultation process, while responsibility for the outcome rests with the consultee (e.g., teacher, school administrator, or parent). The goal of consultation is to indirectly improve the client or situation by empowering and directly developing the knowledge, skills, and abilities of the consultee.

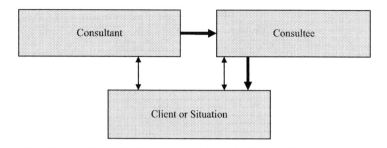

**Figure 2.2 The process of consultation.**

The triadic (i.e., consultant > consultee > client or situation) nature of the consultation process is illustrated in Figure 2.2. The thick arrows indicate the primary structure of the consulting process (Dougherty, 2013), and the thin arrows indicate interactions that may take place in some consulting situations in the schools between the consultant or the consultee and the client system at a given time for assessing needs, clarifying information, asking questions.

In addition to understanding the structure of consulting relationships, school counselors understand the importance of the consultation process. The consultation process is flexible and generally involves four unique stages that can interact and overlap with consultants often moving backward and forward through stages and phases (Dougherty, 2013).

Stage one is known as the *entry stage*, which involves physically and psychologically entering the system and establishing a rapport with all involved. During the entry stage the school counselor identifies desired outcomes, explores needs, and negotiates a contract. Stage two, the *diagnosis stage*, involves four interconnected phases. During the diagnosis stage the school counselor gathers information and data, analyzes and defines the problem, establishes goals, and identifies possible interventions. Stage three is the *intervention stage*. This stage involves selecting and implementing an intervention and developing, implementing, and evaluating a plan.

Stage four, the *disengagement stage*, is the final stage of consulting. During the disengagement stage, the consultation process is evaluated, the consultant's involvement is reduced, and relationships are terminated while creating a plan for post-consultation (i.e., maintaining achieved goals).

> **STAGES AND PHASES**
>
> You are a school counselor engaging in the consultation process. You have identified and clarified the problem and established goals for consultation. While working on creating a plan, you decide to tweak a couple of your interventions while continuing to move forward with plan development. What stage(s) and phase(s) of consultation are you in?

Providing consultation services to enhance the knowledge and skills of important others in a student's personal and academic life allows the school counselor to make a significant difference in student outcomes. School counselors are in an ideal position to offer consulting services in the schools because of their knowledge of the school's unique culture and student needs.

School counselors are sensitive to the needs of culturally diverse consultees and client systems when applying models of consultation. Models of consultation are generally ethnocentric; therefore, school counselors adjust consultation models and services to accommodate individual worldviews and bridge cultural differences.

The school counselor's decision to engage in either consultation or collaboration is often a matter of comfort level with a particular approach. Both approaches have resulted in positive outcomes in the school setting with a wide variety of client issues and situations. In addition to preference, the school counselor considers the contextual nature of the issue, desired goals, and the knowledge, skills, and abilities of those who may be involved or who may need to be involved in the helping process.

> **THE STALEMATE**
>
> The school counseling advisory team that you established is holding its third meeting to discuss the progress of the bully prevention program that the team began working on two months ago. Two months ago, sub-teams of individuals were established with specific tasks. You find out that the program has not made much progress because the two advisory team members who were to develop a

> draft of the program goals and objectives have been unable to reach agreement. One of the team members is an Asian male, who owns a local restaurant and volunteered to be a part of the advisory team to give back to the community and students who support his business. He wants to see a more collaborative program reflected in the goals and objectives. The other member is a Caucasian female who is a stay-at-home parent of one of the students in the elementary school. She said she wants a systems focus, but she believes that the extent of collaboration that the other member is suggesting is not going to be efficient. How would you approach this issue? Are there unique worldviews to consider based on cultural differences? Would collaboration or consultation be the best way to go?

## Referral

Parents and teachers are often the first to recognize the needs of students as a result of daily interactions. For this reason, parents and teachers often refer students to the school counselor and offer unique insights into the student's world both at home and in the classroom. School administrators, too, refer students who have been brought to their attention because of truancy, suspensions, discipline, and other issues that might otherwise go undetected by the school counselor. Students, too, refer themselves to the school counselor for any number of reasons related to personal, social, emotional, academic, and career concerns.

In turn, during interactions with students a school counselor may find that a given student's needs are best met by way of referral within or outside the school. For example, the school counselor may believe the student would benefit from tutoring services to aid in academic development, which may be available in the school or in the community. School counselors may refer students for additional career support. For example, students interested in joining the military may be referred to a recruiter for a specific military branch.

It is important to reiterate that when providing the direct services of individual and small group counseling, the school counselor is careful not to practice outside of their scope of expertise or outside of the scope of school counseling practices (see Chapter 1) and the *ASCA Ethical Standards for School Counselors* (2022a). When a student's need warrants more in-depth counseling and potentially extended counseling, the school counselor makes use of referrals as part of a comprehensive school counseling program.

In such cases school counselors may refer students to outside counselors for social, emotional, and mental health issues not limited to suicide ideation, substance abuse, eating disorders, abuse, violence, and depression. School counselors may strongly encourage parents to seek family counseling, providing parents with a list of potential counseling agencies. School counselors maintain a growing list of potential resources to assist parents in getting the help needed that is not available within the school division. Resource lists contain contacts/agencies that address a broad range of services (e.g., family counseling, parenting education, mental health counseling, counseling for victims of abuse or sexual abuse, substance abuse counseling, support groups for children, support groups for parents with special needs, crisis–suicide intervention centers and numbers).

In some cases, professional counseling may be required before a student can return to school in cases where it is believed that the student is in danger of harming self and/or others. The use of referral enables the school counselor to fully meet the holistic needs of students, who may require more assistance than a school counselor can provide within the school setting. Referrals may also provide school counselors with the opportunity to collaborate/consult with important others on behalf of students and families.

## Assess: program assessment and school counselor assessment and appraisal

Program assessment is the most widely used method of research in the schools, providing school counselors with information about what works, demonstrating *evidence* over *effort*—and answering the pressing question: "How are students different as a result of the school counseling program?" Program assessment keeps school counselors out of the shadows and in the sunlight.

Assessment of educational practices in K-12 school settings has a long history. In a growing climate of accountability and justified pressure for positive student learning outcomes, assessment clearly has a secure and infinite shelf life with a continued demand that is as certain as death and taxes. In fact, over the past decades the colossal influx of broadened assessment demands have left school counselors feeling their way as though in the midst of a blinding assessment sandstorm in the Taklamakan Desert. *You know*—the one that legend says once you enter you can never leave. So, we remain in the sandy dunes of assessment, but with water, camels, and guides supplied by way of the ASCA National Model (2019a) and ASCA's supplemental handbooks (2019d, 2022b).

The *Assess* component of the ASCA National Model (2019a) describes how school counselors collect and analyze data in order to evaluate program effectiveness and demonstrate how students are different as a result of the school counseling program. Assessment information also reveals program areas of strength and/or areas in need of improvement for creating both short-term and long-term improvement plans. ASCA provides an example of the program assessment tool (2019a), recommending that it be used annually toward the end of each school year and has a manual dedicated to managing and assessing the school counseling program with detailed examples (ASCA, 2019c).

Program assessment is viewed as an ethical responsibility of school counselors who adhere to educational research practices and school district policies while ensuring the confidentiality of students during assessment processes as per the *ASCA Ethical Standards for School Counselors* (ASCA, 2022a). As an essential competency, professional best practice, and ethical responsibility, it is important that program assessment becomes an integral component of the comprehensive school counseling program's assessment, review, and feedback structure.

As the axiom goes, "We are drowning in information, but starved for knowledge." Ongoing assessment satisfies that hunger by collecting and analyzing data that increases knowledge. That is, program assessment demonstrates outcomes pertaining to the effectiveness and/or successful implementation of services in measurable terms.

### TROY

You are a seasoned elementary-school counselor mentoring Troy, your itinerant, first-year elementary school counselor. Troy wants to demonstrate the helpfulness of the small group intervention he created because it has become so popular and many students are asking to be a part of future groups. He asks you what method he should use to demonstrate how the groups have helped students. You reply

> a. Program assessment to demonstrate effectiveness in meeting objectives.
> b. Service logs to demonstrate the how many students and groups have been conducted.
> c. Both a and b.
> d. None of the above.

Program assessment is the school counselor's bread and butter. Data gleaned from the analysis of research and assessment are essential in order to

- Identify best practices that contribute to academic success and the personal–social and career development of students.
- Develop empirically supported curriculum.
- Engage in professional advocacy.
- Provide reliable consultation services.
- Make programming decisions.
- Enhance accountability.
- Shape policy in the schools and at the local, state, and federal levels.
- Inform and sustain the profession.

Effective practices sustain and strengthen the school counseling profession. Continuous assessment allows school counselors a means by which to demonstrate the effectiveness of school counseling programming. Toward this end, school counselors are called to document and share program outcomes with stakeholders using annual *results reports*.

## Classroom-group and closing-the-gap results reports

School counselors share the outcomes of program assessment in order to inform the profession and to demonstrate program effectiveness. Inquiring minds want to know *how* we make a difference in the lives of students. *Results reports* are the medium used to accomplish this communication.

Student change and the level of change as a result of the application of school counseling program interventions and strategies are demonstrated on the results report. For example, the report may indicate that the students' test scores improved as a consequence of participation in small group counseling on the topic of test-taking strategies.

ASCA (2019a) recommends the use of two types of results reports: 1) Classroom and group Mindsets & Behavior results reports and Closing-the-gap results reports. These reports are married to the lesson plans/action plans created as a part of the *Manage* component of the ASCA National Model. Thus, participation, Mindsets & Behaviors, and outcome data used for results reports was collected via implementation of the Classroom and Group Mindsets & Behaviors actions plans and Closing-the-gap action plans and/or lesson plans during the *Deliver* component of the ASCA National Model. The Classroom and Group Mindsets & Behaviors Results Report includes a minimum of the following components (ASCA, 2019a, 2019c):

- Identification of service delivered (Classroom Lesson, Unit, or Small Group).
- Grade level.
- Topic.
- Targeted ASCA student standards (Mindsets & Behaviors).
- ASCA student standards pre-post assessment item (two per standard).
- Participation data (number of students; number and length of lessons/sessions).
- Student standards pre-post outcomes (responses to items).
- Outcome data (baseline data, final data, percentage of change).
- Reflection.

The Closing-the-Gap Results Report includes the following components (ASCA, 2019a, 2019c):

- Annual student outcome goal.
- ASCA Mindsets & Behaviors with pre-post assessment items for each.
- Interventions supporting achievement of the annual student outcome goal.
- Systemic focus.
- Baseline and results data (anticipated and actual).
- Mindsets & Behaviors pre-post assessment results.
- Outcome data plan and results (baseline and final data).
- Reflection.

Data collected through program assessment and shared by way of results reports demonstrates how school counselors are contributing to positive student outcomes. Stakeholders review data collected through program assessment to make determinations about the value of the school counseling program in meeting student needs and the needs of the collective. School administrators use results reports to justify resource allocations and the existence of school counseling programs and to demonstrate accountability, which is permeating every molecule of the school counseling profession.

> **DEMONSTRATING RESULTS**
>
> You are a school counselor at Weecanduit High School. Your principal lets you know at the start of the school year that he wants you to be prepared to make a presentation during the spring open house demonstrating how the school counseling program has made a difference in the lives of the students at Weecanduit High School. How will you be able to demonstrate positive student outcomes to stakeholders at the open house?
>
> a. Share action plans.
> b. Highlight program assessment outcomes.
> c. Review the management agreement.
> d. Emphasize the work of the advisory council.

Pre- and post-assessments are essential elements of assessment and begins with the first component of the ASCA National Model. At the assessment stage, it becomes clearly visible how all four of the components of the ASCA National Model come together to create an interdependent plan for measuring how we make an impact on the lives of students and the school community. The student standards (Mindsets & Behaviors) were selected (***Define***) and documented on action plans/lesson plans (***Manage***) that identified pre-post measures, then delivered (***Deliver***) with pre-post measures administered, and the outcome of the pre-post measure is being documented in results reports (***Assess***).

ASCA recommends no more than three to five items per measure and encourages school counselors to tweak items over time until you have nailed the intention of the question/prompt (2019c). They say *Rome wasn't built in a day*. It is no more likely that the perfect pre-post item will be built in a day. Well, unless your one of those brainiac school

### Table 2.8 Pre-Post Methods for Collecting Mindsets & Behaviors Data

| Mindsets & Behaviors | Pre-Post Methods for Data Collection |
|---|---|
| Attitudes/Beliefs | Scaling Technique<br>Likert Scale<br>Card Sorts |
| Knowledge | Likert Scale<br>Recount Fact<br>Define<br>Describe<br>List |
| Skills | Likert Scale<br>Demonstrate<br>Illustrate<br>Role Play<br>Give an Example<br>Solve a Problem |

*Source*: Adapted from *ASCA National Model Implementation Guide: Manage and Assess* (2019c).

counselors! I never fell, or even stumbled, into that category. While not exhaustive, Table 2.8 provides pre-post methods for measuring the attitudes, knowledge, and skills of the ASCA Mindsets & Behaviors.

Use of these pre- and post-measures immediately prior to and immediately following school counseling curriculum/intervention can help to demonstrate a correlation and potentially a causal link between school counseling programs and student change. These measures plainly answer the significant question: "Did it work?"

### PRINCIPAL SHOME

Your principal, Dr. Shome, is not convinced that interrupting a teacher's instructional time with a school counseling lesson is beneficial. He has come to you requesting data that shows "how" your school counseling curriculum instruction in the classroom is making a positive difference in the lives of students. Which of the following types of program assessment methods would be most useful in responding to your principal's request?

> a. Results of a student and teacher survey assessing their perceptions of a classroom lesson delivered by the school counselor.
> b. Results of pre-post measures of previous classroom instruction delivered by the school counselor and annual results reports.
> c. Results of a pre-classroom lesson measure that asks students what they hope to learn from the lesson, and a post-lesson measure that asks students what they learned from the lesson.
> d. A post-classroom lesson measure that asks students to describe what they liked about the lesson delivered by the school counselor and their suggestions for how the lesson may have made more of a positive difference for them.

Sadly, some school divisions are questioning the need for school counseling programs. Assessment may very well be the lifeline for those programs hovering over the brink of extinction. And, although program assessment does not equal accountability it does precede it as a means by which to demonstrate positive outcomes and credible data-driven practices supported by standards, data, and research. Just as assessment practices necessitate that school counselors become savvy consumers and producers of data, demonstrating outcome-based practices and accountability to stakeholders requires that school counselors become efficient consumers of research.

## Proximal and distal measures

Proximal measures assess specific constructs such as the ASCA Mindsets & Behaviors *immediately before and immediately after* intervention or program delivery. The administration of proximal assessments allows school counselors to establish correlations and, in some cases, depending upon the strength of the research design, a causal link between school counseling instruction/intervention and outcomes.

Distal measures do not generally take place immediately following the program or intervention, but it is possible depending upon research design. Distal evaluation outcomes alone do not definitively link school counseling programming to student change because of the great number of factors (i.e., extraneous variables) that impact student development over time (i.e., between phases of evaluation).

There has been some debate over the significance of proximal (immediate) versus distal (over time) program assessment in linking school counseling program activities to what students know and can do as a result of the intervention or program. Proximal evaluation methods, then, are primarily used to establish correlation, if not causality, whereas distal evaluations are often used as a means of cross validation to further support, or call into question, proximal evaluation outcomes and/or to demonstrate lasting change. For example, perhaps a school counselor administered a classroom instructional unit that resulted in improved attendance. Reviewing the outcome date (i.e., attendance) over time would help to determine whether the change that occurred was lasting. Also, reviewing data over time will help school counselors to identify patterns that could indicate gaps and/or systemic concerns potentially related to equity and access.

### DARE TO SAY NO

A middle-school counselor created a classroom instructional unit that involves two visits to the health and PE classrooms over a period of two weeks to cover a drug and alcohol prevention program to supplement the DARE and Just Say No programs at their school. During the first visit, the school counselor administered two questionnaires developed from the Mindsets & Behaviors student standards and supporting curriculum. One of the questionnaires included items that would be covered during this first lesson; the other questionnaire included content that would be covered in the entire two-day program. On the second visit, the school counselor administered a questionnaire that included items that would be covered during this second lesson. One week following the unit, the school counselor returned to the classrooms to administer a questionnaire that was identical to the one administered during the first lesson, which included content that would be covered in the entire two-day program. This is an example of the following type of assessment measure:

a. Proximal.
b. Distal.
c. Outcome.
d. Proximal and distal.

### Table 2.9 Frequently Used Outcome Research Designs

| |
|---|
| **Non-experimental (or Pre-experimental)** |
| Pretest–posttest (one group only) |
| Case study (examination of one individual or group) |
| **Quasi-experimental** |
| Pretest–posttest (two or more groups) |
| Non-equivalent control group (use of a control group and a pre-post measure to understand similarities and differences of groups prior to intervention) |
| Time series design (no control group; one sample with multiple measures on three or more occasions) |
| **True experimental** |
| Randomized pretest–posttest with control group |
| Randomized posttest only with control group |

## Assessment design

Program assessment is a type of field-based outcome study, or applied research often referred to as *action research*. It is frequently used as the *evidence base* for building ASCA lesson plans (2019a). There are many other types of outcome research designs that could be used to measure any number of research questions. The fact is that an infinite number of possibilities exist. Table 2.9 lists the three most commonly used designs (i.e., non-experimental, quasi-experimental, and true experimental) (Erford, 2019).

There are basic differences in the three designs. The true experimental design uses random sampling and control groups; the quasi-experimental design shares similar characteristics of the true experimental design but does not use random assignment. The quasi-experimental design involves multiple groups or multiple measures. Non-experimental designs are generally one-time surveys and single observations. The true experimental design is the strongest for assessing cause and effect, with non-experimental designs having the least value for determining cause and effect between the intervention and the outcome.

> **IS PEER HELPING—HELPING?**
>
> A school counselor conducts a program evaluation that assesses the impact of a peer-helping program in five classrooms over a four-week period of time. This methodology is considered to be
>
> a. True experimental design.
> b. Non-experimental design.
> c. Quasi-experimental design.
> d. All of the above.

Non-experimental and quasi-experimental designs do not allow school counselors to absolutely conclude that observed changes were due to their intervention. Nonetheless, these designs are invaluable in the educational setting where true experiments are extremely difficult because of vast number of uncontrollable variables and the ethical concerns of randomly assigning children and adolescents to treatment conditions and control groups. In the educational setting, the non-experimental and quasi-experimental pre-post program assessment is the most widely used assessment design. Pre-post assessments allow school counselors to gain an understanding of how students are different as a result of the program/intervention implemented. For example, if the school counselor administers a pre-assessment immediately prior to the start of a classroom lesson, then administers the *same* assessment immediately following the classroom lesson, the school counselor could claim with some certainty that the change was due to the classroom lesson.

### Assessment and appraisal of the school counselor

The *Assess* component of the ASCA National Model would not be complete if it did not include a means by which to evaluate the individual school counselor. Toward the end, ASCA created the ASCA School Counselor Professional Standards & Competencies Assessment and the School Counselor Professional also includes the assessment of school counselor competencies and School Counselor Performance Appraisal Template (2019c). Assessing and appraising the school counselor is a multi-faceted process that includes both self-assessment and an annual performance appraisal conducted by the school counselor's administrator.

> ### ASCA Position on The School Counselor and Annual Performance Appraisal
>
> The annual performance appraisal of school counselors should accurately reflect the unique professional training and practices of school counselors working within a pre-K–12 school counseling program. These written appraisals should use forms and tools specifically designed for school counselors, based on documents such as the ASCA School Counselor Professional Standards & Competencies and the School Counselor Performance Appraisal from the ASCA National Model.
>
> *Position statement adopted 1978; reaffirmed 1984; revised 1986, 1993, 2003, 2009, 2015; reviewed 1999, 2021*

The ASCA School Counselor Professional Standards & Competencies Assessment is intended to be used by school counselors, school administrators, and counselor educators (ASCA, 2019a). ASCA anticipates that school counselors might use the standards and competencies as a self-assessment tool and a tool for creating professional development plans based on self-perceptions. Administrators might use the standards and competencies for school counselor recruitment and/or performance evaluation. Counselor educators might find the standards and competencies useful for establishing course/program benchmarks and course curriculum (2019a). The ASCA School Counselor Professional Standards and Competencies are delineated as: 1) Mindsets, 2) Professional Foundation Behaviors, 3) Direct and Indirect Student Services Behaviors, and 4) Planning and Assessment Behaviors.

The School Counselor Performance Appraisal Template (2019a) is a substantial document that is designed to be used alone or in combination with the school and/or district approved appraisal documents. Essentially, the appraisal document assesses the school counselor on the extent to which a comprehensive data-informed, data producing, and outcome driven, school counseling program has been designed and implemented with appropriate allocation of time to direct and indirect student services and closing the gap activities/intervention.

# Chapter 2 Case conceptualization responses

## Comprehensive school counseling programs

### Vision or mission statement?

This statement is an example of an excerpt from a vision statement. This statement has a clear future orientation, describing what students will be/do after participating in the school counseling program.

### Jennifer's score

The correct response is "b." Jennifer took a norm-referenced assessment, which is a standardized, formal assessment.

### My student may have a disability

The correct response is "d." School counselors advocate for student appraisal that draws from multiple sources of both formal and informal assessments to promote practices that reduce premature or inaccurate diagnoses of learning disabilities.

### The college dream

Carolyn's GPA would indicate that she is academically successful. For this reason, the school counselor may wish to inquire as to why the parent believes her daughter will "flunk out" of college. It is important for the parent to know that the SAT is an aptitude test as well as a college entrance exam, which aids in predicting Carolyn's future performance as a college student. Also, providing the parent with an SAT fee waiver may help with the financial burden. Finally, walking the parent through the steps needed to complete and submit the Free Application for Federal Student Aid, or providing her with a contact that will assist her is crucial to guiding the parent of a first-generation college student. This parent could also use some college preparation and financial aid information. Finally, considering the family's financial challenges and Carolyn's GPA, there may be scholarships available, so offering to assist Carolyn with the scholarship search and identifying colleges of interest is critical to helping Carolyn to realize the college dream. It would also be prudent to explore Carolyn's thoughts regarding attending college.

## Meeting Andre's needs

Andre's grade equivalent score on the mathematics test indicates that he has performed at the level of an average fifth-grade student, three months into the school year. Andre's persistent achievement in all subject areas indicates the need for a more rigorous or advanced curriculum to keep Andre motivated toward academics. The school counselor may want to recommend Andre for accelerated learning and enrichment programs such as the school's gifted and talented program and the Governor's School, as well as summer enrichment experiences. The school counselor may want to reassess Andre's need for intervention pertaining to his misbehavior until he has engaged in these extracurricular activities. Andre's misbehavior may be due to boredom or frustration with the nondescript pace of the on-grade-level curriculum.

## Dropout prevention

The correct response is "b." The school counselor is demonstrating school counseling practices that are both data driven (e.g., he or she reviewed data to identify and create a program based on student need) and data producing (e.g., he or she evaluated the program to obtain data that supports the effectiveness of the program).

## Aymee's BASIC ID

The correct response is "d." BASIC ID is a comprehensive, non-standardized, informal, and subjective assessment method that identifies a student's specific strengths and needs, which allows the school counselor to tailor counseling to meet those needs.

## The divorce of Geoffrey's parents

(S)ubjective Observations
Anger (self-report), helplessness/depression (counselor observed).
(O)bjectives Observations
Poor hygiene, sitting slumped over, hands clinched, crying.
(A)ssessment
Geoffrey appears to be somewhat depressed and anxious as a result of his parents' divorce. He also appears to be experiencing a sense of hopelessness about the future based on his statement that he wants to quit school because he does not understand the point of it.

(P)lan

The school counselor might provide Geoffrey with anger management techniques and combat possible depression with cognitive behavioral strategies. The school counselor might also offer strengths-based counseling to build resiliency and identify internal and external resources. Person-centered counseling, too, will allow Geoffrey the opportunity to express his emotions and gain insight into his emotional experiencing. Geoffrey would likely benefit from the support of a small group with other students whose parents are divorcing or already divorced. It would also be prudent to suggest parent involvement with Geoffrey.

## *Is peer helping—helping?*

The correct response is "c." This is an example of a quasi-experimental design because the methodology of the evaluation examines multiple groups as well as multiple measures.

## *Dr. Datarules*

Creating a needs assessment(s) that could be administered to both teachers and students would be warranted in this case. Teachers are in the best position to identify instructional strategies that work; students are in the best position to identify instructional strategies that are enjoyable. You can use a comparative analysis to provide Dr. Datarules with data that identifies instructional strategies that are both effective and enjoyed by students.

## *Principal Shome*

The correct response is "b." Dr. Shome is asking for *outcome* data. By administering a pre-post lesson measure created from lesson content and lesson objectives, you can measure your lesson outcome. Because you are administering the measure immediately before and immediately following the lesson (proximal evaluation), you can claim with some certainty that change is due to your intervention. Furthermore, showing your principal the annual results report will help to drive the point home. Hopefully, you will already be sharing results reports with your administrators each year so your principal already knows the positive impact the school counseling curriculum is having on students and the school community.

## DARE to say no

The correct response is "d." This is an example of both proximal (immediate) and distal (over time) evaluations.

## Troy

The correct response is "a." Troy wants to demonstrate how his small group has helped students. Service logs will only show the number of times the group has been facilitated. Demand for the group does not mean that it is effective. Student may just really like Troy, the group experience, or getting out of class. Troy needs to conduct a program assessment to determine the outcome of his efforts.

## Can this be measured?

The correct response is "d." This option provides the needed components of an ASCA recommended outcome goal, which are: baseline data, target data, and percentage of change. Options "a" and "b" cannot be measured as written, reading more like goals than objectives. Option "c" is an activity that will take place to support the goal, but completing the worksheet does not demonstrate that the student has learned healthy ways to express anger.

## Whitney's behavior

The correct response is "b." The level at which Whitney's academic and behavioral performance has declined places her at high risk, requiring that the school counselor work at the tier three level to help Whitney to be successful. At the tier three level, students are provided intense individualized attention and referred for additional school or community services. In Whitney's case, in-school supports and referrals have not been successful, calling for more intense support from outside of the school.

## Kyleigh's mother

The correct response is "b." Children of Kyleigh's age may experience difficulty labeling and expressing the emotions they are experiencing as a result of the death of a loved one. School counselors can help Kyleigh to identify, label, and express what she is feeling. As counselors, we do not tell clients "everything will be okay" (response option "a"). Everything may not be okay.

## April's IEP

The correct response is "b." You are providing indirect services to April through direct services to those who are working directly with April. As the teachers and parents implement strategies that you helped to put into place for April, you are assisting April, albeit in an indirect manner.

## Stages and phases

You are currently in the implementation stage of the consultation process. Because you are working toward creating the plan while also working on the interventions, you are moving back and forth between phases I and II on the implementation stage.

## The stalemate

A combination of both consultation and collaboration may be the best course of action at this time. Taking into consideration the unique and possibly opposing worldviews of these two members (Eastern and Western cultural philosophies), while listening to and validating their thoughts pertaining to the direction for the program, will promote a trusting and safe climate for sharing ideas. Having these two members begin by sharing their ideas allows the school counselor to observe their interactions and identify commonalities upon which to encourage their positive relations. Also, invite the other team members to engage in positive communications about the program's direction and empower the entire team to begin the program planning process by establishing a primary goal(s) for the program and knocking around some measurable objectives. This would also be a good time to make use of team building strategies (e.g., mediation, problem solving, and negotiation) and engage in collaborative consultation, that is, offering your ideas based on your training and experience in school counseling programming and student development as well as your knowledge of the school and student population. It is important to revisit the data that is driving the program in order to stay focused on meeting the needs of the students and school community and maintaining the shared focus.

## Demonstrating results

The correct response is "b." Program assessment outcomes provide school counselors with the evidence needed to demonstrate how the school counseling program is making a positive difference to the lives of students. Action plans and management agreements may depict what the school counselor is planning to implement and how the program or activity is to be evaluated, but these documents do not provide outcome data. Discussing the good work of the council is not the same as providing outcome data assessing the program's effectiveness.

# Chapter 2 Simulation: Collaboration

## Brief case description

The principal of your high school asks you, the school counselor, to develop and deliver an Internet safety and cyberbullying program to the entire student body. Due to heightened incidences, time is critical, and the expertise of others would be helpful in this endeavor. So, you collaborate with others within and outside of the school.

### Section A: Collaboration

Which of the following best describes your function in relation to other members of the team during the collaboration process?
   (Choose ONLY ONE in this section.)

| | | |
|---|---|---|
| ____A—1. | Expert |
| ____A—2. | Equal |
| ____A—3. | Advisor |
| ____A—4. | Educator |
| ____A—5. | Coordinator |

### Section B: Collaboration

A teacher hears that you are developing an Internet safety program and comes to you about a student in her class, Kenji, who she believes is a victim of cyberbullying, based on the student's behaviors. She is not sure how to approach the issue or what resources she can provide. When she brings up the subject, the student has little to say. What information should you obtain from the teacher before proceeding?
   (Select as many as you consider indicated in this section.)

| | |
|---|---|
| ____B—1. | What behaviors indicate that the student is a victim of cyberbullying |
| ____B—2. | What friends say about the student's situation |

| _____B—3. | Frequency of behaviors |
|---|---|
| _____B—4. | Magnitude of behaviors and emotions |
| _____B—5. | Level of academic functioning |
| _____B—6. | The duration of specific behaviors |
| _____B—7. | Extracurricular activity involvement |
| _____B—8. | What the student has expressed |

## Section C: Collaboration

The teacher offers some insight into the situation, which depicts Kenji in considerable distress this morning in her class. You believe that giving the teacher resources may not be active enough in this situation. Kenji seems highly and negatively impacted by text messages he is receiving from an unidentified other. Which course of action would be most appropriate at this time?
   (Select ONLY ONE in this section.)

| _____C—1. | Refer the case to peer mediation |
|---|---|
| _____C—2. | Involve the assistant principal |
| _____C—3. | Take away the cell phone |
| _____C—4. | Recommend an immediate school counseling session with Kenji |
| _____C—5. | Refer the student to the police |
| _____C—6. | Talk to the student's friends |
| _____C—7. | Recommend a school counseling session with Kenji during this teacher's block tomorrow after receiving parent permission |

## Section D: Collaboration

The teacher insists that you contact the parents because Kenji is Asian, and the parents need to be involved. The teacher says, "It is the Asian way." The culturally sensitive school counselor might respond in the following manner:

(Select as many as you consider indicated in this section.)

| | | |
|---|---|---|
| \_\_\_\_D—1. | "You are correct, I will call the parents" |
| \_\_\_\_D—2. | "Yes, however, I would not want to stereotype Kenji based on his culture" |
| \_\_\_\_D—3. | "You are quite culturally diverse" |
| \_\_\_\_D—4. | "I appreciate your sharing; however, the Asian culture is also very respectful of parents, so Kenji may not wish to involve them at this point" |
| \_\_\_\_D—5. | "Kenji is a typical teen; we get too caught up in cultural differences" |
| \_\_\_\_D—6. | "Does Kenji have Asian friends we can talk to?" |

## Section E: Collaboration

After speaking with Kenji, you learn that he is a senior and 18 years old next month. Kenji is not distressed as a result of cyberbullying, but because he and his girlfriend of three years, who is not Asian and who is also a senior, are not accepted by his parents. They have been having some issues related to their families. As a culturally sensitive counselor, how would you help Kenji?

(Select as many as you consider indicated in this section.)

| | | |
|---|---|---|
| \_\_\_\_E—1. | Advise Kenji to sit down and chat with his family |
| \_\_\_\_E—2. | Ask Kenji to let his parents know what is going on |
| \_\_\_\_E—3. | Find quality time to sit down with his girlfriend because texting is not the best way to resolve their issues |
| \_\_\_\_E—4. | Call in Kenji's girlfriend and talk with both of them at the same time |
| \_\_\_\_E—5. | Encourage Kenji to understand the importance of family to his culture and take into consideration what his parents are advising |
| \_\_\_\_E—6. | Express your concern for him and invite him to share the issues and possible solutions he has considered |

# Chapter 2 Simulation responses: Collaboration

## Brief case description

The principal of your high school asks you, the school counselor, to develop and deliver an Internet safety and cyberbullying program to the entire student body. Time is critical, and the expertise of others would be helpful in this endeavor. So, you decide to collaborate with others within and outside of the school.

## *Section A: Collaboration*

Which of the following best describes your function in relation to other members of the team during the collaboration process?
   (Choose ONLY ONE in this section.)

| | | |
|---|---|---|
| A—1. | Expert<br>No<br>Generally, this is the function taken on by the school counselor as a consultant | |
| A—2. | Equal<br>Yes<br>During the collaboration process, the school counselor works with others within and outside of the school as an equal member of the team, sharing knowledge as well as task and outcome responsibility | |
| A—3. | Advisor<br>No<br>Although the school counselor may offer advice during the collaboration process, this is not the distinguishing function of the school counselor during collaboration | |
| A—4. | Educator<br>No<br>The school counselor is certainly an educator during the process of collaboration; however, this is not the distinguishing function of the school counselor during collaboration | |
| A—5. | Coordinator<br>No<br>The school counselor may coordinate tasks and activities during collaboration; however, this is not the distinguishing function of the school counselor during collaboration | |

## Section B: Collaboration

A teacher hears that you are developing an Internet safety program and comes to you about a student in her class, Kenji, who she believes is a victim of cyberbullying, based on the student's behaviors. She is not sure how to approach the issue or what resources she can provide. When she brings up the subject, the student has little to say. What information should you obtain from the teacher before proceeding?

(Select as many as you consider indicated in this section.)

| | |
|---|---|
| B—1. | What behaviors indicate that the student is a victim of cyberbullying<br>Yes<br>Clarifying "behaviors" that the teacher has specifically observed as "behaviors" is important to understanding Kenji's situation |
| B—2. | What friends say about the student's situation<br>No<br>It is inappropriate for the teacher and school counselor to begin questioning the student's friends about Kenji's situation |
| B—3. | Frequency of behaviors<br>Yes<br>Gaining a greater understanding of how often the observed behaviors occur is critical to behavioral assessment and timely intervention |
| B—4. | Magnitude of behaviors and emotions<br>Yes<br>Gaining a greater understanding of the level of behavioral and emotional disturbances is vital to timely behavioral and emotional assessment and intervention |
| B—5. | Level of academic functioning<br>No<br>There is no indication for assessing academic functioning at the present time. The teacher has not indicated concern in this area.<br>Should the issue persist, assessing its impact on academic functioning may be warranted |
| B—6. | The duration of specific behaviors<br>Yes<br>Understanding how long behavioral and emotional disturbances have been present is useful in providing timely behavioral and emotional assessment and intervention |

| B—7. | Extracurricular activity involvement |
| | No |
| | There is no indication for assessing extracurricular involvement at the present time. The teacher has not indicated concern in this area. Should the problematic behaviors persist or worsen, it may useful to assess change in this area (e.g., the student's lack of interest in extracurricular activities that the student had considered enjoyable in the past) |
| B—8. | What the student has expressed |
| | Yes |
| | Understanding what the student has to say about the situations is critical |

## Section C: Collaboration

The teacher offers some insight into the situation, which depicts Kenji in considerable distress this morning in her class. You believe that giving the teacher resources may not be active enough in this situation. Kenji seems highly and negatively impacted by text messages he is receiving from an unidentified other. Which course of action would be most appropriate at this time?

(Select ONLY ONE in this section.)

| C—1. | Refer the case to peer mediation |
| | No |
| | Peer mediation requires two identifiable others. More information is needed before considering mediation |
| C—2. | Involve the assistant principal |
| | No |
| | At some point, this may become necessary, but this is not the best course of action at the present time |
| C—3. | Take away the cell phone |
| | No |
| | Although texting should not be allowed during instructional time, this will not mediate Kenji's distress |
| C—4. | Recommend an immediate school counseling session with Kenji |
| | Yes |
| | This is the best course of action at the present time. The teacher has observed that Kenji is in considerable distress and believes that it is linked to bullying. The school counselor needs to assess Kenji's emotionality and explore the situation. Bullying and cyberbullying has been linked to suicide and homicide. Immediate contact with the student is warranted |

| C—5. | Refer the student to the police<br>No<br>This may become necessary. More information is needed |
|---|---|
| C—6. | Talk to the student's friends<br>No<br>It is not appropriate to involve Kenji's friends at this point in this situation |
| C—7. | Recommend a school counseling session with Kenji during this teacher's block tomorrow, after receiving parent permission<br>No<br>The teacher has shared that Kenji presents with considerable distress today. The school counselor may be able to mediate Kenji's distress, and acting immediately could save lives |

## Section D: Collaboration

The teacher insists that you contact the parents because Kenji is Asian, and the parents need to be involved. The teacher says, "It is the Asian way." The culturally sensitive school counselor might respond in the following manner:

(Select as many as you consider indicated in this section.)

| D—1. | "You are correct, I will call the parents"<br>No<br>Parent involvement is not indicated at the present time. Hearing what the student has to say first is the appropriate action at this time |
|---|---|
| D—2. | "Yes, however, I would not want to stereotype Kenji based on his culture"<br>Yes<br>This statement is indicative of a culturally sensitive school counselor |
| D—3. | "You are quite culturally diverse"<br>No<br>The school counselor would be reinforcing the teacher's stereotyping behavior |
| D—4. | "I appreciate your sharing; however, the Asian culture is also very respectful of parents, so Kenji may not wish to involve them at this point"<br>Yes<br>This is the response of a culturally sensitive school counselor |

| D—5. | "Kenji is a typical teen; we get too caught up in cultural differences" |
| --- | --- |
| | No |
| | Sensitivity to cultural, individual, and developmental differences is critical to effective counseling |
| D—6. | "Does Kenji have Asian friends we can talk to?" |
| | No |
| | It is inappropriate to involve Kenji's friends in this situation at this time |

## Section E: Collaboration

After speaking with Kenji, you learn that he is a senior and 18 years old next month. Kenji is not distressed as a result of cyberbullying, but because he and his girlfriend of three years, who is not Asian and who is also a senior, are not accepted by his parents. They have been having some issues related to the families. As a culturally sensitive counselor, how would you help Kenji?

(Select ONLY ONE in this section.)

| E—1. | Advise Kenji to sit down and chat with his family |
| --- | --- |
| | No |
| | Kenji is a young adult capable of making this decision. Exploring the level of family involvement Kenji would like to have and/or exploring possible support systems within and outside of the family is warranted |
| E—2. | Ask Kenji to let his parents know what is going on |
| | No |
| | Kenji is a young adult capable of making this decision. Exploring the level of parent involvement Kenji would like to have and/or exploring possible support systems within and outside of the family is warranted |
| E—3. | Find quality time to sit down with his girlfriend because texting is not the best way to resolve their issues |
| | No |
| | The school counselor does not provide solutions to Kenji's issues but allows Kenji to explore and discover his own solutions |
| E—4. | Call in Kenji's girlfriend and talk with both of them at the same time |
| | No |
| | It is not appropriate in this situation for the school counselor to pull Kenji's girlfriend out of class and away from instructional time to engage in personal counseling related to their relationship |

| E—5. | Encourage Kenji to understand the importance of family to his culture and take into consideration what his parents are advising |
| --- | --- |
| | No |
| | Counselors do not espouse their own values onto the student, nor do counselors advise students with regard to the student's behavior in relation to the student's culture. Counselors work within the worldview of the student |
| E—6. | Express your concern for him and invite him to share the issues and possible solutions he has considered |
| | Yes |
| | Empathizing and validating Kenji's concerns are warranted. Also, encouraging Kenji to explore the situation and solutions within his own worldview is appropriate |

## Chapter 2: Guided reflection

Describe a comprehensive school counseling program.

Describe the components of each of the four quadrants of the ASCA National Model:

1) Define

2) Manage

3) Deliver

4) Assess

What are the ASCA Mindsets & Behaviors for Student Success?

What is the difference between direct and indirect student services? Name at least two of each.




What are the ASCA Student Standards and the ASCA Profession Standards?




Explain what a needs assessment is and create one item that might be on a needs assessment for each of the following:

   (1) elementary students



   (2) middle-school students



   (3) parents




Compare individual and program assessment. Then, describe the differences between assessing individual needs (or student appraisal) and assessing program needs.

Compare and contrast formal and informal assessments. Give examples of each.

Describe proximal and distal measures. How are they different?

Discuss the role of data in school counseling. What does it mean to be data-driven and data-producing?

What are the three types of data as described in the ASCA National Model? Briefly denote the differences.

Name at least two data sources that when examined can identify access, attainment, and achievement gaps.

What are action plans? What are the components of an action plan?

Define achievement gap. Name the populations of students that have been identified as part of the national achievement gap.

What are closing the achievement gap action plans? What are the components of a closing the achievement gap action plan?

Why are actions plans needed in school counseling?

What are results reports? What are the components of a results report?

What are closing the achievement gap results reports? What are the components of a closing the achievement gap action plan?

Why are results reports needed in school counseling?

What are the three most commonly used research designs?

What are the most commonly used research designs in the school setting? Why?

If you use the pre-post research design to measure the outcome of a school counseling classroom lesson, can you claim with complete certainty that change was due to your lesson? Why or why not?

What does the acronym RTI stand for? Create one example to illustrate an RTI strategy.

What does the acronym MTSS stand for, and how does it relate to RTI?

Define and describe the importance of instructional strategies and classroom management, and when they would most likely be used in school counseling.

What is a school counseling advisory council? What is the purpose of such a council?

What are the types of calendars school counselor should keep? What are their purposes?

Compare collaboration and consultation. Then define both in a way that demonstrates the differences, including the nature of relationships.

Explain the stages of consultation, identifying key activities at each stage. Create two examples that illustrate when it would be appropriate to engage in consultation as a school counselor.

**170** ■ *Comprehensivs school counseling programs*

What is the purpose of referrals? What types of referrals might you make as a school counselor?

What is the difference between appraisal and advisement?

Name at least two student appraisal approaches/techniques.

After examining the construct, summarize (rewrite in your own words) what is meant by life-saving appraisal. Then, discuss the importance of individual assessment in the following critical situations:

Child abuse and neglect

Substance abuse

Self-harm

What types of counseling might be considered outside the scope of school counseling? What do the ASCA Ethical Standards have to say on the matter?

Describe the function of the school counselor with regard to diagnosing students in the school setting.

# Chapter 3
# Primary developmental domains

School counselors attend to the unique developmental needs of students. Comprehensive school counseling programs and the ASCA *Mindsets & Behaviors for Student Success* (2021) recognize the following three broad areas of development: 1) social/emotional development, 2) career development, and 3) academic development. The approach school counselors take to meeting the complex and contextual needs of students is grounded in a sound understanding of developmental theories discussed in a previous chapter.

Students at the elementary level are more closely supervised and sheltered and parents tend to be more actively involved during the elementary school years. Consequently, parents are a fabulous resource, and it is important to find ways to involve parents and make them feel welcomed in the classrooms and schools. The school counselor and parent have a major commonality—you both want the best for their children! The majority of the elementary school counselor's time is spent facilitating small groups and classroom lessons and responding to students' immediate needs with responsive services strategies and programming. The elementary student's developmental level limits the application of counseling models to the more active approaches that do not require significant insight and self-awareness. Behavioral approaches are more often used at the elementary level while students are beginning to learn appropriate behavioral patterns and expectations.

During the middle-school years, students demonstrate much-improved language skills, heightened individuality, and begin to engage in unparalleled self-exploration. The need to begin high school academic preparation and postsecondary career decision making increases the demand for individual counseling in order to effectively cope with transitions and other social and emotional issues that tend to come up on the maturing road to early adulthood. And, of course, academic and career planning heightens as students begins to envision a more independent life outside of the K-12 school environment.

Behavioral approaches that may have dominated the school counselor's repertoire at the elementary level are now supplemented with counseling approaches that make use of the more sophisticated cognitive processes developmentally available during adolescence. Adolescents, too, have the relational ability to connect with the counselor and engage in self-analysis. Counseling approaches that encourage responsible living, decision making, and problem solving, and the impact of cognitions on emotions and behavior are particularly beneficial for the adolescent.

Developmentally, elementary- and middle-school students are in two very different places. Although elementary students generally aim to please, treating us like a celebrity when spotted in the grocery store, the adolescent will make every effort to avoid us, as though we are merely annoying creatures to be endured. So, keep in mind the adolescent's unique developmental issues and personal characteristics when selecting counseling approaches and techniques. Developmental constructs are important guides but not all-inclusive, so also be careful not to use a cookie-cutter approach based on widely recognized developmental characteristics and milestones of adolescence.

Parent involvement at the middle-school level is often dependent upon the adolescent. Developmentally, adolescents are seeking independence from parents, and may, therefore, be apprehensive about having their parent in the school. Nonetheless, school counselors continue to encourage parents to engage in their adolescent's education both at home and at school, while negotiating responsibility and independence. There is an abundance of research linking parent involvement with improved academic achievement and attendance, as well as reduced dropout rates (Wright & Stegelin, 2002).

The high-school counselor spends the majority of his or her time with high-school students implementing responsive services and providing academic, career, and individual counseling. Their primary responsibilities include student scheduling, administration of assessments, providing career and college information, and addressing individual student concerns and assisting with the decision-making process, primarily as it relates to school and postsecondary opportunities.

Generally speaking, high-school students will tend to view the school counselor as their friend and equal. Some will even attempt to call us by our first names. Keeping boundaries while maintaining an effective school counselor–high-school student relationship can be a challenge, particularly for school counselors from a neighboring generation.

Assuming normal developmental levels, high-school students are fully capable of understanding abstract concepts, analyzing, synthesizing, and relating. Advanced developmental levels allow school counselors to apply virtually any counseling approach appropriate to the school setting and fitting to the student and the presenting issue.

Parent involvement is generally low compared to the family's involvement at the elementary- and middle-school levels. Developmentally, high-school students have established their independence, for the most part, and are making many of their own decisions. School counselors are called upon to continue to encourage parent involvement at the high-school level because research connecting academic achievement to parent involvement pertains to the high school and college years as well as the earlier school years.

### THE PARENTS DO NOT TRUST ME

A school counselor is in a professional development program at his school. A teacher sitting beside him is experiencing her first year at the elementary level. The teacher had just served five years at the high-school level. The teacher is concerned because she is getting so many visits and calls from parents to help in the classroom. The teacher remarks to the school counselor that perhaps she has done something that has caused the parents not to trust her with their children or perhaps they believe because she came from the high-school level that she will not be able to relate to the children. How might you respond to the teacher's concerns?

# Social/emotional development

One of the three broad developmental domains of a CDSCP and the ASCA *Mindsets & Behaviors for Student Success* (2021) is *social/emotional development*. School counselors help students to overcome social and emotional challenges so that they can focus on learning, and develop the fortitude for wellness needed to become contributing members of society.

---

*ASCA Position on The School Counselor and Social/Emotional Development*

School counselors deliver school counseling programs that enhance student growth in three domain areas: academic, career, and social/emotional development. As a part of that program, school counselors implement strategies and activities to help all students enhance their social/emotional development – the mindsets and behaviors students need to manage emotions and learn and apply interpersonal skills - while recognizing that growth in all three domains is necessary for students to be successful now and later in life.

*Position statement adopted 2017; revised 2023*

---

School counselors use a variety of clever strategies to promote the development of morality including character education activities, bibliotherapy, ethical case discussions, current and past events, and role plays to help students to understand the impact of our actions and inactions on others. School counselors foster moral development by encouraging reflection, reasoning, self-esteem, positive social interactions, peaceable schools, respect for others, and appreciation for differences. And, don't forget the significant impact of *positive role models*!

School counselors, who partner with families, teachers, and community members, are better able to identify supports that strengthen protective factors and enhance resilience, empower students, and help students to discover unique personal strengths (Smith, Beck, Bernstein & Dashtguard, 2014). Developing students' resilience enables them to overcome threats to educational success and to successfully engage life's challenges.

CDSCPs that include interventions that place responsibility for success within the student are educational, empowering, and help develop coping skills that can be accessed into adulthood (Gilchrist-Banks, 2009).

School counselors assist teachers, parents, and administrators in developing behavioral interventions and classroom management strategies. Unlike administrators and teachers, however, school counselors do not engage in the discipline of students.

## ASCA Position on The School Counselor and Discipline

School counselors have specialized training and skills in promoting appropriate student behavior and preventing disruptive student behavior. School counselors are not disciplinarians but should be a resource for school personnel in developing individual and schoolwide discipline procedures. School counselors collaborate with school personnel and other stakeholders to establish policies encouraging appropriate behavior and maintaining safe schools where effective teaching and learning can take place.

*Position statement adopted 1989; revised 1993, 1999, 2001, 2007, 2013, 2019*

Emotional and social needs at the elementary level primarily revolve around the child's egocentric nature, adjustment to the concept of attending school, establishing a sound academic, personal–social, and career development foundation, and the transition to middle childhood. Emotional and social programming is generally focused on cooperation, taking turns, making friends, sharing, character education, caring, resolving conflict, and helping.

Classroom instruction and small group instruction and/or small group counseling are primary methods of program delivery at the elementary level. These systems-focused delivery methods are ideal during middle childhood for promoting positive peer interactions and healthy personal development in a social context that is facilitated and closely monitored by the school counselor. The development of social skills and positive peer relationships during middle childhood enhances the likelihood of positive peer relationships during adolescence, which has been identified as critical to prosocial personality development (Schellenberg, 2000).

The middle-school years are a time of intense emotions associated with rapid physical changes and identity development. The adolescent is no longer a child, but not yet an adult, growing away from the family of origin and into the family of man. Peer relationships are extremely influential in the development of identity, self-esteem, and positive interpersonal functioning.

Responsive to this challenging developmental stage, the social/emotional domain of a comprehensive school counseling program focuses programming on the transition to middle school from elementary school and from middle school to high school. The school counseling program also focuses on dealing with bullying, problem solving, responsible decision making, conflict resolution, interpersonal relationships, violence, and Internet safety. In addition, school counselors may include prevention programming that addresses teen dating, teen pregnancy, sexually transmitted disease, and chemical dependency.

---

### ASCA Position on The School Counselor and Prevention of Sexually Transmitted Disease

The school counselor supports educational efforts related to the prevention of sexually transmitted infections (STIs), including human immunodeficiency virus (HIV) and acquired immune deficiency syndrome (AIDS), through engagement with students, families, school staff and the community to prevent infection and the spread of these infections. The school counselor collaborates with other school health personnel in these efforts, while recognizing the importance of student/family confidentiality. The school counselor provides support, counseling and referral services to students and their families affected by these infections.

*Position statement adopted 1988; revised 1993, 1999, 2001, 2006, 2012, 2018*

Social/emotional programming and counseling services for high-school students are a continuation of the areas of focus noted for middle-school students. High-school counselors continue to focus on a successful transition into high school from middle school, providing services for incoming freshmen to promote social and emotional well-being and academic success in high school, while also continuing to prepare students for postsecondary careers and higher education.

## Transitioning

I don't know who said *the one constant in our lives is change* but I agree with this shrewd proclamation. Change does not sit idle, and the vast number of personal, social, emotional, and physical changes that take place, particularly in the lives of children and adolescents, can be anxiety producing. Even welcomed change upsets homeostasis with some discomfort experienced until balance is regained. Helping clients, and in our case, students, to successful navigate change is at the heart of counseling.

Transitioning has been conceptualized in a variety of ways. There are, however, three common points of agreement among specialists in transitioning theory: (1) transition involves grieving the loss of the old and finding stability in the new, (2) successful transition is generally achieved when approached intentionally and with an understanding of the associated challenges, and (3) transition is more likely to succeed when a support system is in place to aid in overcoming challenges and adjusting to the new (Turner, 2007).

Transitions, both welcome and unwelcome, have been identified as a source of stress for children and adolescents—and adults. Developing the attitudes and skills for successful transitioning at an early age is critical to continued health and well-being during periods of change. Framing the experience of transition and change (and life!), largely dependent upon our attitudes, helps students to understand that they control the processes, perceptions, and outcomes of their internal experiences and are victims or victors of their attitudes.

School counselors begin by helping students to normalize change, that is, to view change as a necessary characteristic of life. School counselors offer programming that identifies and helps students to develop competencies essential to successful transitions and continued growth, including support systems, self-care, stress management, decision making, problem solving, communication, and positive attitude.

School counseling programs and activities include transition programs for those students who are entering middle school and high school. Successful transitioning programs invite parent participation, identify social supports, highlight positive aspects of the new setting, underscore increased freedoms and choices associated with maturity, and address the following frequently identified fears of students entering secondary school (Akos, 2002):

- Bullying by older students.
- New rules.
- Forgetting locker combinations.
- Switching classes.
- Getting lost.
- Not succeeding academically.
- Increased responsibility.
- Understanding class scheduling.

Transition programs also provide students with faculty, staff, and school information as well as a map of the school. This information helps students to identify who to go to and how to get there. New students are often reluctant to ask for help. For this reason, during the transition program, school counselors present the concept of asking for help as a positive and strength-building characteristic, reminding students that even the greatest of men recognize and confess that "no man is an island" (Donne, n.d.). School counselors collaborate with students to establish and coordinate peer-mentoring programs for transfer students. This is particularly helpful for students who are coming from culturally and linguistically different backgrounds.

School counselors encourage parents and teachers to look for maladaptive behaviors or behaviors that are not typical for the student (personal, emotional, social, and academic), which may be indicators of unsuccessful transitioning. School counselors work individually with students who are experiencing transition difficulties using a variety of counseling techniques and approaches, as well as family and peer support systems.

## School violence and bullying

Safe and prosocial school environments are essential to academic success and student safety. However, aggressive student interactions often permeate a school's culture and create hostile learning environments that stifle the academic productivity and student success and well-being (Schellenberg, 2000).

---

### ASCA Position on The School Counselor and Bullying/Harassment Prevention and the Promotion of Safe Schools

School counselors recognize the impact a safe and caring environment has on student achievement and social/emotional development. To foster a positive school climate, school counselors work to identify and remove systemic barriers that hinder a safe and caring school environment and culture. School counseling programs promote anti-bullying, anti-harassment and violence-prevention programs, schoolwide positive behavior interventions and support, along with comprehensive conflict-resolution programs to foster a positive school climate.

*Position statement adopted 1994/2000; revised 2005, 2011, 2016, 2022*

---

School counselors seek to implement programs that foster a positive climate and optimal learning environment that respects diversity to promote peaceable schools. One of the most widely used programs for promoting peaceable schools and prosocial behavior is character education. *Character education* involves, first and foremost, modeling. Educators impact the character development of their students through their own attitudes, expectations, and behaviors. Character education involves shaping students' thoughts, emotions, and behaviors to reflect core values of caring citizenship, which may include characteristics such as responsibility, respect, courage, perseverance, fairness, trust, integrity, honesty, cooperation, empathy, and acceptance.

> ### ASCA Position on The School Counselor and Character Education
>
> School counselors endorse and actively support character education programs and include them in the implementation of a comprehensive school counseling program. The school counselor also promotes the infusion of character education in the school curriculum by encouraging the participation of the entire school community.
>
> *Position statement adopted 1998; revised 2005, 2011, 2016, 2022*

Another approach that is often used in the schools is *conflict resolution*. ASCA calls for conflict resolution as a vital component of a comprehensive school counseling program. *Peer mediation* is a type of peer helping program (discussed earlier) whereby students, trained by the school counselor in conflict resolution strategies, help their peers to resolve interpersonal problems peacefully. Peer mediation provides students with a safe place in which to resolve interpersonal conflict peacefully while learning effective communication, conflict resolution, problem solving, appreciation for differences, and relationship building. Research identifies a link between peer mediation programs and school-wide violence reduction. Development of students' knowledge and skills related to conflict resolution strategies and prosocial behaviors paves the way for increased academic performance (Schellenberg, Parks-Savage, & Rehfuss, 2007).

Bullying, too, often unresponsive to peer mediation and conflict resolution, poses a threat to school safety and to the physical and emotional well-being of others. Let us not forget that bullies are victims unto themselves, requiring intervention that disrupts the self-destructive path and aids in charting a new course.

School counselors work with teachers, administrators, and law enforcement officers to create programs that deliver strong anti-bullying messages using everyday examples of the paralyzing atrocities and life-destroying impacts of bullying on named children and adolescents too often leading to gun violence in the school.

---

### ASCA Position on The School Counselor and Prevention of School-Related Gun Violence

School counselors collaborate with school staff and the community to ensure students attend schools where the environment is conducive to teaching and learning. To support the work of school counselors and school staff, schools and communities should be free from gun violence and threats. School counselors support safe schools and are responsive in crises as emphasized in the Safe Schools and Crisis Response (2019) position statement.

*Position statement adopted 2018; revised 2019*

---

School counselors educate students regarding bullying and teach strategies for dealing with bullies, such as maintaining a confident demeanor; making eye contact; delivering strong, assertive, non-emotional communication to the bully; and confiding in a trusted adult.

## Internet safety and cyberbullying

Advances in technology have heightened the need for school counselors to educate students on issues related to Internet safety, *cyberbullying*, and the misuse of cell phones. Programming pertaining to Internet and cell phone use and safety should include Internet addictions, illegal download of music and clipart, stalking and luring, access to illicit drugs, inappropriate chat rooms, invasion of privacy, safeguarding personal information, identity theft, sexting (e.g., the texting/transmission of sexually explicit language/materials), the misuse of personal pictures and information, and school policies pertaining to cyberbullying during and outside of school (Huda, et al., 2017).

ASCA recommends that school counselors provide educators and parents with guidelines for the appropriate use of technology by students, for example, keeping computers (with electronic filtering and monitoring programs installed) in a room that is clearly visible by responsible adults; strongly encouraging children and teens to discuss anything they have received that is confusing, uncomfortable, or frightening; and establishing rules for the use of available technologies. It is also critical that parents understand and relay to their children and adolescents the ethical and legal implications of electronic actions and words and the dangers of giving out personal information and photographs in an electronic environment that is often permanent and irreversible.

---

### ASCA Position on The School Counselor and Student Safety with Digital Technology

Digital technology (e.g. cell phones/mobile devices, gaming platforms, social media, and the internet) is a useful tool in creating equitable and developmental learning opportunities to enhance student academic, career, and social/emotional development. School counselors educate students and families about responsible use, digital citizenship, cultural, ethical, and legal considerations and collaborate with families, educators and law enforcement officials to alert students to risks technology poses.

*Position statement adopted 2000; revised 2006, 2012, 2017, 2023*

---

School counselors include cyberbullying as an essential topic when discussing Internet safety. Cyberbullying is a disturbing issue of grave concern with dire consequences. Cyberbullies often perceive themselves to be invisible, believing that their communications are anonymous and that they will not be caught or held responsible in cyberspace. Ensuring that students understand that all communications online can be tracked may have an immediate and lasting impact on the reduction of cyberbullying.

It is also important that students understand that cyberbullying is considered by law to be a criminal offense when it (1) involves repeated or excessive harassment with or without threats, (2) encourages/suggests suicide, (3) threatens harm to a person or their property, (4) threatens to commit a crime, and/or (5) posts private information in a public forum (Willard, 2006). Actions that can be taken by students to defend against cyberbullies include blocking the sender, avoiding chat rooms where the attacks occur, saving and sharing communications with parents and law enforcement, and changing passwords/accounts. As with other types of bullying, students are encouraged to send a strong, assertive, non-emotional message to the bully along with the action to be taken if the messages continue.

> **WILL I GO TO JAIL?**
>
> Steven, a high-school junior, comes to you very upset because he was angry with his best friend. He said that he sent a nude picture of his girlfriend to his best friend's cellphone because his friend did not believe that Steven's girlfriend would ever take her clothes off for him. His friend spread the picture around, and someone loaded it to Facebook, and his girlfriend's parents called the police. He said, "It isn't fair—she said I could take the picture, and I'm not the one who spread the picture around school or created the Facebook page." The student asks, "Will I go to jail"? If you were Steven's school counselor, how would you respond?

The school counselor's technological literacy and knowledge of human development intersect to provide students with developmentally appropriate technological interventions and training. Students must not leave high school without proficiency in the use of technology, which drives every aspect of our computerized world of work. Section A.14.a. of the ASCA *Ethical Standards for School Counselors* (ASCA, 2022a) calls for school counselors to "demonstrate appropriate selection and use of technology and software applications to enhance students' academic, career and social/emotional development. Attention is given to the ethical and legal considerations of technological applications, including confidentiality concerns, security issues, and potential limitations and benefits and communication practices in electronic media."

Some of the more common information and networking technologies may include e-mail, Internet, blogs, electronic bulletin boards, text messaging, video conferencing, chat rooms, gaming devices, graphics software, websites, and SMART technologies. School counselors introduce these and other more sophisticated technologies and related terminology to enhance students' readiness for entry into today's workforce. ASCA provides an e-newsletter, *ASCA Aspects*, to association members in order to stay abreast of current technologies and tools on the Internet. School counselors incorporate information and networking technologies into all methods of service delivery.

## Substance use, abuse, addiction

School counselors collaborate with local police officers, community agencies, and other school personnel (e.g., school nurses, coaches, and school psychologists) to implement a variety of primary, secondary, and tertiary prevention strategies that promote healthy and drug-free lives in an effort to get ahead of substance use, substance abuse, and addiction. Addiction can be categorized as process addiction and substance addiction (Capuzzi & Stauffer, 2019). Process addiction refers to behavioral patterns, and addictions may include gambling, shopping, Internet usage, eating, working, sex, and more. Substance addiction refers to the ingestion of mood-altering substances such as alcohol and other drugs, including anabolic steroids, which is a growing concern in high-school athletic circles. School counselors do not treat addiction. In the school setting, emphasis is on understanding substance abuse and addiction, identifying students suffering from substance abuse and/or addiction, and referring those students for specialized treatment.

School counselors implement nationally recognized *primary prevention* programs such as Just Say No and Drug Abuse Resistance Education (DARE) programs within the schools. Founded in 1983, the DARE program is the most widely used drug prevention program in our schools today. The DARE program's mission is to provide students with skills and education to live drug and violence free. The program is focused on abstinence from drug use and is generally delivered by law enforcement officers during the school day with a curriculum that is sequentially designed for grades K-12. The program now offers community-based programs as well to promote parent involvement and to provide after school activities and support for families.

The Just Say No to Drugs campaign was championed by then First Lady Nancy Reagan in the 1980s in response to the War on Drugs movement. This primary prevention program, grounded in the prevention efforts of the National Institutes of Health, enlists the support of other nationally recognized organizations such as the Girl Scouts of America and the Kiwanis Club. The program is intended to educate and inoculate students on the negative impact of drug use and to provide students with skills for resisting peer pressure and drug experimentation.

School counselors also develop curriculum geared toward primary prevention in order to thwart drug use, which may include parent and teacher education aimed at recognizing the signs and symptoms of substance abuse and addiction as well as resources for treatment. In-school drug testing is a growing strategy in today's schools, resulting in early treatment for students who test positive. There are legal considerations, including parental consent, and schools will need community support before implementing drug-screening strategies. In-home drug testing is fast becoming a commonly practiced strategy that aids parents in early identification of substance use.

In addition to primary prevention strategies, school counselors implement *secondary prevention* strategies, which target students who may be at risk for substance use, substance abuse, and addiction. School counselors are in an ideal position to identify students who are already demonstrating negative attitudes and risky behaviors. Secondary prevention programs may include small groups on topics related to living responsibly, health and *wellness*, the effects of drug consumption and healthy choices.

Recognizing the signs and symptoms of addiction is essential to *tertiary prevention*, which involves identifying students who are already routinely ingesting chemical substances and are displaying behavior patterns associated with process addiction. Signs and symptoms of addiction include neglecting responsibilities, increased tolerance, preoccupation with the substance or behavior, engaging in risky behaviors such as stealing and driving under the influence, changes in levels of social interaction or a change of friends, abandonment of hobbies and activities that use to be enjoyable, mood swings, paranoia, irritability, interference with daily functioning (e.g., sleep, diet, hygiene), and a general change in what was considered typical behavior for the individual.

### THE BEST FOOTBALL PLAYERS

You are the high-school counselor at Crossroads High School. The physical education (PE) teacher has asked you to meet with a group of six male students on the football team because he overheard them chatting about giving anabolic steroids a try to build muscles and be the best football players on the team. The PE teacher said he already spoke to the parents of the students, who are in agreement with the students meeting with the school counselor. How should you proceed, and is this an example of primary, secondary, or tertiary prevention?

There are many models that attempt to explain the etiology of addiction (Capuzzi & Stauffer, 2019). Psychological models look to cognitive-behavioral, psychodynamic, personality, and learning models for explanations for addiction. Sociocultural models suggest that addiction is contextual and related to the social and cultural environment in which an individual interacts. The disease model holds the addiction as an incurable and progressive disease that one is powerless over, once contracted. Family models suggest that addiction is behaviorally based, with the family interactions and members reinforcing the addiction, either consciously or unconsciously. Biological models hold genetics and our brain's chemical reactions as creating predispositions to addiction. Finally, the moral model holds addiction as a matter of personal choice. As a society, we have now, for the most part, rejected the idea that addiction is the result of immorality. At the present time, our society and our public health system embraces a multi-causal model that considers the interaction of the individual, environment, and the substance or process.

Chapter 2 discussed school counselor appraisal approaches for identifying students who may be suffering from substance abuse and addiction. Once identified, school counselors work with parents and community agencies to secure appropriate counseling services for the student and family.

## *Divorce*

Divorce rates in America hover around 50 percent for first marriages with higher percentages for second and third marriages (Centers for Disease Control and Prevention, 2023). Over one million children and adolescents are affected by parental divorce each year in the United States, where the divorce rate is the highest in the world (Cohen & Weitzman, 2016).

Generally speaking, research suggests that children of divorce adjust well if divorce is accompanied by amiable parental interactions, quality parenting, and reassurance of continued contact after separation and divorce and if the divorce does not substantially impact lifestyle (e.g., finances, discipline, transitions). Other characteristics that are linked to positive adjustment after divorce include level of resiliency and preexisting personal assets (discussed in greater detail in the *Strengths-Based Counseling* section of the next chapter). Age and gender, too, are associated with the level of adjustment for children of divorce; however, the link is largely contextual.

On the other hand, compared to children and adolescents from intact healthy functioning families, children of divorce often demonstrate a variety of issues (Cohen & Weitzman, 2016; Schaan & Vogele, 2016). These issues include:

- Sadness and depression.
- Anxiety and fear.
- Rejection.
- Anger.
- Insecurity.
- Drug and alcohol use.
- Misbehavior.
- Feelings of grief and loss.
- Poor academic performance.
- Interpersonal problems.
- School dropout.

The issues listed above can last well into adulthood. School counselors help children and adolescents to adjust to divorce with a variety of interventions that build protective factors and resilience and allow students to express and work through emotions, share experiences, resolve self-blame, and accept divorce. Small group counseling for children of divorce provides mutual support and allows students to normalize divorce (Corey, 2022). Also, encouraging students to engage in positive school and community activities and build relationships with trusted adults outside of the home helps to build protective factors. School counselors assist parents by providing community resources, including family counseling services, and the research noted above depicts the factors that have been associated with positive adjustment for children of divorce.

## Parenting style

Parenting is not instinctual but requires specific knowledge and skills to raise a well-adjusted adult and contributing member of society. Parenting style has a profound impact on child and adolescent development.

The four widely recognized parenting styles with which school counselors are knowledgeable are authoritative (collaborative, respectful, reasonable consequences), authoritarian (strict, demanding, harsh punishment), permissive (lenient, indulgent), and uninvolved (detached, neglectful). The authoritative parenting style has been found to be the most beneficial to the child, resulting in a well-adjusted, confident, self-controlled, and academically successful child. Inconsistency, ignoring, and intimidation associated with the permissive, uninvolved, and authoritarian parenting styles, respectively, have been linked to the development of emotional, social, psychological, behavioral, and academic problems (Rothrauff, Cooney, & Shin An, 2009).

School counselors provide parental consulting and parenting workshops identifying different parenting styles and the impact of each on child development. Additionally, they help parents to realize that each sibling is an individual and so what works for one may not work for another. Also, they help parents to realize that a child's performance is not an indicator of self-worth and that mistakes are a part of learning and misbehavior a part of childhood, and they prepare the parent for the realities of parenthood. Parenting is a job—likely the most difficulty and high-stress job on the planet.

## Career development

Another of the three broad developmental domains of a CDSCP and ASCA *Mindsets & Behaviors for Student Success* (2021) is *career development*. School counselors create activities that are career specific and developmentally appropriate.

---

*ASCA Position on The School Counselor and Career Development*

School counselors deliver school counseling programs that enhance student growth in three domain areas: academic, career, and social/emotional development. As a part of that program, school counselors implement strategies and activities to help all students enhance their career development – the mindsets and behaviors students need to understand the connection between school and the world of work, plan for and make a successful transition to postsecondary education and work across the life span – while recognizing that growth in all three domains is necessary for students to be successful now and later in life.

*Position statement adopted 2017; revised 2023*

---

School counselors adhere to the professional competencies and ethical issues involved in providing career counseling services to minors. School counselors are well advised to become familiar with the Multicultural Career Counseling Minimal Competencies (National Career Development Association [NCDA], 2009) provided by the NCDA, a division of ACA, as well as the ASCA Model's student competencies for the career development domain.

There are three fundamental differences in career development at each level of K-12 education: career awareness, career exploration, and career planning. At the elementary level, school counselors promote career awareness. *Career awareness* activities might include exposing students to diverse occupations through career day/week guided activities. These activities might include speakers from a variety of occupations, displays of books in the library dedicated to diverse occupations, dressing like a favorite occupation, and mystery career games whereby students guess the occupation based on a description. Any activity that supports the student's curiosity and develops their sense of self and the world of work is appropriate at the elementary level.

Career exploration is the focus at the middle-school level, while career planning, also referred to as career orientation or career preparation, is the focus at the high-school level. Secondary school counselors engage students in career development activities that typically combine counseling, education, and the administration and interpretation of career development inventories (e.g., interests, skills, work values). This comprehensive approach to career development at the secondary level emphasizes the importance of going beyond trait and factor theory to understand the whole person and explore the many internal and external variables that influence a student's career decision making.

Delivering effective career development programs in the schools necessitates that the school counselors apply *career counseling* and *career development* theories and strategies; stay abreast of relevant legislation, research, trends, and resources; identify and administer interest, values, and skills inventories, and other career-related assessments; and understand the influences on career development.

## Influences on career decision making

Helping students to identify personally satisfying career paths requires the application of career development theory, techniques, sound counseling practices, and information. School counselors blend career counseling, assessment, and career education to aid students in (1) understanding and preparing for transition into the world of work, (2) selecting a career path that will be meaningful and satisfying, and (3) ultimately becoming productive members of society.

School counselors engage in career counseling with a sound understanding of the diverse influences on career choice. School counselors aid students in understanding these influences to make informed decisions about their future. Career choice influences include, but are not limited to, family of origin, access to career information, socialization (beliefs and values), personality (including *multiple intelligences* discussed later in this chapter), parent's employment and educational status, early work experiences, economy, socioeconomic status, gender, ethnicity, and development level of functioning.

Research indicates that children begin to limit their career aspirations as early as first grade based on gender, ethnicity, race, and social class (Porfeli, Hartung, & Vondracek, 2008). For example, let us consider the impact of socialization on career choice with regard to gender. Traditionally, women have been guided toward occupations such as teacher, cosmetologist, and nurse, while males have been encouraged to pursue careers such as doctor, mechanic, and scientist.

For this reason, school counselors are now developing programs that educate students with regard to these historical trends, who may not realize how early social interactions have influenced their career decision making. As a result, males are beginning to pursue careers in nursing, accounting, and other occupations that have historically been occupied by females. Females are beginning to pursue careers in science and math and in occupations that have traditionally been dominated by males. There is now a growing trend toward promoting *nontraditional occupations* at every level of education.

In addition to promoting nontraditional career paths, school counselors promote a variety of postsecondary career paths. Our society has come to realize that college is not for everyone and that because a student does not want to attend college it does not mean that the student will not have a successful and fully satisfying career. Student's career choices may take them on a journey down one of five paths after high school: apprenticeship, college (two or four year), technical/trade school, employment, or military service. Well, there is always couch-warming and channel surfing—oh, how parents will rejoice!

## Career development theory and career counseling

School counselors apply career development theory to help students make sense of their experiences and how those experiences influence career decision making. Career counseling grounded in sound theoretical principles, offers education, insight, and alternatives during the process of career planning. Like counseling theories, there are a multitude of career development and career counseling theories, models, and approaches. This section highlights the major theories, theorists, and key constructs. Figure 3.1 is provided to promote the learning and recall of this material.

In general, there are two camps to consider when conceptualizing career development theories (Savickas, 2000): objectivist and constructivist. The objectivist school of thought may also be referred to as the traditional ideology, the positivistic approach, or the established theoretical view, depending upon the company of career theorists you are keeping. The objectivist ideology, as the name implies, is an objective and measurable construct that matches individuals to occupations based on personality and occupational work environment. The constructivist school of thought, also known in certain circles as the emerging postmodern ideology, views career development as an ever-changing, contextual, and dynamic process that is driven by personal perceptions, interactions, and experiences. Figure 3.1 places the variety of career development theories in the respective categories to aid you in the cognitive organization of the many career theories.

The objectivist school of thought began with Frank Parsons. Parsons (1909), who became known as the father of vocational guidance, developed the trait and factor theory, which matches individual traits (e.g., aptitudes, interests, and abilities) to job factors. The trait and factor theory has dominated the field of career development since its inception some one hundred years ago.

John Holland's (1966, 1985) typology is an example of a trait and factor approach that is still widely used today. Holland's constructs include six broad occupational environments. RIASEC is the acronym used to represent Holland's work place environments and points on his well-known hexagon. Holland theorizes that individual personalities can be matched to work place environments for a "good occupational fit." For example, "R" represents the "Realistic" environment, which is the more physically demanding jobs working with tools, machines, automobiles, animals. Realistic personality types are those who enjoy working with

| Objectivist Ideology (Traditional) | Constructivist Ideology (Emerging Models) |
|---|---|
| Traits and work environment match<br>Administers assessment instruments<br>Objective reasoning/measurement are key | Socially constructed, dynamic, ever-changing<br>Individuals' interactions and experiences<br>Subjective intention and perspectives in context |
| **\*Frank Parsons: Trait and Factor**<br>Match individual traits with job factors<br>Focus on 3-step process<br>Understanding self, diverse occupational characteristics, and relationship of the two | **\*\*David Tiedeman: Career Construction**<br>Career choice based on evolving ego/self-development--total cognitive development and processes of decision making<br>Focus on differentiation (evaluating self and self in the world) and integration (find congruence in world of work); parallels Erikson's stages of development |
| **John Holland: Typology**<br>Individuals express self through career<br>Focus on assigning individuals and work environments into 6 categories | **Larry Cochran: Narrative**<br>Individual "tells story" about past and present career experiences and related interactions; counselor assists in creating future career story<br>Focus on phases, episodes, plots:<br>making meaning out of narrative; enacting the role; and crystallizing a decision |
| **Donald Super: Life Span-Life Space** Career choice is an expression of self concept and changes across life span<br>Focus on 5 major life stages; career maturity; career determinants; role of self-concept | |
| **Linda Gottfredson: Self-Creation**<br>Career choice based on social-psychological self, created by heredity-biological factors<br>Focus on self-concept, cognitive maps, circumscription and compromise | **Mark Savickas: Narrative**<br>Individual "tells story" about past and present career experiences and related interactions; counselor assists in creating future career story<br>Focus on four areas:<br>vocational personality (uses Holland's typology); developmental tasks (uses Super's Life Stages); adaptability; life themes (mattering) |
| **Anne Roe: Personality Development**<br>Career choice based on psychological needs derived from parent-child relationships<br>Focus on relating six attitudes of parent-child interactions to specific occupational groups | **Duane Brown: Values-Based**<br>Work values influence occupational choice Focus on the importance of cultural values and differences |
| **Susan Phillips Developmental-Relational**<br>Career choice based on relationships with important others--family, friends, teachers<br>Focus on two themes:<br>Actions of others and self-directedness | **John Krumboltz: Social Learning**<br>Career choice based on cumulative interactions and experiences with people and environment<br>Focus on behavior and cognitions; teaching career decision making techniques |

*Parsons is considered father of vocational guidance
\*\* Tiedeman is considered the author/engineer of the first post-modern career theory

**Figure 3.1** Career development theories: objectivist and constructivist schools of thought.

their hands and interacting with things versus people. "I" represents "Investigative" environments, requiring scientific and mathematical problem solving. Investigative personalities enjoy solving puzzles and researching for solutions. "A" or "Artistic" work environments prize creativity and match to personalities that enjoy free expression often inherent in occupations associated with music, art, theater, and writing. "S" represents the "Social" work environment that involves interaction with other individuals. Social environments often appeal to those who wish to help and provide human services to others, which may include teaching, counseling, and medical professions. "E" encompasses the "Enterprising" work environments that attract those who wish to lead, persuade, sell, and gain positions that provide a level of power. Enterprising individuals are drawn to politics, real estate, business, insurance, and the stock market. "C" is the "Conventional" work environment, which are often office positions. Individuals who enjoying organizing and performing tasks related to accounting, clerical, and record keeping are good fits for the conventional work setting. It is important to note that no one work environment fits one specific type, but involves a combination of types. Therefore, no one personality type fits squarely into one work environment. Instead, an individual's personality may be well-suited to multiple occupational environments. Holland created a career interest inventory known as the *self-directed search* (SDS) for this purpose (Holland, 1974). The SDS is discussed later in this chapter in the section titled "Assessment Instruments and Career Information Delivery Systems."

Donald Super's (1949, 1970, 1980) work in career development may be the most extensive of all the career development theorists, particularly pertaining to the career development of children and adolescents. Major constructs defining Super's lifespan–life space approach includes life stages, career maturity, life-career rainbow, self-concept, and the archway of career determinants. Super's model of career development in children contends that, driven by curiosity, children explore the environment and interact with others, thereby maturing and developing self-control and time perspectives that lead to planful career decision making and implementation of self-concept. Super provides school counselors with a sound theoretical foundation from which to plan and implement developmentally appropriate career activities.

Linda Gottfredson (1981), too, emphasized self-concept in her theory of career development, which focused on childhood and adolescence. Gottfredson's theory of self-creation through interactions with the environment underscores the role of prestige, gender, and cognitive development in career decision making. Other theoretical constructs include circumscription (i.e., eliminating alternatives perceived as inappropriate due to societal expectations, prestige, gender) and compromise (i.e., giving up desired alternatives for those that are more accessible). Gottfredson's views magnify the need for school counselors to address historical trends in career development programming and to explore with students what might be perceived and self-imposed and obstacles to desired careers.

> ### I WANT TO BE A NURSE
>
> You are the elementary school counselor delivering career awareness classroom instruction to first graders. You are holding up pictures of an array of people dressed in attire that depicts specific occupations. You hold up a card of a male who is dressed in a nursing uniform, and the class begins to guess the occupation. Some of the students shouted out "doctor." You said, "Well, it could be that this person is a doctor, but the card said that he is a 'nurse.'" One of the male students said quietly, "I wanted to be a nurse, but my father said that I could not be a nurse because that was a job for girls." According to Gottfredson's theory, is this an example of compromise or circumscription?

Anne Roe (1957) provides school counselors with a career development theory that is grounded in personality development. Roe suggests that there are six parent attitudes toward, or away from, their children that impact a child's personality development. As such, Roe contends that a child's career choice is based on psychological needs derived from these early interactions. School counselors can help students to identify how early interactions with parents may have impacted their career development.

Broadening Roe's parent–child interactions, Susan Phillips postulates that career choices are grounded in interactions with all important others (Phillips, Christopher-Sisk, & Gravino, 2001). Phillips created categories of relational responding, suggesting that others impact our career choices either by inviting themselves into our career decision making (i.e., actions of others) or our inviting others into our career decision making (i.e., self-directedness). It is important to help students identify the strengths and weaknesses of career decision-making influences.

In this section, we have covered the key career theories from the objectivist school of thought. The theories that follow are grounded in the ideologies of the constructivist school of thought.

David Tiedeman (1961) has been credited for engineering the constructivist ideologies, earning himself the title of author, or engineer, of the first postmodern career theory. Tiedeman broke away from traditionalist thought, declaring that career decision making is far more personal and subjective because it is created from an individual's unique perceptions and *worldview*. Tiedeman's theory holds career decision making as an evolving process across developmental stages that parallel those of Erikson. Tiedeman's major constructs included differentiation (i.e., evaluating self and self in the world) and integration (i.e., finding congruence in the world of work). School counselors use Tiedeman's developmental perspectives and theory of the evolving ego, or self, to encourage students at specific developmental stages to consider how this unique self would fit into a variety of occupations.

Larry Cochran (1997), following Tiedeman's theory of the evolving self, provides school counselors with a constructivist approach that allows students to tell their story about career and related interactions. Together, the school counselor and student create a future career story that is a more ideal career narrative, which Cochran refers to as crystallizing a decision. Major theoretical constructs include phases, episodes, plots, narratives, characters, and enacting a role.

Mark Savickas (1997, 2000) also supports the narrative approach in career counseling, believing that clients construct their own career in unique, subjective, and complex ways. He departs a bit from Cochran in his integration of objectivist theories such as Super's life stages and Holland's typology. Savickas focuses on four areas in his theory of career development: vocational personality, developmental tasks, adaptability, and life themes. Savickas integrates Holland's typology in vocational personality and Super's life stages in his developmental tasks. Mattering is a key construct of Savickas' life themes, that is, Savickas explores life themes to determine that which matters to an individual. Mattering, according to Savickas, brings purpose and meaning to work, while adaptability melds the vocational self with an occupational role.

Duane Brown (2015) presents a theory that focuses on the impact of contextual variables on career decision making, satisfaction, and success. Brown's contextual variables include values, gender, family, socioeconomic status, and discrimination. Key constructs are Brown's values-based theoretical propositions.

John Krumboltz (1994) presents a career theory that is grounded in social learning theory. Krumboltz contends that career decisions are made based on an interaction of genetic endowment, learning experiences, environment (e.g., conditions and events), and task approach skills. School counselors who conceptualize career development using Krumboltz theory will likely use traditional behavioral interventions in career counseling, such as role playing, simulation, reinforcement, and role modeling.

> **TED'S FUTURE**
>
> You are a high-school counselor meeting with Ted, who is uncertain about his career path. During your session you are focused on teaching Ted career decision-making strategies. Which of the career development theories discussed in this section are you implementing?

## Career and college transitions

Although career development and college preparation has remained a primary function of the school counselor since the guidance movement, there has been a resurgence in popularity and support over the past two decades. Many school systems are hiring school counselors to specifically serve as career counselors at the high school level with an emphasis on preparing today's students for tomorrow's world of work.

Primary legislation pertaining to the school-to-work movement includes *Goals 2000 (1994): Educate America Act, National Skills Standards Act*, and the *School-to-Work Opportunities Act of 1994*. This legislation, simply stated, promotes the development of occupational standards and an integration of vocational and educational competencies so that students will be well prepared to enter and be successful in our multifaceted and technologically advanced workforce.

School counselors are creative in meeting school-to-work initiatives using a variety of strategies to integrate occupational information and college readiness activities using classroom instruction, small groups, and individual counseling/planning. Activities at the elementary level designed to introduce students to the world of work and college may include career day/week, videos, activity sheets, books, skits, field trips, and tutoring at local colleges.

Activities at the secondary level designed to assist students in exploring and planning for college and career include job shadowing and internships; college and career fairs; collaboration with college access professionals; financial aid workshops; scholarship application process and resources; athletic eligibility; college entrance exams, dates, and procedures; college essay writing; mock interviewing; college tour fieldtrips; and panel presentations by former high-school students sharing career and college success stories.

---

### ASCA Position on The School Counselor and College Access Professionals

School counselors play a critical role in preparing all students for lifelong learning and success. To ensure students have the opportunity to reach their full potential, school counselors collaborate and consult with community-based organizations, including college access organizations and college access professionals, within the framework of a school counseling program.

*Position statement adopted 2016; revised 2022*

---

Many high-school counselors partner with community colleges to offer students the opportunity to take the ACT-sponsored WorkKeys assessments. Students who pass the three WorkKeys assessments (i.e., applied mathematics, locating information, and reading for information) earn the national Career Readiness Certificate. The certification is gaining recognition as a viable screening, hiring, and promotion tool among prospective employers.

Students can now earn industry certifications in many high schools. Industry certifications are generally attached to specific elective courses. For example, students taking culinary arts may be eligible to take the National Occupational Competency Testing Institute (NOCTI) assessment, leading to certification in commercial foods. Students taking marketing classes may be eligible to take the NRF assessments, leading to certifications in customer service and sales. Students can earn industry certifications in specific software packages while attending high school to demonstrate advanced levels of competence in technology. Industry certification assessments such as Brainbench and Microsoft Office Specialist are attached to numerous elective courses in business and technical education. Passing the course and assessment leads to certification in a variety of Adobe and Microsoft software packages. School counselors take the lead in ensuring that students gain information and opportunities to participate in industry certifications that match students' post-secondary areas of interest.

---

### ASCA Position on The School Counselor and Career and Technical Education

School counselors provide all students with counseling that facilitates academic, career and social/emotional development, helping all students develop plans for choosing a career. School counselors demonstrate their understanding of rigorous career technical education (CTE) programs when they join with other CTE stakeholders to advocate for these programs, which are designed to guide students to success in their chosen careers.

*Position statement adopted 2018*

---

School counselors make students aware of WorkKeys and industry certifications during course scheduling. School counselors often go to the classrooms to promote the benefits of these voluntary certifications, which may include course credit and additional diploma seals. Certifications also demonstrate a commitment on the part of the student toward a specific occupation and earnestness about postsecondary employment and/or education.

The ASCA *Ethical Standards for School Counselors* (ASCA, 2022a) emphasize the responsibilities of school counselors in creating a culture of postsecondary preparedness that also addresses transition readiness. As such, school counselors partner with students and collaborate with important others (e.g., parents, administrators, teachers) to develop personalized academic and career goals and a plan for transitioning to ready students for postsecondary opportunities not just academically and physically, but mentally as well.

During collaborative activities, school counselors remain mindful of issues related to confidentiality and compliance with FERPA. For example, school counselors often write letters of recommendation for students seeking postsecondary school or job opportunities. While this is supported by ASCA and by schools in general, school counselors must write such letters in a manner that adheres to ethical standards and FERPA.

## ASCA Position on The School Counselor and Letters of Recommendation

School counselors work ethically when writing letters of recommendation for students. To guide their work, school counselors rely on the ASCA Ethical Standards for School Counselors (2022) and the Family Education Rights and Privacy Act (FERPA; 1974), which is a federal statute protecting parents' and students' rights regarding educational records (Stone, 2022).

*Position statement adopted 2020*

School counselors are often the first contact and coordinator for postsecondary opportunity activities within and outside of the school. This may include job fairs, college/university fairs, apprenticeship program opportunities, and career and technical education internships.

## ASCA Position on The School Counselor and Student Postsecondary Recruitment

School counselors encourage and promote positive and equitable reception of career and postsecondary educational institution recruiters into the school setting. These recruiters may include individuals from organizations such as, but not limited to:

- apprenticeship programs
- athletic programs
- career and technical education institutions
- colleges and universities
- financial aid and scholarship programs
- military branches

*Position statement adopted 2004;
revised 2009, 2015, 2021*

---

Most states have adopted requirements pertaining to the formal creation of academic and career plans. The plan, generally, begins in middle school and is updated annually through the senior year of high school. The plan identifies the courses, specialized programs, and steps needed for the student to attain their desired career and postsecondary education and training.

---

### ASCA Position on The School Counseling and Individual Student Planning for Postsecondary Preparation

School counselors recognize that each student possesses unique interests, abilities and goals, which will lead to various future life and career opportunities. Collaborating with students, families, educational staff and the community, the school counselor works to ensure all students develop an academic and career plan reflecting their interests, abilities and goals and including rigorous, relevant coursework and experiences appropriate for the student.

*Position statement adopted 1994; revised 2000, 2006, 2012, 2013, 2017*

---

Transitioning from school to work or to any of the other postsecondary career options presents unique challenges for young adults. In addition to the general transitioning support noted earlier in this chapter, school counselors can help students to make successful transitions to work and college by offering programming on topics such as workplace skills, job market trends, resume and cover letter writing, interviewing, application completion, networking, securing mentors, managing time and money, and balancing social and academic/work life.

## Career assessment instruments and career information delivery systems

School counselors will often begin the career development process with career-related inventories that assess student's interests, work values, and skills. Information gleaned from these career assessments aids in the career planning process, providing both the counselor and student with valuable information from which to identify possible career paths and establish career goals. Like other student appraisal instruments, however, school counselors do not rely on the results of career assessment alone to guide students' career planning because such instruments do not provide a comprehensive conceptualization of individual complexities. Additionally, some of these instruments lack cultural validity, that is, not all appraisal instruments consider worldviews that differ from the dominant culture.

The three most commonly used career inventories in the schools are the *SDS*, the *SII*, and the *KOIS*. All three inventories are based on John Holland's theory of typology and yield Holland codes. The SDS (Holland, 1974) helps students to identify preferences for specific activities, matching personality type with six workplace environments using the three-letter Holland code. Information about the SDS is available at www.self-directed-search.com. The SII (Strong & Campbell, 1974) provides information about careers that match students' codes and is available at www.cpp.com/products/strong/index.asp. The KOIS (Kuder, 1964) suggests occupations and college majors based on students' interest patterns. Information about the KOIS is available at www.kuder.com.

It is not necessary to memorize all the different types of assessment instruments and tests. It is important, however, for the purpose of school counseling exams, to know the difference between career assessments, personality assessments, intelligence test, aptitude tests, and other types of assessments, inventories, and tests, as well as situations in which you might administer a particular type of assessment over another.

Career development instruments are often included in career information delivery systems (CIDS), also referred to as *computer-assisted career guidance systems* (CACGS), to aid students in career planning. This Internet-based career development tool is available 24-7 to help students plan postsecondary careers and education.

There are many CIDS available for school counselor and student use. Some of the most widely used systems in school counseling include Choices Explorer, Choices Planner, SIGI Plus, DISCOVER, Bridges' Paws in Jobland, and Career Trek. In brief, Bridges' Paws in Jobland is used with elementary-school students. Career Trek is primarily used for grades four through middle school. Choices Explorer is generally used with middle-school students. Choices Planner is appropriate for career planning at the high-school level. DISCOVER is used at both the middle- and high-school levels, and SIGI Plus is often used for college-bound juniors and seniors, students in two- and four-year colleges, and adult populations.

There is often some overlap with regard to the developmental level within which these systems are used. For example, although DISCOVER is often used at the middle-school level, it may also be used by some school counselors at the high-school level. For this reason, selection of one particular system over another is often a matter of school counselor and student preference.

Nationally recognized resources include the *Occupational Outlook Handbook* (OOH) and *Occupational Information Network* (O*Net). The OOH provides information about the job market and specific information about hundreds of occupations. O*Net is a national, interactive database that allows you to explore and search hundreds of occupations and to participate in assessment instruments to aid in career decision making.

Card sorts, too, are an informal and fun way to gain insight into possible occupational choices and can be used with students of all ages. School counselors provide students with a stack of cards. Each card identifies a specific occupation. The student begins placing cards in categories such as (1) "I might consider," (2) "I would not consider," and (3) "I am not sure if I would consider." Once the student sorts the stack of cards, the school counselor explores the student's reasons for the selections (e.g., education, training, characteristics of the job, salary).

## Academic development

The domain of *academic development* has evolved over the past decade. Efforts to change the direction of school counseling have placed considerable emphasis on academic-focused practices in school counseling. Academic development gained considerable ground when new vision school counseling shifted the paradigm from individual- and mental health-focused practices to systems- and academic-focused practices. This shift to an academic focus recognizes the school counselor's professional identity of *counselor* and the importance of that identity in maintaining our role of counselor and our chief function and specialization of counseling. However, the academic focus does call upon our shared role of *educator* to aid in aligning the school counseling program with the fundamental mission of schools: academic achievement.

---

### ASCA Position on The School Counselor and Academic Development

School counselors deliver school counseling programs that enhance student growth in three domain areas: academic, career, and social/emotional development. As a part of that program, school counselors implement strategies and activities to help all students enhance their academic development – the mindsets and behaviors students need to maximize their ability to learn - while recognizing that growth in all three domains is necessary for students to be successful now and later in life.

*Position statement adopted 2017; revised 2023*

---

Topics related to academic development during the elementary school years emphasize paying attention, focusing, following directions, listening, completing classwork and homework, organization, goal setting, study and test taking skills, and mediating testing anxiety. School counselors at the secondary level generally focus on goal setting, time management, study skills, test taking skills, test anxiety, identifying learning styles, course selection, college admission success, post–high-school athletic programs, financial aid for college, college testing requirements, and identification of academic programs at the postsecondary level.

Like a well-played game of chess, we are strategically planning our moves and positioning ourselves to check the king and seize academic success for all. Hand in hand with teachers and administrators, school counselors assist in identifying systemic areas of academic deficits and specific low-achieving student populations. Programming is tailored to target those academic needs while simultaneously meeting the personal, social, and career development needs of all students. School counselors deliver services aimed at enhancing knowledge of testing and test preparation programs, developing test-taking skills, reducing testing anxiety, teaching study methods, and identifying sources for test preparation and tutoring.

## ASCA Position on The School Counselor and Test Preparation Programs

School counselors understand the impact of testing and test scores on college admissions, industry credentialing and other areas pertaining to students' postsecondary plans and goals. School counselors assist students in preparing for standardized tests by promoting opportunities designed to increase knowledge and improve test-taking skills. School counselors help students and their families become knowledgeable about test preparation programs and assist them as they decide which programs best meet their needs.

*Position statement adopted 1989; revised 1993, 1999, 2001, 2006, 2012, 2018*

School counselors apply their knowledge of human development, behavior and learning theories, and principles of motivation to enhance student academic achievement and attitudes toward school. Believing in the capacity of all students to obtain high levels of academic achievement, school counselors help to prepare students for meaningful futures in a global economy and technologically advanced world. In the words of Journey's timeless, sleep-deprived classic that took the midnight train to the number one digital track of all time—*Don't Stop Believin*.

## Curriculum development

School counselors create curriculum and/or use or modify existing curricula to address specific developmental areas. School counselors must first understand which areas needs to be targeted in order to develop goals and lesson objectives discussed in Chapter 2. Once this is complete, lesson content that aligns with stated objectives is created and pre- and post-assessment items are developed to measure curriculum effectiveness. For example, if the goal is to improve student test scores, a measurable objective supporting this goal might be: students will identify five strategies for overcoming test-taking anxiety. The curriculum will include research-supported content and activities specific to achieving this objective. That is, the content will, in some fashion, introduce five research-supported strategies for reducing test-taking anxiety.

> **SCHOOL CLIMATE**
>
> The school counselor, Fernando, is creating a video program to enhance the school's social climate, identified as an area of need on the recently completed needs assessment. One of the program's measurable objectives is "Students will identify and apply three strategies for improving social skills." What would the video program content need to include?

Let us consider the concept of self-esteem. Negative self-esteem has had a long and prosperous career of invading minds, hearts, and souls with self-destructive rubbish, making self our worst enemy. The benefits of positive self-esteem are as widely recognized as the entertaining Geico gecko for offering an insurance policy that kicks in when life serves up spontaneous catastrophe, making self our best friend and wellness bodyguard.

Relying on research, school counselors reveal the link between self-esteem and personal, social, career, and academic development. The school counselor will particularly underscore the relationship between academic success and self-esteem to demonstrate a clear alignment with the academic mission of schools. Once this link is established, research-supported interventions that have been successful in building a positive self-esteem are identified. The following questions help to guide school counselors toward this end:

- Does a correlation exist between self-esteem and academic performance?
- What does the research say about the academic proficiency of students who have negative self-esteem versus those who have positive self-esteem?
- Is poor self-esteem considered a barrier to academic achievement? If so, would it be logical to conclude that programs that enhance self-esteem remove a barrier to academic achievement?
- Which counseling and instructional interventions have been used in the past with positive outcomes?
- With what populations were the counseling and instructional interventions successful?

When developing curriculum, school counselors are sensitive to the diverse *learning styles* of their target population, as discussed in Chapter 1. School counselors are also mindful of the theory of *multiple intelligences* when seeking to create lessons and group sessions that are geared toward holistic student development. Howard Gardner (1983) proposed the theory of multiple intelligences, contending that human cognition is made up of eight independent, yet interactive, intelligences across a variety of disciplines. Gardner defines intelligence as "biopsychological potential to process information that can be activated in a cultural setting to solve problems or create products that are of value in a culture" (Gardner & Moran, 2006, p. 1). The eight intelligences (i.e., linguistic, logical–mathematical, musical, spatial, bodily kinesthetic, naturalistic, interpersonal, and intrapersonal) along with possible counseling strategies for students with a propensity toward a particular intelligence are summarized in Table 3.1.

The interactive nature of multiple intelligences offers insight into the workings of the human mind. Whether intriguing or deeply disturbing, this information is nothing less than invaluable in developing and delivering curriculum that nurtures the diverse intelligences for optimal cognitive and affective learning experiences. Also noted in Chapter 2, identifying students' propensities toward specific intelligences provides information useful in career decision making.

**Table 3.1 Overview of Gardner's Multiple Intelligences and School Counseling Strategies**

| Intelligence | Description | Counseling Strategies |
|---|---|---|
| Linguistic | Reliance on spoken and written words; individuals generally adept in reading, writing, and speaking | Narrative counseling, storytelling, journaling, letter writing, sentence completion, bibliotherapy |
| Logical–mathematical | Reliance on reasoning, numbers, and logic; individuals generally adept in scientific thinking, investigation, and making complex calculations | Genograms, games, strategic planning, objectifying, outlining, exploring, topic specific crossword or word search activities |
| Musical | Reliance on rhythmic sounds, pitch, and tones; individuals generally adept in singing, playing musical instruments, and composing music | Creating lyrics to music, moving to music, musical motivation (e.g., during homework, classwork); musical meditation (e.g., meditation that involves soothing tunes) |
| Spatial | Reliance on the mind's eye; individuals generally adept in design, puzzles, navigation | Cognitive mapping, visualization/imagery, pretend |
| Bodily kinesthetic | Reliance on touch and movement; individuals generally adept in dance and sports | Role playing, psychodrama, exercise, Yoga, dance, interactive games/play |
| Naturalistic | Reliance on nurturing and that which is associated with nature; individuals generally adept at classifying organisms and understanding of the natural environment | Outdoor activities, discussions and observations related to natural consequences and human nature |
| Interpersonal | Reliance on interactions with others; individuals generally adept at identifying the needs of others and working cooperatively with others | Role play, group counseling, collaborative work/play |
| Intrapersonal | Reliance on introspection, intuition, and self-reflection; individuals generally adept in understanding self and self-control | Questioning, journaling, studying, meditation, self-play, quiet time |

*Source*: Adapted from Gardner, H., & Moran, S. (2006). *Educational Psychologist, 41*(4), 227–232.

## Closing the achievement gap

The school counselor's role in academic development includes assisting in meeting the mandates of *No Child Left Behind* (NCLB) (United States Department of Education, 2023b). NCLB is considered by many to be the most significant and controversial of educational reform legislation in our nation's history. The primary goal of NCLB was to ensure that all students obtain proficiency in mathematics and language arts by 2013–2014.

All in all, educators agree with NCLB legislation; however, there are some who view NCLB as equivalent to encounter with the Ebola virus. Disenchantment with NCLB does not appear to be grounded in its philosophies and goals, but in the tough realities of its implementation based on limited human and material resources. Driven to do what is best for children, educators are nevertheless giving it their all and hammering out positive results with moderate or minimal provisions.

The TSCI and ASCA support the primary objectives of NCLB. These objectives include closing the achievement gap, demonstrating accountability, and providing students with a safe and positive learning environment. Under NCLB, schools must establish timelines for closing achievement gaps and tracking student progress toward meeting standards, ensuring adequate yearly progress (AYP) toward academic proficiency.

Achievement gaps exist between males and females and between students from underprivileged backgrounds and those from more affluent backgrounds. Achievement gaps have also been identified between students whose native languages differ and between students of differing ability levels. Achievement gaps vary from school to school and state to state. The most consistently documented achievement gap is based on national data. This data indicates an achievement gap between races, namely Caucasian students and African Americans, Latinos, and Native Americans.

Efforts to close the achievement gap are the impetus behind the call for school counselors to engage in practices that more clearly focus on academic achievement. Historically, school counselors have viewed their function as indirectly increasing academic achievement. School counselors have done this by removing physical, personal, social, emotional, behavioral, and environmental obstacles to learning. School counselors create programs, classroom lessons, and facilitate small groups that teach strategies that help students to master the skills needed for academic success and self-directed learning (e.g., testing taking, studying, note taking, time management, goal setting).

Communications with school administrators, however, depict the belief that school counselors should take a more *direct* role in helping students to achieve academically (Shoffner & Williamson, 2000). ASCA, too, encourages school counselors to develop programs that demonstrate a direct impact on academic achievement and a more overt alignment with the mission of schools. ASCA resources (2019a, 2019c, 2022b) walk school counselors through the process of identifying gaps and planning programming to remediate those gaps by way of closing the gap action plans and results reports, discussed in Chapter 2.

## Specialty and alternative education programs

Specialty and alternative education programs have multiple identities such special education programs, nontraditional education programs, gifted education, and the list goes on. These programs may entail home schooling, online learning, enrichment courses, and multilingual instruction. Specialty and alternative education programs are geared toward any number of special needs student populations (e.g., students with IEPs, students with 504 plans, students with limited English proficiency, students who are at risk of dropping out of school, advanced functioning students).

Specialty and alternative education programs are goal-focused to meet the special needs of a specific student or student population and generally involve more individualized instruction, alternative methods of instruction, smaller class sizes, and/or alternative learning environments. School counselors are diligent in maintaining current information, programs, policies, and legislation as it pertains to specialty programs, approaches, and activities.

### Homeschooling

Homeschooling is the education of a student by the parent or a tutor outside of the traditional public or private school setting. Homeschooling has grown in popularity in recent years for a variety of reasons. Some of the most common reasons noted by parents include issues associated with bullying, negative peer pressure, school violence, a desire to provide religious-based education, a lack of confidence in academic instruction, and/or as a matter of convenience.

Parents' homes are sovereign nations where instruction can be customized to the unique learning style and ability level of their child and around the family's schedule. Homeschooling also allows unlimited freedom to provide instruction in a manner that is consistent with family values and religious beliefs. The homeschooling environment is controlled by the parent, who takes on the responsibility for their child's education. The parent, too, provides opportunities for adequate social interaction to promote personal and social development.

Generally, children who are homeschooled tend to spend more time with parents, which can be a double-edged sword. This increased time together can result in a strengthening of family relationships or it can strain the ties that bond. School counselors understand the pros and cons of home schooling and consider the unique personality and abilities of the child when discussing this as an educational program option. Sharing information and resources and speaking candidly about the realities of home-schooling help parents to make the best decisions for their children and family.

## The virtual classroom

Virtual classrooms offer online instruction outside of the school building, generally at the high-school level. Not all schools offer online instruction; however, the forecast is favorable for continued growth. There are a variety of reasons that a student might wish to take classes in this manner. Some students have an illness that may hinder their ability to participate in daily classes at school, whereas others simply do not like the in-school experience. Still others may wish to take additional courses or advanced courses for college credit supplementing a full daily in-class schedule.

Virtual learning environments require a self-disciplined and self-motivated mind. Online courses are designed to be just as rigorous as those in the traditional school setting, and students will need to be self-motivated time managers. Students also need to possess the skills to manipulate the online environment with basic computer skills (e.g., word processing, e-mail, Internet), or more advanced computer skills, depending upon the educational management system used. While some students flourish in the online learning environment, others learn quickly that it is not the Utopia they had envisioned. Instead, they find themselves mourning the loss of the four classroom walls.

School counselors are becoming increasingly involved in the enrollment and coordination of virtual learning programs and deliver online school counseling virtually. For this reason, school counselors are called upon to understand the nature of online learning and counseling in relation to the characteristics of students who would most likely succeed in this unique and challenging environment.

## ASCA Position on The School Counselor and Virtual School Counseling

School counselors working in a virtual setting provide a school counseling program with the same standards and adherence to ethics as school counselors in an in-person setting. In virtual environments, school counselors work collaboratively with school, family and community partners to ensure equity and access to opportunities that positively affect students' academic, career and social/emotional development.

*Position statement adopted 2017; revised 2023*

### Programs for students with disabilities

Students with documented physical, emotional, social, and learning challenges require differentiated instructional strategies, often in a more structured environment with smaller class sizes or placement in *inclusion classrooms*. Special education students who have an IEP and students who have 504 plans are by law entitled to special accommodations to ensure their educational success and well-being (see Chapter 1).

National legislation, enacted under the Rehabilitation Act of 1973, also referred to as Section 504, and the IDEA, ensures that all students receive *free appropriate public education* (FAPE). Additionally, students who are LEP or use ESL are entitled to specialized instructional and testing accommodations. Students with special needs are guaranteed access to general and specialized educational aids and services to meet their individualized learning needs.

## ASCA Position on The School Counselor and Students with Disabilities

School counselors encourage and support all students' academic, career and social/emotional development through school counseling programs. School counselors are committed to helping all students realize their potential and meet or exceed academic standards with consideration for both the strengths and challenges resulting from disabilities and other special needs.

*Position statement adopted 1999; revised 2004, 2010, 2013, 2016, 2022*

---

School counselors ensure that instructional strategies include accommodations for students with special needs (i.e., students with an IEP, 504 plan, *medical plan*, and/or LEP students). Accommodations may include alternative testing programs; extended time on classwork, homework, and tests; the use of translators and bilingual or multilingual instruction; resources in a variety of languages, large print, or Braille; reduced assignments and homework; special seating arrangements; and specialized equipment.

The IEP of special education students experiencing behavior problems will include a *BIP*. The IDEA also requires that the special education student's IEP include a comprehensive transition plan to prepare the student for life after high school. At the present time, transition plans are not required as a component of the 504 plan.

Educators seek to provide special needs students with accommodations that will promote success while doing so in the *least restrictive environment*. Therefore, many special needs students are placed in general education classrooms while also participating in resource classes to provide additional academic support.

### FAPE

You are a school counselor and member of the child study team at your school. During today's meeting, a parent became quite upset and roared, "I am going to seek legal advisement ... you are denying my child a free and appropriate education." The parent is likely referring to which legislation:

a. IDEA.
b. ADA.
c. FERPA.
d. McKinney-Vento Act.

IEPs and 504 plans are reviewed upon parent request and updated at least annually to assess progress toward goal attainment and appropriateness of accommodations as the student grows and matures. Accommodations vary by student need and can range from extended time on a test to a personal assistant throughout the school day. School counselors apply their knowledge of child development and learning theories to advocate for balanced accommodations, that is, they identify accommodations that provide the optimal level of assistance: not too little, not too much—just right.

**THE INCLUSION CLASSROOM**

Genita is an elementary-school student who has an IEP. The parent visited the school to discover that Genita was in a regular classroom with about 20 other students. The parent went directly to the school counselor, who had been a part of the IEP meeting, and asked why her daughter was not in a special education classroom. The school counselor said that Genita was performing very well in the inclusion classroom and receiving the IEP accommodations needed to be successful, so there was no need for a more restrictive environment. Is the school counselor correct?

*ESL programs*

Students who are limited in their ability to speak English because English is not their native language are referred to as LEP students. ELL has also been used to identify students whose native language is not English. LEP students may qualify for English as a second language (ESL) services/ programs. To identify learning needs, LEP students participate in a home language survey. If indicated, students will then be assessed in reading, writing, listening, and speaking to determine their level of English proficiency and thus identify their needs for specialized instruction and accommodation.

Like students with IEPs and 504 plans, LEP students receive special accommodations and services to promote academic success and total student development. The goal of the ESL program is to help LEP students to achieve English proficiency while accommodating their needs to promote academic success until such proficiency is attained. LEP students are monitored and routinely assessed using both formal and informal measures to determine their progress toward achieving English proficiency. Adjustments to instruction and accommodation are made accordingly.

The educational approach selected for assisting LEP students is at the discretion of the school division. Educational approaches are driven by best practices and the number of LEP students in the school as well as the level of English proficiency for the LEP population to be served. Some schools use: (1) immersion in the general classroom with interpreters, (2) ESL courses taught entirely by bilingual instructors, or (3) individual tutoring. Any combination of multiple approaches may be adopted to meet the needs of LEP students.

For example, limited language development at the elementary level calls for the use of more expressive approaches such as *play therapy*, discussed in the next chapter, to communicate and promote interaction between the student and school counselor. I recall one of the first times I engaged in play therapy as a new elementary-school counselor. I was sitting with the most adorable first grader on the planet. She was beaming with pure delight while describing her adventures while collecting fireflies in a jar. As we squeezed and manipulated Play-Doh, I could hear the faint sounds of jubilant students singing *We Are the World* in preparation for that evening's PTA performance. completely out of harmony. Although, the tune carried by the children was utterly inharmonious, it was an endearing moment that solidified my career choice and I recall thinking, *they pay me to do this—suckers*! A few days later, the monsoon hit my utopian world. Sparing you the details, I recall thinking, *they don't pay me enough to do this—I'm a stooge!* As my esteemed colleagues will attest, this is the ebb and flow of professional school counseling that we would not trade for a million chocolate frogs.

School counselors are familiar with the process for identifying and meeting the needs of LEP students. School counselors advocate for LEP student participation in all educational programs regardless of their level of English proficiency. School counselors also make every effort to ensure that LEP students receive the accommodations needed in order to participate in the variety of educational programs.

## Enrichment programs

Students who are more advanced cognitively need to be intellectually challenged. Advanced functioning students benefit from participation in gifted and talented programs such as Governor's School and/or advanced placement and summer enrichment classes.

When school counselors hear "gifted student" our antennas begin to flail and hum in readiness to pick up on any frequency of distress, because cognitively advanced students are often the suffer-in-silence type. Gifted students may experience a host of social, emotional, and behavioral difficulties unique to the characteristics of giftedness calling for both preventive and responsive services that take into consideration the academic pressures, intellectual excitabilities, and heavy commitments that may lead to stress, depression, and career uncertainty (Elijah, 2011).

---

### ASCA Position on The School Counselor and Gifted and Talented Student Programs

The school counselor delivers a comprehensive school counseling program as an integral component of the school's efforts to meet the academic and developmental needs of all students. Gifted and talented students have unique and diverse needs that are addressed by school counselors within the scope of the comprehensive school counseling program and in collaboration with other educators and stakeholders.

*Position statement adopted 1988; revised 1993, 1999, 2001, 2007, 2013, 2019*

---

Students with exceptional abilities require differentiated instruction within a more rigorous and engaging curriculum that allows for higher order cognitive skills and more complex problem solving. Meeting the advanced capacities of gifted students is essential to encouraging their full potential.

Enrichment programs begin as early as kindergarten. The names and types of programs offered vary from state to state, school division to school division, and even school to school. Some of the more common programs include the Governor's School for the Arts, Science and Technology Academy and the International Baccalaureate program. Honors and advanced placement courses are also designed to meet the exceptional needs of this special population.

---

**I WANT TO BE A PERFORMANCE ARTIST**

Angela is a new school counselor at a large suburban high school. Yesterday, Angela met with Tamika, a tenth-grade student who has a GPA of 3.9 and had some questions regarding the PSAT. Tamika came into Angela's office very excited because she just got her first part in the community theatre. Tamika said, "I'm so happy—I want so badly to be a performance artist!" Which of these programs might be the most appropriate to discuss with Tamika at this time?

a. ESL program.
b. Homeschooling.
c. Virtual classroom.
d. Governor's School.

---

Advanced functioning students are sometimes identified as those students in a class that are exhibiting social, emotional, and behavioral problems. With more neurons in the human brain than planets in our Milky Way galaxy, the voltage of billions of transmitting neurons alive in the minds of geniuses at any given time must be astronomical. With this kind of neuroactivity, our most brilliant prodigies could go supernovae. For this simpleton, that kind of inner-galactic energy is mind-boggling.

We can understand, then, why classroom observations often explain the behavioral mishaps of gifted children and adolescents. Advanced functioning students tend to experience boredom with the general education curriculum, viewing it as mundane. Finishing tasks more quickly than peers, gifted students seek ways to occupy an overactive mind until the transition to a new subject. During this time, the gifted child may engage in activities that disrupt class. School counselors collaborate with teachers and students to find creative ways to fill this time with activities that stimulate and challenge the student's intellect and creativity.

The academically high functioning and asynchronous development of gifted students may also manifest itself as affective disturbances such as feelings of loneliness, anxiety, and depression, as well as social isolation and poor relational skills (Elijah, 2011). However, because of their independent and self-sufficient nature, the need to maintain a perfectionist image, and/or the belief that they may disappoint important others, gifted students often do not ask for help.

## GED programs

Keeping students in school is our goal as educators and as a society. Despite all attempts at intervention, the school setting and structured school day are a struggle for some students. For this reason, school counselors provide students who are at risk of dropping out of school with alternative educational program options. Some programs lead to a high-school diploma, while others result in obtaining a GED.

GED-track programs vary in eligibility requirements from state to state but generally require that students are at risk of dropping out of school and are at least 16 years old. Students generally take an official GED practice test with an established minimum score criteria for entrance into the GED-track program. GED-track programs through the public schools can take weeks to years to complete, although it is generally about one month to 12 months depending upon the program. Some programs offer a track to the high-school diploma or the GED, such as Job Corps. Job Corps is a nationally recognized, highly structured program directed by the Department of Labor that provides at-risk teens, beginning at age 16, with residential housing, allowances, and vocational training. Completion of the Job Corps program generally takes eight months to two years.

School counselors are resource agents. Knowledge of a single resource can make the difference between a student dropping out of school or gaining an education, securing a satisfying career, and becoming a contributing member of society.

> **I WANT MY HIGH-SCHOOL DIPLOMA**
>
> Reginald is a high-school junior who has failed 11th grade twice. He told you, his high-school counselor, that he hates school and just does not know what to do. He said his mom is about to move in with her mom, and he does not know what is going to happen to him because there is not enough room for him and his sisters and brothers at his grandmother's house. His mother suggested that he get his GED and get a job. Reginald said he thinks he will just quit school but that he really wanted a diploma and a career. Which of the following programs may meet Reginald's needs at this time?
>
> a. Governor's School.
> b. Virtual classroom.
> c. Job Corps.
> d. GED track.

*Dropout*
School dropout is a national issue of growing concern. The most recent data, which was reported in 2021 by the National Center for Education Statistics (2023) reports two million statusrates nationally among all races between the ages of 16 and 24. It is essential that school counselors continue to act as programming pit bulls to reclaim the graduation march for our nation's challenged students—pomp and circumstance for all!

In 2021, there were 2.0 million status dropouts between the ages of 16 and 24. Understanding that which places students at risk for not completing school is the first step to developing creative programming to keep our students in school. Risk factors for dropping out of school are as diverse as the student body and become more salient predictors of dropout when found in combination. These risk factors, which can be indicators of dropout as early as elementary school, include poor academic performance; negative attitude toward school; hostile school climate; low parental involvement; low student involvement; behavioral problems; poor teacher–student relationships; low socioeconomic status; educational levels of parents; and personal, social, and emotional issues (Dupere et al., 2015; Parr & Bonitz, 2015).

Addressing these barriers to graduation requires programming that (1) supports student and parent involvement in the school, (2) enhances academic performance with supplemental knowledge and skill building, (3) promotes a more encouraging school climate, (4) links school to career and life after high school, (5) provides counseling services to mediate life's challenges, (6) mediates behavioral problems, (7) addresses the needs of students in financially challenged homes, and (8) focuses on early intervention. Programming to keep students in school requires collaboration within and outside of the school with a variety of stakeholders.

# Chapter 3 Case conceptualization responses

## Primary developmental domains

### The parents do not trust me

The school counselor explains to the teacher that parent involvement at the elementary level is far greater than at the high-school level and that due to their child's developmental level parents tend to be much more protective and engaged in the elementary schoolchild's school years.

### Will I go to jail?

Steven's school counselor cannot comment on what the law may or may not do in his case. The school can educate Steven, by letting him know that what he did is considered "sexting" and that sexting is against the law with some state prosecutors charging teens with felonies, including child pornography. It is important that Steven explores his actions, assumes responsibility for his actions, and considers the consequences of his actions on others.

### The best football players

Although the PE teacher has touched base with the parents, the school counselor, too, will want informed consent from the parents due to the sensitive nature of the topic and the limited confidentiality of a counseling group as a matter of best practices. Meeting with the students to determine their motivation toward group participation is critical as well. Participating in the group to merely satisfy the coach is not sufficient. If the students are motivated and give assent to counseling, they should be given signed consent forms for parental approval to participate in counseling related to this topic. The group would be considered secondary prevention because the students are currently at risk for engaging in the behavior.

### I want to be a nurse

According to Gottfredson, this is an example of circumscription. The first-grade student is ruling out nursing because his father has signified the occupation as socially unacceptable based on gender.

## Ted's future

You are applying Krumboltz's social learning theory, which focused on actions and cognitions and teaching career decision-making techniques.

## School climate

Fernando's video program content would need to introduce students to at least three strategies for improving social skills and demonstrate the application of those strategies.

## FAPE

The parent is referencing the language used in the IDEA, which ensures that students receive a FAPE.

## The inclusion classroom

Yes, the school counselor is advising the parent correctly. By law, special education students are to be in the least restrictive environment with supports as listed in the student's IEP.

## I want to be a performance artist

The correct response is "d." Tamika has the academic performance and a passion for the performing arts that makes her a prime candidate for the Governor's School for the Arts enrichment program.

## I want my high-school diploma

The correct response is "c." The GED track, although an option for Reginald, it is not the best response choice. Reginald has been clear that he really wants his high-school diploma. Job Corps offers students the opportunity to earn either a GED or a high-school diploma. Reginald also wants a career. Job Corps teaches a variety of occupational skills, and upon earning his high-school diploma, Reginald can go to college. Finally, Job Corps can offer Reginald a structured living environment, providing him with a place to live, which is a concern for him at the current time.

# Chapter 3 Simulation: High school career development

## Brief case description

You are a high-school counselor creating a career development classroom instruction unit to target ninth-grade students. Your lesson objectives include (1) increasing student knowledge of self in relation to career, (2) enhancing knowledge of resources available for career exploration and decision making, and (3) creating a career and academic plan.

### Section A: High school career development

What information about the ninth-grade student population would be helpful to know when developing your curriculum?

(Select as many as you consider indicated in this section.)

| | |
|---|---|
| _____A—1. | Gender |
| _____A—2. | Attendance |
| _____A—3. | Developmental level of functioning |
| _____A—4. | Retentions |
| _____A—5. | Ethnicity |
| _____A—6. | Discipline |
| _____A—7. | Grades |
| _____A—8. | Course selections |

### Section B: High school career development

Which Internet-based career information system might you consider most appropriate to introduce to ninth-grade students in your classroom instruction lesson?

**224** ■ *Primary developmental domains*

(Choose ONLY ONE in this section.)

| | | |
|---|---|---|
| \_\_\_\_B—1. | WISC |
| \_\_\_\_B—2. | Choices Planner |
| \_\_\_\_B—3. | MBTI |
| \_\_\_\_B—4. | SDS |
| \_\_\_\_B—5. | Stanford–Binet |

## Section C: High school career development

You want to include an activity in your career development program curriculum that will aid students in developing an understanding of how they come to make career decisions over time, including developmental interests and self-control. Which career theorist's model or approach would be the most useful in helping you to develop your activity?

(Select ONLY ONE in this section.)

| | | |
|---|---|---|
| \_\_\_\_C—1. | Parsons |
| \_\_\_\_C—2. | Super |
| \_\_\_\_C—3. | Krumboltz |
| \_\_\_\_C—4. | Savickas |
| \_\_\_\_C—5. | Holland |
| \_\_\_\_C—6. | Gottfredson |

## Section D: High school career development

When delivering culturally sensitive career development programs to a diverse student population, school counselors consider the following influences on career choice.

(Select as many as you consider indicated in this section.)

| | |
|---|---|
| ____D—1. | Allocentrism |
| ____D—2. | Social relationships |
| ____D—3. | Availability of occupation information |
| ____D—4. | Beliefs and values |
| ____D—5. | Favorite meal |
| ____D—6. | Gender |
| ____D—7. | Personal appearance |
| ____D—8. | Job factors |
| ____D—9. | Socioeconomic status |
| ____D—10. | Developmental level of functioning |

## Section E: High school career development

What other strategies might be introduced in your curriculum to aid students in exploring diverse careers?

(Select as many as you consider indicated in this section.)

| | |
|---|---|
| ____E—1. | Resume and cover letter writing |
| ____E—2. | Community service |
| ____E—3. | Job shadowing |
| ____E—4. | Developing a career portfolio |
| ____E—5. | Informational interviewing |
| ____E—6. | Creating a career and academic plan |
| ____E—7. | Obtaining a part-time/summer job |

## Section F: High school career development

Which interest inventory might you consider including in your curriculum to aid students in understanding self and the work environments for which they may be best suited?
   (Choose ONLY ONE in this section.)

| _____F—1. | SDS |
| _____F—2. | Connors scale |
| _____F—3. | ASVAB |
| _____F—4. | Career beliefs inventory |
| _____F—5. | WISC |
| _____F—6. | Vineland |

## Section G: High school career development

Once your unit is implemented, your principal, who emphasizes accountability and outcomes, would like to know how effective you were in meeting lesson objectives aimed at enhancing student development and career readiness. What information would you provide?
   (Select as many as you consider indicated in this section.)

| _____G—1. | The number of students who participated in the lessons |
| _____G—2. | Pre-post measure of knowledge of career resources |
| _____G—3. | Pre-post measure of student attendance and participation |
| _____G—4. | Feedback from students about the lessons' usefulness |
| _____G—5. | The number of students who completed a career and academic plan |
| _____G—6. | Pre–post measure of students' knowledge of self related to career |
| _____G—7. | Measure of academic performance pre- and post-lesson implementation |

# Chapter 3 Simulation responses: High school career development

## Brief case description

You are a high-school counselor creating a career development classroom instruction unit to target ninth grade students. Your lesson objectives include (1) increasing student knowledge of self in relation to career, (2) enhancing knowledge of resources available for career exploration and decision making, and (3) creating a career and academic plan.

## *Section A: High school career development*

What information about the ninth-grade student population would be helpful to know when developing your curriculum?

(Select as many as you consider indicated in this section.)

| A—1. | Gender |
| --- | --- |
| | Yes |
| | Gender is applicable when considering the promotion of nontraditional occupations and the enhancement of student knowledge of self in relation to career. It is also critical that school counselors understand and provide information to students related to gender and the world of work (e.g., gender-role stereotyping, gender segregation, bias in occupational information). Such information enhances student knowledge for career decision making and understanding self in relation to career, two of the objectives identified for this classroom lesson |
| A—2. | Attendance |
| | No |
| | Attendance is not a factor for consideration because it has no bearing on the objectives identified for this classroom lesson |
| A—3. | Developmental level of functioning |
| | Yes |
| | Students' levels of social and cognitive functioning is important to consider when creating and delivering a developmentally appropriate educational curriculum. Otherwise, students may not be capable of grasping the material presented, and the school counselor is unable to meet the objectives of the lesson |
| A—4. | Retentions |
| | No |
| | Knowing which students have been retained or the number of students with retentions is not a factor for consideration because it has no bearing on the objectives identified for this classroom lesson |

**228** ■ *Primary developmental domains*

| A—5. | Ethnicity |
|---|---|
| | Yes |
| | Ethnicity is a consideration when creating any curriculum that is sensitive to the needs of a diverse population. It is important for school counselors to understand how ethnicity impacts career decision making and critical that school counselors provide students with information related to culturally diverse individuals and the world of work (e.g., stereotyping, discrimination, affirmative action, bias in occupational information). Such information enhances student knowledge for career decision making and understanding self in relation to career, two of the objectives identified for this classroom lesson |
| A—6. | Discipline |
| | No |
| | Discipline is not a factor for consideration because it has no bearing on the objectives identified for this classroom lesson |
| A—7. | Grades |
| | No |
| | Grades are not a factor for consideration because they have no bearing on the objectives identified for this classroom lesson |
| A—8. | Course selections |
| | No |
| | Although students will be identifying courses and programs as part of the curriculum for this classroom lesson (e.g., creating a career and academic plan), knowing students' current course selections is not a factor for consideration because it has no bearing on the objectives identified for this classroom lesson |

## Section B: High school career development

Which Internet-based career information system might you consider most appropriate to introduce to ninth grade students in your classroom lesson? (Choose ONLY ONE in this section.)

| B—1. | WISC |
|---|---|
| | No |
| | The WISC is often used in schools for diagnostic testing to assess level of intelligence |
| B—2. | Choices Planner |
| | Yes |
| | Choices Planner is a comprehensive career information system for career planning at the high-school level and the single best selection for this item |

| B—3. | MBTI |
| --- | --- |
| | No |
| | The MBTI, although sometimes used in career counseling, it is considered a personality test |
| B—4. | SDS |
| | No |
| | The SDS is a career interest inventory |
| B—5. | Stanford–Binet |
| | No |
| | The Stanford–Binet is an intelligence test often used in the schools for diagnostic testing |

## Section C: High school career development

You want to include an activity in your career development program curriculum that will aid students in developing an understanding of how others influence career decision making. Which career theory, model, or approach would be the most useful in helping you to develop your activity?

(Choose ONLY ONE in this section.)

| C—1. | Cochran's narrative career counseling theory |
| --- | --- |
| | No |
| | This theory focuses on one's narrated story based on perceived interactions with the world. Although one's story may include important others in the individual's life, the instructions stated to select "only one" and this is not the most relevant response among the choices provided |
| C—2. | Super's lifespan theory |
| | Yes |
| | This model demonstrates how childhood career development evolves |
| C—3. | Krumboltz's social learning theory |
| | No |
| | Social learning theory emphasizes the role of behavior and cognitions in career decision making. Important others may have served as role models or important reinforcers of behavior, however, relationship is not the single most applicable construct for this theory or response for this item |
| C—4. | Savickas' career construction approach |
| | No |
| | Seeks to identify meaningful life themes and one's adaptation to the environment and unique situations |

| C—5. | Cognitive information-processing approach |
| --- | --- |
| | No |
| | Emphasizes how one's thoughts influence career development |
| C—6. | Gottfredson's theory of circumscription and compromise |
| | No |
| | Focus is on developmental processes in career decision making |

## Section D: High school career development

When delivering culturally sensitive career development programs to a diverse student population, school counselors consider the following influences on career choice.

(Select as many as you consider indicated in this section.)

| D—1. | Allocentrism |
| --- | --- |
| | Yes |
| | It is important to understand the way the student views career selection |
| D—2. | Social relationships |
| | Yes |
| | Career choice is influenced by important others in student's life |
| D—3. | Availability of occupation information |
| | Yes |
| | Students from low-socioeconomic environments do not have the same access to career information and career development tools |
| D—4. | Beliefs and values |
| | Yes |
| | Understanding how one's general and work-related beliefs and values impact occupational choices is critical to aiding individuals in making decisions that result in satisfying careers |
| D—5. | Favorite meal |
| | No |
| | This would not be relevant to career decision making |
| D—6. | Gender |
| | Yes |
| | Gender influences career selection. Encouraging students to consider nontraditional careers is a growing trend in today's schools |

| D—7. | Personal appearance<br>No<br>A student's appearance does not impact career decision making. However, it is important to consider that how students feel about themselves (e.g., appearance, intelligence) may impact career decision making |
|---|---|
| D—8. | Job factors<br>Yes<br>Job factors (e.g., salary, environment, physical ability, education, and training) influence career decision making |
| D—9. | Socioeconomic status<br>Yes<br>Students may rule out particular careers (ruling in others) based on socioeconomic status. Also, students from low socioeconomic backgrounds may not be knowledgeable of all the different career opportunities due to limited career resources and information |
| D—10. | Developmental level of functioning<br>Yes<br>A student's ability to perform the occupation of choice must be considered |

## Section E: High school career development

What other strategies might be introduced in your curriculum to aid students in exploring diverse careers?

(Select as many as you consider indicated in this section.)

| E—1. | Resume and cover letter writing<br>No<br>Resumes and cover letters are important tools for applying for colleges, jobs, military, apprenticeships, and technical schools. However, students will not find these tools useful for exploring diverse careers |
|---|---|
| E—2. | Community service<br>Yes<br>Community service is a valuable way for students to learn about different occupations while also providing a valuable service to the community |
| E—3. | Job shadowing<br>Yes<br>Job shadowing allows students to observe, first-hand, the characteristics of specific occupations from which to further development career interests |

| E—4. | Developing a career portfolio |
| --- | --- |
| | No |
| | Career portfolios are important tools for enhancing application to colleges, jobs, military, apprenticeships, and technical schools. However, students will not find this tool useful for exploring diverse careers |
| E—5. | Informational interviewing |
| | Yes |
| | Informational interviewing provides students with relevant and real-world information about specific occupations. Informational interviews allow students an opportunity to ask valuable questions that might not be asked in a job interview for fear of revealing a lack of knowledge to a prospective employer |
| E—6. | Creating a career and academic plan |
| | No |
| | Creating a career and academic plan is an objective of the career development program. However, it is not a strategy that will aid students in exploring diverse careers. It will aid students in identifying future course selections and programs based on identified careers of interest |
| E—7. | Obtaining a part-time/summer job |
| | Yes |
| | Part-time and summer jobs are excellent ways for students to explore a variety of occupations and work environments |

## Section F: High school career development

Which interest inventory might you consider including in your curriculum to aid students in understanding self and the work environments for which they may be best suited?

(Choose ONLY ONE in this section.)

| F—1. | SDS |
| --- | --- |
| | Yes |
| | Holland's SDS assigns individuals and work environments into six categories using a three-letter code |
| F—2. | Connors Scale |
| | No |
| | The Connors Scale is an instrument used to assess for ADHD |

| F—3. | ASVAB |
| --- | --- |
| | No |
| | The ASVAB, often used to identify areas of strength, can drive career decision making, but it does not yield information about self and the work environment |
| F—4. | Career beliefs inventory |
| | No |
| | Krumboltz's career beliefs inventory identifies problematic self-perceptions and worldviews |
| F—5. | WISC |
| | No |
| | The WISC is often used in schools for diagnostic testing to assess level of intelligence |
| F—6. | Vineland |
| | No |
| | The Vineland measures levels of personal and social functioning and is considered to be a personality test |

## Section G: High school career development

Once your unit is implemented, your principal, who emphasizes accountability and outcomes, would like to know how effective you were in meeting lesson objectives aimed at enhancing student development and career readiness. What information would you provide?

(Select as many as you consider indicated in this section.)

| G—1. | The number of students who participated in the lessons |
| --- | --- |
| | No |
| | The number of participants does not indicate the lesson's effectiveness in meeting the identified objectives for this career development program |
| G—2. | Pre-post measure of knowledge of career resources |
| | Yes |
| | Pre- and post-lesson assessments of knowledge gains related to career resources measure one of the lesson's objectives (i.e., enhancing knowledge of resources available for career exploration and decision making) and would be valuable information to submit to your principal in a results report |

| | |
|---|---|
| G—3. | Pre–post measure of student attendance and participation<br>No<br>Student attendance and participation does not indicate the lesson's effectiveness in meeting identified objectives for this career development program |
| G—4. | Feedback from students about the lessons' usefulness<br>No<br>Feedback from students' pertaining to their perceived value of the lesson is useful information for program improvement and/or continuance. However, it is not useful information to submit to your principal, who is requesting outcome data related to meeting the program's objectives |
| G—5. | The number of students who completed a career and academic plan<br>Yes<br>Creating a career and academic plan is an objective of the program. For this reason, providing your principal with the number of students who created a plan is appropriate to his or her request. In this situation, it would be appropriate to provide the number of participants as well because participation provides a point for comparison (i.e., number of participants and number of participants who completed a career and academic plan) |
| G—6. | Pre-post measure of students' knowledge of self related to career<br>Yes<br>Increasing student knowledge of self in relation to career is an objective of the program. For this reason, providing your principal with this outcome data is appropriate to his or her request |
| G—7. | Measure of academic performance pre- and post-lesson implementation<br>No<br>Enhanced academic performance is not an objective of this program |

# Chapter 3: Guided reflection

What are the three primary developmental domains addressed by school counselors using a comprehensive developmental school counseling program? Describe each.

*Developmentally, elementary- and middle-school students are in two very different places.* Support this statement.

Name at least two of the most frequently identified fears of students entering secondary school.

High-school counselors spend most their time with students providing which types of services?

What is *character education*? Why is this important that character education be addressed in schools at every level? What types of characteristics are addressed in character education programs (name at least four in your response)?

What is peer programming and why is it important in schools at every level? Name three types of peer programming appropriate to the school setting.

Explain the significance of academic development in school counseling.

The following are critical issues/incidents associated with the academic development of students in the school setting. Define each critical incident and identify related constructs and their significance to school counseling:

Curriculum development

Closing the achievement gap

Specialty and alternative programs including:

Homeschooling

*Primary developmental domains* ■ **237**

The virtual classroom

Programs/services for students with disabilities

ESL program

Enrichment programs

GED program

Explain the significance of social/emotional development in school counseling.

## 238 ■ Primary developmental domains

The following are critical issues/incidents associated with the social/emotional development of students in the school setting. Define each critical incident and identify related constructs and its significance to school counseling:

Transitioning

Crisis management

School violence and bullying

Internet safety and cyberbullying

Substance use, abuse, addiction

Divorce

Parenting styles

Explain the significance of career development in school counseling.

The following are critical issues/incidents associated with the career development of students in the school setting. Define each critical incident and identify related constructs and their significance to school counseling:

Influences on career decision making (include at least two in your response)

Career development theory and career counseling (include at least two theories and include the theorists and major constructs of each theory)

Career and college transitions

**240** ■ *Primary developmental domains*

Assessment instruments (include at least two in your response)

Career information systems (include at least two in your response)

When is cyberbullying considered by law to be a criminal offense? Should this be shared with students in your school? If so, how might a school counselor address this in the school?

What are the differences between Substance Use, Abuse, Addiction?

Name at least four signs/symptoms of addiction.

Is the treatment of addiction within the scope of school counseling? Why or why not?

What is the difference between primary, secondary and tertiary prevention? Give examples of scenarios whereby the use of each would be appropriate.

According to research, children of divorce often demonstrate a variety of issues. Name at least four potential issues experienced by children of divorce.

What are the four widely recognized parenting styles? Which has been found to be most beneficial to raising a well-adjusted, confident, self-controlled, and academically successful child? Which parenting style(s) has been linked to the development of emotional, social, psychological, behavioral, and academic problems and why?

*Chapter 4*

# Theories and techniques for school settings

There are hundreds of counseling and psychotherapy theories, models, and approaches (Wedding & Corsini, 2013). The theoretical approach(es) a school counselor elects to use will depend on the topic and goals of counseling, student characteristics (e.g., culture, developmental level), and the comfort level of the school counselor with a specific approach.

School counselors are well advised to consider the principle of reductionism when considering the complexities of a student's case, that is, the child is but one part of an intricate system of multiple interacting parts. Systems theory necessitates that school counselors consider students in the context of their relationship to other family members because each part (individual) influences the whole (family). When there is evidence of a family dysfunction, school counselors strongly encourage parents to consider counseling by a licensed marriage and family therapist.

The sections that follow will cover nine of the most widely used theories and associated techniques for counseling children and adolescents in the schools. For ease of learning and recall, each theory will be summarized in a chart that includes the following: theorist and philosophy, therapeutic relationship, key concepts and techniques, and multicultural responsiveness. The following theories are covered in this section:

- Adlerian.
- Behavioral.
- Cognitive behavioral.

- Gestalt.
- Person-centered (also called Rogerian and humanistic).
- Rational emotive behavior therapy (REBT).
- Reality.
- Solution-focused brief counseling.
- Strength-based counseling.

## Adlerian

Developed by Alfred Adler (1925), Adlerian counseling, also referred to as individual psychology, is defined by its encouraging, goal-driven approaches that focus on immediate behavioral change (Table 4.1). School counselors with Adlerian orientations often rely on play therapy methods to induce communication, interaction, and problem solving while acting out appropriate responding and behavioral expectations (e.g., differentiating good behavior from bad behavior).

### Table 4.1 Adlerian Counseling

| Theorist and philosophy | Alfred Adler's theoretical philosophy holds internalized feelings of inferiority/inadequacy and resulting frustration and discouragement as the source of difficulties and misbehavior. The underlying belief is that social interest/inherent human desire for success drives behavior. Counseling is directive |
|---|---|
| Therapeutic relationship | School counselor is supporter, encourager, facilitator |
| Key concepts/ techniques | Self-awareness is encouraged. Using structured questions, confrontation, and *play therapy*, students share perceptions of their lives, family history, and social interactions. Students identify unconstructive behaviors by catching oneself and more constructive alternatives. Together, goals are established toward creating a desired lifestyle that gives students a sense of equality. *Inferiority complex* (an advanced sense of inability and inequality in meeting life's demands) is a concept born out of Adler's work |
| Multicultural responsiveness | Focus on individuality is not compatible with some cultures; individualized approach is culturally sensitive and accommodates the student's frame of reference/worldview; focus on the holistic approach and social responsibility is compatible with some cultures; focus on shared goal setting is culturally sensitive |

## Behavioral

B. F. Skinner (1971) developed behavioral counseling. The defining characteristics of behavioral counseling (see Table 4.2) involve identifying behavioral influences and helping students to eliminate problematic behavior and learn more functional behaviors. School counselors who practice from a behavioral orientation view behavior as learned and therefore focus on teaching new behaviors.

Three approaches are generally associated with behavioral theory. The first, *stimulus–response*, which applies to involuntary behaviors illustrated by the classical experiments with Pavlov's dogs, is not covered in this study guide. The stimulus–response method is rarely, if ever, applied in the school setting because educators are more concerned with voluntary behaviors. The other two approaches, *operant conditioning* and *social-cognitive*, are covered in this study guide and are often used by school counselors to bring about behavioral change.

**Table 4.2 Behavioral Counseling**

| Theorist and philosophy | B. F. Skinner's philosophy holds environmental factors responsible for creating dysfunctional behaviors. Behavior is learned; therefore, behaviors can be unlearned and modified. Counseling is directive |
|---|---|
| Therapeutic relationship | Counselor is teacher, collaborator, advisor, facilitator, and reinforcer |
| Key concepts/ techniques | Operant conditioning using a behavior modification technique that involves introducing a *stimulus* (activating event), applying (positive) or withdrawing (negative) a reinforcer or punisher to elicit a desired or undesired *consequence* that changes behavior (extinguishes undesired/promotes desired), particularly when using schedules of reinforcement (repeated over time). Other techniques used toward collaboratively established goals include *behavioral rehearsal* (practicing desired behavior), *assertiveness training* (reducing anxiety in appropriate emotional expression), and *contingency* or *behavioral contracts* (identifies target behavior and rewards/punishments involved) |
| Multicultural responsiveness | Focus on behavior versus feelings is compatible with many cultures; focus on shared goal setting is culturally sensitive; focus on collaboration is empowering for many cultures; the definition of "appropriate" behavior may differ across cultures; passivity is revered in some cultures |

Operant conditioning, more recently referred to as applied *behavioral analysis*, applies punishment or reward to specific behaviors to reduce or eliminate undesirable behaviors and to promote desirable behaviors. Operant conditioning is exemplified when the school counselor applies intrinsic and extrinsic rewards in an attempt to modify behavior. Chapter 1 describes the process of *behavior modification* using operant conditioning and the use of intrinsic and extrinsic rewards in greater detail.

The social-cognitive approach is grounded in the concept of *modeling*, that is, students learn new behaviors by observing the behaviors of others. Observational learning is a powerful phenomenon that has a lasting impact on a student's behavior. School counselors apply the social-cognitive approach in peer-helping programs, mentor programs, and by exposing students to prominent current and historical figures and community participants during career week.

> **LEARNING TO RESOLVE CONFLICT**
>
> During a small group session, an elementary school counselor introduces the students to a conflict resolution strategy and names several historical figures who used conflict resolution to deflect war and improve lives. Members of the group take turns role-playing the strategy. This is referred to in behavioral counseling as
>
> a. Teaching new behavior.
> b. Rehearsal.
> c. Social-cognitive learning.
> d. All of the above.

# Cognitive behavioral

Aaron Beck (1979) developed cognitive behavioral counseling, "also referred to as cognitive behavioral theory/therapy (CBT). Beck has been referred to in cerebral circles" as the father of cognitive therapy. Beck developed a banquet of self-report measures related to the assessment of thoughts and feelings associated with depression, hopelessness, anxiety, and suicide. The defining characteristics of cognitive behavioral counseling (see Table 4.3) involve viewing counseling as learning and emphasizing the role of cognitions and internal dialogue (i.e., thinking) in

**Table 4.3 Cognitive Behavioral Counseling**

| | |
|---|---|
| Theorist and philosophy | Aaron Beck's philosophy holds that one's thoughts determine one's feelings and behaviors. Dysfunction is a result of faulty cognitions. Directive approach to counseling |
| Therapeutic relationship | Counselor is teacher and collaborator |
| Key concepts/ techniques | *Cognitive restructuring* (replacing maladaptive thoughts with more functional thoughts) is a core technique in this psychoeducational model that is direct, goal driven, and structured. Other techniques include identifying faulty thinking that leads to self-defeating behaviors; using *reframing* (alternative perceptions), cognitive modeling (self-talk), *Socratic dialogue* (how questioning); and *thought stopping* (yelling STOP or visualizing a STOP sign when the target thought surfaces) to change thought patterns. *Stress inoculation* (teaching cognitive and physical skills for heading off future stress and identifying automatic thoughts—triggers), *guided imagery* (mental picture—past, present, or future), and problem-solving (step-by-step process) aid in reducing stress, relieving anxiety, and gaining alternative perceptions of events and direction. Homework is often assigned as a strategy to change and practice new thought processes and behaviors |
| Multicultural responsiveness | Focus on thinking versus feelings is compatible with many cultures; focus on teaching and learning is better suited to cultures that hold a negative view of mental health counseling; challenging belief systems may not be compatible with some cultures |

bringing about emotional and behavioral responses (i.e., doing). In other words, our emotions and behaviors are slave to our thoughts. School counselors used this structured and time-sensitive approach to teach and practice new skills and behaviors, problem-solving approaches, and to promote self-control.

# Gestalt

Gestalt theory, developed by Fritz Perls (1969), focuses on here-and-now processes (i.e., thinking, perceiving, feeling, acting) of the whole (Table 4.4). The whole is considered more than the sum of its parts but the unification of those parts as observed by the relationship between those parts. School counselors help students to identify what they are doing and how they can change while gaining insight and learning to appreciate the self.

**Table 4.4 Gestalt Counseling**

| | |
|---|---|
| Theorist and philosophy | Fritz Perls' philosophy holds that disturbance may be due to any number of issues such as overintellectualizing (i.e., out of touch with emotions); unresolved or unfinished business; loss of contact with environment or overinvolved in the environment and loss of contact with self; pulled in too many directions; conflict between what one wants to do and what one feels like they should do |
| Therapeutic relationship | The therapeutic relationship is considered critical to successful outcomes; counselor is caring, warm, accepting, and nonjudgmental |
| Key concepts/ techniques | Counselor helps students to resolve current life problems; to meet needs to achieve homeostasis; to become more self-aware; to develop holistically (mind, body, emotions, sensations); and to identify, clarify, and take responsibility for behaviors using direct experiencing with techniques such as *psychodrama* (enacting conflicts), *empty chair* (enacting dialogues), *I Take Responsibility* (student completes sentences pertaining to an issue with "I take responsibility for it"), and *confrontation* (counselor challenges student's actions or words) |
| Multicultural responsiveness | Working within students' values and acceptance of uniqueness and diverse worldviews appreciates cultural differences; focus on holistic development is compatible to some cultures |

School counselors may rely on gestalt theory to assist students in crisis and to help students get in touch with their emotions through self-exploration and in-the-moment experiencing. School counselors might use gestalt techniques to aid students in resolving past problems so that they might move toward the future, to meet needs as they arise in order to regain a sense of balance, and to recognize that the future is impacted by our choices in the present.

# Person-centered

Carl Rogers (1961, 1969) developed person-centered counseling, also referred to as humanistic and Rogerian counseling. The defining characteristics of person-centered counseling (see Table 4.5) involve viewing the student as having the capacity for growth and self-direction, as well as the potential to understand and resolve life problems.

School counselors may apply person-centered counseling to help students gain a greater understanding of self and daily experiences and

**Table 4.5 Person-Centered (Humanistic) Counseling**

| | |
|---|---|
| Theorist and philosophy | Carl Rogers' philosophy holds that disturbance is due to incongruence between the real and ideal self. Nondirective approach to counseling |
| Therapeutic relationship | Therapeutic relationship is considered essential to effective outcomes; counselor is nurturing, warm, and genuine and exhibits unconditional positive regard for the client |
| Key concepts/ techniques | Counselor promotes self-exploration in a safe climate with *active listening*, reflecting feelings, *paraphrasing*, and clarifying so that client recognizes barriers to performance and growth and identifies new aspects of self |
| Multicultural responsiveness | Working within students' values appreciates cultural differences; focus on feelings may not be compatible to some cultures; some cultural populations desire more activity |

work through brief situational stress and anxiety. School counselors rely on the person-centered approach to establish positive, nurturing counselor–student relationships that allow for the incorporation of more directive counseling techniques and approaches.

# Rational emotive behavior therapy

Ellis and Dryden (1997) developed rational emotive behavior therapy (REBT), born out of cognitive behavioral theory. The defining characteristics of REBT (see Table 4.6) involve encouraging clients to confront and gather evidence to dispute irrational beliefs and faulty assumptions that are believed to result in negative emotional and behavioral consequences.

> **MEAN GIRLS**
>
> Elijah comes to you, the elementary school counselor, very upset. He said that a group of girls on the playground were teasing him, so he is never going to talk to girls again because girls are so mean. Which counseling approach might best describe Elijah's thoughts in this case, and how might the school counselor apply this approach to help Elijah?

**Table 4.6 Rational Emotive Behavior Therapy**

| Theorist and philosophy | Albert Ellis' cognitive-behavioral theoretical philosophy holds that faulty/irrational thinking is the cause of dysfunction. Directive approach to counseling |
|---|---|
| Therapeutic relationship | Collaborative |
| Key concepts/ techniques | Use the A-B-C Model to debunk irrational thinking. The process involves identifying the activating event and the faulty belief about the event that contributes to the consequence, or self-defeating behavior. Counselors challenge faulty assumptions using questioning and identify alternatives to change internal dialogues and previously held beliefs, and, consequently, emotional and behavioral responses |
| Multicultural responsiveness | Working within the student's values appreciates cultural differences |

School counselors use REBT to promote change and choice by helping students to better understand their thought processes and the relationship between those processes and emotional and behavioral responding. School counselors seek to ultimately empower students to apply REBT in daily living for self-regulation of emotions and behaviors.

# Reality counseling

William Glasser (1998) developed reality therapy, also referred to as *control* or *choice* theory, to promote effective decision making and responsible living. The defining characteristics of reality counseling (see Table 4.7) involve helping students to identify inappropriate decisions and honestly evaluate and take responsibility for their current self-defeating behaviors. As Shakespeare proclaimed—*to thine own self be true!*

School counselors may find reality counseling helpful for students who have a pattern of making poor choices, exhibiting an external locus of control, and lacking realistic goals. School counselors use choice theory to help students understand that they are in control of their lives and possess the ability to change, grow, and achieve, using self-evaluation and relevant planning (Gilchrist-Banks, 2009).

**Table 4.7 Reality Counseling**

| Theorist and philosophy | William Glasser's theoretical philosophy holds unmet needs due to unproductive/ineffective behaviors as the source of dysfunction and that all behavior is an attempt to control the environment to meet our needs. Directive approach to counseling |
|---|---|
| Therapeutic relationship | Facilitator |
| Key concepts/ techniques | Focusing on responsibility, choice, and doing, the counselor asks the student: (1) *What do you want?* (2) *What are you doing to get what you want?* (3) *Is it working?* Counselor challenges current behaviors and encourages students to self-evaluate and judge the quality of their behaviors toward getting what they want. Together, a workable plan is established to change unproductive behaviors to more productive behaviors that guide future direction and meet needs/desires |
| Multicultural responsiveness | Focus on students' evaluation of self within their own cultural frame of reference prizes diversity and accommodates differing worldviews; focus on personal responsibility for change does not account for external factors of discrimination and racism; individualized approach is culturally sensitive |

# Solution-focused brief counseling

Solution-focused brief counseling (SFBC), introduced by Steve de Shazer (1985), is a growing and promising approach particularly suited to school counseling because of its brief nature. SFBC has been vigorously inducted into the not-so-secret society of positive psychology discussed in the next section. The defining characteristics of solution-focused brief counseling (see Table 4.8) involve focusing on solutions versus problems based on what the student is already doing that works, nurturing internal assets, and involving important others (e.g., teachers, parents).

In addition to brevity, SFBC is particularly useful with children and adolescents because of its focus on developmental stages, social support, appropriate use of humor, and active techniques. School counselors identify developmental struggles and help students to identify internal and external resources to create realistic solutions germane to the developmental stage.

**Table 4.8 Solution-Focused Brief Counseling**

| | |
|---|---|
| Theorist and philosophy | Steve de Shazer's solution-focused brief counseling focuses on a student's strengths and abilities rather than weaknesses and inabilities and on solutions rather than problems. Time-limited, directive approach to counseling |
| Therapeutic relationship | Collaborative |
| Key concepts/ techniques | Students' inner and external resources with attention to developmental level are accessed. The counselor identifies what has worked for the student in the past and focuses on goals. Techniques may include the *miracle question* (if magic happened and the problem was gone, what would be different), *exceptions* (identify times where the problem is not present—what does it look like), *scaling* (on a scale of 1–10, with 10 being the hardest day and 1 being after the miracle, where would you be right now), *mindmapping* (e.g., identify what you did that made you successful in the past), *reframing* (viewing problems in more positive terms), and *assigning behavioral tasks* (e.g., doing more of the exceptions). |
| Multicultural responsiveness | Compatible to some cultures that prefer time-limited, practical applications; viewing the student as the expert and working within the student's frame of reference are culturally sensitive and accommodate differing worldviews; using developmentally appropriate, flexible interventions congruent to students' culture is culturally responsive |

# Strengths-based counseling

Strengths-based counseling, an emerging positive psychology pioneered by Martin Seligman, accesses inherent strengths to identify the student's resources and supports for addressing the problem. The strengths-based approach underscores the value of protective factors in combating *risk factors* and enhancing resilience, embracing the philosophy that treatment is not just about fixing what is broken, but nurturing what is best within ourselves (Seligman, 2004). Defining characteristics of strengths-based counseling (see Table 4.9) involve identifying current and past successes to address future challenges.

Unlike many theories focused on deficit reduction, school counselors use strengths-based counseling to build on students' unique assets to empower, strengthen, instill hope, and strengthen resilience. The Search Institute (2007) has developed lists of *Developmental Assets* for early childhood, middle childhood, and adolescence. These lists are available at www.search-institute.org/developmental-assets/lists. Each list depicts

## Table 4.9 Strengths-Based Counseling

| Theorist and philosophy | Martin Seligman espoused that strengths-based counseling is a therapeutic approach that is grounded in the belief that personal strengths enable individuals to achieve, change, and grow. Counseling is directive |
|---|---|
| Therapeutic relationship | Collaborative; counselors are guides |
| Key concepts/ techniques | Accesses students' unique, inherent strengths and builds upon those strengths to empower, promote change, and encourage self-help. This is often found in what has generally been identified as a weakness. For example, being very talkative and opinionated is viewed, instead, as having great passion, conviction, and being communicative |
| Multicultural responsiveness | Working within the client's values appreciates cultural differences; focusing on inner strengths, assets, and resources is compatible to many cultures |

40 Developmental Assets considered to be building blocks for healthy development, which include eight categories:

1. Support.
2. Empowerment.
3. Boundaries and expectations.
4. Constructive use of time.
5. Commitment to learning.
6. Positive values.
7. Social competencies.
8. Positive identity.

In turn, Developmental Assets will aid in preventing and mediating problems and promote change. School counselors may find strengths-based counseling particularly helpful for students with low self-esteem, marginal academic performance, and a lack of self-confidence and motivation.

### THE MEANING OF LIFE

Kafi is a middle-school student whom you meet for issues associated with low motivation and poor self-esteem. During today's session, Kafi remarks, "My life just has no meaning… who am I… what can I do about anything anyway… what kind of future could I possibly have?" Which category of the Developmental Assets likely needs to be the focus of this counseling session?

# Play therapy techniques

Deemed critical to the personal, social, and cognitive development of a healthy child, incorporating play therapy as a staple technique into counseling services is another consideration for school counselors (Santrock, 2014). Play therapy may be directive, nondirective, or a combination of approaches. Play therapy has been associated with enhanced social skills, communication, attention, self-control, and self-esteem, as well as reduced levels of *aggression*, depression, anxiety, and *antisocial* and delinquent behaviors. Play therapy has also helped many children and adolescents to work through emotional, personal, and interpersonal issues associated with trauma (e.g., grief, abuse, disaster) and family issues (e.g., divorce, adoption, deployment). Play therapy also enhances cognitive and psychosocial functioning in students with disabilities and is used as a diagnostic tool to appraise psychosocial functioning (Kottman & Meany-Walen, 2015).

During play therapy, the school counselor systematically applies one or more of the theoretical approaches covered in this chapter. Toys are used and often represented in categories such as nurturing, aggressive, scary, expressive, and pretend. Some of the toys may fit into several categories, which are listed in the following paragraphs (Kottman & Meany-Walen, 2015). Nurturing toys help students to express and act out relationships and past, present, or future events. School counselors are careful to include dolls that represent different cultures for exploring differences and similarities. Nurturing toys may include the following:

- Dolls or people puppets (some with anatomical parts and removable clothing).
- Child-size furniture (e.g., kitchen sink, stove, refrigerator).
- Kitchenware (e.g., plates, pots, pans, cups).
- Doll clothing.
- Blankets.
- Stuffed animals.

Aggressive toys help children and adolescents to express feelings of anger appropriately or symbolically. School counselors often elect not to include aggressive toys in their office, preferring to avoid conveying a message that violence of any kind is acceptable. Aggressive toys may include

- Punching bag.
- Rubber mallet.
- Soft boxing gloves.
- Foam bats.

Scary toys help children and adolescents to express fear; to symbolically represent abusive, frightening, or past traumatic situations; and to practice ways in which they can keep themselves safe. Scary toys may include

- Plastic insects.
- Rubber snake.
- Plastic dinosaur, shark, rat, alligator.
- A variety of puppets and stuffed toys representative of scary animals (e.g., lion, gorilla, bear, wolf, tiger).

Toys that allow children to pretend, or fantasize, promote behavioral and emotional expression, communication, role exploration, and the reenactment of past and present life events. Students use these toys for metaphorical expression of ideas and experiences. These toys may include

- Clothing.
- Jewelry.
- Telephones and computers.
- Puppets and puppet stage.
- Blocks.
- Masks.
- Kits (e.g., doctor, geologist).
- Hats.
- Magic wands.
- Fantasy creatures (e.g., unicorn, leprechaun, witch, troll, fairy princess).
- Superheroes (e.g., Superman, Spiderman, Batman).
- Villains (e.g., Joker, Riddler, Dr. Doom).

Expressive toys help students to communicate difficult emotions through actions and symbols while finding the appropriate vocabulary for verbal expression of emotions. Expressive toys also help students gain a greater understanding of themselves, their environment, and the self in relation to others. Use of expressive toys with children has been linked to enhanced problem solving, self-confidence, creativity, self-control, and emotional and cognitive expression. Expressive toys include

- Games.
- Musical instruments.
- Paint.
- Play dough.
- Blocks.
- Books.
- Sand and water trays.
- Stuffed animals.
- Beads.
- Construction paper, tape, scissors, pencils, glue sticks, markers.
- Yarn.

### PLAY THERAPY

Yasmin is an eight-year-old female student whose grandfather died suddenly last week. Yasmin's teacher reports that Yasmin is very quiet and withdrawn. Also, her classwork is not completed, which is not typical for Yasmin. The parent and teacher have asked the school counselor to meet with Yasmin. What toys might be particularly helpful to Yasmin at this time?

a. Scary.
b. Nurturing.
c. Expressive.
d. Aggressive.
e. Pretend.

# Chapter 4 Case conceptualization responses

## Theories and techniques for the school setting

### Play therapy

The correct response is "c." Yasmin would likely benefit from expressive toys that will allow her to work through a variety of emotions. The school counselor can explore metaphorical and symbolical expressions of emotions that may be associated with grief, helping Yasmin to identify and work through difficult emotions.

### Learning to resolve conflict

The correct response is "d." All the possible responses in this scenario are examples of behavioral counseling. *Behavioral rehearsal* involves teaching new behaviors (i.e., conflict resolution) and having students practice those behaviors in some fashion (i.e., role play). Introducing historical figures as models of a specific behavior is a social-cognitive learning approach used in behavioral counseling.

### Mean girls

Albert Ellis might describe Elijah's thoughts as irrational. Elijah is overgeneralizing the behavior of girls based on the behavior of a few select girls in one situation. Debunking Elijah's irrational thoughts using the A–B–C model of REBT might be helpful for Elijah.

### The meaning of life

The school counselor should focus on the Developmental Assets category of "positive identity," empowering Kafi and encouraging her to be an explorer of her world and all the possibilities.

# Chapter 4 Simulation: Esther

## Brief case description

You are an elementary school counselor. A parent refers her third-grade daughter to you. She said she does not have the money to pay for counseling right now and understands that you meet with students for a limited number of individual sessions. This year, Esther, her daughter, began picking her arms so badly that they bleed. She took her daughter to the family physician, and he said it did not appear to be allergies or a rash but seems to be more emotionally driven. When she asks Esther what is wrong, she says, "I don't know." The parent adds that her grades have continued to be good, and the problem does not seem to be related to friendship issues because Esther has positive relations with peers at home and at school.

## *Section A: Esther*

What information might be useful from the parent at this time?
  (Select as many as you consider indicated in this section.)

| | |
|---|---|
| _____A—1. | Frequency of behavior |
| _____A—2. | Student's diet |
| _____A—3. | Duration of behavior |
| _____A—4. | Medical history |
| _____A—5. | Onset of behavior |
| _____A—6. | Family events |
| _____A—7. | School events |
| _____A—8. | Student–family relations |
| _____A—9. | Mother's relationship with father |
| _____A—10. | Student's hobbies |
| _____A—11. | Living arrangements |
| _____A—12. | Time spent on the computer |

## Section B: Esther

You meet with Esther and notice that she is a small third grader and very shy. You ask a few open-ended questions related to friends and family, but Esther just gives a quick response that offers you no substantial insight. What approach might be the best to use with Esther at this time?
(Choose ONLY ONE in this section.)

| | |
|---|---|
| _____B—1. | Strengths-based counseling |
| _____B—2. | Cognitive behavioral counseling |
| _____B—3. | Play therapy |
| _____B—4. | Gestalt |
| _____B—5. | REBT |

## Section C: Esther

During the second session, Esther enters the room and walks over to the toys, and selects a female doll and a plastic shark off your toy shelf. Esther sits on the mat on the floor and proceeds to have the shark eat the head off the female doll. What might be the most appropriate communication by you in order to gather needed information about this behavior?
(Select as many as you consider indicated in this section.)

| | |
|---|---|
| _____C—1. | Esther, you seem to be angry at that doll |
| _____C—2. | Esther, do you like sharks? |
| _____C—3. | Esther, who is that doll? |
| _____C—4. | Esther, what is that shark doing? |
| _____C—5. | Esther, that is a mean shark, why did you choose to play with it? |
| _____C—6. | Esther, why are you angry? |
| _____C—7. | Esther, who is that shark? |

## Section D: Esther

During the third session, Esther expresses her anger toward her mother stating, "Mom doesn't love me, all she cares about is my getting good grades." Which counseling approach might be the most useful at this time to help Esther confront this irrational thought?

(Choose ONLY ONE in this section.)

| | |
|---|---|
| _____D—1. | Reality |
| _____D—2. | Solution-focused |
| _____D—3. | Strength-based |
| _____D—4. | Behavioral |
| _____D—5. | REBT |
| _____D—6. | Person-centered |

## Section E: Esther

As Esther enters your office for her fourth session, you notice that her arms are really picked and she is picking at her arms as she walks into your office. You ask her if she realizes that she is picking her arms. She says, "Yes." You ask her what she has been thinking about today. She says, "My test." You realize that this morning third-grade students took an important standardized test. You ask, "What are you thinking about the test?" She responds, "I am so scared that I did not make an A, so mom is going to take away my birthday party this summer." You ask, "Have you talked about this with your mother?" Esther says, "No, I'm afraid she will get mad and yell at me." What might be the best course of action at this time?

(Choose ONLY ONE in this section.)

| | |
|---|---|
| _____E—1. | Friendship group |
| _____E—2. | Self-esteem building |
| _____E—3. | Encourage role-play communication with mother |
| _____E—4. | Strategies for reducing test-taking anxiety |
| _____E—5. | Study-skills group |
| _____E—6. | Encourage and role-play communication with teacher |

# Chapter 4 Simulation responses: Esther

## Brief case description

You are an elementary school counselor. A parent refers her third-grade daughter to you. She said she does not have the money to pay for counseling right now and understands that you meet with students for a limited number of individual sessions. This year, Esther, her daughter, began picking her arms so badly that they bleed. She took her daughter to the family physician, and he said it did not appear to be allergies or a rash but seems to be more emotionally driven. When she asks Esther what is wrong, she says, "I don't know." The parent adds that her grades have continued to be good, and the problem does not seem to be related to friendship issues because Esther has positive relations with peers at home and at school.

## *Section A: Esther*

What information might be useful from the parent at this time?
  (Select as many as you consider indicated in this section.)

| | |
|---|---|
| A—1. | Frequency of behavior<br>Yes<br>Frequency of behavior is important to assessing the severity of the issue |
| A—2. | Student's diet<br>No<br>This is not indicated at this time because the student has already seen a physician |
| A—3. | Duration of behavior<br>Yes<br>Duration of behavior is important to assessing the severity of the issue |
| A—4. | Medical history<br>No<br>The student has already visited the physician. The school counselor might suggest that the parent consider a second opinion by a medical doctor |

| | |
|---|---|
| A—5. | Onset of behavior<br>Yes<br>Onset of the behavior may help to identify precipitating events or triggers that may be causing or contributing to the behavior |
| A—6. | Family events<br>Yes<br>Family events may help to identify life changes or triggers that may be causing or contributing to the behavior |
| A—7. | School events<br>Yes<br>School events may help to identify life changes or triggers that may be causing or contributing to the behavior |
| A—8. | Student–family relations<br>Yes<br>Changes in relationships can have a significant impact on functioning and behavioral patterns |
| A—9. | Mother's relationship with father<br>Yes<br>Changes in marital relationships impact family dynamics, functioning, and behavior |
| A—10. | Student's hobbies<br>No<br>Exploring the student's hobbies is not indicated at the present time. The student's physician would have explored exposure to skin irritants |
| A—11. | Living arrangements<br>Yes<br>It is important to gain an understanding of the student's environment in order to better understand the student |
| A—12. | Time spent on the computer<br>No<br>Time spent on the computer would not offer insight into Esther's behavior at this time |

## Section B: Esther

You meet with Esther and notice that she is a small third grader and very shy. You ask a few open-ended questions related to friends and family, but Esther just gives a quick response that offers you no substantial insight. What approach might be the best to use with Esther at this time? (Choose ONLY ONE in this section.)

| B—1. | Strengths-based counseling |
| --- | --- |
|  | No |
|  | Promoting Esther's strengths is certainly useful; however, it is difficult to identify and access those strengths without counselor–client communication |
| B—2. | Cognitive behavioral counseling |
|  | No |
|  | The CBT focus on thought processes could be useful in this case, but the school counselor must first promote counselor–client communication and build trust with this student |
| B—3. | Play therapy |
|  | Yes |
|  | Play therapy is an excellent choice at this time for Esther because play often promotes communication and relationship building between the client and counselor. This is also particularly helpful in cases where the child is reluctant to express thoughts and emotions and is in the initial stages of counseling |
| B—4. | Gestalt |
|  | No |
|  | Gestalt is certainly a good choice for helping students to resolve current life issues to become more self-aware and offers practical techniques for daily living. However, the school counselor will need to first establish communications with Esther |
| B—5. | REBT |
|  | No |
|  | Perhaps Esther's issues are related to faulty thinking or irrational beliefs, but REBT would not be indicated at this time |

## Section C: Esther

During the second session, Esther enters the room and walks over to the toys selecting a female doll and a plastic shark off your toy shelf. Esther sits on the mat on the floor and proceeds to have the shark eat the head off the female doll. What might be the most appropriate communication by you in order to gather needed information about this behavior?

(Select as many as you consider indicated in this section.)

| C—1. | Esther, you seem to be angry at that doll |
| --- | --- |
| | No |
| | The school counselor does not want to presume this emotion without exploring how the student perceived the action |
| C—2. | Esther, do you like sharks? |
| | No |
| | Focus on the action and what may be implied by the action in the child's world |
| C—3. | Esther, who is that doll? |
| | Yes |
| | This will help the school counselor to understand who the doll represents in the child's world |
| C—4. | Esther, what is that shark doing? |
| | Yes |
| | This is a good choice as it will help the school counselor to interpret the child's thoughts and emotions |
| C—5. | Esther, that is a mean shark, why did you choose to play with it? |
| | No |
| | Focus on the action and what may be implied by the action in the child's world |
| C—6. | Esther, why are you angry? |
| | No |
| | The school counselor does not want to presume this emotion without exploring how the student perceived the action |
| C—7. | Esther, who is that shark? |
| | Yes |
| | This will help the school counselor to understand who or what the shark signifies in the child's world |

## Section D: Esther

During the third session, Esther expresses her anger toward her mother stating, "Mom doesn't love me, all she cares about is my getting good grades." Which counseling approach might be the most useful at this time to help Esther confront this irrational thought?

(Choose ONLY ONE in this section.)

| D—1. | Reality<br>No<br>Reality counseling is a great approach for examining how current behaviors are meeting or not meeting client needs, but this may or may not be related to irrational thoughts |
|---|---|
| D—2. | Solution-focused<br>No<br>It is important to focus on solutions to the problem, but at the present time addressing Esther's irrational belief would be appropriate |
| D—3. | Strengths-based<br>No<br>Focusing on Esther's strengths to encourage self-help is important, but she had expressed an irrational thought that the school counselor would be wise to address before moving on |
| D—4. | Behavioral<br>No<br>Behavioral counseling, which focuses on learned behaviors, is not indicated at this time |
| D—5. | REBT<br>Yes<br>REBT will provide the school counselor with the approach needed to debunk Esther's irrational belief |
| D—6. | Person-centered<br>No<br>Although the nurturing and warm approach of person-centered counseling is useful in Esther's case, it is not the best choice for countering irrational beliefs |

## Section E: Esther

As Esther enters your office for her fourth session, you notice that her arms are really picked and she is picking at her arms as she walks into your office. You ask her if she realizes that she is picking her arms. She says, "Yes." You ask her what she has been thinking about today. She says, "My test." You realize that this morning third-grade students took an important standardized test. You asked, "What are you thinking about the test?" She responds, "I am so scared that I did not make an A, so mom is going to take away my birthday party this summer." You ask, "Have you talked about this with your mother?" Esther says, "No, I'm afraid she will get mad and yell at me." What might be the best course of action at this time?

(Choose ONLY ONE in this section.)

| E—1. | Friendship group |
| | No |
| | Peer relationship issues have not been identified |
| E—2. | Self-esteem building |
| | No |
| | Although Esther is shy, her issues are not presented as related to self-esteem. Esther's issues are more likely related to her lack of candid communication with her parent and her respect for her parent's feelings |
| E—3. | Encourage role-play communication with mother |
| | Yes |
| | Esther is having difficulty communicating with her mother. Empowering Esther to communicate her thoughts and emotions with her parent is critical to continued family communications. Esther's behavior appears to be related to stress associated with the performance pressure she perceives from her mother |
| E—4. | Strategies for reducing test-taking anxiety |
| | No |
| | This is not the immediate course of action, but the school counselor may want to consider this intervention after communication between Esther and her mother |
| E—5. | Study-skills group |
| | No |
| | This is not the immediate course of action, but the school counselor may want to consider this intervention after communication between Esther and her mother |
| E—6. | Encourage and role-play communication with teacher |
| | No |
| | Esther has not identified communications issues with her teacher |

## Chapter 4 Guided reflection

The following are the most widely used counseling theories by the school counselor in the school setting. For each theory below, identify: theorist, philosophy, therapeutic relationship, key concepts and techniques, and multicultural responsiveness.

Adlerian

Behavioral

Cognitive behavioral theory

Gestalt

Person-centered

Rational emotive behavior therapy

Reality counseling

Solution-focused brief counseling

Strengths-based counseling

What is play therapy? Discuss the importance of play therapy with regard to providing school counseling services.

Name at least three play therapy techniques and in what types of scenarios might each technique be beneficial and why.

**268** ■ *Theories and techniques for school settings*

In play therapy, what are considered to be *expressive toys*?

---

Describe how the school counselor generally engages in individual assessment in the school setting.

# Chapter 5
# Diversity, equity, and advocacy

Never in the history of school counseling have our student populations been more lusciously diverse than they are at the present time. Multilingual, multiethnic, and multicultural students are the majority in many of our schools. In order to continue to practice effectively, professionally, and ethically, school counselors must be culturally competent with a sound commitment to understanding how unique student characteristics impact learning and educational experiences.

Diversity has many faces. It has been defined as the array of cultures and subcultures that characterize attitudes, values, beliefs, rituals, norms, symbols, conventions, customs, ideologies, and behaviors (Sue & Sue, 2019). School counselors spread the aroma of respect and value for diverse individuals and groups, seeking to eliminate hostility and inappropriate language. Inclusive language, too, is modeled to foster a nonjudgmental environment where diversity is embraced and celebrated.

### ASCA Position on The School Counselor and Cultural Diversity

School counselors have a professional and ethical responsibility to expand personal multicultural and social justice advocacy, awareness, knowledge and skills to be an effective, culturally competent school counselor. School counselors work toward cultural competence and cultural humility to provide culturally sustaining school counseling. School counselors demonstrate responsiveness by collaborating with students and stakeholders in support of a school and community climate that embraces cultural diversity and helps to promote all students' academic, career and social/emotional development.

*Position statement adopted 1988; revised 1993, 1999, 2004, 2009, 2015, 2021*

School counselors advocate for the acceptance, respect, and fair and equal treatment of all people (ASCA, 2019a). The Tucson shootings and the youth camp massacre in Norway are recent reminders of the international scope and magnitude of the need for a call to arms of the people to advocate for one another, to honor differences, and to ensure equality—in our homelands and across oceans.

## Advocacy and equity

School counselors are the rock stars of advocacy, belting out the lyrics of equity for quality curricula, programs, and educational and career resources for all. Equity and advocacy begin with compassion and an appreciation of diversity.

*ASCA Position on The School Counselor and Equity for All Students*

School counselors recognize and distinguish individual and group differences and strive to equally value all students and groups. School counselors are advocates for the equitable treatment of all students in school and in the community.

*Position statement adopted 2006; revised 2012, 2018*

School counselors model and teach an appreciation for difference, not just a tolerance of differences. School counselors advocate for equality and justice regardless of socioeconomic standing/background, religion, family and community, race, culture, gender, ethnicity, sexuality, levels of intelligence and functioning, and citizenship status.

---

### ASCA Position on The School Counselor and Working with Students Experiencing Issues Surrounding Undocumented Status

School counselors promote equal opportunity, a safe and nurturing environment and respect for all individuals regardless of citizenship status, including undocumented students and students with undocumented family members, understanding that this population faces a unique set of stressors. School counselors work to eliminate barriers that impede student development and achievement and are committed to the academic, career and social/emotional development of all students. "School counselors demonstrate their belief that all students have the ability to learn by advocating for an education system that provides optimal learning environments for all students" (ASCA, 2022, p. 1).

*Position statement adopted 2017; revised 2019*

---

School counselors understand that issues related to diversity impact learning and academic achievement as well as students' personal, social, emotional, and career development. The goal is to create encouraging and safe learning environments perfumed with social consciousness and compassion for all.

---

### ASCA Position on The School Counselor and Gender Equity

School counselors are committed to creating an emotionally, intellectually and physically safe environment for all students and to using inclusive language and positive modeling of gender equity. Creating this environment facilitates and promotes the development of each individual by removing bias and stereotypes for all students in school.

*Position statement adopted 1983; revised 1993, 1999, 2002, 2008, 2014, 2020*

The culturally sensitive school counselor, discussed later in this chapter, is able to identify prejudicial attitudes and stereotyping that permeates and poisons school communities. School counselors actively challenge oppressive conditions, teach social responsibility, promote climates of acceptance and safety, and seek to remove barriers to success for all individuals.

---

### ASCA Position on The School Counselor and Anti-racist Practices

School counselors work toward cultural competence and engage in anti-racist actions by advocating to change racist policies, procedures, practices, guidelines and laws contributing to inequities in students' academic, career and social/emotional development.

*Position statement adopted 2021*

---

Low SES poses unique challenges for schools, families, and communities. Low SES can have a negative impact on family structures, housing, individual identity, self-esteem, health, and access to educational and career resources. School counselors act as advocates for social change, social responsibility, and social justice in the school and community, providing students from low SES and impoverished backgrounds with much-needed consideration to ensure equity to services and programming. Advocacy and equity for students from low SES environments necessitates active participation, action, and unity. Toward this end, school counselors coordinate and engage in community efforts to combat poverty, empower, support, and give a voice to diverse student populations and the family system.

### JEREMIAH'S CONCERN

Jeremiah is a high-school counselor who is quite versed in Web applications and website development. He created an outstanding website for the school counseling program. The website has all the information deemed important for school counseling websites. His director was pleased since they no longer have to spend time, energy,

> and any of the budget to maintain the binders that housed summer and special programs, scholarships, study abroad, after school jobs, and more. The director was pleased that now students and parents only need to look at the website. Jeremiah had an ethical concern about his school counseling director's response. What do you think it is?

Advocacy is driven by school counselors' compassion for others and their conviction to social justice that embraces equity. *Social justice* is an ideological approach to the professional and ethical practice of professional school counseling. ASCA *Ethical Standards for School Counselors* (ASCA, 2022a) calls school counselors to engage in activities that assess and grow their cultural competence and ability to effectively address social justice.

Six elements have been identified as key to implementing a social justice approach in school counseling. The following six Cs of school counseling encompass the life-force of social justice (Holcomb-McCoy, 2022):

- Counseling and intervention planning.
- Consultation.
- Connecting schools, families, and communities.
- Collecting and utilizing data.
- Challenging bias.
- Coordinating student services and support.

---

## ASCA Position on The School Counselor and LBGTQ Youth

School counselors promote equal opportunity and respect for students regardless of sexual orientation, gender identity or gender expression. School counselors recognize the school experience can be significantly more difficult for students with marginalized identities. School counselors work to eliminate barriers impeding LGBTQ+ student development and achievement.

*Position statement adopted 1995; revised 2000, 2005, 2007, 2013, 2014, 2016, 2022*

The ASCA *Ethical Standards for School Counselors* (ASCA, 2022a) reiterates school counselors' responsibilities as advocates and leaders in providing equitable educational access and success by connecting their school counseling programs to the district's mission and improvement plans.

The ACA adopted *Advocacy Competencies* (Lewis, Arnold, House, & Toporek, 2003), which aid school counselors in better understanding our roles associated with advocacy and how Advocacy Competencies apply vis-à-vis school counseling. Table 5.1 provides a brief overview of the

**Table 5.1 Advocacy Competencies**

| Community collaboration | Their ongoing work with people gives counselors a unique awareness of recurring themes. Counselors are often among the first to become aware of specific difficulties in the environment. |
|---|---|
| | Advocacy-oriented counselors often choose to respond to such challenges by alerting existing organizations that are already working for change and that might have an interest in the issue at hand. |
| | In these situations, the counselor's primary role is as an ally. Counselors can also be helpful to organizations by making available to them our particular skills: interpersonal relations, communications, training, and research |
| Systems advocacy | When counselors identify systemic factors that act as barriers to their students' or clients' development, they often wish that they could change the environment and prevent some of the problems that they see every day. |
| | Regardless of the specific target of change, the processes for altering the status quo have common qualities. Change is a process that requires vision, persistence, leadership, collaboration, systems analysis, and strong data. In many situations, a counselor is the right person to take leadership |
| Public information | Across settings, specialties, and theoretical perspectives, professional counselors share knowledge of human development and expertise in communication |
| | These qualities make it possible for advocacy-oriented counselors to awaken the general public to macrosystemic issues regarding human dignity |
| Social/ political advocacy | Counselors regularly act as change agents in the systems that affect their own students and clients most directly. This experience often leads toward the recognition that some of the concerns they have addressed affected people in a much larger arena |
| | When this happens, counselors use their skills to carry out social/ political advocacy |

*Source*: Adapted from Lewis, J., Arnold, M., House, R., & Toporek, R. (2003). *Advocacy competencies*. Retrieved 7 March 2011, from www.counseling.org/resources

Advocacy Competencies for each of the six domains. For a detailed listing of the competencies for each domain go to the ACA website at www.counseling.org.

## Access, attainment, and achievement

Data and assessment are the instruments used to identify and remove obstacles to student success and to challenge oppressive policies and practices. Emphasis is placed on social justice, empowerment, and equality, creating opportunities to promote students' strengths and academic, career, and personal–social development. School counselors apply systems-focused practices and leadership while collaborating and consulting with important others both within and outside of the school on behalf of students and families.

Access, attainment, and achievement gaps are identified by disaggregating data from a variety of sources. Disaggregating data by race, ethnicity, special needs, gender, and teacher (ASCA, 2019d, 2022b; Erford, 2019; Schellenberg, 2019) allow school counselors to identify and remove obstacles to student success and wellbeing. Data give school counselors the leverage needed to challenge oppressive policies and practices that perpetuate access, attainment, and achievement inequities. Table 5.2 provides a listing of school-wide data sources that when examined can identify access, attainment, and achievement gaps.

Systems-focused practices are paramount to addressing and/or resolving sometimes deeply rooted practices and policies that perpetuate access, attainment, and achievement gaps. The school counselor needs to collaborate and consult with important others both within and outside of the school on behalf of students and families. Challenging deep-seated inequitable practices and policies may mean asking for help. Advocacy is an enormous job and having a team of courageous and creative advocates who share common goals and actively participate to achieve a shared purpose can bring about change.

Opening others' eyes to injustices illuminated by data also opens the doors and hopefully flood gates of change. Admittedly, during my years as a practicing school counselor, the fierce growl of my inner bear would emerge in the face of injustice. Hey, it happens. Plus, most of the snarls were equivalent to a quake of no more than a 2.0 in seismic energy on the Richter scale. So, with about 8000 quakes of this size each day across the nation, at times, the growl was barely noticeable. When the bear is riled, we simply (and sometimes not so simply) keep the explicatives to

## Table 5.2  Access, Attainment, and Achievement Gap Identification

| | |
|---|---|
| Access (or Opportunity) | Enrollment patterns and participation in:<br>■ AP, IB, honors, college preparation, and enrichment classes<br>■ Special education programs<br>■ 504 Plans<br>■ Gifted and talented programs<br>■ Student Council<br>■ Governor's School<br>■ ESL/ELL learner classes/programs |
| Attainment | ■ Attendance<br>■ Dropout rates and graduation rates<br>■ Promotion and retention rates<br>■ Homework completion rates<br>■ Course completion and pass rates<br>■ Non-traditional program tracks (GED, Job Corps)<br>■ In-school and out-of-school suspensions and expulsion rates<br>■ Study abroad<br>■ Parent participation rates<br>■ GED attainment rates<br>■ College/postsecondary acceptance patterns<br>■ College application completion<br>■ FAFSA completion<br>■ Scholarship submissions<br>■ Participation in Individual Planning with the School<br>■ Rates of participation in interest inventories, career development activities, college entrance testing, industry certifications, learning style inventories, academic portfolios development |
| Achievement | ■ Grade point averages<br>■ Scores on classroom assignments end-of-course tests<br>■ Scores on standardized achievement tests<br>■ Scores on homework assignments<br>■ Scores on aptitude tests<br>■ Course grades in all subjects |

ourselves as if performing a soliloquy, ask for strength from our Creator, and stay mindful that the inner bear, too, works responsibly, professionally, and ethically with others to affect change. That is, we show our teeth, but we are careful not to bite anybody!

ASCA *Ethical Standards for School Counselors* (ASCA, 2022a) reminds us that when working in situations whereby practices and policies do not reflect the ethics of our profession, school counselors collaborate with others going through the correct channels in a responsible and professional manner. School counselors labor under the philosophy that it really does *take a village*—and sometimes a bear.

Resolving identified inequities may involve reviewing and making suggestions for more inclusive classrooms, and changes to curricula, instructional strategies, textbooks, and classroom management approaches. Addressing inequities may involve spearheading changes to local and state policy. Challenging the system in this manner may result in resistance and disequilibrium, necessitating that the school counselors aid the system in working through difficult changes and rediscovering new balance.

> **HELP ME TO REACH MY POTENTIAL**
>
> Jameel, a tenth-grade student, comes to you, his new school counselor, to discuss college opportunities. You notice that Jameel's classes are not rigorous and may limit his college options, while his GPA is consistent with a high-functioning student. Upon further investigation, you notice that students from low socioeconomic backgrounds and ethnically diverse students are underrepresented in rigorous courses. This is an example of:
>
> a. Access gap.
> b. Attainment gap.
> c. Achievement gap.
> d. None of the above.

Promotion, retention, and placement of students are additional areas that may prove to be problematic. School counselors are called to monitor these systems by participating on various committees (e.g., child study, student assistance, early intervention, RTI) that review individual student needs and provide specialized instruction to meet those needs.

## ASCA Position on The School Counselor and Retention, Social Promotion, and Age-Appropriate Placement

School counselors recognize that decisions on student retention, promotion and placement are best made when the student's needs are at the forefront of the decision and after considering multiple factors. School counselors also recognize that retention and social promotion decisions have a disproportionate impact on students from culturally, linguistically and otherwise diverse backgrounds. School counselors oppose laws or policies requiring social promotion or retention and advocate for laws and policies that consider individual student needs regarding age-appropriate placement.

*Position statement adopted 2006; revised 2012, 2017, 2023*

Confronting barriers that may lead to inequities is essential. This may simply mean identifying and providing resources and creating sensitive ways that students and parents can directly communicate needs. School counselors can take the lead in establishing strategies that will help to remove some of the more common barriers to parents' participation in school activities, such as:

- Brainstorming ways to welcome parent participation.
- Providing childcare during school meetings and events.
- Arranging school bus transportation to school events.
- Developing needs assessments.
- Coordinating carpools.
- Providing information regarding bus transportation.
- Offering multiple times for program presentations including weekends.

# Multicultural competence

Culturally competent school counselors have the ability to work proficiently across cultures to promote equity by advocating for a system that justly serves the needs of all students. The alternative is continual access, attainment, and achievement School counselors understand how students' self-perceptions and worldviews (e.g., conceptualization of the world) are shaped by culture and cultural experiences. In addition to bridging gaps, culturally sensitive responsive services and competent *multicultural counseling* are used to clarify feelings, promote self-understanding and self-esteem, and develop the personal, social, and emotional well-being of students from all cultures and backgrounds.

ASCA *Ethical Standards for School Counselors* (ASCA, 2022a) emphasizes that school counselors are to avoid imposing personal beliefs or values such as those related to religious, spiritual or political beliefs, culture, and ethnicity. Toward this end, school counselors should become familiar with the Multicultural Counseling Competencies and Standards developed by the Association of Multicultural Counseling and Development (AMCD), a branch of the ACA. The Multicultural Counseling Competencies and Standards are available at www.amcdaca.org.

**Table 5.3 Four Categories of the Culturally Competent School Counseling Program**

| | |
|---|---|
| Culturally Inept | School counseling program preserves and supports the inequitable status quo and does not engage in any activities to enhance cultural responsiveness, reduce achievement or opportunity gaps, or promote equity. School counselors support school personnel who elect to blame *the gaps* on students and families who *don't care* thereby continuing to promote success only for those students who are performing well |
| Culturally Blind | School counseling programming minimizes or negates cultural differences, grouping all students into a single one-size-fits-all category. Although the program may engage in activities to close the achievement gap, the one-size-fits-all mindset reflects a bias in favor of the dominant cultures' norms, values, and practices |
| Culturally Sensitive | Diversity, discrimination, power, and privilege are acknowledged in the program mission statement, in designing and delivering the core school counseling curriculum, and during consultation and counseling. Data is used to develop program goals that support all student populations. There is commitment to enhancing the cultural competence of the school counseling program |
| Culturally Competent | The program seeks, invites, values, and involves parents/guardian and community leaders who represent the student body's various cultural identities. The program mission statement, goals, and evaluation reflect a commitment to equity and cultural responsiveness. The program facilitates systemic changes and prioritizes the eradication of inequitable school polies and practices in order to promote and support success for all students |

*Source*: Adapted from Terrell & Lindsey (2009).

School counselors who wish to gain a greater understanding of the knowledge and skills areas needed to provide culturally competent counseling should refer to the *School Counselor Multicultural Competence Checklist* (Holcomb-McCoy, 2004). The checklist is also helpful in heightening self-awareness of current levels of cultural competence and assessing the school's policies, procedures, and programs for cultural competence. As noted above, Section B.3.i. of the ASCA *Ethical Standards for School Counselors* (ASCA, 2022a) underscores the importance of the school counselor's self-knowledge and an understanding of oppression and the development of racial identity and worldviews as key to multicultural competence.

Reducing and, moreover, eliminating issues associated with *encapsulation* and developing the ability to provide students from diverse backgrounds with the optimal environment for success call for a keen sense of one's cultural self (dominant and minority cultures) and the affirmation of nondominant cultures, which involves:

- Awareness of one's own assumptions, racial biases, and attitudes.
- Awareness of the environmental forces that have impacted minority students.
- Understanding the importance of worldviews and the similarities and differences between the school counselor and the culturally different student and how those characteristics impact the counseling process.
- Understanding differences in language, terminology, and communication styles.
- Possessing an empathetic attitude.
- Possessing a knowledge of a variety of counseling theories and techniques and their strengths and weaknesses with diverse cultures.
- Possessing a knowledge of racial identity development.
- Learning a variety of languages.
- Participating in multicultural development workshops.
- Staying abreast of current literature on topics related to counseling the culturally different.
- Participating in cultural immersion experiences.

School counselors realize that racial identity development is a multifaceted process and, as such, they are careful not to conceptualize students within a universal grouping based on culture or subculture. In other words, they avoid stereotyping.

Individuality is multifaceted and influenced by numerous personal and environmental factors. Models of racial identity development affirm varying levels of enculturation among members of a particular race or culture. That is, on the basis of social and cultural influences, some students feel a stronger identification with their culture than others, which, in turn, impacts acculturation, which is the individual's personal struggle to adapt to a new and unfamiliar culture (Matsumoto & Juang, 2016).

School counselors are aware that students who enter a school where the dominant culture is different from their own will experience varying levels of adjustment based on the strength of their enculturation. The internal process of acculturation is influenced by assimilation, a process external to the individual and determined by the dominant cultures' acceptance of the individual from a new and unfamiliar culture (Matsumoto & Juang, 2016), which can be negatively impacted by *encapsulation.*

---

**THE FISH MARKET**

Kwame, a new student from Ghana, is sitting in his new American fifth-grade elementary-school class. While the teacher is conducting the mathematics lesson, she notices that Kwame appears confused and asks him if he understands what she is teaching. He responds that he does not understand and that this is really different from the way he learns in his home country. He goes on to say that he learned math by selling fish. The class laughs, and the teacher, taking Kwame's remark as a personal affront, tells him that math instruction is not the time to be joking around. The teacher's response is an example of:

   a. Assimilation.
   b. Acculturation.
   c. Encapsulation.
   d. Enculturation.

---

Recognizing that culture impacts a student's thoughts, beliefs, view of self, problem-solving and decision-making processes, orientation to time, and verbal and nonverbal communications—their very being—school counselors are students and teachers of multiculturalism. In addition to becoming culturally competent, school counselors teach cultural sensitivity to teachers and students using systemic approaches such as classroom instruction, school-wide presentations, transitioning programs, and small groups. The following topics are recommended when teaching others to be sensitive to those from culturally diverse backgrounds (Erford, 2019):

- Affirming differences.
- Using accurate multicultural terminology.
- Exploring one's own biases.
- Learning about ethnic and racial identity models.
- Understanding diverse worldviews.
- Challenging oppression.
- Understanding the dangers of stereotyping.
- Exploring racial, ethnic, and cultural histories.

Affirming cultural diversity within and outside of the school setting aids students of the nondominant culture in developing a strong racial identity. A strong racial identity is a protective factor that promotes resiliency.

### LOOK AT ME WHEN I AM TALKING TO YOU

Maya, an Asian high-school student, comes to you, her alphabet counselor, because the student assistance counselor is out with the flu. She discusses an important family issue with you, hoping to make some critical decisions related to the issue. When the student assistance counselor returns, you let her know about your brief session with Maya. The student assistance counselor immediately knows who you are referring to and says that she, too, met with Maya once for about ten minutes, and adds, "Did you notice how little eye contact she makes with you—it's a cultural thing." The alphabet counselor replies, "I did not notice." The student assistance counselor is making a generalization based on Maya's culture, which is considered:

a. Acculturation.
b. Encapsulation.
c. Assimilation.
d. Stereotyping.

## Spirituality

Spirituality continues to be a *taboo* topic in the public school system as a result of the separation of church and state. However, heightened emphasis on the importance of spirituality in the ethical and culturally competent practice of counseling is opening the school doors for the return of spirituality as a topic crucial to holistic student development.

Spiritual development is a critical aspect of human development, a cultural agent, and a natural component for exploration in the counseling process that significantly impacts the student's worldview and the counseling relationship (Kimbel & Schellenberg, 2014). How can you study Naples, Italy, and disregard the pizza pie?

Kimbel and Schellenberg (2014) created School Counselor Spiritual and Religious Competencies to aid school counselors in integrating spirituality and religion into counseling services in K-12 schools in a manner that is ethical, legal, and culturally sensitive. Those competencies were published by ASCA in their journal, *Professional School Counseling*, and featured in their magazine, *ASCA School Counselor*, underscoring the importance and appropriateness of spiritual development as part of a comprehensive school counseling program.

ASCA *Ethical Standards for School Counselors* (ASCA, 2022a) call for the respect of individual and family values, beliefs, and cultural background cautioning against imposing personal values on students or their families. Uncertain as to how to address the sensitive topic of spirituality in a manner that would be considered by parents, students, and administrators to be ethical, professional, and legal, school counselors have elected to avoid the topic.

Like the path to multicultural competence, becoming a school counselor competent in addressing matters of spirituality begins with identifying personal biases with regard to spiritual and religious beliefs and traditions and a commitment to learning more about the spiritual and religious practices of others. Socrates, a Greek thinker and architect of Western philosophies, is viewed by some as a martyr for moral virtue. Socrates emphasized the importance of not being blind to our own (and others') deeply-seated beliefs and presuppositions. Like Socrates, school counselors are heartened to live by the truism "To know thyself," seeking a path for ourselves and our students in what Italians refer to as living *la dolce vita*, or the good life.

Helping students to gain insight into their worldviews and working within the worldviews of students necessitates cultural diplomacy. That is, having a dialogue about how religious or spiritual beliefs, as well as tradition, lifestyle, ideas, beliefs, and values, may impact the student's personal–social, academic, and career decisions. For example, it is virtually impossible to understand Indians apart from their religion because it is so deeply ingrained in everyday personal and public living.

Allow teaching versus preaching to be the guiding philosophy (Wolf, 2004). That is, objectively educate students about spirituality and religion by (1) being descriptive and unbiased in the information presented, (2) teaching respect and appreciation of diversity, and (3) introducing literature or current events that involve spirituality, religion, personal beliefs, and values for class or group discussion. Discussing issues related to spirituality is both constitutional and ethical in accordance with the First Amendment of the Constitution and the ASCA Code of Ethics, respectively (Wolf, 2004). Just as former first lady, Michelle Obama has the right to *bare arms*, school counselors have the right to remove the sleeves that cover critical areas of human development in our efforts to provide culturally competent counseling services.

Maintaining objectivity in school counseling activities related to spirituality and religion begins with an understanding of the differences between spirituality and religion. Religion is more of an organized practice that involves specific beliefs. Religion generally involves worship by groups of individuals in a ritualized fashion and in a bricks-and-mortar establishment such as a church. Spirituality is broad, unstructured, and focused on the individual's essence of being in relation to nature and the universe and may include religion. Fundamental principles of spirituality include hope, meaning in life, and compassion.

In addition to teaching, school counselors might also consider participating in student-initiated spiritual and religious events such as the annual *See You at the Pole* prayer meeting. Section 8524(a) of the *Elementary and Secondary Education Act* (ESEA) of 1965 constitutionally protects prayer and religious expression in public schools (United States Department of Education, 2023). School counselors who explore issues of spirituality with students are engaging in both ethically responsible and culturally sensitive counseling practices.

> **AN INTERNATIONAL BROUHAHA**
>
> When former first lady, Michelle Obama, reached out to the conservative Indonesian government official to invite him to shake her hand this was widely criticized as a culturally insensitive gesture grounded in a lack of knowledge pertaining to the Indonesian culture. This would also demonstrate the profound impact of the following religious beliefs in shaping the cultural customs and identity of many Indonesian people:
>
> a. Muslim.
> b. Christian.
> c. Protestant.
> d. None of the above.

School counselors are mindful of the culturally diverse populations being served in the schools. Culture impacts our thought processes and the manner in which a given situation or problem is perceived. Thus, cultural sensitivity and multicultural competence is crucial to establishing shared goals and achieving desired outcomes.

## Chapter 5 Case conceptualization responses

## Diversity, equity, and advocacy

### Jeremiah's concern

The ASCA *Ethical Standards for School Counselors* (2022a) calls for school counselors to "advocate for equal access to technology for all students." Jeremiah is rightfully concerned that many of the students in his school will not get access to this important information because some do not have home computers and some with home computers do not have Internet access.

### Help me to reach my potential

The correct response is "a." Jameel has not been given access to rigorous coursework despite his ability to succeed in advanced placement classes. School counselors are called to consider the student's ability and aptitude based on past academic performance and take future career and college desires into consideration when determining core and elective course placements.

### The fish market

The correct response is "c." The teacher's response is demonstrative of encapsulation and a lack of cultural sensitivity. The teacher is encapsulated in the Western culture whereby mathematics is taught in a formal educational institution and classroom. In Ghana, many children learn math in the community, through the elderly, and in trades such as marketing fish.

### Look at me when I am talking to you

The correct response is "d." The student assistance counselor is stereotyping. Generally speaking, the Asian culture views direct eye contact with elders and with those in authority as rude and confrontational. Maya's lack of eye contact could be related to culture and her way of showing the school counselor respect. However, it may not be related to culture; the alphabet counselor did not notice a lack of eye contact when speaking with Maya.

Consequently, some secondary schools divide school counselor load by alphabet, and those school counselors are often referred to as the alphabet counselor. Other schools may assign students to school counselors by grade level, in which case the school counselor is often referred to as the grade level counselor.

## An international brouhaha

The correct response is "a." Many, if not most, of the people of Indonesia practice the Muslim faith. This real-world case drives home the importance of spirituality and religion in shaping the practices and worldview of individuals, which must not be ignored in counseling and in the specialty of school counseling as well as in the teachings in our schools. Whether we are of the majority or minority population of a Western or non-Western culture, we need to learn about (or in this case, be advised on) the cultures with whom we are interacting to develop positive relations.

# Chapter 5 Simulation: The newbie

## Brief case description

You are a newly practicing elementary-school counselor developing your first classroom lesson for fifth graders.

## Section A: The newbie

One of the teachers informs you that the principal requires that special education students be pulled out of class to be with resource teachers for academic tutoring during the school counselor's classroom instruction. The teacher said the principal announced this practice during a faculty meeting a few years ago, as a way to provide special education students with extra academic support and improve test scores. What is your response?

(Select ONLY ONE in this section.)

| | |
|---|---|
| _____A—1. | Comply with the principal's requirements and develop the curriculum for the general education student population at that grade level |
| _____A—2. | Go to the principal and explain how this practice is not equitable and limits access to important programming for special education students |
| _____A—3. | Strongly encourage the teacher to keep special education students in class during school counselor delivered classroom instruction |
| _____A—4. | Talk to the special education teachers to ensure that classroom instruction delivered by the school counselor is a part of the students' IEP so that students are included in the lessons |

## Section B: The newbie

Now that school counselor delivered classroom lessons will be provided to both general education and special needs students, which of the following applies?
(Select as many as you consider indicated in this section.)

| _____B—1. | Curriculum should be developed based on the grade level of the student regardless of special needs status to ensure access to a rigorous, age-appropriate curriculum |
|---|---|
| _____B—2. | Curriculum should be modified to meet the special needs of each student in the classroom |
| _____B—3. | Because it is impossible to meet the special needs of all students, develop a curriculum that meets the needs of the majority |
| _____B—4. | Make every effort to ensure special needs students sit grouped together so that you can better monitor their understanding of the lesson's content |
| _____B—5. | Teachers need to inform school counselors of the needs of the special education students in their class because school counselors are not privy to this information |

## Section C: The newbie

One of the teachers, whose class is receiving your lesson, informs you that one of her students, Sabrina, will not be a part of the classroom lesson because she is an ESL student and her translator is out on the day of the lesson. Your response is:
(Select ONLY ONE in this section.)

| _____C—1. | All students need to be present for the lesson, so you will reschedule the lesson |
|---|---|
| _____C—2. | You will meet with Sabrina and her translator individually on another day to deliver the content of the lesson |
| _____C—3. | Have Sabrina participate in the lesson without her translator to ensure equity and access to all programming |

## 290 ■ Diversity, equity, and advocacy

| | |
|---|---|
| _____C—4. | Identify others in the building who can translate for Sabrina and see if he or she can translate on the day of the lesson while also talking to the principal about getting a substitute |
| _____C—5. | Tape the lesson so that Sabrina and her translator can watch it together when the translator returns |

## Section D: The newbie

During the lesson, a female student sitting by herself answers a question you posed. You notice that the student has an olive complexion, is very soft-spoken, and has an accent. Her response is uncommon, so you let her know that her response is interesting and offers a unique perspective. Another female student blurts out in a sarcastic tone, "Yea, you mean a weird perspective," and she and the girl next to her laugh along with the rest of the class. How would you respond?

(Select as many as you consider indicated in this section.)

| | |
|---|---|
| _____D—1. | Continue the lesson, careful not to give the girls an audience |
| _____D—2. | Stop the lesson and have the two girls removed from the class |
| _____D—3. | Reassure the student that the response she gave was appropriate and worthwhile |
| _____D—4. | Tell the girls that those comments are unacceptable and mean-spirited, redirecting the lesson to one of diversity appreciation, respect, and the power of words |
| _____D—5. | Continue the lesson, and ask to see the two girls after class |
| _____D—6. | Tell the girls that those comments are unacceptable and mean-spirited and then continue the planned lesson |
| _____D—7. | Come back the following week to teach a lesson on appreciation of diversity |

## Section E: The newbie

The day after the lesson, the student comes to you to thank you and lets you know that the girls have been nicer to her. She begins to share some family and personal issues that are bothering her. As a culturally sensitive counselor, how might you proceed?

(Select ONLY ONE in this section.)

| | |
|---|---|
| _____E—1. | Let the student know that you are not familiar with her culture, express your interest in learning about her culture, and ask her to educate you |
| _____E—2. | Sensitive not to make the student uncomfortable about her culture, just listen and reflect her feelings |
| _____E—3. | Ask her to identify her culture and to come back later, so you can find out more about her culture before she returns |
| _____E—4. | Let the student know that you are not familiar with her culture, so she should talk to her parents about her concerns to ensure cultural sensitivity |
| _____E—5. | Let her know that you are not familiar with her culture, and share with her how the dominant culture handles those types of issues |
| _____E—6. | Let her know that you are unfamiliar with her culture, but offer your thoughts and beliefs on the issues |

# Chapter 5 Simulation responses: The newbie

## Brief case description

You are a newly practicing elementary school counselor developing your first classroom lesson for fifth graders.

## Section A: The newbie

One of the teachers informs you that the principal requires that special education students be pulled out of the class to be with resource teachers for academic tutoring during the school counselor's lessons. The teacher said the principal announced this practice during a faculty meeting a few years ago, as a way to provide special education students with extra academic support and improve test scores. What is your response?

(Select ONLY ONE in this section.)

| | |
|---|---|
| A—1. | Comply with the principal's requirements and develop the curriculum for the general education student population at that grade level <br> No <br> School counselors advocate for equity and access in educational programming |
| A—2. | Go to the principal and explain how this practice is not equitable and limits access to important programming for special education students <br> Yes <br> School counselors advocate for equity and access in educational programming |
| A—3. | Strongly encourage the teacher to keep special education students in class during school counselor delivered classroom instruction <br> No <br> This puts the teacher in the position of disobeying the principal's directives |
| A—4. | Talk to the special education teachers to ensure classroom instruction by the school counselor is a part of the students' IEP so that students are included in the lessons <br> No <br> Access to general education programming for special education students does not need to be in their IEP. It is the right of all students to participate in this programming |

## Section B: The newbie

Now that school counselor delivered classroom lessons will be provided to both general education and special needs students, which of the following applies?

(Select as many as you consider indicated in this section.)

| B—1. | Curriculum should be developed based on the grade level of the student regardless of special needs status to ensure access to a rigorous, age-appropriate curriculum |
| --- | --- |
| | No |
| | The school counselor needs to consider the special accommodations of special needs students when planning and delivering classroom instruction |
| B—2. | Curriculum should be modified to meet the special needs of each student in the classroom |
| | Yes |
| | Like teachers, school counselors must follow students' IEP's, 504 Plans, and the accommodations afforded to those students whose primary language is not English. Also, there may be students in the class who are under a temporary medical plan (e.g., broken finger) |
| B—3. | Because it is impossible to meet the special needs of all students, develop a curriculum that meets the needs of the majority |
| | No |
| | School counselors create curriculum to meet the needs of all students to whom the curriculum is being implemented |
| B—4. | Make every effort to ensure special needs students sit grouped together so that you can better monitor their understanding of the lesson's content |
| | No |
| | School counselors and teachers do not segregate students based on ability, disability, gender, ethnicity, and so on |
| B—5. | Teachers need to inform school counselors of the needs of the special education students in their classes because school counselors are not privy to this information |
| | No |
| | School counselors may ask teachers to identify special needs students so that they can pull those students' IEP, 504 Plan, or ESL plans for compliance. Many school counselors have access to the special needs status of students in every classroom via student information systems |

## Section C: The newbie

One of the teachers, whose class is receiving your lesson, informs you that one of her students, Sabrina, will not be a part of the classroom lesson because she is an ESL student and her translator is out on the day of the lesson. Your response is:

(Select ONLY ONE in this section.)

| | |
|---|---|
| C—1. | All students need to be present for the lesson, so you will reschedule the lesson <br> No <br> All students cannot always be present for every classroom lesson |
| C—2. | You will meet with Sabrina and her translator individually on another day to deliver the content of the lesson <br> No <br> School counselors do not meet with students individually to make up a classroom instruction missed. The swollen counselor-to-student ratio makes it virtually impossible to provide this service to students unless mandated by student IEP and 504 Plan or is a part of Sabrina's LEP services plan |
| C—3. | Have Sabrina participate in the lesson without her translator to ensure equity and access to all programming <br> No <br> It is not equity and access to have Sabrina participate without the accommodations she needs to comprehend the material presented |
| C—4. | Identify others in the building who can translate for Sabrina and see if he or she can translate on the day of the lesson while also talking to the principal about getting a substitute <br> Yes <br> Advocating on behalf of the student for her rightful accommodations in order to access programming is an important function of the school counselor |
| C—5. | Tape the classroom lesson so that Sabrina and her translator can watch it together when the translator returns <br> No <br> Viewing the lesson as a spectator is not the same as interacting with other students and being a part of the lesson. However, in the event that a translator is not made available to Sabrina, then this would be an alternative to her missing the lesson entirely |

## Section D: The newbie

During the classroom lesson, a female student sitting by herself answers a question you posed. You notice that the student has an olive complexion, is very soft-spoken, and has an accent. Her response is uncommon, so you let her know that her response is interesting and offers a unique perspective. Another female student blurts out in a sarcastic tone, "Yea, you mean a weird perspective," and she and the girl next to her laugh along with the rest of the class. How would you respond?

(Select as many as you consider indicated in this section.)

| D—1. | Continue the lesson careful not to give the girls an audience<br>No<br>This is bully behavior and needs to be addressed |
|---|---|
| D—2. | Stop the lesson and have the two girls removed from the class<br>No<br>This action would not teach the girls appropriate behavior |
| D—3. | Reassure the student that the response she gave was appropriate and worthwhile<br>Yes<br>This is appropriate in addition to intervention in the moment |
| D—4. | Tell the girls that those comments are unacceptable and mean-spirited, redirecting the lesson to one of diversity appreciation, respect, and the power of words<br>Yes<br>Use this as an immediate opportunity (a teachable moment) to demonstrate a zero tolerance for bullying and to promote a climate of compassion and acceptance |
| D—5. | Continue the lesson, and ask to see the two girls after class<br>No<br>This is a teachable moment for all, and counselors address behavior but not as a disciplinarian. |
| D—6. | Tell the girls that those comments are unacceptable and mean-spirited and then continue the planned lesson<br>No<br>Chances are, the girls already know that what they are saying and doing is bullying. Continuing with your lesson as planned after pointing out the obvious will not eliminate the problem or appeal to the support of the group or to the human compassion of the "mean" girls |

## Diversity, equity, and advocacy

| D—7. | Come back the following week to teach a lesson on appreciation of diversity |
| --- | --- |
| | No |
| | The teachable moment will have passed. School counselors are flexible. You may be able to cover your intended lesson as well as the unexpected lesson |

## Section E: The newbie

The day after the lesson, the student comes to you to thank you and lets you know that the girls have been nicer to her. She begins to share some family and personal issues that are bothering her. As a culturally sensitive counselor, how might you proceed?

(Select ONLY ONE in this section.)

| E—1. | Let the student know that you are not familiar with her culture, express your interest in learning about her culture, and ask her to educate you |
| --- | --- |
| | Yes |
| | This is the culturally sensitive response. The student will recognize that you want to help and appreciate your honesty |
| E—2. | Sensitive not to make the student uncomfortable about her culture, just listen and reflect her feelings |
| | No |
| | This will only take you so far, and you risk the student misinterpreting your lack of knowledge about her culture as not being genuine or worse |
| E—3. | Ask her to identify her culture and to come back later, so you can find out more about her culture before she returns |
| | No |
| | The student is asking for assistance now, and it may have taken much courage to come to you on her own. Now is the moment |
| E—4. | Let the student know that you are not familiar with her culture, so she should talk to her parents about her concerns to ensure cultural sensitivity |
| | No |
| | The student came to you, not her parents. She may not want her parents to know because what she is experiencing is contrary to deeply held cultural beliefs |

| E—5. | Let her know that you are not familiar with her culture, and share with her how the dominant culture handles those types of issues |
| --- | --- |
| | No |
| | You are espousing your personal beliefs onto your client. This is against our code of ethics |
| E—6. | Let her know that you are unfamiliar with her culture, but offer your thoughts and beliefs on the issues |
| | No |
| | You are espousing your personal beliefs onto your client. This is against our code of ethics |

## Chapter 5 Guided reflection

Why is it important that school counselors be multiculturally competent?

How does a school counselor become multiculturally competent and maintain multicultural competency?

What does it mean to be a culturally sensitive school counselor?

What is one of the best ways to learn about the culture of your client/student?

Compare and contrast acculturation, assimilation, encapsulation, and stereotyping.

*Diversity, equity, and advocacy* ■ 299

Reducing the likelihood of issues associated with *encapsulation* in an effort to provide students from diverse backgrounds with optimal learning environments calls for a keen sense of one's cultural self and the affirmation of others' cultures. Name at least two strategies for accomplishing this.

Should school counselors address the religious beliefs and spirituality of students in public school settings? If so, when would this be appropriate? If so, how might a school counselor do this in a culturally sensitive, legal, and ethical way? What school counseling program delivery methods would be used and how?

What does research say about school counseling and the topic of religion and spirituality in the public-school setting?

Define the following constructs as they relate to school counseling:

Advocacy


Equity

## Diversity, equity, and advocacy

Access




Attainment




Achievement




Name two types of advocacy competency.




Give one example of a strategy to address each: 1) access gap, 2) attainment gap, and 3) achievement gap.




Name three ways school counselors can help to remove common barriers to parents' participation in school activities.

## Chapter 6

# Leadership

ASCA (2019a) underscores the role of leadership in building a systems-focused comprehensive school counseling program, calling on school counselors to be leaders who positively impact student learning outcomes and holistic student development. As leaders, school counselors build strong foundations that clearly define what students will learn as a result of the program (2019a). School counselors accomplish this by attaching program activities to standards, namely the ASCA Mindsets & Behaviors (ASCA, 2021) as well as core academic standards and collaborating with others toward this end. ASCA supports the following characteristics and practices to operationally define school counselor leadership (Young & Kneale, 2013):

- Use multiple strategies and resources to solve problems.
- Build partnerships and engage all stakeholders.
- Navigate through the politics of systems.
- Advocate for equitable services for marginalized and all students with a courageous stance.
- Excel in the use of appropriate accountability strategies to challenge status quo.
- Persuade colleagues and build consensus.
- Identify and accomplish goals with confidence.
- Exceed expectations when accomplishing tasks.
- Accept the responsibility to lead.
- Acquire a leadership mindset.

Building a capacity for leadership begins during the education and training of school counselors and continues throughout the career of a school counselor in the form of continued education, workshops,

DOI: 10.4324/9781032634500-6

networking, and conference participation. Cashwell and others (2013) surveyed members of ACA identifying the following five characteristics and practices that are recommended for building counselor leadership:

- Resourceful problem solving.
- Systemic collaboration.
- Interpersonal influence.
- Social justice advocacy.
- Professional efficacy.

School counselor leaders know how to clearly define school counselor roles and functions and know and use the language of the profession. School counselors are able to clearly articulate their vision and beliefs and illustrate how those vision and beliefs align with the mission of schools and drive their leadership philosophy. Visionary school counselor leaders are reflective practitioners who engage in self-examination on a regular basis in order to identify areas of strength and areas needing improving in order to build leadership abilities.

As leaders, school counselors support a comprehensive school counseling program by: (1) developing vision and mission statements that align with that of the school, (2) using data to create equitable services for all students, (3) skillfully delivering direct and indirect services, (4) reflecting on the outcomes of services delivered in meeting the needs of all students, improving programming, and promoting systemic change, and (5) engaging in continuous self-improvement with professional development and continuous evaluation.

In the throes of a leadership identity crisis, our profession is blazing the trail and making progress toward clearly establishing a profile for school counselor leadership (Mason, Ockerman, Chen-Hayes, 2013; Ockerman, Patrikakou & Hollenbeck, 2015). Once we can look at leadership as an honor versus a responsibility, perhaps we can come to fully embrace our role as leader. Many of us lead every day and do not even realize that we are already leaders! John Quincy Adams summed it up nicely: *If your actions inspire others to dream more, learn more, do more, and become more, you are a leader.*

## Leadership attributes, styles, and practices

ASCA provides the following list of leadership characteristics and practices indicative of an effective school counselor leader capable of promoting change and implementing a successful comprehensive school counseling program:

- Visionary thinking.
- Challenging inequities.
- Shared decision making.
- Collaborative processing.
- Modeling excellence.
- A courageous stance.

Triumphant school counseling leadership has been linked to enhanced student learning and includes specific attributes and skills, that can be used to supplement those named by ASCA (Young, Dollarhide, & Baughman, 2015). These skills and attributes include:

- A clear vision (there's that *vision* word again—must be important).
- A realistic, goal-focused plan of action.
- Clearly defined school counselor roles.
- Ability to build a support system.
- Ability to work through and grow from resistance.
- A sense of responsibility for program effectiveness.
- Ability to encourage, motivate, and empower others.
- Actively seeking out supervision.
- Willingness to continue to develop leadership skills.
- Tackling tasks with determination.

In addition to possessing specific leadership attributes, leadership style is important. Erford (2019) names four styles of leadership found to be present in effective school counselors: (1) structural leadership, (2) human resources leadership, (3) political leadership, and (4) symbolic leadership. Structural leadership involves creating a plan for change and an approach for putting that plan into action. Human resources leadership is built upon the construct of empowerment. School counselors leading from this perspective seek to motivate and inspire students toward career and academic achievement and social/emotional well-being. Political leadership relies on the school counselor's ability to understand systems processes and effectively compromise and advocate using persuasive, convincing arguments with those in powerful positions. Last, symbolic leadership involves effectively communicating a vision of change/growth to all, including those in powerful positions. Clearly, a combination of leadership styles could be most helpful, enabling the school counselor leader to not only help students directly, but indirectly as well by winning the support of others both within and outside of the school.

Traditionally, school counselors have practiced from a *transformational leadership* framework, whereby the school counselor is a visionary acting singularly as change agent endeavors to *transform* the system by understanding and respecting the unique roles of other stakeholders both within and outside of the school. The school counselor as transformational leader seeks to influence and inspire these important others toward a common goal. More recently school counselors have begun to practice from a *participatory* and/or *distributed* leadership framework, which is much more collaborative with a focus on democracy instead of a single leader tapping into the plethora of skills of the collective, who share responsibilities, bringing diverse backgrounds, experience, and perspectives to the table as a leadership body. This group may include general and special education teachers, administrators, parents, and specialization personnel such as the diagnostician, social worker, psychologist, nurse, speech therapist, academic testing coordinator, and specialties within the school's community. Like transformational leadership, *servant leadership* entails a single school counselor acting as a shepherd using integrity, empathy, and humility, to empower and guide the flock toward becoming servant leaders as well. Finally, there is *transformative leadership*, which focuses on the outcomes of leadership versus the other frameworks which focus on process. Transformative leadership is most aligned with the ASCA National Model in its focus on equity and social justice with the inclusion of those who have been traditionally minoritized (Goodman-Scott & Ziomek-Daigle, 2022; Shields, Dollarhide & Young, 2017).

Regardless of school counseling leadership approaches it is key to focus on school climate, community, and collaboration, and to understand the importance of practicing within the professional hierarchy of the system. That is, school counselors remain mindful of the educational and political forces involved at the school and community levels.

School counselor leadership practices include providing educational programming to both parents and teachers, who are the ones, after all, that spend the most time with students. Offering topics to parents and teachers not limited to identifying signs of suicide ideation and homicide ideation, substance use/abuse, addiction, cutting, abuse/neglect, eating disorders and early signs/symptoms of potentially serious emotional-social behavioral issues aids in meeting the desired outcomes of the school counseling program and promotes student wellbeing, student-teacher relations, and family relations and wellness.

> **PROFESSIONAL DEVELOPMENT**
>
> A high-school counselor is planning to implement a teacher workshop during staff development day on the topic of bullying. The principal has announced that the workshop is mandatory, due to the high incidence of bullying in the school. The teachers are complaining that they should not be required to attend a workshop when they are not experiencing any problems with bullying in their classrooms and when it is not related to teaching and learning, but the "job of the school counselor." The school counselor asks the principal if she can speak during the next faculty meeting to let the teachers know a bit more about the bullying workshop that will be presented during staff development. The school counselor shares with the teachers the hidden aspects of victims of bullying, and how it is often the "silent killer" that only teachers can detect given the substantial amount of time they spend with the students in their classes and in light of the special relationship teachers have with their students. The school counselor goes on to say that the workshop will offer some ways to identify and intervene on behalf of these students and involve the school counselor so that teachers can get back to the important task of teaching. Which leadership strategy is the school counselor using with the teachers?
>
> a. Role modeling.
> b. Overcoming resistance.
> c. Empowering.
> d. All of the above.

Research has identified parent workshops as highly effective prevention and intervention strategies in the schools. Parent education has been linked to heightened involvement in the schools and improved parent–child relations (Wright & Stegelin, 2002). Parenting style is critical to child and adolescent development as discussed in Chapter 3. Therefore, educating parents on the differing types of parenting styles in relation to developmental outcomes is an essential topic for consideration by the school counselor when preparing a topic agenda for parent education. Additionally, parents often lack the resources to fully understand the many services that are available to support them as they seek to meet the unique needs of their children and raise a healthy child to become a well-adjusted contributing member of society. Improving the life of a student that extends into the home supports the entire school community.

## Use of technology

The technological literacy of school counselors is becoming increasingly important in order to: (1) meet the demands of the information age, (2) enhance the learning environment, (3) effectively manage and promote the school counseling program, and (4) to promote the safe use of technology by students, parents, and teachers. Recognizing that counselors need to be leaders in the use of technology, ACES (2007) has identified twelve technology competencies that should be covered during master's level counselor education programs (see Table 6.1).

The use of technology may well be the mechanism that determines the level of success of school counseling programs and student learning outcomes. School counselors use technology to:

- Deliver education and special education accommodations.
- Communicate with the masses.
- Share and disseminate information.
- Coordinate activities.
- Consult and collaborate.
- Advocate for students, families, and the profession.
- Broaden service delivery.
- Expedite tasks.
- Simplify data analysis and reporting.
- Fortify accountability efforts.
- Provide supervision and mentoring.
- Engage in video conferencing.
- Conduct research.
- Participate in professional development.

**Table 6.1 Technology Competencies**

| | |
|---|---|
| 1. | Be able to use productivity software to develop Web pages, word processing documents (letters, reports), basic databases, spreadsheets, and other forms of documentation or materials applicable to practice |
| 2. | Be able to use such audiovisual equipment as video recorders, audio recorders, projection equipment, video conferencing equipment, playback units, and other applications available through education and training experiences |
| 3. | Be able to acquire, use, and develop multimedia software (i.e., PowerPoint/keynote presentations, animated graphics, digital audio, digital video) applicable to education, training, and practice |
| 4. | Be able to use statistical software to organize and analyze data |
| 5. | Be able to use computerized and/or Internet-based testing, diagnostic, and career decision-making programs with clients |
| 6. | Be able to use e-mail |
| 7. | Be able to help clients search for and evaluate various types of counseling-related information via the Internet, including information about careers, employment opportunities, educational and training opportunities, financial assistance/scholarships, treatment procedures, and social and personal information |
| 8. | Be able to subscribe, participate in, and sign off on counseling-related listservs or other Internet-based professional communication applications |
| 9. | Be able to access and use counseling-related research databases |
| 10. | Be able to use the Internet to locate, evaluate, and use continuing education, professional development, and supervision options in counseling |
| 11. | Be able to perform basic computer operation and maintenance tasks |
| 12. | Be knowledgeable about legal, ethical, and efficacy issues associated with delivery of counseling services via the Internet |

*Source*: Adapted from Association for Counselor Education and Supervision (2007). *Technical competencies for counselor education students: Recommended guidelines for program development.* https://acesonline.net/wpcontent/uploads/2018/11/2007-ACES-TechnologyCompetencies.pdf

In addition to mastering the use of technology for enhancing student development, academic achievement, and a comprehensive school counseling program. School counselors lead the charge in providing students, parents, and teachers with information pertaining to the safe use of technology. This is particularly critical in light of the increased prevalence of cyberbullying, seduction by Internet predators, and the misuse of cell phones. *Internet safety and cyberbully* is thoroughly covered in Chapter 3 along with the school counselor's responsibility for providing students, parents, and teachers with education related to the potential threats posed when using technology to include cell phones.

## School counseling websites

School counselors are encouraged to make use of technology to develop a presence on the Internet. Leadership entails taking the technology bull by the horns to create a departmental website and/or an independent professional website that provides information about you as a professional and the school counseling program. This is a cost-effective way to get information and resources to parents, students, and the community. When advertising your website remember your ethical mandate to identify ways that students and parents without Internet access can get this valuable information. Ideally, school counseling department websites communicate:

- Information about the comprehensive school counseling program.
- Information related to the counseling process, including referral, signed consent, and confidentiality.
- School counselor roles and functions.
- Links to ASCA's ethical standards and professional competencies.
- The school counselors' education, training, and credentials.
- Information regarding professional associations.
- Current trends and developments in the profession (the ASCA National Model, TSCI).
- Mission statements and program goals that clearly connect school counseling to the academic achievement mission of schools.
- Program outcome data, including efforts to close the achievement gap.
- Parent, student, teacher, and community resources.
- Opportunities for school involvement.

Information and resources listed on school counseling websites have the potential to enhance student development and well-being and help to support healthy schools, homes, and communities. Some students are reluctant to ask for help and do not actively seek out support. It is the professional responsibility of school counselors as leaders in the school to be creative in getting meaningful information to stakeholders for sound decision making, problem solving, and family support (Nelson, Tarabochia, & Koltz, 2014). Web-based information and resources might include information on:

- Crisis response information.
- Support programs.
- Parenting programs.
- Tutoring contacts and test preparation.
- Substance use/abuse.
- Eating disorders.
- Counseling services.
- Problem solving, communication, and conflict resolution.
- Self-mutilation.
- Suicide and homicide ideation.
- Financial aid and scholarships.
- Summer programs and study abroad.
- Special events.
- Warning signs of troubled youth.

## School, family, and community partnerships

School administrators across the nation have made tremendous progress in promoting community and school relations, particularly through the AASA Stand Up for Public Education call to action. Such partnerships multiply the players and broadens the playing field, resulting in more funding and increased material and human resources.

Well-planned and organized school-family-community partnerships help school counselors to meet demanding student caseloads while building the foundation upon which systemic change can be realized and positive student outcomes are achieved. School counselors are leaders who work both independently and interdependently with important others within and outside the school community on a daily basis to promote the academic, career, and social/emotional development of students.

## ASCA Position on The School Counselor and School-Family-Community Partnerships

School counselors have an essential and unique role in promoting, facilitating and advocating for collaboration with parents/guardians and community stakeholders. These collaborations are an important aspect of implementing school counseling programs that promote all students' successful academic, career and social/emotional development.

*Position statement adopted 2010; revised 2016, 2022*

Parents often remain an untapped resource in schools where human resources are generally limited. School counselors are encouraged to establish or tap into a school-based *Parent–Teacher–Student Resource Center* (PTSRC). PTSRCs provide information and resources that promote student development and family well-being. Who better than parent volunteers to oversee daily PTSRC operations. Parents, familiar with the community, are in an ideal position to coordinate requests for information and maintain the informational flow. Many parents want to get in the game but for a variety of reasons do not step up to the plate. Extend an invitation to parents and be specific about the position for which they are being recruited—with the bases loaded and the batter up, there is sure to be a home run!

In addition to parents, the level of success of the school counseling program is dependent upon the involvement and support of community businesses and agencies. These are your educational soul mates—individuals and agencies impacting, or impacted by, the schools. Many school systems have institutionalized the soul mate philosophy, adopting Partners-in-Education programs. These programs are often facilitated by school counselor leaders who link the school to specific local organizations and businesses. The organization unites with the school to support school improvement and student learning by providing invaluable human, financial, and consumable resources. Organizations (e.g., retail stores, banks, hospitals, fire stations, and restaurants) proudly display certificates of appreciation from the schools they support, which helps their business to prosper as parents and members of the community offer patronage in appreciation.

# Systemic change

In addition to possessing leadership skills, mastering the ability to be a collaborative leader is essential to systemic change that leads to enhanced student learning and well-being as well as strong, safe school environments that exude the scent of community. The collaborative concept of leadership is akin to the transformational leadership that positions the leader in an egalitarian role with power shared by other stakeholders. This view of leadership is collaborative and supports student learning and aids in meeting the mental health needs of students, aligning with contemporary school counseling practices that support a systems-focused comprehensive school counseling program (Capp, 2015).

Collaborative leaders possess teambuilding skills, serving as community and school liaisons who are able to establish and maintain cohesive relationships with important others in a student's life. Teambuilding strategies may include (Dougherty, 2013):

- Conflict resolution.
- Mediation.
- Empowerment.
- Cross-cultural training.
- Analysis of member interaction.
- Facilitation.
- Coordination.
- Problem solving.
- Brainstorming.
- Encouragement.
- Negotiation.

### TEAMBUILDING

You are a school counselor collaborating with parents to establish a parent resource center at your school. Two of the parents are having a significant disagreement, which is interfering with progress. You are engaging your conflict resolution skills by providing mediation services to these parents with the hope that they will be able to negotiate a resolve. Conflict resolution, mediation, and negotiation

> are teambuilding skills that are helpful during the process of collaboration. Other team-building skills identified as helpful are:
>
> a. Brainstorming.
> b. Empowerment.
> c. Cross-cultural training.
> d. All of the above.

In an effort to enhance teambuilding, school counselors participate in the school leadership team invaluable to gaining a greater understanding of the subsystems operating within the school as well as areas of strength and challenge related to the school's unique student population and climate. Membership on the school leadership team allows school counselors to have a voice on important issues impacting the students and community we serve.

School counselors are agents for systems change, identifying groups of students (versus a select few) who are not being successful and intervening to remove obstacles or provide additional support to promote success. Toward this end, leadership skills and a mindset that embraces the constructs of advocacy, equity, collaboration, consultation, and referral as well as an active passion toward identifying and closing access, attainment, and achievement gaps is essential. Serving as an agent for systemic change also necessitates an understanding of strategic planning and the principles of systems theory discussed in Chapter 4.

Schools are both systems and subsystems in a web of interconnectedness that makes virtually everyone a stakeholder and a client. Systemic school counseling programs are those that encompass programming that is purposeful in its intentions to provide prevention and intervention to the entire student body and other stakeholders within and outside of the school.

The ASCA National Model exemplifies such a systems-focused model. Only through systems-focused practices can the school counselor fully eliminate access, achievement, and attainment gaps.

Leadership that views schools through the lens of the systems perspective acknowledges that important others with whom the student interacts have a tremendous influence on the student's career and academic development and personal, social, physical, and emotional well-being. These powerful interactions transcend the family system as the student and family interact with school personnel, all of whom interact with the community. School counselors interact collaboratively within the varied systems with which students interact to influence *each part* of the system in order to bring about systemic change. In this regard, we are systems hackers. Understanding the profound impact of the interactions that influence an individual is paramount to understanding the individual—a good leader seeks to understand more so than to be understood.

# Chapter 6 Case conceptualization responses

## Leadership

### *Professional development*

The correct response is "b." The teachers are displaying resistance to the idea of mandatory training on a topic that they perceive as unrelated to teaching. The school counselor, in a non-confrontational manner, helps teachers to understand how the topic of bullying is connected to the role of teacher and the importance of that role.

### *Teambuilding*

The correct response is "d." All of the strategies listed have been identified as helpful in the collaboration process.

Leadership ■ 315

# Chapter 6 Simulation: School counselor leader

## Brief case description

You are a middle-school counselor whose principal has requested that you assist him in designing interview questions that may help him to hire a school counselor leader to replace one of your fellow school counselors who has decided to go back to school full-time to get his doctoral degree.

### Section A: School counselor leader

First, your principal asks you to identify a few leadership practices that are indicative of an effective school counselor.
   (Select as many as you consider indicated in this section.)

| | | |
|---|---|---|
| _____ | A—1. | Models excellence |
| _____ | A—2. | Engages in individual processing |
| _____ | A—3. | Does not challenge inequitable processes that upsets status quo |
| _____ | A—4. | Challenges processes that are inequitable |
| _____ | A—5. | Engages in shared decision making |
| _____ | A—6. | Engages in visionary thinking |
| _____ | A—7. | Creates clear mission statements that are distinct from the school's mission statement |

### Section B: School counselor leader

Your principal asks you to confirm the percentage of time that a school counselor should be spending in the delivery of both direct and indirect student services. The following response is accurate in accordance with the ASCA National Model.

(Select ONLY ONE in this section.)

| | |
|---|---|
| _____ B—1. | 80% |
| _____ B—2. | 20% |
| _____ B—3. | 50% |
| _____ B—4. | 75% |
| _____ B—5. | 25% |

## Section C: School counselor leader

You suggest that the new school counselor be responsible for developing and maintaining a web site that you were in the process of creating. Your principal asks what types of things are appropriate for inclusion on the school counseling website.

(Select as many as you consider indicated in this section.)

| | |
|---|---|
| _____ C—1. | Program outcome data |
| _____ C—2. | Students' grades |
| _____ C—3. | School counselor roles and functions |
| _____ C—4. | Most promising teachers and their areas of expertise |
| _____ C—5. | Parent, teacher, student, community resources |

## Section D: School counselor leader

The principal likes the idea of a school counseling program website, and also wants the new school counselor to serve primarily as the student assistance counselor, responding to the immediate needs of students. The two delivery methods critical to this position would include:

(Select ONLY ONE in this section.)

| | | |
|---|---|---|
| _____ | D—1. | Individual counseling and academic planning |
| _____ | D—2. | Small group counseling and core school counseling curriculum group activities |
| _____ | D—3. | Individual counseling and classroom instruction |
| _____ | D—4. | Individual counseling and small group counseling |
| _____ | D—5. | Group counseling and classroom instruction |

## Section E: School counselor leader

In addition to specific school counselor leadership practices, the principal asks as to whether there are specific characteristics counseling literature and research has identified as essential to supporting an effective comprehensive school counseling program:

(Select as many as you consider indicated in this section.)

| | | |
|---|---|---|
| _____ | E—1. | Visionary thinking |
| _____ | E—2. | Careful not to challenge inequities |
| _____ | E—3. | Shared decision making |
| _____ | E—4. | Collaborative processing |
| _____ | E—5. | A courageous stance |

# Chapter 6 Simulation responses: School counselor leader

## Brief case description

You are a middle-school counselor whose principal has requested that you assist him in designing interview questions that may help him to hire a school counselor leader to replace one of your fellow school counselors who has decided to go back to school full-time to get his doctoral degree.

## *Section A: School counselor leader*

First, your principal asks you to name a few leadership practices that have been identified via counseling literature and research as indicative of an effective school counselor.

(Select as many as you consider indicated in this section.)

| A—1. | Models excellence<br>Yes<br>School counselors model that which they teach/desire to develop in others |
|---|---|
| A—2. | Engages in individual processing<br>No<br>School counselors engage in collaborative processing |
| A—3. | Does not challenge inequitable processes that upsets status quo<br>No<br>School counselors courageously challenge processes that are not equitable in a professional manner understanding that it may upset the status quo |
| A—4. | Challenges processes that are inequitable<br>Yes |
| A—5. | Engages in shared decision making<br>Yes<br>School counselors invite other stakeholders into the decision-making process |

| A—6. | Engages in visionary thinking<br>Yes<br>School counselors are visionaries, who fully articulate the school counseling program vision |
|---|---|
| A—7. | Creates clear mission statements that are distinct from the school's mission statement<br>No<br>School counselors create clear mission statements that are aligned and support the school's mission statement |

## Section B: School counselor leader

Your principal asks you to confirm the percentage of time that a school counselor should be spending in the delivery of both direct and indirect student services. The following response is accurate in accordance with the ASCA National Model.

(Select ONLY ONE in this section.)

| B—1. | 80%<br>Yes |
|---|---|
| B—2. | 20%<br>No |
| B—3. | 50%<br>No |
| B—4. | 75%<br>No |
| B—5. | 25%<br>No |

## Section C: School counselor leader

You suggest that the new school counselor be responsible for developing and maintaining a web site that you were in the process of creating. Your principal asks what types of things are appropriate for inclusion on the school counseling website.

(Select as many as you consider indicated in this section.)

| | |
|---|---|
| C—1. | Program outcome data <br> Yes <br> Reporting program outcome data on the website allows stakeholders to review the effectiveness of the school counseling program. Include efforts to close the achievement gap as well |
| C—2. | Students' grades <br> No <br> School counselors to not post students grades to the website |
| C—3. | School counselor roles and functions <br> Yes <br> It is important to de-mystify the school counseling process. Educating important others on the roles and functions of the school counseling, including training and credentials helps to improve program understanding and supports your qualifications to work with students, parents, teachers, and the community |
| C—4. | Most promising teachers and their areas of expertise <br> No <br> School counselors do not elevate one teacher over another and leaves it to the teachers to create their own internal/external web pages |
| C—5. | Parent, teacher, student, community resources <br> Yes <br> School counselors are resource agents who provide information and referral resources on a variety of topics related to academic, career, and social/emotional development. As leaders, school counselors provide credible resources that aid stakeholders in sound decision making, problem solving, and family support |

## Section D: School counselor leader

The principal likes the idea of a school counseling program website, and also wants the new school counselor to serve primarily as the student assistance counselor, responding to the immediate needs of students. The two delivery methods critical to this position would include:

(Select ONLY ONE in this section.)

| D—1. | Individual counseling and academic planning |
| --- | --- |
| | No |
| | Individual counseling is a responsive service that would be widely used by a student assistance counselor intending to meet the immediate needs of students and to intervene in crisis situations. Academic planning, however, is more preventative and used to aid students in development academic, post-secondary career plans, and life goals |
| D—2. | Small group counseling and core school counseling curriculum group activities |
| | No |
| | Small group counseling is a responsive service that would be widely used by a counselor intending to meet the immediate needs of students and to intervene in crisis situations. Group activities are part of the core school counseling curriculum that is provided to all students as part of prevention vs. intervention |
| D—3. | Individual counseling and classroom instruction |
| | No |
| | Individual counseling is a responsive service that would be widely used by a counselor intending to meet the immediate needs of students and to intervene in crisis situations. Classroom instruction is part of the core school counseling curriculum that is provided to all students as part of prevention vs. intervention |
| D—4. | Individual counseling and small group counseling |
| | Yes |
| | Both individual counseling and small group counseling are responsive service that would be widely used by a counselor intending to meet the immediate needs of students and to intervene in crisis situations |
| D—5. | Group counseling and classroom instruction |
| | No |
| | Group counseling is a responsive service that would be widely used by a counselor intending to meet the immediate needs of students and to intervene in crisis situations. Classroom instruction is part of the core school counseling curriculum that is provided to all students as part of prevention vs. intervention |

## Section E: School counselor leader

In addition to specific school counselor leadership practices, the principal asks as to whether there are specific characteristics counseling literature and research has identified as essential to supporting an effective comprehensive school counseling program:

(Select as many as you consider indicated in this section.)

| | |
|---|---|
| E—1. | Visionary thinking<br>Yes |
| E—2. | Careful not to challenge inequities<br>No. School counselor leaders absolutely challenge inequities using appropriate channels and professionalism |
| E—3. | Shared decision making<br>Yes |
| E—4. | Collaborative processing<br>Yes |
| E—5. | A courageous stance<br>Yes |

# Chapter 6 Guided reflection

Define leadership and describe its significance in school counseling.

Connect school counseling leadership and learning.

What is the role of leadership in promoting systemic change?

Name two leadership attributes/practices named by ASCA as indicative of the effective school counselor who is capable of promoting change.

Name and describe the four leadership styles of effective school counselors.

Summarize how school counselors make use of technology to enhance professional practices and student learning. Create an example of an activity to illustrate (1) a school counselor making use of technology to enhance professional practices, and (2) a school counselor making use of technology to improve student learning.

## 324 ■ Leadership

Identify the importance of professional school counseling websites and identify the recommended information for website inclusion.

Discuss the school counselor's responsibility with regard to the students' use of technology.

Discuss the importance of school, family, and community partnerships.

Name partnership strategies that may result in improved academic achievement and positive student development.

Name at least four teambuilding strategies used by collaborative leaders.

What is a PTSRC?

# Full-length practice exam

## Full-length practice exam Simulation One: *College readiness*

### Brief case description

You are a high-school counselor reviewing student surveys that were collected from tenth- and 11th-grade students, which indicate that 85 percent of the students in these grades plan to attend a four-year college. However, an analysis of 10th- and 11th-grade academic performance records reveals that only 35 percent currently have the academic standing needed to get into college.

### *Section A: College readiness*

What information would help you to identify that which may be contributing to this gap?

(Select as many as you consider indicated in this section.)

| | | |
|---|---|---|
| _____ | A—1. | Access to enrichment activities |
| _____ | A—2. | Promotion and retention rates |
| _____ | A—3. | Hobbies |
| _____ | A—4. | Course enrollment patterns |
| _____ | A—5. | Time spent on the computer |
| _____ | A—6. | Standardized test scores |
| _____ | A—7. | Attendance rates |

| | |
|---|---|
| _____ A—8. | College application completion |
| _____ A—9. | Career assessment participation |
| _____ A—10. | FAFSA completion |
| _____ A—11. | Course completion rates |
| _____ A—12. | Parent participation rates |

## Section B: College readiness

What types of programming or strategies might you consider to help students to understand the connection between grades and getting into college and to close the gap between college goals and college readiness?

(Select as many as you consider indicated in this section.)

| | |
|---|---|
| _____ B—1. | Classroom lessons on career planning |
| _____ B—2. | Student participation in a small group on study skills |
| _____ B—3. | College visitations/field trips |
| _____ B—4. | Individual academic advising |
| _____ B—5. | SAT and ACT preparation program |
| _____ B—6. | Peer tutoring program |
| _____ B—7. | Development of a career and academic plan |
| _____ B—8. | Encourage participation in SCA |
| _____ B—9. | Parent involvement programs |

## Section C: College readiness

During your analysis of the school data, you find that there are high numbers of tenth-grade students failing the same required English class taught by the same teacher for the past three years. You pointed this out to your school counseling director, who said she has talked to the teacher several times about this, but the teacher just gets angry. What would be the best course of action at this time?

(Select ONLY ONE in this section.)

| ____ C—1. | Ask for a meeting with the teacher and principal |
| ____ C—2. | Try to talk with the teacher again |
| ____ C—3. | Bring this data to the attention of the principal |
| ____ C—4. | Ask for a meeting with the teacher and school counseling director |
| ____ C—5. | Do not fight this battle |
| ____ C—6. | Encourage students to take a different English teacher during scheduling |

## Section D: College readiness

Further data analysis reveals an alarming number of absences among the tenth- and 11th-grade student population. After talking to these grade level teachers, you find that many students are performing poorly or failing classes due to excessive absences that result in missing homework and failing course tests, although they are passing the standardized tests. The majority of absences do not qualify for extenuating circumstances. What might you want to consider as possible courses of action to address this issue?

(Select as many as you consider indicated in this section.)

| ____ D—1. | Phone calls to parents from the attendance office after a specified number of days |
| ____ D—2. | Phone calls to parents from the teacher after a specified number of days |
| ____ D—3. | Send letters home after a specified number of days |
| ____ D—4. | Grade level assemblies to stress the importance of attendance to academic success and college entrance |
| ____ D—5. | Administer a needs assessment to the tenth-and 11th-grade students asking them to identify perceived obstacles to school attendance and to provide suggestions to improve attendance |
| ____ D—6. | Develop harsher penalties for unexcused absences |
| ____ D—7. | Strengthen attendance policy with fewer absences allowed each year |

## Section E: College readiness

Further analysis revealed a pattern. Hundreds of students identified needs at home as the reason for missing so much school. Most of those reasons included after school jobs to help parent(s) pay bills and staying home to take care of younger siblings while the parent worked. You also find out that these students do not have materials at home to complete homework and study (e.g., calculators, paper, pencils, study space). These students do not have a home computer, printer, or Internet access in order to conduct required research and type papers. It is difficult, if not impossible, for these students to go to the library due to demands at home. Transportation is also an issue if they miss the bus. What can you, the school counselor, do to help these students?

(Select as many as you consider indicated in this section.)

| | | |
|---|---|---|
| _____ | E—1. | Reduce homework for these students |
| _____ | E—2. | Sponsor school-wide drives for school supplies |
| _____ | E—3. | Work with community agencies to identify resources to help parents with child care and financial burdens |
| _____ | E—4. | Coordinate partnerships with local businesses to provide supplies |
| _____ | E—5. | Provide after school homework assistance for these students |
| _____ | E—6. | Work with the principal to develop an academic enrichment class as a resource/elective course or to develop a component to an existing course with content that would help these and other students prepare for post-high-school opportunities |
| _____ | E—7. | Give a list of student names needing school supplies to local media to "adopt a student" |
| _____ | E—8. | Do not require homework for these special needs students |
| _____ | E—9. | Apply for a grant to assist students in your school in "achieving the college dream" |

# Full-length practice exam Simulation Two: School violence

## Brief case description

A teacher comes to you, the eighth-grade middle-school counselor, because she has three male students in her science class who are entirely disengaged, quiet, and only hang out with each other. She saw them at lunch today sitting only with each other and not eating lunch. No other students were anywhere near them. The students dress in black most every day and routinely appear tired and unkempt. A student observed the teacher gazing at the three male students during lunch and said, to the teacher, "I hope someone looks more closely at those guys-they are so scary and make gestures when anyone gets near them while teachers are not looking."

## Section A: School violence

What information might you want to gather about the students at this point in time?

(Select as many as you consider indicated in this section.)

| | | |
|---|---|---|
| _____ | A—1. | Current and past grades |
| _____ | A—2. | Attendance patterns |
| _____ | A—3. | Parents' knowledge of student behavior as reported by teachers |
| _____ | A—4. | After—school activities |
| _____ | A—5. | Information from other students |
| _____ | A—6. | Observations of these students by their other teachers |
| _____ | A—7. | Educational history from student records |
| _____ | A—8. | Time spent on the computer at home and school |
| _____ | A—9. | More information from the student who talked to the teacher about the three male students in the lunchroom |
| _____ | A—10. | Disciplinary infractions |
| _____ | A—11. | Relationship with siblings and parents |

## Section B: School violence

The information you gathered demonstrates a pattern of increasingly negative behavior by all three of the students despite school and parent intervention. One of the three students was expelled during middle school for threatening to kill a teacher. Based on the information you have gathered; you decide on the following course of action:
  (Choose ONLY ONE in this section.)

| | |
|---|---|
| _____ B—1. | Request an intervention by the principal |
| _____ B—2. | Request an intervention by the schools' resource officer |
| _____ B—3. | Meet with the students together |
| _____ B—4. | Meet with the students individually |
| _____ B—5. | Contact the students' parents for an urgent meeting |

## Section C: School violence

The art teacher comes to you the next morning with a picture one of the three male students drew during art class. The picture appears to be of the school cafeteria with all the doors closed. There are people lying face down on the floor and others that appear to be dead with blood on the floors and walls. There are three individuals on three sides of the cafeteria with guns pointed toward other individuals. The art teacher said the student tried to hide the picture and did not want to show it to her, but she demanded to see it. The art teacher had the student walk with her to the school counseling office during which time he continued to reassure her that it was "just a picture and nothing more." Your concern is heightened because you know that this was the student who had threatened to kill his teacher during middle school. What is the best course of action at this time?
  (Select ONLY ONE in this section.)

| | |
|---|---|
| _____ C—1. | Involve the resource officer |
| _____ C—2. | Involve the principal |
| _____ C—3. | Talk to the student about the meaning of the picture |
| _____ C—4. | Pull the other two students from class to discuss the picture |

| _____ C—5. | Contact the student's parents |
|---|---|
| _____ C—6. | Contact local police |
| _____ C—7. | Contact Child Protective Services |

## Section D: School violence

The following day, you called the home of the student, who had been suspended, to offer the parent counseling resources for her son. In conversation, the parent noted that she could give those to her son, who had just left with his two friends to come to the school to get some books he needed to complete some assignments while on the three-day suspension. You confirmed the names of his friends and let the parent know that suspended students were not allowed on school property during the suspension period, so you would be letting the principal know. Although the parent appeared unalarmed, you checked attendance on the other two students to find that they had been reported absent by the teachers. What action should you take at this point?

(Select ONLY ONE in this section.)

| _____ D—1. | No action required |
|---|---|
| _____ D—2. | Call the parents of the other two students to report their absences |
| _____ D—3. | Go directly to the truancy officer |
| _____ D—4. | Notify the resources officer |
| _____ D—5. | Go directly to the school principal to report this information |
| _____ D—6. | Call the local police |

## Section E: School violence

The resource officer sees two students letting the suspended student in the hall door that is locked. He recognizes the three students and sees suspiciously bulky zipped jackets. He quickly notifies the principal via the two-way radio, who immediately calls a lockdown. The resource officer yelled to the students while the lockdown was being called, but the students darted down the halls in separate directions. After some gunfire throughout the halls of the school, the police swarm the school, apprehend the three students, and secure the school. As the school counselor, what intervention would you consider after such an incident has occurred?

(Select ONLY ONE in this section.)

|  |  |
|---|---|
| _____ E—1. | Begin meeting with small groups of students until you have met with all students school wide |
| _____ E—2. | No action required at this time by the school counselor |
| _____ E—3. | Just have teachers report any behavioral changes in students |
| _____ E—4. | Visit all classes in the building to invite students to see the school counselor to talk about what they experienced |
| _____ E—5. | Encourage students to resume their normal activities so as not to draw attention to the incident |

# Full-length practice exam Simulation Three: *Student appraisal*

## Brief case description

Timmy, a fifth-grade male, has been referred to the Child Study Team by his teacher because of both behavioral concerns and academic performance. You are the school counselor and chair of the Child Study Team. Based on the information presented in the meeting, the team decides testing is needed. The school counselor explains to Timmy's mother, who is present at the meeting, that the team will administer a series of assessments that will include assessing personality, achievement, aptitude, intelligence, and adaptive and social functioning.

## *Section A: Student appraisal*

The parent inquires as to how personality tests will get to the root of Timmy's behavior. The school counselor responds that understanding Timmy's personality is important to helping the team to more fully understand Timmy's behavior because the assessment reveals the following information:

(Select as many as you consider indicated in this section.)

| | |
|---|---|
| _____ A—1. | Emotional functioning |
| _____ A—2. | Level of knowledge |
| _____ A—3. | Motivation |
| _____ A—4. | Social functioning |
| _____ A—5. | Skills |
| _____ A—6. | Attitude |
| _____ A—7. | Abilities |
| _____ A—8. | Level of achievement |

## Section B: Student appraisal

The parent asks the school counselor to identify the personality assessment that will be administered to her son. The school counselor identifies the following standardized personality test for the school setting at the elementary level:
(Choose ONLY ONE in this section.)

| | |
|---|---|
| _____ B—1. | SII |
| _____ B—2. | Kuder |
| _____ B—3. | SAT |
| _____ B—4. | Vineland |
| _____ B—5. | ACT |

## Section C: Student appraisal

The parent also asks which achievement test will be used. The school counselor replies, identifying the following standardized achievement test:
(Select ONLY ONE in this section.)

| | |
|---|---|
| _____ C—1. | MBTI |
| _____ C—2. | Woodcock-Johnson |
| _____ C—3. | Vineland |
| _____ C—4. | Stanford-Binet |
| _____ C—5. | SDS |
| _____ C—6. | ASVAB |
| _____ C—7. | SAT |

## Section D: Student appraisal

The parent requests that the team also includes an aptitude test because she is worried about her son's potential for learning. The school

counseling identifies the following standardized aptitude test appropriate for Timmy's age:
(Select ONLY ONE in this section.)

| | |
|---|---|
| _____ D—1. | ACT |
| _____ D—2. | Kaufman Assessment Battery |
| _____ D—3. | Vineland |
| _____ D—4. | Woodcock-Johnson |
| _____ D—5. | WISC |
| _____ D—6. | GATB |

## Section E: Student appraisal

The team decides that meeting with the school counselor individually would also be beneficial. The school counselor gathers information using the following nonstandardized approaches to better understand Timmy and his situation:
(Select as many as you consider indicated in this section.)

| | |
|---|---|
| _____ E—1. | Observation |
| _____ E—2. | WISC |
| _____ E—3. | Portfolio |
| _____ E—4. | ACT |
| _____ E—5. | Counseling notes |
| _____ E—6. | Consulting with teachers |
| _____ E—7. | School records |
| _____ E—8. | SAT |
| _____ E—9. | GATB |

## Section F: Student appraisal

After four sessions, the school counselor becomes concerned about Timmy's increasingly flat affect, sense of worthlessness, excessive absences, inability to focus, lack of personal hygiene, and frequent injuries. The school counselor cannot get Timmy to communicate. The school counselor calls a meeting with Timmy and his mother. When his mother arrives, she is agitated and expresses what a terrible inconvenience this is, reiterating that she was just here a month ago. During the meeting, the school counselor identifies the following behaviors, coupled with the information she already has, as indicators of child abuse or neglect:

(Select as many as you consider indicated in this section.)

| | | |
|---|---|---|
| _____ | F—1. | Mother smells of alcohol |
| _____ | F—2. | Mother asks school counselor to be sensitive to her son |
| _____ | F—3. | Mother and son rarely make eye contact |
| _____ | F—4. | Mother is apathetic |
| _____ | F—5. | Mother allows son to control the conversation |
| _____ | F—6. | Mother is indifferent toward son |
| _____ | F—7. | Mother and son appear secretive |
| _____ | F—8. | Frequent touch between mother and son |
| _____ | F—9. | Son flinches when mother turns in his direction |

## Section G: Student appraisal

After the meeting, the school counselor suspects that Timmy is being neglected and abused. The school counselor should take the following course of action:

(Select ONLY ONE in this section.)

| | | |
|---|---|---|
| _____ | G—1. | Contact local police |
| _____ | G—2. | Contact Timmy's dad |
| _____ | G—3. | Contact the emergency contact on Timmy's health card |
| _____ | G—4. | Contact CPS |
| _____ | G—5. | Ask the principal for appropriate course of action |
| _____ | G—6. | Inform the mother of her suspicions, and say if it continues she will report her |

# Full-length practice exam Simulation Four: *Early intervention*

## Brief case description

You are a middle-school counselor. Your principal comes to you concerned about the disproportionately high number of students identified as special education and students with a 504 Plan as compared to other schools in the district of similar size and population. He asks for suggestions that could reduce the number of students identified as special needs in your school while still providing students with the assistance that is needed to be successful. The principal also expresses his concern with the lack of referrals to the school-wide early intervention team, which you chair.

## *Section A: Early intervention*

You provide the principal with the following suggestion:
   (Choose ONLY ONE in this section.)

| | |
|---|---|
| _____ A—1. | Require that teachers refer students to the early intervention team prior to referral to the 504 or child study teams, unless a parent objects |
| _____ A—2. | Pay teachers for the time they spend in early intervention team meetings |
| _____ A—3. | Require a minimum number of early intervention team meetings each academic year |
| _____ A—4. | Require teachers and parent to refer students to the early intervention team prior to referral to a 504 or the child study committee |
| _____ A—5. | Require particular grade levels to go through the early intervention team prior to going through child study or the 504 team |

## *Section B: Early intervention*

Joshua, a sixth-grade student, was referred to the early intervention team for academic difficulties. His teacher expressed that he is well liked by other students and he is cooperative and that she has not noticed any other concerns apart from academic performance. What type of information or data would be important to acquire from the teacher and parents during the initial team meeting to assess Joshua's issues?

(Select as many as you consider indicated in this section.)

| | | |
|---|---|---|
| _____ | B—1. | Hobbies and interests |
| _____ | B—2. | Past and present social functioning |
| _____ | B—3. | Sleeping habits |
| _____ | B—4. | Medical information |
| _____ | B—5. | Behavioral records |
| _____ | B—6. | Family income |
| _____ | B—7. | Past and present academic performance |
| _____ | B—8. | Subjects with which the student is struggling |
| _____ | B—9. | Past and present emotional functioning |
| _____ | B—10. | Student's eating habits |
| _____ | B—11. | Environmental factors |

## Section C: Early intervention

During the team meeting, an individualized intervention plan is established to target Joshua's areas of academic difficulty. After the early intervention team meeting, as the team's chair you would do the following:

(Select ONLY ONE in this section.)

| | | |
|---|---|---|
| _____ | C—1. | Distribute a copy of the intervention plan to all the members of the team, the students' teachers, the parents, and to the student's record |
| _____ | C—2. | Provide only the intervention team members and parents with a copy of the intervention plan |
| _____ | C—3. | Meet with principal regarding the meeting outcome |
| _____ | C—4. | Ensure that the intervention plan does not become a part of the student's educational record |

## Section D: Early intervention

Two weeks later, the team reconvenes at the request of the teacher who reports that although Joshua's academics have improved slightly, Joshua is displaying behavioral issues such as agitation and bullying of other students, which is out of character for Joshua, according to his teacher. During the meeting, the parent shares that she and her husband are going through a divorce, which began just about the time that Joshua's academic performance declined. Based on this new information, Joshua's intervention plan was modified to include participation in a small group on divorce. The following permissions must be obtained:
(Select ONLY ONE in this section.)

| | | |
|---|---|---|
| _____ | D—1. | Informed consent from the parents of all group members |
| _____ | D—2. | Because small groups are a primary method of school counseling program delivery, parental consent is assumed |
| _____ | D—3. | Informed consent of parents of all group members and participants |
| _____ | D—4. | Informed consent only from Joshua's parent because the activity is connected to an intervention plan |
| _____ | D—5. | No informed consent is required |

## Section E: Early intervention

During your first group session, one of the most important issues you want to discuss with these adolescents relates to:
(Select ONLY ONE in this section.)

| | | |
|---|---|---|
| _____ | E—1. | Goals |
| _____ | E—2. | Topic |
| _____ | E—3. | Member rights |
| _____ | E—4. | Confidentiality |
| _____ | E—5. | Informed consent |
| _____ | E—6. | Termination |
| _____ | E—7. | Process |
| _____ | E—8. | Emergency contact information |

## Section F: Early intervention

During the third group session, one of the group members becomes very angry and says, "I never even got to tell the jerk what I thought of him before he left us." Which counseling techniques might be useful at this time to mediate the student's emotional distress and work through the issue presented?

(Select as many as you consider indicated in this section.)

| _____ F—1. | Clarifying |
| _____ F—2. | Empty chair |
| _____ F—3. | Paraphrasing |
| _____ F—4. | Relaxation techniques |
| _____ F—5. | Guided imagery |
| _____ F—6. | Stress inoculation |
| _____ F—7. | Behavior contract |

# Full-length practice exam Simulation Five: *Academic achievement*

## Brief case description

You are a school counselor at a large, pluralistic elementary school. Twenty percent of the student body is special education and ESL students. Nearly half of the student body receives free or reduced lunch. Your school did not make AYP last year, so everyone is academic-focused and implementing programs that will result in the immediate improvement of standardized test scores.

## Section A: Academic achievement

What information do you need in order to begin planning strategies to improve academic achievement?

(Select as many as you consider indicated in this section.)

| | |
|---|---|
| _____ A—1. | Parent support |
| _____ A—2. | Student interests |
| _____ A—3. | Past successes |
| _____ A—4. | School and community resources |
| _____ A—5. | Target populations |
| _____ A—6. | Students' favorite subjects |
| _____ A—7. | Subject areas of weakness |
| _____ A—8. | Subject areas of strength |

## Section B: Academic achievement

Which data sources would provide useful information for creating classroom lessons to target specific grade levels and subjects?

(Select as many as you consider indicated in this section.)

| | |
|---|---|
| \_\_\_\_ B—1. | Standardized test score reports |
| \_\_\_\_ B—2. | School report card |
| \_\_\_\_ B—3. | School-wide attendance patterns |
| \_\_\_\_ B—4. | Individual disciplinary records |
| \_\_\_\_ B—5. | Family structure |
| \_\_\_\_ B—6. | Each student's academic record |

## Section C: Academic achievement

Data analysis reveals grade 3 math and grade 5 English as areas of specific weakness, particularly among the special education and ESL populations and African American males. Which intervention would be most useful for providing responsive services for these struggling students?

(Select ONLY ONE in this section.)

| | |
|---|---|
| \_\_\_\_ C—1. | Small group on study skills |
| \_\_\_\_ C—2. | Classroom lesson on study skills that crosswalks school counseling standards and core academic standards |
| \_\_\_\_ C—3. | Small group on study skills that crosswalks school counseling standards and math and English standards |
| \_\_\_\_ C—4. | Small group on test taking skills that crosswalks school counseling standards and core academic standards |
| \_\_\_\_ C—5. | Classroom lesson on test taking skills that crosswalks school counseling standards and core academic standards |
| \_\_\_\_ C—6. | Small group on test taking |

## Section D: Academic achievement

While chatting with your school's test coordinator, you discover that many special education students have not been given special accommodations during standardized testing. When you voiced your concern to the test coordinator, she said that as long as examiners and proctors are in short supply and because teachers are not always giving these students the accommodations during the school year, then she is not going to worry about it at testing time. What is the best course of action to take at this time?

(Select ONLY ONE in this section.)

| | |
|---|---|
| _____ D—1. | Let the test coordinator know that you will be making the principal aware of these unlawful instructional and standardized testing practices |
| _____ D—2. | Let the test coordinator know that you will be making the principal aware of these questionable instructional and standardized testing practices |
| _____ D—3. | Let the test coordinator know that if this continues you will need to notify the principal |
| _____ D—4. | Call a meeting of the teachers, test coordinator, and principal about these practices |
| _____ D—5. | Voice your concerns to the test coordinator and trust her to correct the standardized testing practices |
| _____ D—6. | Notify the school division's testing administrator about these questionable standardized testing practices |

## Section E: Academic achievement

The actions of the teachers and test coordinator concerned you, so you reviewed some of the special education students' IEPs to find that several students were given special accommodations only on standardized tests, not on classroom tests. When you spoke to one of the teachers of these students, he said that this was an IEP team decision that included the principal and that the decision was based on the lack of manpower during the school day. What is the best course of action to take at this time?

(Select as many as you consider indicated in this section.)

| | |
|---|---|
| _____ E—1. | Talk to the principal about ways that these students can get the accommodations during the school day, not just on standardized testing days |
| _____ E—2. | Contact the school division's test administrator |

| _____ E—3. | Discuss with the principal your concern about setting the students up for failure on standardized testing day if they have not been pulled out of the class the entire year for testing |
|---|---|
| _____ E—4. | Contact the State Department of Education |
| _____ E—5. | Let the principal know that if he does not do something about this then you are going to contact the Department of Education |
| _____ E—6. | Contact your school division's supervisor of instructional practices so that he or she can talk to the principal about these practices |
| _____ E—7. | Request to be a part of the IEP meetings, so that you can have a voice in the creation of students' IEPs |

# Full-length practice exam Simulation Six: *Assessment*

## Brief case description

You are a high-school counselor. Terrance is a junior at the high school whose parent has requested that you pull his record and go over the grades and assessments with her so that she might better understand his academic status and level of functioning. She wants to know if her son, Terrance, has the grades and intelligence to get into a four-year college and to be successful in college. She said Terrance has identified seven colleges that offer majors in communication, which is his area of interest.

## Section A: Assessment

The first assessment you came to was the WAIS-II. You explained that Terrance has a verbal IQ score of 95 and a performance IQ score of 85, giving Terrance a full-scale IQ of 90. Terrance's mother responds, "I don't know what that means." What information would you share with the student's mother?

(Select as many as you consider indicated in this section.)

| | | |
|---|---|---|
| _____ | A—1. | Most individuals have an IQ score between 85 and 115 |
| _____ | A—2. | Because the assessment uses a 95% confidence level, Terrance's score could, at any given time, fall within five points in either direction |
| _____ | A—3. | Terrance's IQ score indicates genius |
| _____ | A—4. | Terrance has an average IQ |
| _____ | A—5. | Terrance has a very low IQ |
| _____ | A—6. | Terrance's IQ indicates mild retardation |

## Section B: Assessment

Terrance's mother also said that Terrance told her that he got a 34 on his ACT test. She began to cry stating that her son would "never get into college with such low scores on his college entrance exams." You look at Terrance's score report from ACT and see that, indeed, Terrance's score on the ACT was 34. What information would you share with this parent?

(Select as many as you consider indicated in this section.)

|  |  |
|---|---|
| _____ B—1. | The average score of the ACT is 21 |
| _____ B—2. | The average score on the ACT is 71 |
| _____ B—3. | Because the high score is 75, Terrance did not do well |
| _____ B—4. | ACT scores range from 1 to 36 |
| _____ B—5. | ACT scores range from 25 to 75 |
| _____ B—6. | Because the high score is 36, Terrance did very well |

## Section C: Assessment

As you go through Terrance's record you notice that there are no SAT scores. His mother said that he is not taking the SAT because he took the ACT. What advice would you give to the parent at this point?

(Select ONLY ONE in this section.)

|  |  |
|---|---|
| _____ C—1. | The ACT is all he needs |
| _____ C—2. | The SAT should be taken and is the most widely used college entrance exam in the country |
| _____ C—3. | The ACT measures the same thing as the SAT |
| _____ C—4. | The SAT is not used very often for college entrance; however, it is a good measure of achievement |
| _____ C—5. | The SAT is the only assessment that should be taken for college entrance |

## Section D: Assessment

Terrance's mother says that she is still a bit concerned about Terrance's choice of major. She worries that it will not be a good match. She adds that she knows Terrance is interested in communication, but she is not sure about his skills and abilities or that the work environment would fit

his personality. The school counselor suggests that the career counselor administer the following career interest inventory:
   (Select ONLY ONE in this section.)

| | |
|---|---|
| _____ D—1. | ASVAB |
| _____ D—2. | Kaufman |
| _____ D—3. | SDS |
| _____ D—4. | Super's model of career development |
| _____ D—5. | WAIS |
| _____ D—6. | Vineland |

## Section E: Assessment

Terrance's mother thanks you for your time and asks, "What do we need to do next because it is the spring of Terrance's junior year?" The following information would be useful for the parent at this time:
   (Select as many as you consider indicated in this section.)

| | |
|---|---|
| _____ E—1. | FAFSA deadlines |
| _____ E—2. | SAT information and deadlines |
| _____ E—3. | ACT information and deadlines |
| _____ E—4. | PSAT information and deadlines |
| _____ E—5. | College fair dates |
| _____ E—6. | GED Official Practice Test information and deadlines |
| _____ E—7. | Scholarship websites |
| _____ E—8. | Financial aid website |

# Full-length practice exam Simulation seven: Special needs and scope of practice

## Brief case description

Julianna is a fifth-grade African American student diagnosed with ADHD, and you are the elementary-school counselor at her school. The teacher and parent report that Julianna consistently presents as hyperactive, restless, argumentative, and impulsive. Julianna's mother reports that the medication Julianna is taking does not appear to be working because Julianna continues to experience academic, social, and behavioral issues. Julianna's mother is a single parent and admits that she does not have much time to spend with Julianna and her other two children to help with their studies because she works two jobs. A 504-committee meeting was just held, and Julianna qualified for a 504 plan due to the academic and social impact related to Julianna's ADHD.

## Section A: Special needs and scope of practice

During the 504 meeting, you identified the following strategies and approaches to help Julianna and her family:

(Select as many as you consider indicated in this section.)

| | | |
|---|---|---|
| _____ | A—1. | Homeschooling |
| _____ | A—2. | Social skills development |
| _____ | A—3. | Reduced television time |
| _____ | A—4. | Parenting skills training |
| _____ | A—5. | Family counseling |
| _____ | A—6. | Reduced computer time |
| _____ | A—7. | Change in diet |
| _____ | A—8. | Increased time spent with friends |
| _____ | A—9. | Counseling |
| _____ | A—10. | Reduced length of academic work |
| _____ | A—11. | Increased length of academic work |
| _____ | A—12. | Providing choices (academic and home tasks) |

## Section B: Special needs and scope of practice

Julianna's mother asks about what other things she can do at home to improve Julianna's behavior and increase cooperation. In addition to organization and maintaining a consistent schedule, you name the following:

(Select as many as you consider indicated in this section.)

| | | |
|---|---|---|
| _____ | B—1. | Positive reinforcement |
| _____ | B—2. | Loss of privileges |
| _____ | B—3. | Allow more computer time |
| _____ | B—4. | Negotiated rewards |
| _____ | B—5. | Contracts |
| _____ | B—6. | Resist setting goals |
| _____ | B—7. | Mild consequences |
| _____ | B—8. | Give specific behavioral feedback |

## Section C: Special needs and scope of practice

What counseling theory might be most useful when working with Julianna?

(Select ONLY ONE in this section)

| | | |
|---|---|---|
| _____ | C—1. | Gestalt counseling |
| _____ | C—2. | Behavioral counseling |
| _____ | C—3. | Reality counseling |
| _____ | C—4. | Person—centered counseling |
| _____ | C—5. | Adlerian counseling |
| _____ | C—6. | Cognitive behavioral counseling |

## Section D: Special needs and scope of practice

Several months into the 504 plan, the teacher and parent report that Julianna's behavioral and peer relations problems have increased, and her academic performance has declined. Julianna is now having full-blown temper tantrums at home, at school, and in the community. She is disobedient and blames others for her actions. The school counselor strongly encourages the following actions to help Julianna and her family:

(Select as many as you consider indicated in this section.)

| | |
|---|---|
| _____ D—1. | Referral to child study for possible testing and special education services |
| _____ D—2. | Homeschooling |
| _____ D—3. | Participation in Governor's School |
| _____ D—4. | Medical examination by the child's physician |
| _____ D—5. | Less time with peers |
| _____ D—6. | Appointment with a child psychiatrist |
| _____ D—7. | More time with peers |
| _____ D—8. | Family counseling |
| _____ D—9. | Resources related to helping children with disruptive behavior issues/disorders |

## Section E: Special needs and scope of practice

Julianna's mother returns to you a few weeks later and says that the psychiatrist has diagnosed Juliann with oppositional defiance disorder and recommended ongoing individual counseling for Julianna and the family. She asks if you would be Julianna's counselor over the next couple of years. Your response is:

(Select ONLY ONE in this section.)

| | |
|---|---|
| _____ E—1. | Of course |
| _____ E—2. | I would like to, as I have enjoyed working with Julianna very much; however, I just do not have time as the only school counselor in the building |

| _____ E—3. | Julianna's needs are beyond the scope of school counseling, but I have a list of counseling resources, which may be helpful in identifying a counselor |
|---|---|
| _____ E—4. | I would not be able to do this during the school day, as it is beyond the scope of school counseling. However, I can provide counseling services to Julianna outside of school hours at your home or mine for a minimal charge |
| _____ E—5. | Oppositional defiance disorder is not really my area of expertise, but I will work with Julianna because she and I already have a positive relationship |

# Full-length practice exam Simulation Eight: Program evaluation

## Brief case description

You are the school counselor at an elementary school. The principal wants to ensure that you are implementing a data- and needs-driven, comprehensive school counseling program. As such, she has requested that you present her with a five-year plan for meeting the needs of stakeholders and evaluating the school counseling program.

## Section A: Program evaluation

What strategies would you include in your plan to ensure that the school counseling program is appropriately evaluated?

(Select as many as you consider indicated in this section.)

|  |  |
|---|---|
| _____ A—1. | Preprogram surveys |
| _____ A—2. | Student names for interview by the principal |
| _____ A—3. | Needs assessment |
| _____ A—4. | Postprogram surveys |
| _____ A—5. | Teacher names for interview by the principal |
| _____ A—6. | Teacher program perception surveys |
| _____ A—7. | Parent reports to the principal |
| _____ A—8. | Student program perception surveys |
| _____ A—9. | Community member names for interview by the principal |
| _____ A—10. | Statistical testing of pre-post data |
| _____ A—11. | Committee meeting involvement |
| _____ A—12. | Website development |

## Section B: Program evaluation

The principal likes the strategies you have designed to include in your five-year plan for accountable school counseling practices. She is uncertain as to how you would objectively measure each classroom lesson and small group activity to ensure that you are making a positive difference in the lives of the students. She is focused on data that will demonstrate how well you have met stated goals, objectives, and standards. Which of the following types of evaluation will yield this data?
   (Choose ONLY ONE in this section.)

| | |
|---|---|
| \_\_\_\_ B—1. | Process evaluation using a pre-and post-measure |
| \_\_\_\_ B—2. | Formative evaluation using a pre-and post-measure |
| \_\_\_\_ B—3. | Outcome evaluation using a pre-and post-measure |
| \_\_\_\_ B—4. | Pre-and postquestionnaire of participants' perceptions of the program |
| \_\_\_\_ B—5. | Program review by teachers |

## Section C: Program evaluation

In a recent faculty meeting, your principal stressed the importance of developing research-supported curriculum. You are about to develop a small group for second-grade students on social skills. What information do you need from the research to develop a research-supported curriculum?
   (Select as many as you consider indicated in this section.)

| | |
|---|---|
| \_\_\_\_ C—1. | Previous successful social skills programs |
| \_\_\_\_ C—2. | Age-grade-specific social skills activities |
| \_\_\_\_ C—3. | Correlation between social skills and academic achievement |
| \_\_\_\_ C—4. | Effectiveness of small group programs for enhancing social skills |
| \_\_\_\_ C—5. | Definition of social skills |
| \_\_\_\_ C—6. | Use of recognized interventions for social skills improvement |

## Section D: Program evaluation

Which of the following resources would be most useful in providing research pertaining to school counseling and school counseling interventions?
   (Select as many as you consider indicated in this section.)

| | |
|---|---|
| _____ D—1. | ASCA Scene |
| _____ D—2. | Wikipedia |
| _____ D—3. | *Counseling Today* |
| _____ D—4. | National Technology Institute for School Counseling |
| _____ D—5. | Peer-reviewed journals |
| _____ D—6. | Center for School Counseling Outcome Research |
| _____ D—7. | Webster Dictionary Online |
| _____ D—8. | NBCC Newsletter |
| _____ D—9. | PSC |

## Section E: Program evaluation

The data collected from your social skills group indicated that the group intervention was not effective in meeting the stated objectives. What type of program evaluation would have been useful to determine the program's strengths and weaknesses and provide information that could be used for program improvement?
   (Choose ONLY ONE in this section.)

| | |
|---|---|
| _____ E—1. | Process evaluation |
| _____ E—2. | Formative evaluation |
| _____ E—3. | Outcome evaluation |
| _____ E—4. | Program evaluation |
| _____ E—5. | Student evaluation |

# Full-length practice exam Simulation Nine: *Alternative educational programs*

## Brief case description

You are a high-school counselor who delivered classroom instruction on career readiness to a career and technical education class. Afterward, a student from the class comes to meet with you. During the session, he tells you that he is going to drop out of school. The student just turned 17 and in the tenth grade. He says that he hates coming to school because his classmates are so immature. He says he hates studying and doing homework.

### Section A: Alternative educational programs

In an effort to prevent this student from dropping out of school, which course of action would be best at this time?
   (Select as many as you consider indicated in this section.)

| | |
|---|---|
| _____ A—1. | Refer the student to the peer tutoring program |
| _____ A—2. | Suggest the student wait until he is 18 years old to drop out of high school |
| _____ A—3. | Share information about the GED track and the pros and cons of a GED versus a high-school diploma, including the potential impact on student's current career choices |
| _____ A—4. | Encourage the student to talk to his parents about his plan to drop out of school |
| _____ A—5. | Share information about Job Corps and other non-traditional educational programs |
| _____ A—6. | Give him the official GED qualifying practice test during the session |

### Section B: Alternative educational programs

The student returns to you the next day and says that his parents got mad because you talked to him about alternative education programs. They told him his is staying in school. Tears in his eyes, the student says, "I'm already almost two years behind. I hate to study, I hate sitting in class, I just hate learning period so I'm failing English and Math." I'm just going to quit school. I don't care what my parents say." What is your best course of action at this time?

(Choose ONLY ONE in this section.)

| _____ B—1. | Help the student to secure a non-peer tutor |
| _____ B—2. | Ask the student to allow you to set up a meeting with the parents with him present as well |
| _____ B—3. | Tell the student you respect his decision and wish him the best. |
| _____ B—4. | Request that the principal contact the student's parents |
| _____ B—5. | Encourage the student to talk to his parents again |

## Section C: Alternative educational programs

Before the meeting with the student's parents, the student tells you that the only alternative he would consider to dropping out of school is the GED track but that he is okay with your sharing all alternative programs with his parents during the meeting. During the meeting you will discuss the following:

(Select as many as you consider indicated in this section.)

| _____ C—1. | A plan for staying in school |
| _____ C—2. | Pros and cons of the GED track in relation to the student's aspirations |
| _____ C—3. | Other alternative education programs available |
| _____ C—4. | The parents' unrealistic expectations of their son |
| _____ C—5. | Apologizing for sharing alternative education program information with their son without their knowledge |

## Section D: Alternative educational programs

During the meeting with the student and his parents, his parents agree to allow him to pursue the GED. What is the next best course of action?

(Choose ONLY ONE in this section.)

| _____ D—1. | Tell the student he no longer needs to attend classes and you will get back to him with a day and time to take the GED. |
|---|---|
| _____ D—2. | Tell the student to continue to attend classes but not to worry about grades since he will be sitting for the GED. |
| _____ D—3. | Give the student a day and time to take the GED practice exams or let him know when you'll get back to him with a day and time. Also, encourage the student to continue to attend classes and do his best work. |

## Section E: Alternative educational programs

The parents then ask what type of postsecondary opportunities may exist for their son with only a GED. You respond with which of the following options?

(Select as many as you consider indicated in this section.)

| _____ E—1. | Apprenticeship |
|---|---|
| _____ E—2. | College |
| _____ E—3. | Vocational school |
| _____ E—4. | Technical school |

# Full-length practice exam responses

## Full-length practice exam Simulation One responses: College readiness

### Brief case description

You are a high-school counselor reviewing student surveys that were collected from tenth-and 11th-grade students, which indicate that 85 percent of the students in these grades plan to attend a four-year college. However, an analysis of tenth- and 11th-grade academic performance records reveals that only 35 percent currently have the academic standing needed to get into college.

### *Section A: College readiness*

What information would help you to identify what may be contributing to this gap?

(Select as many as you consider indicated in this section.)

| | | |
|---|---|---|
| A—1. | Access to enrichment activities<br>Yes<br>Struggling students need access to enrichment activities to improve performance | |
| A—2. | Promotion and retention rates<br>Yes<br>This information will help school counselors to identify which populations of students are being successful in meeting their college goals and which are not | |
| A—3. | Hobbies<br>No<br>Hobbies will not provide useful information for identifying reasons for the gap | |
| A—4. | Course enrollment patterns<br>Yes<br>This information is helpful in providing insight into low GPAs | |
| A—5. | Time spent on the computer<br>No<br>This information would not be helpful in identifying that which is contributing to the gap in this scenario | |

| | |
|---|---|
| A—6. | Standardized test scores<br>Yes<br>Scores on these assessments will help to identify areas of struggle for targeted intervention |
| A—7. | Attendance rates<br>Yes<br>Poor attendance can be a factor in low GPAs |
| A—8. | College application completion<br>No<br>This information will not be helpful in identifying what may be contributing to the gap, which is related to academic performance prior to college application |
| A—9. | Career assessment participation<br>Yes<br>Students who connect learning to real life and career aspirations are more likely to achieve at higher levels and experience higher levels of academic motivation |
| A—10. | FAFSA completion<br>No<br>This information will not be helpful in identifying what may be contributing to the gap, which is related to academic performance prior to FAFSA and college application completion |
| A—11. | Course completion rates<br>Yes<br>If students are not successful in the courses in which they enroll, this needs to be identified and mediated. This data may also reveal specific classes in which masses of students are not being successful, indicating a problem with the course structure, content, and/or instructor |
| A—12. | Parent participation rates<br>Yes<br>Students whose parents are involved in their education generally experience higher levels of academic achievement |

## Section B: College readiness

What types of programming might you consider to help students to understand the connection between grades and getting into college and to close the gap between college goals and college readiness?

(Select as many as you consider indicated in this section.)

| B—1. | Classroom lessons on career planning |
| --- | --- |
| | Yes |
| | Connecting academic performance to college entrance and career goal attainment has been linked to heightened academic achievement |
| B—2. | Student participation in a small group on study skills |
| | Yes |
| | Study skills have been linked to improved academic achievement |
| B—3. | College visitations/field trips |
| | Yes |
| | Campus tours help to motivate students toward college attendance and provide students with the opportunity to further understand the importance of high-school grades and college admission |
| B—4. | Individual academic advising |
| | Yes |
| | Individual academic advising is a primary delivery method used by school counselors |
| B—5. | SAT and ACT preparation program |
| | No |
| | This strategy will not be a helpful strategy for closing the gap that exists between students' school performance and college entrance (e.g., high-school GPA and required GPA for college entrance) |
| B—6. | Peer tutoring program |
| | Yes |
| | Peer tutoring may be helpful for some of the population of tenth-and 11th-grade students that are struggling due to a specially challenging subject matter |
| B—7. | Development of a career and academic plan |
| | Yes |
| | Students benefit from a plan of action that lays out exactly what courses and types of training are needed to meet postsecondary goals |
| B—8. | Encourage participation in SCA |
| | No |
| | Participation in SCA would not necessarily be helpful in mediating the academic gap indicated in this scenario |
| B—9. | Parent involvement programs |
| | Yes |
| | Parent involvement has been linked to higher levels of academic achievement |

## Section C: College readiness

During your analysis of the school data, you find that there are high numbers of tenth-grade students failing the same required English class taught by the same teacher for the past three years. You pointed this out to your school counseling director, who said she has talked to the teacher several times about this, but the teacher just gets angry. What would be the best course of action at this time?

(Select ONLY ONE in this section.)

| C—1. | Ask for a meeting with the teacher and the principal<br>No<br>This may result in the teacher feeling "cornered" |
|---|---|
| C—2. | Try to talk with the teacher again<br>No<br>Because your director already tried on multiple occasions, all indications are that the teacher will not heed your concern either. Meanwhile, more students continue to experience closed college doors |
| C—3. | Bring this data to the attention of the principal<br>Yes<br>The principal will be able to address this with the teacher individually, allowing the teacher a private forum in which to communicate. These actions are indicative of student advocacy—a critical role for school counselors |
| C—4. | Ask for a meeting with the teacher and the school counseling director<br>No<br>The teacher has already dismissed the concerns of your director. A meeting with you and the director may result in the teacher feeling "ganged-up" on |
| C—5. | Do not fight this battle<br>No<br>This is a battle worth fighting. Addressing issues of equity in access, attainment, and achievement for students is a critical aspect of the role of the school counselor in systems support, leadership, and advocacy |
| C—6. | Encourage students to take a different English teacher during scheduling<br>No<br>This will not resolve the issue as some students will still have to take the required course with this teacher once other English classes reach capacity |

## Section D: College readiness

Further data analysis reveals an alarming number of absences among the tenth- and 11th-grade student population. After talking to these grade level teachers, you find that many students are performing poorly or failing classes due to excessive absences that result in missing homework and failing course tests, although they are passing the standardized tests. The majority of absences do not qualify for extenuating circumstances. What might you want to consider as possible courses of action to address this issue?

(Select as many as you consider indicated in this section.)

| | |
|---|---|
| D—1. | Phone calls to parents from the attendance office after a specified number of days<br>Yes<br>Tracking student attendance and keeping parents informed is critical to helping to keep students in school |
| D—2. | Phone calls to parents from the teacher after a specified number of days<br>Yes<br>Tracking student attendance and keeping parents informed is critical to helping to keep students in school. This also gives the teacher a chance to share the impact of attendance issues on the students' performance with the parent |
| D—3. | Send letters home after a specified number of days<br>No<br>This is not cost-effective, and there is no way to be sure that parents will receive the letters |
| D—4. | Grade level assemblies to stress the importance of attendance to academic success and college entrance<br>Yes<br>Assemblies offer a systems-focused approach to informing the masses |
| D—5. | Administer a needs assessment to the tenth-and 11th-grade students asking them to identify perceived obstacles to school attendance and to provide suggestions to improve attendance<br>Yes<br>If you want to know why masses of students are not attending school-ask them! |
| D—6. | Develop harsher penalties for unexcused absences<br>No<br>The penalty is already harsh-students are not performing academically and not meeting their postsecondary goal to get into college |

| D—7. | Strengthen attendance policy by reducing the number of absences allowed each year |
| --- | --- |
| | No |
| | Because students cannot meet the attendance expectations as they are now, this action will likely result in increased numbers of students out of compliance with the attendance policy |

## Section E: College readiness

Further analysis revealed a pattern. Hundreds of students named *needs at home* as the reason for missing so much school. Most of those reasons included after school jobs to help parent(s) pay bills and staying home to take care of younger siblings while the parent worked. You also find out that these students do not have materials at home to complete homework and study (e.g., calculators, paper, pencils, study space). These students do not have a home computer, printer, or Internet access in order to conduct required research and type papers. It is difficult, if not impossible, for these students to go to the library due to demands at home. Transportation is also an issue if they miss the bus. What can you, the school counselor, do to help these students?

(Select as many as you consider indicated in this section.)

| E—1. | Reduce homework for these students |
| --- | --- |
| | No |
| | Rigorous standards still need to be maintained, and without a special need (e.g., ESL, 504, IEP), students do not receive special accommodations |
| E—2. | Sponsor school-wide drives for school supplies |
| | Yes |
| | Collaborating with student groups to donate school supplies is helpful |
| E—3. | Work with community agencies to identify resources to help parents with child care and financial burdens |
| | Yes |
| | Parents appreciate this support and may not have the time or resources to identify the assistance needed |
| E—4. | Coordinate partnerships with local businesses to provide supplies |
| | Yes |
| | Generally, businesses are responsive to the needs of the schools in their communities and understand the interdependent nature of the system |

| E—5. | Provide after-school homework assistance for these students |
|---|---|
| | No |
| | These students have identified transportation and after school jobs and caring for younger siblings as barriers. This might work for some, if transportation was also provided, and you find significant interest. Further information would be needed before implementing this strategy |
| E—6. | Work with the principal to develop an academic enrichment class as a resource/elective course or to develop a component to an existing course with content that would help these and other students prepare for post-high-school opportunities |
| | Yes |
| | This course could prove to be more valuable than some elective courses in helping students to prepare for postsecondary opportunities, particularly for this school's student population |
| E—7. | Do not require homework for these students |
| | No |
| | Rigorous standards still need to be maintained, and without a special need (e.g., ESL, 504, IEP), students do not receive special accommodations |
| E—8. | Apply for a grant to assist students in your school in "achieving the college dream" |
| | Yes |
| | There are many education grants available for the asking; you have the data to support your need, and your grant could include many items (e.g., transportation, supplies, equipment, child care) |

# Full-length practice exam Simulation Two responses: *School violence*

## Brief case description

A teacher comes to you, the eighth-grade middle-school counselor, because she has three male students in her science class who are entirely disengaged, quiet, and only hang out with each other. She saw them at lunch today sitting only with each other and not eating lunch. No other students were anywhere near them. The students dress in black most every day and routinely appear tired and unkempt. A student observed the teacher gazing at the three male students during lunch and said, "I hope someone is finally going to look more closely at those guys-they are so scary and make gestures when anyone gets near them while teachers are not looking."

## *Section A: School violence*

What information might you want to gather about the students at this point in time?
   (Select as many as you consider indicated in this section.)

| A—1. | Current and past grades |
| --- | --- |
| | Yes |
| | It is important to look for educational impact to understand how students' behavior may be affecting other areas of life or vice versa |
| A—2. | Attendance patterns |
| | Yes |
| | It is important to look for impact on daily functioning to understand how students' behavior may be affecting other areas of life or vice versa |
| A—3. | Parents' knowledge of student behavior as reported by teachers |
| | Yes |
| | Understanding how involved parents are in the students' lives and their level of support provides the school counselor with insight, resources, and direction |
| A—4. | After-school activities |
| | No |
| | Although this may become important at a later time, this information at this time would not be useful |

| | |
|---|---|
| A—5. | Information from other students<br>No<br>Perhaps in a time of crisis it may become necessary to elicit information about the three students from peers, but it is not warranted or appropriate at this time |
| A—6. | Observation of these students by their other teachers<br>Yes<br>It is important for the school counselor to explore how these students interact with other teachers and in diverse classroom settings in order to establish patterns of behaviors and to understand the frequency and magnitude of behaviors |
| A—7. | Educational history from student records<br>Yes<br>It is important for the school counselor to explore the students' history of academic performance and behavior in order to establish patterns of behaviors and to understand the frequency, magnitude, and onset of behaviors |
| A—8. | Time spent on the computer at home and school<br>No<br>Although time spent on the computer would not be useful at this time, what the students are doing on the home computer (school computers are generally monitored) may be useful (e.g., violent video games, disturbing communications in chat rooms and blogs, disturbing Facebook pages) |
| A—9. | More information from the student who talked to the teacher about the three male students in the lunchroom<br>No<br>Perhaps in a time of crisis it may become necessary to elicit information about the three students from peers, but it is not warranted or appropriate at this time |
| A—10. | Disciplinary infractions<br>Yes<br>A history of disciplinary actions aids the school counselor in identifying patterns, frequency, and magnitude of behaviors in order to adequately assess level, immediacy, and type of intervention needed |
| A—11. | Relationship with siblings and parents<br>No<br>This information may be important at a later time, but it is not useful at this particular moment |

## Section B: School violence

The information you gathered demonstrates a pattern of increasingly negative behavior by all three of the students despite school and parent intervention. One of the three students was expelled during middle school for threatening to kill a teacher. Based on the information you have gathered you decide on the following course of action:
(Choose ONLY ONE in this section.)

| | |
|---|---|
| B—1. | Request an intervention by the principal <br> No <br> The principal understands that some students may have a history of disciplinary infractions by the time they get to high school. The principal looks to the school counselor to mediate behavioral issues with counseling interventions |
| B—2. | Request an intervention by the school's resource officer <br> No <br> The resource officer is a valuable resource; however, there is no action for the officer to take at this time |
| B—3. | Meet with the students together <br> No <br> Together, the students will not likely openly communicate |
| B—4. | Meet with the students individually <br> Yes <br> This is the most appropriate course of action to take at this time. Individually, the students may openly communicate, and you can explore each student's unique situation/issues |
| B—5. | Contact the students' parents for an urgent meeting <br> No <br> At the present time there is no indication of urgency, and the academic history records parental awareness of each disciplinary incident to date |

## Section C: School violence

The art teacher comes to you the next morning with a picture one of the three male students drew during art class. The picture appears to be one of the school cafeteria with all the doors closed. There are people lying face down on the floor and others that appear to be dead with blood on the floors and walls. There are three individuals on three sides of the cafeteria with guns pointed toward other individuals. The art teacher said the student tried to hide the picture and did not want to show it to her, but she demanded to see it. The art teacher had the student walk with her to the school counseling office during which time he continued to reassure her that it was "just a picture and nothing more." Your concern is heightened because you know that this was the student who had threatened to kill his teacher during middle school. What is the best course of action at this time?

(Select ONLY ONE in this section.)

| C—1. | Involve the resource officer |
| --- | --- |
| | No |
| | The artwork should be viewed as an illustration of threat to others, particularly when coupled with the student's past disciplinary infractions and present behavioral concerns reported by the teacher. For this reason, the threat must be brought to the attention of the building head |
| C—2. | Involve the principal |
| | Yes |
| | This student's actions in context with other behavioral issues call for immediate action and must be taken seriously despite his contention that it is "just a picture and nothing more" |
| C—3. | Talk to the student about the meaning of the picture |
| | No |
| | This is a matter of school—wide safety that will likely result in disciplinary actions, which should be handled by the principal/assistant principals |
| C—4. | Pull the other two students from class to discuss the picture |
| | No |
| | The school counselor cannot assume to know who the other two individuals in the picture are and should not pull additional students out of class to discuss the actions of the other in this case. The principal's investigation may call for this, but it would not be an appropriate responsibility of the school counselor |
| C—5. | Contact the student's parents |
| | No |
| | The principal will make this determination after talking with the student |
| C—6. | Contact local police |
| | No |
| | The principal will make this determination after talking with the student |

| C—7. | Contact Child Protective Services |
|---|---|
| | No |
| | The principal will make this determination after talking with the student. Child Protective Services is generally involved in cases of abuse, neglect, and suicide threat or ideation that implicate the parent or guardian |

## Section D: School violence

The following day, you called the home of the student, who had been suspended, to offer the parent counseling resources for her son. In conversation, the parent noted that she could give those to her son, who had just left with his two friends to come to the school to get some books he needed to complete some assignments while on the three-day suspension. You confirmed the names of his friends and let the parent know that suspended students were not allowed on school property during the suspension period, so you would be letting the principal know. Although the parent appeared unalarmed, you checked attendance on the other two students to find that they had been reported absent by the teachers. What action should you take at this point?

(Select ONLY ONE in this section.)

| D—1. | No action required |
|---|---|
| | No |
| | Action on your part is absolutely required because this information indicates a violation of suspension and could indicate a school-wide threat |
| D—2. | Call the parents of the other two students to report their absences |
| | No |
| | Although this would be appropriate, it is not the most appropriate action at this time |
| D—3. | Go directly to the truancy officer |
| | No |
| | This would not be the most appropriate action at this time, and generally truancy officers get involved after a specific number of unexcused absences |
| D—4. | Notify the resource officer |
| | No |
| | This would not be the most appropriate action at this time because the principal/assistant principals determine actions related to suspension and school threat |

| D—5. | Go directly to the school principal to report this information |
| --- | --- |
| | Yes |
| | This is the most appropriate action to take at this time. The principal should determine the next course of action |
| D—6. | Call the local police |
| | No |
| | The principal will make this determination |

## Section E: School violence

The resource officer sees two students letting the suspended student in the hall door that is locked. He recognizes the three students and sees suspiciously bulky zipped jackets. He quickly notifies the principal via the two-way radio, who immediately calls a lockdown. The resource officer yelled to the students while the lockdown was being called, but the students darted down the halls in separate directions. After some gunfire throughout the halls of the school, the police swarm the school, apprehend the three students, and secure the school. As the school counselor, what intervention would you consider after such an incident has occurred?

(Select ONLY ONE in this section.)

| E—1. | Begin meeting with small groups of students until you have met with all students school wide |
| --- | --- |
| | No |
| | There are many students who will not need intervention and would rather not participate in counseling |
| E—2. | No action required at this time by the school counselor |
| | No |
| | The school counselor needs to be proactive in reaching out to students who may need counseling to process what they experienced |
| E—3. | Just have teachers report any behavioral changes in students |
| | No |
| | Although it is important for teachers to report such changes in behavior to the school counselor as a possible indicator for counseling, this action is not enough because some students may not overtly display stress reactions |

| E—4. | Visit all classes in the building to invite students to see the school counselor to talk about what they experienced |
| --- | --- |
| | Yes |
| | This would be the most appropriate action at this time. This would allow the school counselor to identify students in need of counseling services based on overt emotional reactions while also encouraging and offering counseling for other experiencing distress |
| E—5. | Encourage students to resume their normal activities so as not to draw attention to the incident |
| | No |
| | Ignoring the emotional reaction will not make it go away and promotes dysfunction. Although resuming daily functioning and activities is the ultimate goal and may be just fine for some students immediately following a stress-inducing incident, it is important to offer the assistance needed and allow students decide when they are ready to resume daily routines |

# Full-length practice exam Simulation Three Responses: Student appraisal

## Brief case description

Timmy, a fifth-grade male, has been referred to the Child Study Team by his teacher because of both behavioral concerns and academic performance. You are the school counselor and chair of the Child Study Team. Based on the information presented in the meeting, the team decides testing is needed. The school counselor explains to Timmy's mother, who is present at the meeting, that the team will administer a series of assessments that will include assessing personality, achievement, aptitude, intelligence, and adaptive and social functioning.

## Section A: Student appraisal

The parent inquires as to how personality tests will get to the root of Timmy's behavior. The school counselor responds that understanding Timmy's personality is important to helping the team to more fully understand Timmy's behavior because the assessment reveals the following information:

(Select as many as you consider indicated in this section.)

| A—1. | Emotional functioning<br>Yes<br>The personality assessment provides this information |
|---|---|
| A—2. | Level of knowledge<br>No<br>The personality assessment does not provide this information. Tests of achievement and intelligence tests measure knowledge |
| A—3. | Motivation<br>Yes<br>The personality assessment provides this information |
| A—4. | Social functioning<br>Yes<br>The personality assessment provides this information |
| A—5. | Skills<br>No<br>The personality assessment does not provide this information. Aptitude tests measure skills |

| A—6. | Attitude<br>Yes<br>The personality assessment provides this information |
|---|---|
| A—7. | Abilities<br>No<br>The personality assessment does not provide this information. Aptitude tests measure abilities |
| A—8. | Level of achievement<br>No<br>The personality assessment does not provide this information Achievement is measured using achievement tests such as Stanford tests of achievement |

## Section B: Student appraisal

The parent asks the school counselor to identify the personality assessment that will be administered to her son. The school counselor identifies the following standardized personality test for the school setting at the elementary level:
   (Choose ONLY ONE in this section.)

| B—1. | SII<br>No<br>The SII measures career interest |
|---|---|
| B—2. | Kuder<br>No<br>The Kuder is used for career exploration and planning |
| B—3. | SAT<br>No<br>The SAT is an aptitude test |
| B—4. | Vineland<br>Yes<br>The Vineland measures levels of personal and social functioning and is considered to be a personality test |
| B—5. | ACT<br>No<br>The ACT is a test of achievement |

## Section C: Student appraisal

The parent also asks which achievement test will be used. The school counselor replies identifying the following standardized achievement test:

(Select ONLY ONE in this section.)

| C—1. | MBTI |
| | No |
| | The MBTI is a personality test |
| C—2. | Woodcock-Johnson |
| | Yes |
| | The Woodcock-Johnson is a test of achievement |
| C—3. | Vineland |
| | No |
| | The Vineland is considered a personality test/test of adaptive behavior |
| C—4. | Stanford-Binet |
| | No |
| | The Stanford-Binet is a test of intelligence |
| C—5. | SDS |
| | No |
| | The SDS is a career interest inventory |
| C—6. | ASVAB |
| | No |
| | The ASVAB is an aptitude test |
| C—7. | SAT |
| | No |
| | The SAT is an aptitude test |

## Section D: Student appraisal

The parent requests that the team also includes an aptitude test because she is worried about her son's abilities and potential for learning. The school counseling identifies the following standardized aptitude test appropriate for Timmy's age:

(Select ONLY ONE in this section.)

| D—1. | ACT |
| | No |
| | The ACT is an achievement test. |
| D—2. | Kaufman Assessment Battery |
| | Yes |
| | The Kaufman Assessment Battery is an aptitude test often used in the schools for ages 3—18. |
| D—3. | Vineland |
| | No |
| | The Vineland is considered a personality test/test of adaptive behavior |
| D—4. | Woodcock-Johnson |
| | No |
| | The Woodcock-Johnson is a test of achievement |
| D—5. | WISC |
| | No |
| | The WISC is often used in schools for diagnostic testing to assess level of intelligence |
| D—6. | GATB |
| | No |
| | The GATB is an aptitude test, but it is intended for students in grades nine and higher |

## Section E: Student appraisal

The team decides that meeting with the school counselor individually would also be beneficial. The school counselor gathers information using the following nonstandardized approaches to better understand Timmy and his situation:

(Select as many as you consider indicated in this section.)

| E—1. | Observation |
| | Yes |
| | School counselors gain valuable information by observing students and their interactions with peers and adults in the classroom, on the playground, at lunch, and so on |
| E—2. | WISC |
| | No |
| | This is a standardized test for intelligence |

| | |
|---|---|
| E—3. | Portfolio<br>Yes<br>Portfolios provide a chronicle of information about a student's interests, strengths, and challenges |
| E—4. | ACT<br>No<br>This is a standardized measure of achievement |
| E—5. | Counseling notes<br>Yes<br>School counselor case notes provide a means by which to follow a student's progress from initial session to final session |
| E—6. | Consulting with teachers<br>Yes<br>Consultation with other school personnel is a valuable means by which to learn more about a student by someone who may know the student better and/or in a different capacity |
| E—7. | School records<br>Yes<br>A thorough review of the student's cumulative record provides the school counselor with insight into the student's health, personal-social, academic, and possibly psychological, social, and emotional functioning |
| E—8. | SAT<br>No<br>The SAT is a standardized measure of aptitude |
| E—9. | GATB<br>No<br>The GATB is a standardized aptitude measure |

## Section F: Student appraisal

After four sessions, the school counselor becomes concerned about Timmy's increasingly flat affect, sense of worthlessness, excessive absences, inability to focus, lack of personal hygiene, and frequent injuries. The school counselor cannot get Timmy to communicate. The school counselor calls a meeting with Timmy and his mother. When his mother arrives, she is agitated and expresses what a terrible inconvenience this is, reiterating that she was just here a month ago. During the meeting, the school counselor identifies the following behaviors, coupled with the information she already has, as indicators of child abuse/neglect:

(Select as many as you consider indicated in this section.)

| F—1. | Mother smells of alcohol<br>Yes<br>Alone this would not be an indicator. However, coupled with other indicators this is considered |
|---|---|
| F—2. | Mother asks school counselor to be sensitive to her son<br>No<br>Generally, abusive parents will encourage the school counselor to use stern punishment |
| F—3. | Mother and son rarely make eye contact<br>Yes<br>Alone this would not be an indicator. However, coupled with other indicators this is considered |
| F—4. | Mother is apathetic<br>Yes<br>Alone this would not be an indicator. However, coupled with other indicators this is considered |
| F—5. | Mother allows son to control the conversation<br>No<br>Generally, the abusive parent will control the conversation |
| F—6. | Mother is indifferent toward son<br>Yes<br>Alone this would not be an indicator. However, coupled with other indicators this is considered |
| F—7. | Mother and son appear secretive<br>Yes<br>Alone this would not be an indicator. However, coupled with other indicators this is considered |
| F—8. | Frequent touch between mother and son<br>No<br>Generally, the abusive parent will not openly display intimacy. Frequent touching and inappropriate or questionable touching could be an indicator of sexual abuse. All to be considered in context and in relation to other signs |
| F—9. | Son flinches when mother turns in his direction<br>Yes<br>This behavior may be associated with physical and sexual abuse |

## Section G: Student appraisal

After the meeting, the school counselor suspects that Timmy is being neglected and abused. The school counselor should take the following course of action:
(Select ONLY ONE in this section.)

| G—1. | Contact local police |
| --- | --- |
| | No |
| | The local police may refer the child to CPS, or make contact with CPS themselves |
| G—2. | Contact Timmy's dad |
| | No |
| | The school counselor cannot be sure that Timmy's dad is not involved or will protect Timmy |
| G—3. | Contact the emergency contact on Timmy's health card |
| | No |
| | School counselors have a legal responsibility to report suspected child abuse to appropriate authorities (i.e., CPS) |
| G—4. | Contact CPS |
| | Yes |
| | This is the professional, ethical, and legal course of action |
| G—5. | Asks principal for appropriate course of action |
| | No |
| | Principals depend upon school counselors to know the appropriate and legal course of action in these situations. Principals generally like to know when calls are made to CPS because social workers often visit the child at the school and go through the front office |
| G—6. | Inform the mother of her suspicions, and say if it continues she will report her |
| | No |
| | This could anger the parent, who, if she is abusive, may take it out on Timmy. Instead of protecting Timmy, you may have placed him in harm's way. The responsible, ethical, and legal course of action is to report suspected child abuse to CPS |

# Full-length practice exam Simulation Four responses: Early intervention

## Brief case description

You are a middle-school counselor. Your principal comes to you concerned about the disproportionately high number of students identified as special education and students with a 504 plan as compared to other schools in the district of similar size and population. He asks for suggestions that could reduce the number of students identified as special needs in your school while still providing students with the assistance that is needed to be successful. The principal also expresses his concern with the lack of referrals to the school-wide early intervention team, which you chair.

## *Section A: Early intervention*

You provide the principal with the following suggestion:
   (Choose ONLY ONE in this section.)

| | | |
|---|---|---|
| A—1. | Require that teachers refer students to the early intervention team prior to referral to the 504 or child study teams, unless a parent objects | |
| | Yes | |
| | This would be the best course of action at this time, allowing for early and least-restrictive intervention that may be all the student needs to be successful | |
| A—2. | Pay teachers for the time they spend in early intervention team meetings | |
| | No | |
| | Attending school-related meetings to help students to be successful is the responsibility of the educator | |
| A—3. | Require a minimum number of early intervention team meetings each academic year | |
| | No | |
| | This would create unwarranted team meetings to meet a quota | |
| A—4. | Require teachers and parents to refer students to the early intervention team prior to referral to a 504 or child study committee | |
| | No | |
| | Parents of children in the public schools have a legal right to make referrals to these committees and at any time | |

| A—5. | Require particular grade levels to go through the early intervention team prior to going through child study or the 504 team |
|---|---|
| | No |
| | This is not equitable access to educational programs |

## Section B: Early intervention

Joshua, a sixth-grade student, was referred to the early intervention team for academic difficulties. His teacher expressed that he is well liked by other students and he is cooperative and that she has not noticed any other concerns apart from academic performance. What type of information or data would be important to acquire from the teacher and parents during the initial team meeting to assess Joshua's issues?

(Select as many as you consider indicated in this section.)

| B—1. | Hobbies and interests |
|---|---|
| | No |
| | This would not be useful to assess Joshua's issues related to academic difficulties |
| B—2. | Past and present social functioning |
| | Yes |
| | Interpersonal relations impact diverse areas of life |
| B—3. | Sleeping habits |
| | Yes |
| | Sleep impacts daily functioning and performance |
| B—4. | Medical information |
| | Yes |
| | There may be a medical explanation for Joshua's academic difficulties |
| B—5. | Behavioral records |
| | No |
| | Behavior is not identified as a concern |
| B—6. | Family income |
| | No |
| | Family income will not provide insight into the student's academic difficulties |

| B—7. | Past and present academic performance |
| --- | --- |
| | Yes |
| | This will help the school counselor to identify the onset of academic difficulties and patterns in academic strengths and weaknesses |
| B—8. | Subjects with which the student is struggling |
| | Yes |
| | It is important to know the academic areas of difficulty in order to target strategies for remediation |
| B—9. | Past and present emotional functioning |
| | No |
| | Emotional disturbance is not identified as a concern |
| B—10. | Student's eating habits |
| | No |
| | Student's eating habits would not offer insight into his academic difficulties at this time |
| B—11. | Environmental factors |
| | Yes |
| | A change in environment may impact academic functioning |

## Section C: Early intervention

During the team meeting, an individualized intervention plan is established to target Joshua's areas of academic difficulty. After the early intervention team meeting, as the team's chair you would do the following:

(Select ONLY ONE in this section.)

| C—1. | Distribute a copy of the intervention plan to all the members of the team, the students' teachers, the parents, and to the student's record |
| --- | --- |
| | Yes |
| | The intervention plan needs to be shared with all those who work with the student, and it becomes a part of the student's permanent school record |
| C—2. | Provide only the intervention team members and parents with a copy of the intervention plan |
| | No |
| | The plan needs to go to all those who work with the student and become a part of the student's academic record |

| C—3. | Meet with principal regarding the meeting outcome |
| --- | --- |
| | No |
| | The principal does not have time to meet and discuss the outcome of every education meeting that takes place in their building |
| C—4. | Ensure that the intervention plan does not become a part of the student's educational record |
| | No |
| | The intervention plan is to become part of the student's educational record |

## Section D: Early intervention

Two weeks later, the team reconvenes at the request of the teacher who reports that although Joshua's academics have improved slightly, Joshua is displaying behavioral issues such as agitation and bullying of other students, which is out of character for Joshua according to his teacher. During the meeting, the parent shares that she and her husband are going through a divorce, which began just about the time that Joshua's academic performance declined. Based on this new information, Joshua's intervention plan was modified to include participation in a small group on divorce. The following permissions must be obtained:

(Select ONLY ONE in this section.)

| D—1. | Informed consent from the parents of all group members |
| --- | --- |
| | Yes |
| | Although school counselors are not legally obligated to obtain parental permission prior to counseling, unless there is a federal or state statute to the contrary, considering that most school divisions do require parental permission for ongoing individual and small group counseling and considering the sensitive nature of the topic and age of the student, parental permission should be secured |
| D—2. | Because small groups are a primary method of school counseling program delivery, parental consent is assumed |
| | No |
| | School counselors do not assume parental consent for student participation in group counseling |
| D—3. | Informed consent of parents of all group members and participants |
| | No |
| | Students can give verbal consent, while the school counselor seeks written consent from parents |

| D—4. | Informed consent only from Joshua's parent because the activity is connected to an intervention plan |
| --- | --- |
| | No |
| | School counselors should secure written consent from parents for student participation in group counseling |
| D—5. | No Informed consent is required |
| | No |
| | Although school counselors are not legally obligated to obtain parental permission prior to counseling, unless there is a federal or state statute to the contrary, most school divisions require parental permission for ongoing individual and small group counseling and when meeting with students on sensitive topics |

## Section E: Early intervention

During your first group session, one of the most important issues you want to discuss with these adolescents relates to:
  (Select ONLY ONE in this section.)

| E—1. | Goals |
| --- | --- |
| | No |
| | Not the most important among the choices |
| E—2. | Topic |
| | No |
| | Not the most important among the choices |
| E—3. | Member rights |
| | No |
| | Not the most important among the choices |
| E—4. | Confidentiality |
| | Yes |
| | It is critical to discuss with students the limits of confidentiality in group work during the first group session |
| E—5. | Signed consent |
| | No |
| | Signed consent should be secured prior to the first session of the group |
| E—6. | Termination |
| | No |
| | Termination is not generally discussed until the final stages of the group |

| | |
|---|---|
| E—7. | Process<br>No<br>Not the most important among the choices |
| E—8. | Emergency contact information<br>No<br>Generally, emergency contact information is on file in the school already |

## Section F: Early intervention

During the third group session, one of the group members becomes very angry and says, "I never even got to tell the jerk what I thought of him before he left us." Which counseling techniques might be useful at this time to mediate the student's emotional distress and work through the issue presented?

(Select as many as you consider indicated in this section.)

| | |
|---|---|
| F—1. | Clarifying<br>No<br>This will not help to mediate the student's emotional distress or help the student to work through the distressing experience |
| F—2. | Empty chair<br>Yes<br>This is an excellent gestalt enacting dialogue technique to assist the student in appropriately experiencing the unresolved issues with his father |
| F—3. | Paraphrasing<br>No<br>This will not help to mediate the student's emotional distress or help the student to work through the distressing experience |
| F—4. | Relaxation techniques<br>Yes<br>This will help the student to self-regulate |
| F—5. | Guided imagery<br>Yes<br>An excellent cognitive behavioral technique that will teach the student to use mental pictures to self-regulate |

| F—6. | Stress inoculation |
| --- | --- |
| | Yes |
| | An excellent cognitive behavioral technique for teaching skills that head off stress and identify triggers to stress |
| F—7. | Behavior contract |
| | No |
| | Behavioral interventions are not indicated for this student at this time |

# Full-length practice exam Simulation Five responses: Academic achievement

## Brief case description

You are a school counselor at a large, pluralistic elementary school. Twenty percent of the student body is special education and ESL students. Nearly half of the student body receives free or reduced lunch. Your school did not make AYP last year, so everyone is academic focused and implementing programs that will result in the immediate improvement of standardized test scores.

### Section A: Academic achievement

What information do you need in order to begin planning strategies to improve academic achievement?

(Select as many as you consider indicated in this section.)

| A—1. | Parent support<br>Yes<br>Parents are resourceful and excellent sources of manpower and creativity |
|---|---|
| A—2. | Student interests<br>No<br>Knowledge of the students' interests will not aid in planning strategies for academic achievement |
| A—3. | Past successes<br>Yes<br>Draw upon what has worked before within the school and with your unique student population |
| A—4. | School and community resources<br>Yes<br>Knowing what resources are available to you is helpful in the planning process |
| A—5. | Target populations<br>Yes<br>School counselors need to know who is to receive the intervention |

| | |
|---|---|
| A—6. | Students' favorite subjects<br>No<br>Knowing which subjects students like best will not, generally, be helpful in planning strategies for academic achievement. However, teaching styles and methods of instruction preferred by students could be helpful |
| A—7. | Subject areas of weakness<br>Yes<br>School counselors need to know the subjects for which students need intervention |
| A—8. | Subject areas of strength<br>No<br>School counselors need to identify subject areas of weakness for intervention planning |

## Section B: Academic achievement

Which data sources would provide useful information for creating classroom lessons to target specific grade levels and subjects?

(Select as many as you consider indicated in this section.)

| | |
|---|---|
| B—1. | Standardized test score reports<br>Yes<br>Standardized test score reports can identify specific students, groups of students, subject areas, content specific to subject areas, and teachers |
| B—2. | School report card<br>Yes<br>Data from school report cards can serve as an indicator of systems-level student needs in specific academic areas |
| B—3. | School-wide attendance patterns<br>Yes<br>Schools with poor student attendance will likely experience low academic performance because the two have been found to be correlated |
| B—4. | Individual disciplinary records<br>No<br>Behavior can be an obstacle to academic performance; however, it would be time-consuming to review every student's disciplinary record and is not indicated for a systems-focused intervention |

| B—5. | Family structure |
| --- | --- |
| | No |
| | Knowing students' family structure would not be particularly useful in planning systems-focused strategies for academic achievement |
| B—6. | Each student's academic record |
| | No |
| | This will allow for individualized intervention; however, it can be time-consuming to review every student's academic record and is not indicated for systems-focused intervention planning |

## Section C: Academic achievement

Data analysis reveals grade 3 math and grade 5 English as areas of specific weakness, particularly among the special education and ESL populations and African American males. Which intervention would be most useful for providing responsive services for these struggling students?

(Select ONLY ONE in this section.)

| C—1. | Small group on study skills |
| --- | --- |
| | No |
| | This would be a useful responsive service for these students; however, it is not the best choice among those listed |
| C—2. | Classroom lesson on study skills that crosswalks school counseling standards and core academic standards |
| | No |
| | Study skills would be useful for this population; however, the target subjects are math and English, which may not be the core subjects covered in this classroom lesson |
| C—3. | Small group on study skills that crosswalks school counseling standards and math and English standards |
| | Yes |
| | Small groups would provide a systems-focused responsive service that targets the two specific areas of need for these students |
| C—4. | Small group on test taking skills that crosswalks school counseling standards and core academic standards |
| | No |
| | Test-taking skills would be useful for this population; however, the target subjects are math and English, which may not be the core subjects covered in this classroom lesson |

| C—5. | Classroom lesson on test taking skills that crosswalks school counseling standards and core academic standards |
| --- | --- |
| | No |
| | Test taking skills would be useful for this population; however, the target subjects are math and English, which may not be the core subjects covered in this classroom lesson |
| C—6. | Small group on test taking |
| | No |
| | This would be a useful responsive service for these students; however, it is not the best choice among those listed |

## Section D: Academic achievement

While chatting with your school's test coordinator, you discover that many special education students have not been given special accommodations during standardized testing. When you voiced your concern to the test coordinator, she said that as long as examiners and proctors are in short supply and because teachers are not always giving these students the accommodations during the school year, then she is not going to worry about it at testing time. What is the best course of action to take at this time?
 (Select ONLY ONE in this section.)

| D—1. | Let the test coordinator know that you will be making the principal aware of these unlawful instructional and standardized testing practices |
| --- | --- |
| | Yes |
| | The principal needs to be made aware that the special education students are not receiving their accommodations as written on the legally binding IEP |
| D—2. | Let the test coordinator know that you will be making the principal aware of these questionable instructional and standardized testing practices |
| | No |
| | These practices are not only questionable but unlawful because they clearly deprive special education students of their rights to testing accommodations |
| D—3. | Let the test coordinator know that if this continues you will need to notify the principal |
| | No |
| | School counselors are student advocates and advocates for social justice. Also, knowing and not doing anything about it can make the school counselor liable as well |

| D—4. | Call a meeting of the teachers, test coordinator, and principal about these practices |
| --- | --- |
| | No |
| | This is the responsibility of the principal/designated school administrator |
| D—5. | Voice your concerns to the test coordinator and trust her to correct the standardized testing practices |
| | No |
| | This is an unlawful practice that must be brought to the attention of the school administrator for immediate correction and possible exploration into past testing impacts and action |
| D—6. | Notify the school division's testing administrator about these questionable standardized testing practices |
| | No |
| | School counselors should follow the chain of command by reporting this information to the school principal |

## Section E: Academic achievement

The actions of the teachers and test coordinator concerned you, so you reviewed some of the special education students' IEPs to find that several students were given special accommodations only on standardized tests, not on classroom tests. When you spoke to one of the teachers of these students, he said that this was an IEP team decision that included the principal and that the decision was based on the lack of manpower during the school day. What is the best course of action to take at this time?

(Select as many as you consider indicated in this section.)

| E—1. | Talk to the principal about ways that these students can get the accommodations during the school day, not just on standardized testing days |
| --- | --- |
| | Yes |
| | School counselors use their leadership skills to partner with school administrators |
| E—2. | Contact the school division's test administrator |
| | No |
| | School counselors partner with their building principals to effect change |

| | |
|---|---|
| E—3. | Discuss with the principal your concern about setting the students up for failure on standardized testing day if they have not been pulled out of the class the entire year for testing<br>Yes<br>Helping the principal to understand the adverse impact that this practice can have on student performance during standardized testing would be beneficial |
| E—4. | Contact the State Department of Education<br>No<br>School counselors can best serve students by working within the school's policies, and because this is an IEP team decision, it is not an unlawful or unethical practice that warrants going over the head of the building principal |
| E—5. | Let the principal know that if he does not do something about this then you are going to contact the Department of Education<br>No<br>Although the situation may adversely impact student scores, the situation is not unlawful and was based on a team decision, which included the parent |
| E—6. | Contact your school division's supervisor of instructional practices so that he or she can talk to the principal about these practices<br>No<br>This action could harm your relationship with your principal, and thus your ability to provide optimal services to students |
| E—7. | Request to be a part of the IEP meetings, so that you can have a voice in the creation of students' IEPs<br>Yes<br>School counselors can advocate for students by taking part in child study, IEP, and other academic-related meetings |

# Full-length practice exam Simulation Six responses: Assessment

## Brief case description

You are a high-school counselor. Terrance is a junior at the high school whose parent has requested that you pull his record and go over the grades and assessments with her so that she might better understand his academic status and level of functioning. She wants to know if her son, Terrance, has the grades and intelligence to get into a four-year college and to be successful in college. She said Terrance has identified seven colleges that offer majors in communication, which is his area of interest.

## Section A: Assessment

The first assessment you came to was the WAIS-II. You explained that Terrance has a verbal IQ score of 95 and a performance IQ score of 85, giving Terrance a full-scale IQ of 90. Terrance's mother responds, "I don't know what that means." What information would you share with the student's mother?

(Select as many as you consider indicated in this section.)

| A—1. | Most individuals have an IQ score between 85 and 115<br>Yes<br>This is accurate and helpful information to give the parent |
|---|---|
| A—2. | Because the assessment uses a 95% confidence level, Terrance's score could, at any given time, fall within five points in either direction<br>Yes<br>This will help the parent to understand how the score might be captured on other similar assessments |
| A—3. | Terrance's IQ score indicates genius<br>No<br>This is not an accurate interpretation of Terrance's score |
| A—4. | Terrance has an average IQ<br>Yes<br>This is an accurate interpretation of Terrance's score |

| A—5. | Terrance has a very low IQ |
| --- | --- |
| | No |
| | This is not an accurate interpretation of Terrance's score |
| A—6. | Terrance's IQ indicates mild retardation |
| | No |
| | This is not an accurate interpretation of Terrance's score |

## Section B: Assessment

Terrance's mother also said Terrance told her that he got a 34 on his ACT test. She began to cry stating that her son would "never get into college with such low scores on his college entrance exams." You look at Terrance's score report from ACT and see that, indeed, Terrance's score on the ACT was 34. What information would you share with this parent?

(Select as many as you consider indicated in this section.)

| B—1. | The average score of the ACT is 21 |
| --- | --- |
| | Yes |
| | This is accurate information that will help the parent to understand the meaning of her son's score |
| B—2. | The average score on the ACT is 71 |
| | No |
| | This is not accurate; the average score on the ACT is 21 |
| B—3. | Because the high score is 75, Terrance did not do well |
| | No |
| | This is not accurate; the high score on the ACT is 36 |
| B—4. | ACT scores range from 1 to 36 |
| | Yes |
| | This is accurate and will help Terrance's mother to understand his score |
| B—5. | ACT scores range from 25 to 75 |
| | No |
| | This is not accurate information; the ACT score range is 1 to 36 |
| B—6. | Because the high score is 36, Terrance did very well |
| | Yes |
| | This is an accurate interpretation of Terrance's ACT score |

## Section C: Assessment

As you go through Terrance's record you notice that there are no SAT scores. His mother said he is not taking the SAT because he took the ACT. What advice would you give to the parent at this point?
   (Select ONLY ONE in this section.)

| C—1. | The ACT is all he needs |
| --- | --- |
|  | No |
|  | It is best to take the one that the college of your choice requires. Many will take either test, but both are encouraged because each tests you in a different way |
| C—2. | The SAT is the most widely used college entrance exam in the country although many colleges accept either the ACT or SAT |
|  | Yes |
|  | This is accurate information. Students should also be advised to take the test required by the college of their choice |
| C—3. | The ACT measures the same thing as the SAT |
|  | No |
|  | This is not accurate information |
| C—4. | The SAT is not used very often for college entrance; however, it is a good measure of achievement |
|  | No |
|  | The SAT is the most widely used college entrance exam in the country |
| C—5. | The SAT is the only assessment that should be taken for college entrance |
|  | No |
|  | Students who do not wish to take both the ACT and the SAT should take the test required by the college of their choice |

## Section D: Assessment

Terrance's mother says that she is still a bit concerned about Terrance's choice of major. She worries that it will not be a good match. She adds that she knows Terrance is interested in communication, but she is not sure about his skills and abilities or that the work environment would fit his personality. The school counselor suggests that the career counselor administer the following career interest inventory:

(Select ONLY ONE in this section.)

| D—1. | ASVAB<br>No<br>The ASVAB is an aptitude test |
|---|---|
| D—2. | Kaufman<br>No<br>The Kaufman is an assessment of cognitive development and not generally used as a career decision-making tool |
| D—3. | SDS<br>Yes<br>The SDS will match Terrance's skills and interests to specific careers |
| D—4. | Super's model of career development<br>No<br>This is a career development model not a career assessment |
| D—5. | WAIS<br>No<br>This is an intelligence test and not generally used to make career decisions |
| D—6. | Vineland<br>No<br>This assessment measures adaptive behavior |

## Section E: Assessment

Terrance's mother thanks you for your time and asks, "What do we need to do next because it is already the spring of Terrance's junior year?" The following information would be useful for the parent at this time:

(Select as many as you consider indicated in this section.)

| E—1. | FAFSA deadlines<br>Yes<br>This form should be completed in January of the student's senior year |
|---|---|
| E—2. | SAT information and deadlines<br>Yes<br>Students are encouraged to take both the SAT and the ACT, unless their school(s) of choice specifies one or the other |

| | | |
|---|---|---|
| E—3. | ACT information and deadlines<br>No<br>The student already took the ACT and scored well | |
| E—4. | PSAT information and deadlines<br>Yes<br>Although this test is generally taken in the ninth and tenth grade years, it is sometimes taken in the 11th-grade year for scholarship awards and as a practice test for the SAT | |
| E—5. | College fair dates<br>Yes<br>This would be beneficial to Terrance, who has not identified a specific college | |
| E—6. | GED Official Practice Test information and deadlines<br>No<br>This is an alternative education route for students who do not desire to graduate from high school or who are at risk of dropping out of high school | |
| E—7. | Scholarship websites<br>Yes<br>This is useful information for college-bound students | |
| E—8. | Financial aid website<br>Yes<br>This is useful information for college-bound students | |

# Full-length practice exam Simulation Seven responses: Special needs and scope of practice

## Brief case description

Julianna is a fifth-grade African American student diagnosed with ADHD, and you are the elementary-school counselor at her school. The teacher and parent report that Julianna consistently presents as hyperactive, restless, argumentative, and impulsive. Julianna's mother reports that the medication Julianna is taking does not appear to be working because Julianna continues to experience academic, social, and behavioral issues. Julianna's mother is a single parent and admits that she does not have much time to spend with Julianna and her other two children to help with their studies because she works two jobs. A 504-committee meeting was just held, and Julianna qualified for a 504 Plan due to the academic and social impact related to Julianna's ADHD.

## Section A: Special needs and scope of practice

During the 504 meeting, you identified the following strategies and approaches to help Julianna and her family:
   (Select as many as you consider indicated in this section.)

| A—1. | Homeschooling<br>No<br>Julianna can benefit from the social interaction and structure of school |
|---|---|
| A—2. | Social skills development<br>Yes<br>Students with ADHD often experience interpersonal relationship issues |
| A—3. | Reduced television time<br>No<br>A reduction in television time is not indicated at this time |
| A—4. | Parenting skills training<br>Yes<br>It is important to help parents to acquire the skills needed to help their children with ADHD |

| | |
|---|---|
| A—5. | Family counseling<br>Yes<br>ADHD is a challenge that impacts the entire family |
| A—6. | Reduced computer time<br>No<br>A reduction in computer time is not indicated at this time |
| A—7. | Change in diet<br>Yes<br>There is much research to support the effectiveness of diet in mediating the symptoms of ADHD. This is an option worthy of further investigation |
| A—8. | Increased time spent with friends<br>No<br>An increase in the amount of time spent with friends is not indicated at this time. Additionally, more time with friends does not equal enhanced social skills. It is possible that more time with friends will lead to more rejection until proper social skills are developed |
| A—9. | Counseling<br>Yes<br>A combination of counseling and medication has been found to be effective in mediating the symptoms of ADHD |
| A—10. | Reduced length of academic work<br>Yes<br>This is a 504 Plan accommodation that has been found to be helpful for students with ADHD |
| A—11. | Increased length of academic work<br>No<br>Lengthening academic work and the time required to complete such assignments is frustrating for a child with ADHD, who is already having difficulty focusing on the work load assigned |
| A—12. | Providing choices (academic and home tasks)<br>Yes<br>Allowing choices for students with ADHD will help them to select a "means to the end" that is best suited for them and helps them to stay on task |

## Section B: Special needs and scope of practice

Julianna's mother asks about what other things she can do at home to improve Julianna's behavior and increase cooperation. In addition to organization and maintaining a consistent schedule, you name the following:

(Select as many as you consider indicated in this section.)

| B—1. | Positive reinforcement <br> Yes <br> Positive reinforcement for following rules at home and school has been used successfully with children and adolescents with ADHD |
|---|---|
| B—2. | Loss of privileges <br> Yes <br> Loss of privileges has been used successfully as a mild consequence to undesired behaviors for children with ADHD |
| B—3. | Allow more computer time <br> No <br> Increasing computer time is not indicated |
| B—4. | Negotiated rewards <br> Yes <br> Allowing choices and negotiating rewards helps children with ADHD to participate in their own behavioral plan |
| B—5. | Contracts <br> Yes <br> Behavior contracts have been found to be useful in mediating the negative behaviors associated with ADHD and provide a clearly defined process of rewards and consequences |
| B—6. | Resist setting goals <br> No <br> Goals are useful for children with ADHD, aiding in directing behavior |
| B—7. | Mild consequences <br> Yes <br> Mild consequences are enough to shape behavior |
| B—8. | Give specific behavioral feedback <br> Yes <br> Specific feedback allows for specific change and clear understanding |

## Section C: Special needs and scope of practice

What counseling theory might be most useful when working with Julianna?

(Select ONLY ONE in this section.)

| C—1. | Gestalt counseling  <br>No  <br>This is not the best counseling approach among those listed here for children with ADHD |
|---|---|
| C—2. | Behavioral counseling  <br>Yes  <br>Behavioral counseling is the approach most widely used with children with ADHD |
| C—3. | Reality counseling  <br>No  <br>This is not the best counseling approach among those listed here for children with ADHD |
| C—4. | Person-centered counseling  <br>No  <br>This is not the best counseling approach among those listed here for children with ADHD |
| C—5. | Adlerian counseling  <br>No  <br>This is not the best counseling approach among those listed here for children with ADHD |
| C—6. | Cognitive behavioral counseling  <br>No  <br>This is not the best counseling approach among those listed here for children with ADHD |

## Section D: Special needs and scope of practice

Several months into the 504 Plan, the teacher and parent report that Julianna's behavioral and peer relations problems have increased, and her academic performance has declined. Julianna is now having full-blown temper tantrums at home, at school, and in the community.

She is disobedient and blames others for her actions. The school counselor strongly encourages the following actions to help Julianna and her family:
(Select as many as you consider indicated in this section.)

| D—1. | Referral to child study for possible testing and special education services<br>Yes<br>It is a good idea to explore possible coexisting conditions |
|---|---|
| D—2. | Homeschooling<br>No<br>The structure provided by attending school and the social interactions with age—appropriate others is beneficial for children with ADHD |
| D—3. | Participation in Governor's School<br>No<br>Governor's School is for students who have been identified as gifted |
| D—4. | Medical examination by the child's physician<br>Yes<br>It is important to rule out medical conditions that may be a contributing factor |
| D—5. | Less time with peers<br>No<br>Less time with peers is not indicated as this time |
| D—6. | Appointment with a child psychiatrist<br>Yes<br>An appointment with a child psychiatrist is indicated based on presenting behaviors and current diagnosis |
| D—7. | More time with peers<br>No<br>More time with peers is not indicated |
| D—8. | Family counseling<br>Yes<br>The entire family is impacted by the behavioral conditions of a family member |
| D—9. | Resources related to helping children with disruptive behavior issues/disorders<br>Yes<br>School counselors provide parents with information and resources related to behavioral and emotional issues |

## Section E: Special needs and scope of practice

Julianna's mother returns to you a few weeks later and says that the psychiatrist has diagnosed Juliann with oppositional defiance disorder and recommended ongoing individual counseling for Julianna and the family. She asks if you would be Julianna's counselor over the next couple of years. Your response is

(Select ONLY ONE in this section.)

| E—1. | Of course |
| --- | --- |
| | No |
| | Julianna's counseling needs are beyond the scope of school counseling |
| E—2. | I would like to, as I have enjoyed working with Julianna very much, however, I just do not have time as the only school counselor in the building |
| | No |
| | Time is not the primary issue |
| E—3. | Julianna's needs are beyond the scope of school counseling, but I have a list of counseling resources, which may be helpful in identifying a counselor |
| | Yes |
| | School counselors do not provide individuals with ongoing counseling for chronic behavioral, emotional, and mental health issues. This type of long-term counseling is beyond the scope of school counseling |
| E—4. | I would not be able to do this during the school day, as it is beyond the scope of school counseling. However, I can provide counseling services to Julianna outside of school hours at your home or mine for a minimal charge |
| | No |
| | This is a dual relationship and an ethical violation |
| E—5. | Oppositional defiance disorder is not really my area of expertise, but I will work with Julianna because she and I already have a positive relationship |
| | No |
| | Practicing outside of your areas of expertise is an ethical violation and could become a legal issue as well |

# Full-length practice exam Simulation Eight responses: Program evaluation

## Brief case description

You are the school counselor at an elementary school. The principal wants to ensure that you are implementing a data- and needs-driven, comprehensive school counseling program. As such, she has requested that you present her with a five-year plan for meeting the needs of stakeholders and evaluating the school counseling program.

### Section A: Program evaluation

What strategies would you include in your plan to ensure that the school counseling program is appropriately evaluated?

(Select as many as you consider indicated in this section.)

| A—1. | Preprogram surveys<br>Yes<br>Preprogram measures provide school counselors with a baseline for assessing change |
|---|---|
| A—2. | Student names for interview by the principal<br>No<br>Principals do not have time to interview students about their perceptions of the effectiveness of the school counseling program. Also, principals are generally more interested in data that identifies the outcome of school counseling practices |
| A—3. | Needs assessment<br>Yes<br>Needs assessments are a time-honored means for collecting data from stakeholders for needs-driven program decision making |
| A—4. | Postprogram surveys<br>Yes<br>Postprogram assessment provides program outcome data. School counselors combine pre-and postprogram measures to assess academic and behavioral change |

| A—5. | Teacher names for interview by the principal |
| --- | --- |
| | No |
| | Principals do not have time to interview teachers about their perceptions of the effectiveness of the school counseling program. Also, principals are generally more interested in data that identifies the outcome of school counseling practices |
| A—6. | Teacher program perception surveys |
| | Yes |
| | Although program outcome data is necessary in today's educational climate that asks how school counselors are making a difference in the lives of students, process data from perception surveys depicts how the school counseling program is viewed by others and may identify areas of strength and weakness for program improvement |
| A—7. | Parent reports to the principal |
| | No |
| | Principals do not have time to read parent reports or receive visits from parents of all the students regarding the school counseling program |
| A—8. | Student program perception surveys |
| | Yes |
| | Program outcome data is critical to answering the important question "How do school counselors make a difference in the lives of students?"; however, process data from perception surveys are helpful in identifying areas of strength and weakness for program improvement |
| A—9. | Community member names for interview by the principal |
| | No |
| | Principals do not have time to interview community members about the effectiveness of the school counseling program |
| A—10. | Statistical testing of pre-post data |
| | Yes |
| | Statistical tests of program data are useful in understanding if changes related to program implementation are significant, which can be documented in results reports to school administrators and stakeholders |
| A—11. | Committee meeting involvement |
| | No |
| | Although school counselors are encouraged to participate in committees and collaborate with others within and outside of the school, membership does not offer insight into the effectiveness of the school counseling program |

| A—12. | Website development |
| --- | --- |
| | No |
| | School counselors are encouraged to have a presence on the Web. However, having a website does not offer insight into program effectiveness |

## Section B: Program evaluation

The principal likes the strategies you have designed to include in your five-year plan for accountable school counseling practices. She is uncertain as to how you would objectively measure each classroom lesson and small group activity to ensure that you are making a positive difference in the lives of the students. She is focused on data that will demonstrate how well you have met stated goals, objectives, and standards. Which of the following types of evaluation will yield this data?

(Choose ONLY ONE in this section.)

| B—1. | Process evaluation |
| --- | --- |
| | No |
| | Process evaluation yields formative information that identifies program strengths and weakness |
| B—2. | Formative evaluation |
| | No |
| | Formative evaluation, also referred to as process evaluation, provides information about program strengths and weaknesses |
| B—3. | Outcome evaluation |
| | Yes |
| | Outcome evaluation yield objective data that demonstrates the effectiveness of the program in meeting stated goals and objectives |
| B—4. | Pre-and post-questionnaire of participants' perceptions of the program |
| | No |
| | Perceptions will not objectively measure program effectiveness. The principal is requesting objective outcome data |
| B—5. | Program review by teachers |
| | No |
| | Teacher reviews will yield perception data, which will not objectively measure program effectiveness |

## Section C: Program evaluation

In a recent faculty meeting, your principal stressed the importance of developing research-supported curriculum. You are about to develop a small group for second-grade students on social skills. What information do you need from the research to develop a research-supported curriculum?

(Select as many as you consider indicated in this section.)

| | |
|---|---|
| C—1. | Previous successful social skills programs<br>Yes<br>Understanding what social skills interventions have worked in the past is helpful to present planning |
| C—2. | Age-grade-specific social skills activities<br>Yes<br>Understanding what social skills interventions have worked in the past for a particular age group is helpful when considering the application of those interventions to the age group of the target population |
| C—3. | Correlation between social skills and academic achievement<br>Yes<br>A brief statement in a school counseling action plan about how social skills connect to academic achievement demonstrates how your intervention relates to academic achievement |
| C—4. | Effectiveness of small group programs for enhancing social skills<br>Yes<br>The school counselor wants to demonstrate with research that small group interventions are effective methods of delivery for social skills development |
| C—5. | Definition of social skills<br>No<br>Defining social skills does not contribute to a research-supported curriculum |
| C—6. | Use of recognized interventions for social skills improvement<br>No<br>"Recognized" interventions may not be research-supported interventions |

## Section D: Program evaluation

Which of the following resources would be most useful in providing research pertaining to school counseling and school counseling interventions?

(Select as many as you consider indicated in this section.)

| D—1. | ASCA Scene |
| --- | --- |
| | Yes |
| | The ASCA Scene provides school counselor with an abundance of resources, which may include research and research-supported interventions |
| D—2. | Wikipedia |
| | No |
| | Wikipedia is a fine resource, but it is not considered scholarly |
| D—3. | *Counseling Today* |
| | No |
| | *Counseling Today*, ACA's magazine, is not considered scholarly and does not generally include research |
| D—4. | National Technology Institute for School Counseling |
| | Yes |
| | School counselors can access this resource for research on a variety of school counseling-related topics |
| D—5. | Peer-reviewed journals |
| | Yes |
| | Peer-reviewed journals are considered the best source for scholarly research |
| D—6. | Center for School Counseling Outcome Research |
| | Yes |
| | School counselors access this resource for school counseling-related research |
| D—7. | Webster Dictionary Online |
| | No |
| | This is a fine resource but does not include scholarly research articles |

| D—8. | NBCC Newsletter |
| | No |
| | The NBCC newsletter provides a wealth of information to members pertaining to the professional of counseling. However, it does not include scholarly research articles |
| D—9. | PSC |
| | Yes |
| | This is ASCA's peer-reviewed journal, which contains the most relevant scholarly research for the profession of school counseling |

## Section E: Program evaluation

The data collected from your social skills group indicated that the group intervention was not effective in meeting the stated objectives. What type of program evaluation would have been useful to determine the program's strengths and weaknesses and provide information that could be used for program improvement?
 (Choose ONLY ONE in this section.)

| E—1. | Process evaluation |
| | Yes |
| | Process evaluation provides data about the strengths and weaknesses of a program |
| E—2. | Summative evaluation |
| | No |
| | Summative evaluation, also referred to as outcome evaluation, provides objective data about the effectiveness of the intervention in meeting stated goals and objectives |
| E—3. | Outcome evaluation |
| | No |
| | Provides data related to program effectiveness |
| E—4. | Program evaluation |
| | No |
| | May be process or outcome, and the school counselor is seeking process data |
| E—5. | Student evaluation |
| | No |
| | Identifies who is participating in the evaluation instead of the type of evaluation |

# Full-length practice exam Simulation Nine responses: Alternative educational programs

## Brief case description

You are a high-school counselor who delivered classroom instruction on career readiness to a career and technical education class. Afterward, a student from the class comes to meet with you. During the session, he tells you that he is going to drop out of school. The student just turned 17 and in the tenth grade. He says that he hates coming to school because his classmates are so immature. He says he hates studying and doing homework.

## Section A: Alternative educational programs

In an effort to prevent this student from dropping out of school, which course of action would be best at this time?
   (Select as many as you consider indicated in this section.)

| A—1. | Refer the student to the peer tutoring program |
| --- | --- |
| | No |
| | Peer tutoring is for additional assistance with specific course material, not an intervention for students who express a desire to drop out of school. Plus, he has already expressed a disinterest in peers perceiving them as *immature* |
| A—2. | Suggest the student wait until he is 18 years old to drop out of high school |
| | No |
| | Although students may be eligible to drop out of school as an adult once the student becomes 18, school counselors strive to keep students in school |
| A—3. | Share information about the GED track and the pros and cons of a GED versus a high-school diploma, including the potential impact on student's current career choices |
| | Yes |
| | School counselors have been identified as resource brokers. As such, the school counselor should provide the student with information about alternative education programs that will result in a diploma or GED rather than risk the student dropping out of school. Critical to the student's decision is understanding his post-high-school plans and career aspirations |

| A—4. | Encourage the student to talk to his parents about his plan to drop out of school |
| --- | --- |
| | Yes |
| | School counselors encourage parent-student communication and empower students to talk to parents about important decisions in their life |
| A—5. | Share information about Job Corps and other non-traditional educational programs |
| | Yes |
| | As a resource broker, the school counselor should provide the student with information about alternative education programs that may result in a diploma or GED, rather than risking the student dropping out of school |
| A—6. | Give him the official GED qualifying practice test during the session |
| | No |
| | Unless the student is an emancipated minor, parent permission is required to test the student. Also, parents need to know that their teen is planning to go the GED track versus traditional education that leads to the high-school diploma |

## Section B: Alternative educational programs

The student returns to you the next day and says that his parents got mad because you talked to him about alternative education programs. They told him his is staying in school. Tears in his eyes, the student says, "I'm already almost two years behind. I hate to study, I hate sitting in class, I just hate learning period so I'm failing English and Math." I'm just going to quit school. I don't care what my parents say." What is your best course of action at this time?

(Choose ONLY ONE in this section.)

| B—1. | Help the student to secure a non-peer tutor |
| --- | --- |
| | No |
| | The student wants to drop out of school; tutoring is not indicated at this time |
| B—2. | Ask the student to allow you to set up a meeting with the parents with him present as well |
| | Yes |
| | The school counselor is a student and family advocate and collaborator. It is time for the family to come together to discuss all options. Discuss this option with the student. Since dropping out of school would not be considered a reason to breach confidentiality, an alliance with the student to be in the meeting with his parents to present his case while you present the parents with alternatives to their son dropping out of school |

| B—3. | Tell the student you respect his decision and wish him the best |
| | No |
| | School counselors empower students toward sound choices and advocate for what is in the student's best interest |
| B—4. | Request that the principal contact the student's parents |
| | No |
| | The principal looks to you, the school counselor, to make parent contacts and apply consultation, collaboration, advocacy, and leadership skills. Plus, this was shared in the context of a counseling session and would breach confidentiality *unless* the student wants to the principal to be the one to contact his parent |
| B—5. | Encourage the student to talk to his parents again |
| | No |
| | The student has tried to communicate with his parents. You do not want the student to drop out or put him in the position to be argumentative with his parents |

## Section C: Alternative educational programs

Before the meeting with the student's parents, the student tells you that the only alternative he would consider to dropping out of school is the GED track but that he is okay with your sharing all alternative programs with his parents during the meeting. During the meeting you will discuss the following:

(Select as many as you consider indicated in this section.)

| C—1. | A plan for staying in school |
| | No |
| | This is not the purpose of the meeting as agreed upon by you and the student |
| C—2. | Pros and cons of the GED track in relation to the student's aspirations |
| | Yes |
| | Just as you have already done with the student, helping the family to understand the GED process and potential limitations of the GED versus a high-school diploma |
| C—3. | Other alternative education programs available |
| | Yes |
| | Although the student has made it clear that he only wants to take the GED, discussing alternative programs is acceptable |

| C—4. | The parents' unrealistic expectations of their son |
| --- | --- |
| | No |
| | While finishing high school and securing a diploma is not unreasonable, unrealistic or not, school counselors respect parents' beliefs and understand that parents (generally) want what is best for their children |
| C—5. | Apologizing for sharing alternative education program information with their son without their knowledge |
| | No |
| | The school counselor acted appropriately, providing the 17-year-old student with alternatives to dropping out of high school |

## Section D: Alternative educational programs

During the meeting with the student and his parents, his parents agree to allow him to pursue the GED. What is the next best course of action?
(Choose ONLY ONE in this section.)

| D—1. | Tell the student he no longer needs to attend classes and you will get back to him with a day and time to take the GED |
| --- | --- |
| | No |
| | The student must make a qualifying score on each of the practice GED exam subject areas, or he cannot pursue the GED, thus needs to continue classes until the practice exams |
| D—2. | Tell the student to continue to attend classes but not to worry about grades since he will be sitting for the GED |
| | No |
| | Student must meet the level of knowledge deemed appropriate before he is permitted to take the official GED test. If the student does not, staying in school may be the only choice until the issue can be revisited with him and his parents |
| D—3. | Give the student a day and time to take the GED practice exams or let him know when you'll get back to him with a day and time. Also, encourage the student to continue to attend classes and do his best work |
| | Yes |
| | Generally, these exams are given by the high-school counselor within the school |

## Section E: Alternative educational programs

The parents then ask what type of postsecondary opportunities may exist for their son with only a GED. You respond with which of the following options?

(Select as many as you consider indicated in this section.)

| E—1. | Apprenticeship<br>Yes |
|---|---|
| E—2. | College<br>Yes |
| E—3. | Vocational school<br>Yes |
| E—4. | Technical school<br>Yes |

# Glossary

**504 Plan**: a written document that identifies special accommodations afforded to students with qualifying conditions pursuant to Section 504 of the Rehabilitation Act of 1973.

**Academic development**: one of three developmental domains within a comprehensive school counseling program, promoting skills, relating learning to life, and enhancing academic success and a positive attitude toward school and learning.

**Accommodation**: adjustments made to instruction, homework, testing, and the physical environment in order to promote the success of students with special needs (e.g., special education, 504, and ESL students), as well as students with temporary conditions (e.g., illness, injury).

**Accountability**: practices that are data-driven, standards-based, research-supported, evaluated for effectiveness and ongoing program improvement, and demonstrate the outcomes of a comprehensive school counseling program.

**Achievement gap**: the disparity in educational performance that exists between specific populations of students, primarily low-income and minority students when compared to peers on a variety of educational measures, namely standardized tests.

**Action plan**: written plans that describe specific programming and how programming will achieve stated objectives, including closing the achievement gap activities.

**Action research**: research conducted for the purpose of enhancing the effectiveness of one's practices and/or measuring program outcomes. Pre-post assessment is the most widely used action research in the K-12 educational setting.

**Active listening**: a basic counseling skill and communication skill that attends to the student's verbal and nonverbal behaviors.

**Addiction**: psychological and/or physiological dependence on a substance or activity.

**Advisory council**: a committee of stakeholders, established by the school counselor, to direct and assist the school counseling program. ASCA recommends an advisory committee as part of the manage component of a school counseling program.

**Advocacy**: a function of the school counselor that involves acting and speaking on behalf of others to support equity and access to programming and to promote student, family, school, and community relations and development.

**Aggression**: verbal, physical, and psychological behaviors intended to cause harm, threat, or pain.

**Americans with Disabilities Act (ADA)**: national legislation that prohibits discrimination against persons with a disability in employment, public institutions, public transportation, and telecommunications. A *qualified individual with a disability* is entitled to reasonable accommodations.

**Anorexia**: an eating disorder that is characterized primarily by a consistent and extreme restriction of food intake and a refusal to maintain minimum normal body weight for age and height.

**Antisocial behavior**: behavior, covert and overt, that disregards the rights and privacy of others and the norms, laws, and standards of a society.

**Appraisal (see also assessment)**: approaches and/or measures (standardized and non-standardized) used to gain a greater understanding of a student's functioning (e.g., intellectual, educational, mental, emotional, social, physical, or occupational).

**ASCA National Model**: the only national model for the profession of school counseling designed to serve as a framework from which to implement a comprehensive, developmental, and primarily preventative school counseling program.

**ASCA Mindsets & Behaviors for Student Success**: standards that define that which students should know and be able to do as a result of a comprehensive school counseling program in three broad developmental areas: career, academic, and social/emotional.

**Assessment (see also appraisal)**: approaches and/or measures (standardized and non-standardized) used to gain a greater understanding of a student's functioning (e.g., intellectual, educational, mental, emotional, social, physical, or occupational).

**Autonomy**: one of Kitchener's five ethical principles that refers to the notion of independence, which encourages the client to exercise freedom of choice and behavior when those actions do not infringe upon the rights and beliefs of others. Autonomy is promoted versus dependence upon the counselor.

**Behavior contract**: a plan of action used for general education students to reduce or eliminate specific, observable, and measurable undesirable behaviors by applying specific interventions and rewards.

**Behavior intervention plan**: a plan of action, often part of an IEP for special education students, aimed at reducing or eliminating specific, observable, and measurable undesirable behaviors by applying individualized interventions and rewards.

**Behavioral rehearsal**: practicing new skills and behaviors for application outside of the counseling environment.

**Beneficence**: one of Kitchener's five ethical principles that refers to the counselor's responsibility to *do good*.

**Bibliotherapy**: the use of books/literature in counseling toward established counseling goals.

**Bulimia**: an eating disorder that is characterized primarily by reoccurring episodes of binging and purging (e.g., vomiting, laxatives) and a preoccupation with body weight.

**Bullying (see also cyberbullying)**: any verbal, nonverbal, or physical behavior intended to intimidate, threaten, harm, or cause physical, emotional, and/or psychological pain.

**Career awareness**: the focus on career development at the elementary level that promotes students' knowledge of the world of work.

**Career counseling**: counseling aimed at career development at a specific time and across the lifespan.

**Career development**: one of three developmental domains of a comprehensive school counseling program that promotes students' identification of, and preparation for, desired post–high-school occupations, education, and training, and relating school and the world of work.

**Career development inventories**: instruments used to enhance a student's knowledge pertaining to occupational choices, self-knowledge (e.g., interests, values, skills), and education and training related to specific careers.

**Career exploration**: a focus at the middle-school level that enhances students' understanding of career opportunities and the link between school and work, developing an academic plan to meet postsecondary career choices.

**Career planning**: a focus at the high-school level that encourages students to continue to update and follow through on established career and academic plans for career readiness.

**Child abuse**: harm toward a child caused by neglect or exploitation and/or physical, emotional, psychological, or sexual mistreatment.

**Child neglect**: failure to provide for the social, psychological, emotional, and biological needs of a child; failure to prevent suffering or to act on behalf of the child that places the child in imminent danger; behaviors that place the child in harm's way.

**Child study**: a team approach to identifying and understanding the needs of a student who is not achieving academically in comparison to peers or who is demonstrating physical, emotional, verbal, or psychological issues that are interfering with daily functioning.

**Closed group**: groups that are no longer open to new membership once group facilitation begins.

**Collaboration**: a function of the school counselor that involves working cooperatively with others toward a common goal.

**Computer-assisted career guidance systems**: electronic systems designed to promote career readiness.

**Conflict resolution**: the process by which students resolve conflict peacefully by engaging a variety of skills (e.g., problem solving, empathy, clarification, questioning, communication, and negotiation).

**Consultation**: a function of the school counselor that involves providing services in their area of expertise to other stakeholders (e.g., teachers, parents, and school administrators).

**Crisis**: traumatic or extremely stressful situations that require immediate action to secure the safety and well-being of students and others (e.g., suicide or homicide risk, post-student suicide, homicide, accidental death, terrorism, natural disaster, and child abuse/neglect).

**Culturally blind**: a category of the culturally competent school counseling program whereby school counseling programming minimizes or negates cultural differences, grouping all students into a single one-size-fits-all category. Although the program may engage in activities to close the achievement gap, the one-size-fits-all mindset reflects a bias in favor of the dominant cultures' norms, values, and practices.

**Culturally competent**: a category of the culturally competent school counseling program whereby the program seeks, invites, values, and involves parents/guardian and community leaders who represent the student body's various cultural identities. The program mission statement, goals, and evaluation reflect a commitment to equity and cultural responsiveness. The program facilitates systemic changes and prioritizes the eradication of inequitable school policies and practices in order to promote and support success for all students.

**Culturally inept**: a category of the culturally competent school counseling program whereby the school counseling program preserves and supports the inequitable status quo and does not engage in any activities to enhance cultural responsiveness, reduce achievement or opportunity gaps, or promote equity. School counselors support school personnel who elect to blame *the gaps* on students and families who *don't care* thereby continuing to promote success for only those students who are performing well.

**Culturally sensitive**: a category of the culturally competent school counseling program whereby diversity, discrimination, power and privilege are acknowledged in the program mission statement, in designing and delivering the core school counseling curriculum, and during consultation and counseling. Data is used to develop program goals that support all student populations. There is commitment to enhancing the cultural competence of the school counseling program.

**Cyberbullying (see also bullying)**: any electronic (e.g., via texting, Internet, email, chat rooms, or social networks) behavior intended to intimidate, threaten, harm, or cause physical, emotional, and/or psychological pain.

**Data analysis**: an examination of information that aids school counselors in identifying stakeholder needs, targeting programming, and determining program effectiveness and areas for improvement.

**Data-driven**: programs, practices, and activities that are created based on an analysis of data.

**Diagnostic test**: an assessment used to identify areas of academic competencies and areas of deficit.

**Disability**: a cognitive/psychological, behavioral, and/or physical impairment that limits one or more daily living functions.

**Educational diagnostician**: an individual employed by school divisions to assess levels of student academic functioning and to suggest interventions to meet individual student needs; often a member of child study teams.

**Emancipated minor**: a minor who has been granted by the courts the decision-making power of an adult with regard to their own affairs. Emancipated minors do not need parental consent to engage in counseling services.

**Encapsulation**: ignorance of one's cultural background and how culture impacts one's total being.

**English as a second language**: students whose primary or native language is not English.

**Equity and access**: equal opportunity to rigorous curriculum and school and community programs.

**Extrinsic motivation**: motivation that is achieved with external rewards (e.g., stickers, certification, treats, or praise).

**Family Educational Rights and Privacy Act (FERPA)**: legislation enacted to protect the privacy of students' academic records and to allow parents and students to inspect academic records and petition for the removal of information perceived as inaccurate. FERPA is also known as the Buckley Amendment.

**Fidelity**: one of Kitchener's five ethical principles that refers to the trusting nature of the therapeutic relationship built upon a demonstrated reliability and authenticity toward the client. Counselors promote fidelity by honoring commitments and obligations to clients.

**Free and appropriate public education**: legislation that ensures individualized curriculum that meets unique student needs and prepares students for post–high-school education, careers, and independent living.

**General equivalency diploma (GED)**: an alternative to a high-school diploma and completion of high school, the GED established mastery of high-school core course content and may be obtained during the high-school years through alternative educational programs or post–high-school for those adults who "dropped out" of high school.

**Guidance counselor**: an outdated title for the counselor in the PK-12 school setting, depicting only one component of the many functions of the contemporary school counselor that is associated primarily with more directive approaches and education and career planning.

**High stakes testing**: standardized testing used to determine passing or failure of select core courses and graduation from high school; it also drives the type of diploma received.

**Human resources leadership**: is built upon the construct of empowerment. School counselors leading from this perspective seek to motivate and inspire students toward career and academic achievement and social/emotional well-being.

**In loco parentis**: a common-law doctrine that allows educators to act as parents, protecting students and their rights while under their care at school.

**Inclusion classroom**: a general education classroom that provides additional supports and accommodations for special education student participation.

**Individual-focused**: school counseling practices that are more focused on intervention for a select individual than on prevention and intervention services for all students.

**Individualized education program**: a written document that identifies specific and individualized strategies for the personal–social, academic, and career success of students with a qualifying disability under IDEA as part of special education services.

**Individuals with Disabilities Education Act (IDEA)**: national legislation that ensures that the educational needs of students with disabilities are met.

**Intelligence quotient**: a score from standardized intelligence tests, which represents one's level of intelligence.

**Intelligence test**: standardized tests intended to assess an individual's cognitive abilities and yield an intelligence quotient score.

**Intervention**: activities and strategies applied with the purpose of reducing or eliminating specific thoughts, actions, or situations.

**Intrinsic motivation**: motivation that is achieved with internal rewards (e.g., specific positive feedback, or earned recognition through accomplishment).

**Justice**: one of Kitchener's five ethical principles that should be conceptualized as treating others equally, but in relation to their individual differences. When treating clients differently in order to meet their unique needs, counselors operate from a sound rationale for such actions.

**Leadership**: the ability to inspire, influence, and persuade others to follow or act.

**Learning profile**: a comprehensive conceptualization that considers an individual's learning styles, predisposition toward specific intelligences (see **multiple intelligences**), as well as cultural and gender differences.

**Least restrictive environment**: special education students are to receive educational services that promote success in the least restrictive manner while receiving accommodations and supports as outlined in the student's IEP; the least restrictive environments in the public-school setting are the general education classrooms (**see also inclusion classroom**).

**Limited English proficient (LEP)**: individuals whose first language is not English and who are therefore restricted in their English-speaking ability.

**Medical plan**: used in schools for students with medical conditions that may warrant special accommodations for a specified amount of time.

**Modeling**: observing and imitating others.

**Motivation**: a force, energy, desire, or state of being that directs thoughts and behavior.

**Multicultural counseling**: counseling that is sensitive to the needs of all people and their unique worldviews grounded in gender, race, ethnicity, culture, social status, economic status, sexual orientation, and religion.

**Multiple intelligences**: eight independent cognitive and affective intelligences working interactively for a holistic understanding of human intelligence.

**Needs assessment**: formal and informational measures that result in the identification of stakeholder needs.

**Negative reinforcement**: removal of a stimulus in an effort to increase a desired behavior or response.

**New Vision School Counseling**: the current movement to transform school counseling into an academic- and systems-focused paradigm.

**No Child Left Behind**: legislation that supports standards-based education between specific classes and racial groups of students.

**Nonmaleficence**: one of Kitchener's five ethical principles that is often defined as "above all do no harm" and viewed by many as the most critical of the five ethical principles. In brief, this concept promotes the idea of avoiding any actions or intentions that may place clients at risk for harm.

**Nontraditional occupation**: occupations in which few individuals of a specific gender generally work. For example, occupations historically dominated by females would be nontraditional occupations for males (e.g., nurse), and occupations historically dominated by males would be nontraditional for females (e.g., mechanic).

**Occupational Information Network**: national database for career information, exploration, assessment, and career decision making.

**Occupational Outlook Handbook**: nationally recognized source for career information and career decision making.

**Open group**: groups that allow new membership once group facilitation begins.

**Outcome evaluation**: program evaluation that determines the effectiveness of a program or intervention in meeting established goals and objectives.

**Paraphrasing**: a basic counseling technique that involves the school counselor restating what a student has shared to communicate understanding.

**Participatory leadership**: sometimes referred to as distributed leadership, is a highly collaborative approach with a focus on democracy instead of a single leader.

**Peer helping/peer support**: programs that involve students helping students (e.g., peer tutoring, peer mentoring, or peer mediation).

**Peer mediation**: a process by which students help students to resolve conflict peacefully by engaging a variety of skills (e.g., problem solving, empathy, clarification, questioning, communication, and negotiation). Peer mediation involves more than two individuals.

**Play therapy**: the use of directive and nondirective play facilitated by the school counselor as a therapeutic medium for emotional expression and communication.

**Political leadership**: relies on the school counselor's ability to understand systems processes and effectively compromise and advocate using persuasive, convincing arguments with those in powerful positions.

**Positive reinforcement**: application of a stimulus in an effort to increase a desired behavior or response.
**Prevention**: activities and strategies applied with the purpose of averting specific thoughts, actions, or situations.
**Primary prevention**: programming that focuses on prevention and wellness for a large population (e.g., the entire student body), who may or may not be potentially at risk for a specific targeted behavior or problem.
**Process addiction**: refers to behavioral patterns, and addictions may include gambling, shopping, Internet usage, eating, working, sex, and more.
**Process evaluation**: program evaluations that assess the program's strengths and weaknesses for program improvement.
**Professional associations**: school counseling related associations that support the profession with resources, professional development opportunities, unification, and advocacy.
**Professional school counselor**: the title that replaced that of guidance counselor due to our emphasis on comprehensive counseling services and holistic student development.
**Program evaluation**: an ongoing component of accountable school counseling practices that results in data that demonstrates program outcomes and answers the question "How do school counselors make a difference in the lives of students?"; also provides information for program improvement.
**Reciprocal determinism**: a term coined by Albert Bandura to describe how behavior is determined by the shared relationship (one acting upon the other) between a person and the environment.
**Reinforcement/reinforcer (see also positive/negative reinforcement)**: a concept used in operant conditioning to refer to a stimulus, positive or negative, to increase the likelihood of desired behaviors or reduce or eliminate undesired behaviors.
**Research-based**: school counseling practices and programming that are supported by research.
**Resilience**: the capacity of an individual to cope with stress and harsh conditions.
**Response to intervention**: an intervention process used to help struggling students to improve behavior and achieve academically.
**Responsive services**: services that meet the immediate needs and distressing issues of students.

**Results report**: written reports that describe the outcomes of specific programming as outlined in action plans, including closing the achievement gap activities.

**RIASEC**: is the acronym used to represent Holland's workplace environments and points on his well-known hexagon.

**Risk factors**: any physical, personal, social, familial, environmental, or economical condition that places students at a disadvantage and serves as an obstacle to well-being, academic achievement, and healthy student development.

**School counselor**: current (as of 2016) contemporary title for the counselor in the PK-12 school setting, depicting a comprehensive counseling specialty that shares the dual roles of educator and counselor and practices using a comprehensive developmental model that attends to the whole child/adolescent/young adult.

**School nurse**: an individual employed by school divisions to attend to student injury, coordinate medical care with physicians, psychologists, and parents, and administer medications during the school day; often a member of child study teams.

**School psychologist**: an individual employed by school divisions to assess levels of student psychological functioning and to suggest interventions to meet individual student needs; often a member of child study teams.

**School social worker**: an individual employed by school divisions to assess levels of student social and family functioning and to suggest interventions to meet individual student needs; often a member of child study teams.

**School-to-Work Opportunities Act**: legislation that seeks to ensure that students will be well prepared to succeed in our multifaceted and technologically advanced workforce.

**Secondary prevention**: programming aimed at mediating a specific behavior or problem that has been identified as a potential threat among a particular population or subgroup of students.

**Section 504**: a part of the ADA, also known as the Rehabilitation Act of 1973, that protects individuals with disabilities from discrimination and allows for equal access to services and the provision of reasonable accommodations related to the disability.

**Servant leadership**: entails a single school counselor acting as a shepherd using integrity, empathy, and humility, to empower and guide the flock toward becoming servant leaders as well.

**Social/Emotional development**: one of three developmental domains within a comprehensive school counseling program that promotes total student well-being through the application of counseling theory and techniques and teaches skills for living (e.g., safety, problem solving, decision making, conflict resolution, and communication).
**Social responsibility**: an ethical ideology that is grounded in the principles of equality, unity, and respect for human rights and acting on behalf of the good of society.
**Special needs students**: students who are limited English proficient or have a 504 Plan or IEP.
**Stakeholder**: any individual or organization that impacts or is impacted by the school.
**Standards**: statements that delineate what students should know and be able to do.
**Strengths-based counseling**: a counseling approach that emphasizes the value of protective factors in combating risk factors and enhancing resilience.
**Structural leadership**: involves creating a plan for change and an approach for putting that plan into action.
**Substance abuse**: repeated use of a chemical substance that may or may not include dependence.
**Substance addiction**: refers to the ingestion of mood-altering substances such as alcohol and other drugs, including anabolic steroids, which is a growing concern in high-school athletic circles.
**Substance use**: repeated use of a chemical substance without dependence.
**Suicide assessment**: screening an individual to determine their risk for suicide.
**Suicide ideation**: thinking about taking one's own life.
**Summarizing**: a basic counseling technique whereby the school counselor condenses into a few brief statements that which the student has conveyed over a period of time during the counseling session.
**Symbolic leadership**: involves effectively communicating a vision of change/growth to all, including those in powerful positions.
**Systems-focused**: school counseling practices that are more focused on prevention and intervention services for all students rather than a select few.

**Teaming**: joining together with other stakeholders to accomplish a common goal.

**Tertiary prevention**: programming that targets a specific population who are already engaging in the at-risk behavior or experiencing a specific problem in order to reduce or eliminate the problem or behavior and improve quality of life.

**Transformational leadership**: the school counselor leader is a visionary acting singularly as change agent endeavors to *transform* the system by understanding and respecting the unique roles of other stakeholders both within and outside of the school. The school counselor as transformational leader seeks to influence and inspire these important others toward a common goal.

**Transformative leadership**: focuses on equity and social justice with the inclusion of those who have been traditionally minoritized and emphasizes the outcomes of leadership versus the process.

**Transforming school counseling initiative**: the movement to change the paradigm of school counseling to one that is academic- and systems-focused.

**Universal Academic Achievement**: academic achievement for all students.

**Wellness**: a sense of personal, social, emotional, physical, and spiritual well-being.

**Worldview**: how an individual conceptualizes and interprets the world, views their relationship with the world, and interacts with the world that is grounded in presupposition, beliefs, and values.

**Zeitgeist**: the thought or spirit of the time in a specified time period or generation.

# References

Adler, A. (1925). *The practice and theory of individual psychology* (P. Radin, Trans., Rev. ed., 1929). London: Routledge.

Akos, P. (2002). Student perceptions of the transition from elementary to middle school. *Professional School Counseling, 5,* 339–345.

American School Counselor Association. (2023a). *ASCA position statements.* Retrieved October 1, 2023, from www.schoolcounselor.org

American School Counselor Association. (2023b). *School counselor roles and ratios.* Retrieved October 1, 2023, from www.schoolcounselor.org

American School Counselor Association. (2022a). *Ethical standards for school counselors.* Alexandria, VA: Author.

American School Counselor Association. (2022b). *ASCA national model implementation guide: ASCA student standards.* Alexandria, VA: Author.

American School Counselor Association. (2021). *Mindsets & behaviors for student success: K-12 college- and career-readiness standards for every student.* Alexandria, VA: Author.

American School Counselor Association. (2019a). *The ASCA national model: A framework for school counseling programs* (4th ed.). Alexandria, VA: Author.

American School Counselor Association. (2019b). *ASCA school counselor professional standards and competencies.* Retrieved September 2, 2023, from www.schoolcounselor.org

American School Counselor Association. (2019c). *ASCA standards for school counselor preparation programs.* Alexandria, VA: Author.

American School Counselor Association. (2019d). *ASCA national model implementation guide: Manage and assess.* Alexandria, VA: Author.

Anderson, L. W., & Krathwohl, D. R. (Eds.). (2001). *A taxonomy for learning, teaching, and assessing: A revision of Bloom's taxonomy of educational objectives.* New York, NY: Longman.

Association for Counselor Education and Supervision. (2007). *Technical competencies for counselor education students: Recommended guidelines for program development.* https://acesonline.net/wpcontent/uploads/2018/11/2007-ACES-TechnologyCompetencies.pdf

Bandura, A. (1969). *Principles of behavior modification.* New York, NY: Holt, Rinehart & Winston.

Bandura, A. (1977). *Social learning theory.* Englewood Cliffs, NJ: Prentice Hall.

Bauman, S. (2008). *Essential topics for the helping professional.* Boston, MA: Allyn & Bacon.

Beck, A. (1979). *Cognitive therapies and emotional disorders.* New York, NY: International Universities Press.

Bernard, J. M., & Goodyear, R. K. (2018). *Fundamentals of clinical supervision* (6th ed.). Boston, MA: Pearson.

Bernard, J. M., & Luke, M. (2015). A content analysis of 10 years of clinical supervision articles in counseling. *Counselor Education and Supervision, 54*(4), 242–257.

Berne, E. (1961). *Transactional analysis in psychotherapy.* New York: Grove Press.

Bloom, B. S. (1953). Thought processes in lectures and discussions. *Journal of General Education, 7,* 160–169.

Brown, D. (2015). *Career information, career counseling, and career development* (11th ed.). Boston, MA: Pearson.

Cameron, S., & Turtle-Song, I. (2002). Learning to write case notes using the SOAP format. *Journal of Counseling & Development, 80*(3), 286.

Capp, G. (2015). Our community, our schools: A case study of program design for school-based mental health services. *Children & Schools, 37*(4), 241–248.

Capuzzi, E., & Stauffer, M. D. (2019). *Foundations of addictions counseling* (4th ed.). Boston, MA: Pearson.

Cashwell, C. S., Young, J. S., Fulton, C. L., Willis, B. T., Giordano, A., Daniel, L. W., Crockett, J., Tate, B. N., & Welch, M. L. (2013). Clinical behaviors for addressing religious/spiritual issues: Do we practice what we preach? *Counseling & Values, 58*(1), 45–58.

Centers for Disease Control and Prevention (2023). National center for health statistics: Marriage and divorce. Retrieved October 13, 2023 from https://www.cdc.gov/nchs/fastats/marriage-divorce.htm

Child Welfare Information Gateway. (2023). *Definitions of child abuse and neglect.* United States department of health and human services, administration for children and families, children's bureau. Retrieved September 2, 2023 from https://www.childwelfare.gov/

Cochran, L. (1997). *Career counseling: A narrative approach.* Newbury Park, CA: Sage.

Cohen, G. J., & Weitzman, C. C. (2016). Helping children and families deal with divorce and separation. *Pediatrics, 138*(6), 103–111.

Corey, G. (2022). *Theory and practice of group counseling* (10th ed.). Belmont, CA: Cengage Learning.

Council for Accreditation of Counseling and Related Educational Programs. (2024). *CACREP Standards*. Alexandria, VA: Author.

Council for the Accreditation of Educator Preparation. (2022). *Knowledge, skills, and professional dispositions*. Retrieved September 14, 2023, from https://mwsu.edu/academics/education/ncate-transition

Cronley, C., & Evans, R. (2017). Studies of resilience among youth experiencing homelessness: A systematic review. *Journal of Human Behavior in the Social Environment, 27*(4), 291–310.

de Shazer, S. (1985). *Keys to solution in brief therapy*. New York, NY: Norton.

Donne, J. (n.d.). *Quotes.net*. Retrieved May 12, 2011, from www.quotes.net/quote/3018

Doran, G. T. (1981). There's a S.M.A.R.T. way to write management's goals and objectives. *Management Review, 70*(11), 35–36.

Dougherty, M. (2013). *Psychology consultation and collaboration in school and community settings* (6th ed.). Belmont, CA: Brooks/Cole.

Dupere, V., Leventhal, T., Dion, E., Crosnoe, R., Archambault, I., & Janosz, M. (2015). Stressors and turning points in high school and dropout. *Review of Educational Research, 85*(4), 591–629.

Education Trust, The (1997, February) *The national guidance and counseling reform program*. Washington, DC: Author.

Elijah, K. (2011). Meeting the guidance and counseling needs of gifted students in school settings. *Journal of School Counseling, 9,* 1–19.

Ellis, A., & Dryden, W. (1997). *The practice of rational emotive behavior therapy*. New York, NY: Springer.

Erford, B. T. (2019). *Transforming the school counseling profession* (5th ed.). Boston, MA: Pearson.

Erikson, E. H. (1950). *Childhood and society*. New York, NY: Norton.

Erikson, E. H. (1959). *Identity and the life cycle*. New York, NY: International Universities Press.

Fowler, J. (1981). *Stages of faith: The psychology of human development and the quest for meaning*. New York, NY: Harper Collins.

Gardner, H. (1983) *Frames of Mind: The theory of multiple intelligences*. New York: Basic Books.

Gardner, H., & Moran, S. (2006). The science of multiple intelligences theory: A response to Lynn Waterhouse. *Educational Psychologist, 41*(4), 227–232.

Gilchrist-Banks, S. (2009). *Choice theory: Using choice theory and reality therapy to enhance student achievement and responsibility*. Alexandria, VA: American School Counselor Association.

Glasser, W. (1998). *Choice theory*. New York, NY: Harper Collins.

*Goals 2000: Educate America Act*, H.R. 1804. (1994). Retrieved September 8, 2009, from www.ed.gov/legislation/GOALS2000/TheAct/index.html

Goodman-Scott, E., & Ziomek-Daigle, J. (2022). School counselors' leadership experiences in multi-tiered systems of support: A phenomenological investigation. *Educational Practice & Theory, 44*(1), 75–94.

Goodman-Scott, E., Betters-Bubon, J., & Donohue, P. (2015). Aligning comprehensive school counseling programs and positive behavioral interventions and supports to maximize school counselor efforts. *Professional School Counseling, 19*(1), 57–67.

Gottfredson, L. S. (1981). Circumscription and compromise: A developmental theory of occupational aspirations. *Journal of Counseling Psychology, 28*(6), 545–579.

Havighurst, R. J. (1972). *Developmental tasks and education.* New York, NY: McKay.

Hobson, S. M., Fox, R. W., & Swickert, M. L. (2000). *School counselor shortages: A statewide collaborative effort in counselor education.* Ypsilanti, MI: Eastern Michigan University. (ERIC Document Reproduction Service No. ED454484).

Holcomb-McCoy, C. C. (2004). Assessing the multicultural competence of school counselors: A checklist. *Professional School Counseling, 7,* 178–183.

Holcomb-McCoy, C. C. (2022). *School counseling to close opportunity gaps: A social justice and antiracist framework for success* (2nd ed.). Thousand Oaks, CA: Corwin Press.

Holland, J. L. (1966). *The psychology of vocational choice.* Waltham, MA: Blaisdell.

Holland, J. L. (1974). *Self-directed search.* Palo Alto, CA: Consulting Psychologists Press.

Holland, J. L. (1985). *Making vocational choices: A theory of personalities and work environments* (2nd ed.). Englewood Cliffs, NJ: Prentice Hall.

Huda, M., Jasmi, A. K., Hehsan, A., Mustari, I. M., Shahrill, M., Basiron, B., & Gassama, S. K. (2017). Empowering children with adaptive technology skills: Careful engagement in the digital information age. *International Electronic Journal of Elementary Education, 9*(3), 698–708.

Kerr, M. M. (2016). *School crisis prevention and intervention.* Long Grove, IL: Waveland Press, Inc.

Kimbel, T., & Schellenberg, R. (2014). Meeting the holistic needs of students: A proposal for spiritual and religious competencies for school counselors. *Professional School Counseling, 17*(1), 76–85.

Kitchener, K. S. (1984). Intuition, critical evaluation, and ethical principles: The foundation for ethical decisions in counseling psychology. *Counseling Psychologist, 12*(3), 43–55.

Kohlberg, L. (1967). Moral and religious education in the public schools: A developmental view. In T. R. Sizer (Ed.), *The roles of religion in public education,* 164–183. Boston, MA: Houghton Mifflin.

Kohlberg, L. (1969). *Stages in the development of moral thought.* New York, NY: Holt, Rinehart & Winston.

Kottman, T., & Meany-Walen, K. (2015). *Partners in play: An Adlerian approach to play therapy* (3rd ed.). Alexandria, VA: American Counseling Association.

Krumboltz, J. D. (1994). Improving career development theory from a social learning theory perspective. In M. L. Savickas & R. W. Lent (Eds.), *Convergence in career development theory*, 9–32. Palo Alto, CA: CPP Books.

Kubler-Ross, E., & Kessler, D. (2014). *On grief and grieving: Finding the meaning of grief through the five stages of loss.* New York, NY: Scribner.

Kuder, G. F. (1964). *Kuder general interest survey: Manual.* Chicago, IL: Science Research Associates.

Lazarus, A. A. (1976). *Multimodal behavior therapy.* New York, NY: Springer.

Lewis, J., Arnold, M., House, R., & Toporek, R. (2003). *Advocacy competencies.* Retrieved March 7, 2011, from www.counseling.org/resources

Lopez, C. J., & Mason, E. C. (2018). School counselors as curricular leaders: A content analysis of ASCA lesson plans. *Professional School Counseling, 21*(1b), 1–12.

Marzano, R. J. (2004). *Building background knowledge for academic achievement: Research on what works in schools.* Alexandria, VA: Association for Supervision and Curriculum Development.

Maslow, A. H. (1970). *Motivation and personality* (2nd ed.). New York, NY: Harper & Row.

Mason, E. M., Ockerman, M., & Chen-Hayes. (2013). Change-agent-for-equity (CAFÉ) model: A framework for school counselor identity. *Journal of School Counseling, 11,* 1–25.

Matsumoto, D., & Juang, L. (2016). *Culture and psychology* (6th ed.). Belmont, CA: Wadsworth Publishing.

McClelland, D. C. (1961). *The achieving society.* Princeton, NJ: Van Nostrand.

McClelland, D. C. (1985). *Human motivation.* Glenview, IL: Scott, Foresman.

McWhirter, J. J., & McWhirter, B. T. (2012). *At-risk youth: A comprehensive response* (5th ed.). Pacific Grove, CA: Brooks/Cole.

Moldovan, O. D. (2014). Intrinsic and extrinsic motivation to primary school children. *Journal Plus Education/Educatia Plus, 10*(1), 203–211.

Morrison, J. (2016). *Diagnosis made easier: Principles and techniques for mental health clinicians* (2nd ed.). New York, NY: Guilford Press.

Moyer, M., & Nelson, K. W. (2007). Investigating and understanding self-mutilation: The student voice. *Professional School Counseling, 11,* 42–48.

Moyer, M., & Yu, K. (2012). Factors influencing school counselors' perceived effectiveness. *Journal of School Counseling, 10,* 1–23.

Murran, S. & Brady, E. (2023). How does family homelessness impact on children's development? A critical review of the literature. *Child & Family Social Work, 28*(2), 291–588.

National Board for Professional Teaching Standards. (2012). *School counseling standards.* Retrieved January 21, 2017, from www.nbpts.org

National Career Development Association. (2009). *Multicultural career counseling minimal competencies*. Retrieved July 1, 2010, from http:// associationdatabase.com/aws/NCDA/pt/sp/guidelines

National Center for Education Statistics (2023). *Digest of education statistics*. Retrieved August 1, 2023, from https://nces.ed.gov/fastfacts/display.asp?id=16

Nelson, M. D., Tarabochia, D. W., & Koltz, R. L. (2014). PACES: A model of student well-being. *Journal of School Counseling, 13*(19), 1–25.

Nye, R. D. (1975). *Three psychologies: Perspectives from Freud, Skinner, and Rogers*. Pacific Grove, CA: Brooks/Cole.

Ockerman, M. S., Patrikakou, E., & Hollenbeck, A. F. (2015). Preparation of school counselors and response to intervention: A profession at the crossroads. *Journal of Counselor Preparation & Supervision, 7*, 161–184.

Page, B., Pietrzak, D., & Sutton, J. (2001). National survey of school counselor supervision. *Counselor Education and Supervision, 41*, 142–150.

Parr, A., & Bonitz, V. S. (2015). Role of family background, student behaviors, and school-related beliefs in predicting high school dropout. *Journal of Educational Research, 108*(6), 504–514.

Parsons, F. (1909). *Choosing your vocation*. Boston, MA: Houghton Mifflin.

Perls, F. S. (1969). *Gestalt therapy verbatim*. Moab, UT: Real People Press.

Phillips, S. D., Christopher-Sisk, E., & Gravino, K. L. (2001). Making career decisions in a relational context. *The Counseling Psychologist, 29*, 193–213.

Piaget, J. (1932). *The moral judgment of the child*. London: Routledge & Kegan Paul.

Piaget, J. (1963). *The origins of intelligence in children*. New York, NY: Norton.

Porfeli, E. J., Hartung, P. J., & Vondracek, F. W. (2008). Children's vocational development: A research rationale. *Career Development Quarterly, 57*, 25–37.

Remley, T., & Herlihy, B. (2019). *Ethical, legal, and professional issues in counseling* (6th ed.). Upper Saddle River, NJ: Pearson.

Roe, A. (1957). Early determinants of vocational choice. *Journal of Counseling Psychology, 4*, 212–217.

Rogers, C. (1961). *On becoming a person: A therapist's view of psychotherapy*. New York, NY: Houghton Mifflin.

Rogers, C. (1969). *Freedom to learn*. Columbus, OH: Merrill Publishing.

Rothrauff, T. C., Cooney, T. M., & Shin An, J. (2009). Remembered parenting styles and adjustment in middle and late adulthood. *The Journals of Gerontology, 64b*, 137–147.

Santrock, J. (2014). *Life-span development* (15th ed.). New York, NY: McGraw-Hill Education.

Savickas, M. L. (1997). Constructivist career counseling: Models and methods. *Advances in Personal Construct Psychology, 4*, 149–182.

Savickas, M. L. (2000). Renovating the psychology of careers for the twenty-first century. In A. Collin & R. A. Young (Eds.), *The future of career*, 53–68. New York, NY: Cambridge University Press.

Schaan, V., & Vogele, V. (2016). Resilience and rejection sensitivity mediate long-term outcomes of parental divorce. *European Child & Adolescent Psychiatry, 25*(11), 1267–1269.

Schellenberg, R. (2000). Aggressive personality: When does it develop and why? *Virginia Counselors Journal, 26*, 67–76.

Schellenberg, R. (2019). *Mindsets and practices of the contemporary school counselor* (3rd ed.). Lanham, MD: Rowman Littlefield Education.

Schellenberg, R., Parks-Savage, A., & Rehfuss, M. (2007). Reducing levels of elementary school violence with peer mediation. *Professional School Counseling, 10*, 475–481.

School-to-Work Opportunities Act, P.L. 103–239. (1994). Retrieved October 1, 2010, from www.fessler.com/SBE/act.htm

Seligman, L. (2004). Diagnosis and treatment planning in counseling. *Professional School Counseling, 2*, 244–247.

Shields, C.M., Dollarhide, C. T., & Young, A. A. (2017). Transformative leadership in school counseling: An emerging paradigm for equity and excellence. *Professional School Counseling, 21*, 1–11.

Shoffner, M. F., & Williamson, R. D. (2000). Engaging preservice school counselors and principals in dialogue and collaboration. *Counselor Education and Supervision, 40*, 128–141.

Skinner, B. F. (1971). *Beyond freedom and dignity*. New York, NY: Vintage Books.

Smith, L., Beck, K., Bernstein, E., & Dashtguard, P. (2014). Youth participatory action research and school counseling practice: A school-wide framework for student well-being. *Journal of School Counseling, 12*(21), 1–31.

Steinmayr, R., Weidinger, A.F., Schwinger, M., & Spinath, B. (2019). The importance of student's motivation for their academic achievement: Replicating and extending previous findings. *Frontiers in Psychology, 10*, 1–11.

Stone, C. (2022). *School counseling principles, ethics, and law* (5th ed.). Alexandria, VA: American School Counseling Association.

Strong, E. K., & Campbell, D. P. (1974). *Strong-Campbell interest inventory*. Stanford, CA: Stanford University Press.

Sue, D. W., & Sue, D. (2019). *Counseling the culturally diverse: Theory and practice* (8th ed.). Hoboken, NJ: Wiley.

Super, D. E. (1949). *Appraising vocational fitness*. New York, NY: Harper & Brothers.

Super, D. E. (1970). *Work values inventory*. Boston, MA: Houghton Mifflin.

Super, D. E. (1980). A life-span, life-space approach to career development. *Journal of Vocational Behavior, 16*, 282–298.

Terrell, R. D., & Lindsey, R. B. (2009). *Culturally proficient leadership: The personal journey begins within*. Thousand Oaks, CA: Corwin.

The Search Institute. (2007). *Developmental assets lists.* Retrieved September 12, 2010, from www.search-institute.org/developmental assets/lists

Tiedeman, D. V. (1961). Decision and vocational development: A paradigm and its implications. *The Personnel and Guidance Journal, 40,* 15–21.

Turner, S. L. (2007). Introduction to special issue: Transitional issues for K-16 students. *Professional School Counseling, 10,* 225–226.

United States Department of Education. (2023a). *Education for Homeless Children and Youth Program title VII, subtitle B of the McKinney-Vento Homeless Assistance Act.* Retrieved September 1, 2023, from https://nche.ed.gov/legislation/mckinney-vento/

United States Department of Education. (2023b). *No Child Left Behind Act of 2001.* Retrieved October 1, 2023, from https://www2.ed.gov/nclb/landing.jhtml

United States Department of Education. (2023c). *Rehabilitation Act of 1973, Section 504.* Retrieved October 1, 2023, from https://www.dol.gov/agencies/oasam/centers-offices/civil-rights-center/statutes/section-504-rehabilitation-act-of-1973

United States Department of Education. (2023d). *Guidance on constitutionally protected prayer and religious expression in public elementary and secondary schools.* Retrieved September 1, 2023, from https://www2.ed.gov/policy/gen/guid/religionandschools/prayer_guidance.html

United States Department of Education. (2023e). *Individuals with Disabilities Act.* Retrieved September 5, 2023, from https://sites.ed.gov/idea/

United States Department of Education. (2023f). *Family Educational Rights and Privacy Act of 1974.* Retrieved September 3, 2023, from https://studentprivacy.ed.gov/?src=fpco

United States Department of Housing and Urban Development (2023). *The 2022 annual homelessness assessment report (AHR) to congress.* Retrieved September 1, 2023, from: https://www.steppingstoneinc.org/wp-content/uploads/2023/01/2022-AHAR-Part-1.pdf

Vygotsky, L. S. (1934). *Thought and language.* Cambridge, MA: Massachusetts Institute of Technology Press.

Vygotsky, L. S. (1978). *Mind and society.* Cambridge, MA: Harvard University Press.

Wedding, D., & Corsini, R. J. (2013). *Current psychotherapies* (10th ed.). Itasca, IL: Brooks Cole.

Whiston, S. C., Tai, W. L., Rahardja, D., & Eder, K. (2011). School counseling out-come: A meta-analytic examination of interventions. *Journal of Counseling & Development, 89,* 37–55.

Willard, N. E. (2006). *Cyberbullying and cyberthreats: Responding to challenge of online cruelty, threats, and distress* (2nd ed.). Eugene, OR: Center for Safe and Responsible Internet Use.

Wolf, J. T. (2004). Teach, but don't preach: Practical guidelines for addressing spiritual concerns of students. *Professional School Counseling, 7,* 363–366.

Wright, K., & Stegelin, D. A. (2002). *Building school and community partnerships through parent involvement* (2nd ed.). Upper Saddle River, NJ: Merrill/Prentice Hall.

Ying, S., Yingzi, H., Yongjie, Z, & Xiwang, F. (2023). Non-suicidal self-injury function: Prevalence in adolescents with depression and its associations with non-suicidal self-injury severity, duration, and suicide. *Frontiers in Psychology, 14*, 1–9.

Young, A., Dollarhide, C. T., & Baughman, A. (2015). The voices of school counselors: Essential characteristics of school counselor leaders. *Professional School Counseling, 19*(1), 36–45.

Young, A., & Kneale, M. M. (2013). *School counselor leadership: The essential practice.* American School Counselor Association.

Youngs, B. B. (1992). *The six vital ingredients of self-esteem: How to develop them in your students.* Torrance, CA: Jalmar Press.

# Acronyms

| | |
|---|---|
| AACD | American Association for Counseling and Development |
| AASA | American Association of School Administrators |
| ACA | American Counseling Association |
| ACES | Association for Counselor Education and Supervision |
| ACSC | ASCA Certified School Counselor |
| ADHD | Attention-Deficit/Hyperactivity Disorder |
| AMCD | Association for Multicultural Counseling and Development |
| AOD | Alcohol and Other Drugs |
| APGA | American Personnel and Guidance Association |
| ASCA | American School Counselor Association |
| ASGW | Association for Specialists in Group Work |
| ASVAB | Armed Services Vocational Aptitude Battery |
| AYP | Adequate Yearly Progress |
| BIP | Behavior intervention plan |
| CACGS | Computer-assisted career guidance systems |
| CACREP | Council for Accreditation of Counseling and Related Educational Programs |
| CAEP | Council for the Accreditation of Educator Preparation |
| CAPTA | Child Abuse Prevention and Treatment Act |
| CBT | Cognitive Behavioral Theory/Therapy |
| CIDS | Career information delivery systems |
| CPCE | Counselor Preparation Comprehensive Examination |
| CPS | Child Protective Services |
| CSCORE | Center for School Counseling Outcome Research and Evaluation |
| ELL | English language learners |
| ESEA | Elementary and Secondary Education Act |

| | |
|---|---|
| ESL | English as a second language |
| FERPA | Family Educational Rights and Privacy Act |
| GATB | General Aptitude Test Battery |
| GED | General equivalency diploma |
| GPA | Grade Point Average |
| HIPAA | Health Insurance Portability and Accountability Act |
| IDEA | Individuals with Disabilities Education Act |
| IEP | Individualized education program/plan |
| KOIS | Kuder Occupational Interest Survey |
| LEP | Limited English Proficient |
| MBTI | Myers-Briggs Type Indicator |
| MOS | Microsoft Office Specialist |
| MTSS | Mutitiered System of Supports |
| NBPTS | National Board for Professional Teaching Standards |
| NCC | National Certified Counselor |
| NCDA | National Career Development Association |
| NCE | National Counselor Examination |
| NCLB | No Child Left Behind |
| NCSC | National Certified School Counselor |
| NCTSC | National Center for Transforming School Counseling |
| NOCTI | National Occupational Competency Testing Institute |
| NRF | National Retail Federation |
| NSCTI | National School Counselor Training Initiative |
| NTE | National Teachers Examination |
| O*Net | Occupational Information Network |
| PIAT | Peabody Individual Achievement Test |
| PSAT | Preliminary Scholastic Aptitude Test |
| PSC | Professional School Counseling |
| PTA | Parent–Teacher Association |
| PTSA | Parent–Teacher–Student Association |
| PTSRC | Parent-Teacher-Student Resource Center |
| RAMP | Recognized ASCA Model Program |
| REBT | Rational Emotive Behavior Therapy |
| RTI | Response to Intervention |
| SCA | Student Council Association |
| SCALE | School Counseling Analysis, Leadership and Evaluation |
| SCOPE | School Counseling Operational Plan for Effectiveness |
| SCORE | School Counseling Operational Report of Effectiveness |

| | |
|---|---|
| SDS | Self-directed search |
| SES | Socioeconomic status |
| SII | Strong interest inventory |
| SOL | Standards of learning |
| TSCI | Transforming School Counseling Initiative |
| WAIS | Wechsler adult intelligence scale |
| WISC | Wechsler intelligence scale for children |

# Index

Locators in *italic* indicate figures, in **bold** tables and in ***bold-italic*** boxes.

504 plans, 504 committee/team 34, 61, 414; practice exam (Julianna) 348, 379–380, 397–398, 400–401; case simulation, Kenneth **35**; counselor as committee member 129; legislative background 34, 212–213; reviews, parental request 214

ACA *see* American Counseling Association
academic achievement, practice exam 341–344, 386–391
academic development 204–221, 414; achievement gaps 209, 275, 312; action plans 94–95, 141, 210, 414; alternative and specialty education programs *see under own heading*; appraisal and advising *see under own heading*; ASCA position on 204; classroom management 6, 51, 105–106, 176, 277; curriculum development 206–207, *207*, 223, 234; differentiated instruction 104–105, 212, 216–217; enrichment programs 216–218; ESL/LEP student programs 214–216; GED-track programs 218, *219*, 222, 355, 356–357, 409–412, 419–420; gifted and talented student test/programs 117, 118, 119, 210, 216–218, **276**; homeschooling 210–211; instruction *see under own heading*; multiple intelligences, types, counseling strategies 207–208, **208**, 421; No Child Left Behind Act 209, 421; parent involvement-achievement link 173–174; self-esteem and 206, 252, ***252***, 256; special needs students *see* special needs students; summarizing counseling technique 53, *53*, 425; virtual classrooms 211–212; *see also* response to intervention (RTI)
accountability 31, 84, 87, 88, 98, 138, 141, 144, 414

acculturation 281, ***281***, **282**; *see also* multicultural competence and counseling
ACES 2, 4, 8, 306
achievement 275–278; achievement motivation theory 54–58, **58**, 62; focus, Transforming School Counseling Initiative (TSCI) 4, 5; gaps 6, 209, 275, **276**, 312, 414; Marzano's Nine Instructional Strategies 49, 52, **53–54**, *54*; parent involvement-achievement link 173–174; practice exam simulation 341–371; role achievement 42; self-esteem-achievement link 206, 252, ***252***, 256; *see also* academic development
achievement tests 115–117, **115**; on high stakes testing 116; high stakes testing 420; on high stakes testing 420; Peabody Individual Achievement Test (PIAT) **115**, 117; Stanford Achievement Test Series ACT **115**, 117; Woodcock–Johnson Test of Achievement (Woodcock–Johnson) **115**, 117, 334, 335, 374, 375
action plans 94–95, 141, 414; classroom-group action plan 94–95; closing-the-gap action plan 94, 95, 141, 210; components 94–95; group mindsets & behaviors actions plans 141; templates, ASCA National Model Implementation Guide: Manage and Assess 94
action research 414
active listening 415
ADA *see* Americans with Disabilities Act (1990)
Adams, J, Q. 302
addiction 415
adequate yearly progress (AYP) 209
Adler, Alfred / Adlerian counseling 243, ***243***
advanced voluntary credentials *see* certification, licensure credentials, (counselors/teachers)

439

# 440 ■ Index

advisory council 98–99, *136–137*, 415
advocacy 415
advocacy and equity 270–275, ASCA position on 270–271, 272; competencies (ACA) 274–275, **274**; social justice 5, 35–36, 269, 272, 273, 275, 302, 304
advocacy competencies (ACA) 274–275
age-appropriate placement 277–278
aggression 415
aggressive toys 253–254; *see also* play therapy techniques
alcohol *see* substance use, abuse, addiction
alternative and specialty education programs: GED-track programs 218, *219*, 222, 355, 356–357, 409–412, 419–420; Job Corps 218, *219*, 222, **276**; practice exam 355–357, 409–413
American Counseling Association (ACA) 3, 4, 11, 96, 110, 274–275, 279, 302
American Personnel and Guidance Association (APGA) 2
American School Counselor Association *see under* ASCA
Americans with Disabilities Act (ADA, 1990) 33–34, 415; 504 Plan 34, 414; Section 504 33–34, 212, 414, 424
annual administrative conference 97
annual performance appraisal, ASCA position on 147, 148
annual student outcome goal plan and statement 92–93, **92–93**, *93–94*, 141, 152
anorexia 57, 128, 415
anti-racist practice, ASCA position on 272
antisocial behavior 254, 415
APGA (American Personnel and Guidance Association) 2
appraisal and advising 112–128, 415; appraisal categories 115, **115**; formal and informal 115–122; *see also* formal and informal appraisal; function and focus 112; level (individual, group, classroom) 114; life-saving 122–128; *see also* life-saving appraisal; practice exam 333–336, 372–378; roots 112; *see also* assessment
aptitude assessments 118–119 *see* ASVAB, GATB, Kaufman Assessment Battery, SAT, PSAT
Armed Services Vocational Aptitude Battery (ASVAB) **116**, 118–119
ASCA: *ASCA Aspects* newsletter 184–185; Recognized ASCA Model Program (RAMP) 4; use of time calculator 97–98, 99
ASCA ethical standards: *ASCA Ethical Standards for School Counselors*, purpose and decision making model 13–14; on alliances and collaborations 18, 130, 277; on confidentiality counselor–student/therapeutic relationship and its records 15, 18, 22, 52, 59, 140; on divorce, custodial and non-custodial parent rights 19; on dual relationships 37; on electronic technology/media use 21, 185; on formal and informal appraisal score, interpretations 113–114; on harm to self/others, student privacy vs parental rights 22; on moonlighting 28, 60; on multicultural competence and bias avoidance 278–279, 280; on postsecondary preparedness, transition readiness 199, 200; on program assessment and student confidentiality 140; on research in schools 36; on scope of practice limitations 28, 29, 60, 137; on sensitive student data transmission 21; on social justice and equitable educational access/success 273, 274; on spiritual and religious respect 283; on student evaluation, assessment, interpretation 29; on supervision 38
ASCA Mindsets & Behaviors for Student Success 84, 172, 415; academic development 204–221; career development 189–203, 223–234; social/emotional development 175–188; *see also under own headings*
ASCA National Model 3–4, 81–85, 415; *ASCA National Model Implementation Guide: Manage and Assess* (2019) 94; recognition as framework 3
ASCA National Model school counseling program components: assess / program assessment and school counselor assessment and appraisal 138–148; define / student and professional standards 84–85; deliver / direct and indirect student services 99–139; manage / program focus and planning 85–99; as academic-and systems-focused school counseling program 3, 4, 9, 176–177, 275, 302, 311–312, 425
ASCA position statements on: academic development 204; annual performance appraisal 148; anti-racist practices 272; career and technical education 199; career development 189; character education 181; child abuse and neglect 24, 25; child abuse and neglect prevention 25; children experiencing homelessness 35–36; college access professionals 198; confidentiality 15; corporal punishment 25; credentialing and licensure 11; crisis response 133; cultural diversity 269–270; digital technology, student safety 183; disabilities, students with 213; discipline 176; equity for all students 270; foster

care students support 27; gender equity 271; gifted and talented student programs 216; group counseling 109; gun violence prevention, school-related 182; harmful or disadvantageous behaviors, identification, prevention and intervention 83; high-stakes testing 116; LBGTQ youth 273; letters of recommendation 200; military-connected students 110; multicultural competence 280; multitiered support systems 101; non-school counseling credentialed personnel to implement school counseling programs 82–83; peer-support programs 132; postsecondary preparation, individual student planning 201; retention, social promotion, age-appropriate placement 277–278; safe schools and bullying/harassment prevention 180; safe schools and crisis response 133; school counseling preparation programs 10; school counseling programs 82; school counselor supervision 38–39; school-family-community partnerships 310; sexually transmitted disease prevention 177; social/emotional development 175; student mental health 27; student postsecondary recruitment 200–201; suicide prevention/awareness 22; suicide risk assessment 127; support staff in school counseling programs 83; test preparation programs 205; trauma informed practices 108; undocumented status, student issues 271; universal screening 103; violence, bullying 180; virtual classrooms/learning environments / virtual school counseling 212; virtual school counseling 212
ASCA School Counselor Professional Standards & Competencies Assessment 147–148
ASGW *see* Association for Specialists in Group Work
assessments and appraisals 99–139, 416; assessment design 146–147; career assessment instruments 202–203; case conceptualization/responses *142*, 151, 152, 154; child abuse or neglect *see* child abuse and neglect; classroom-group and closing-the-gap results reports 139–144; competencies *see* competencies, school counselors; cultural bias 113; distal (over time) measures/evaluation 144–145, *145*, 152; formal/informal, instruments *see* formal and informal appraisal; life-saving appraisal 122–129; measurement concepts 113, **113**; needs assessments 89–90, **90**, 151, 421; practice exam 345–347, 392–396; pre-/post-assessments (programs, interventions) 142–143, **143**, 206, 233; program assessment 138, 139–140, 141, 141–142, 144; proximal (immediate) measures/evaluation 144–145, *145*, 151, 152; school counseling programs 147; school counselor 147–148; student assessment and appraisal *see* formal and informal appraisal; substance abuse *see* substance use, abuse, addiction; suicide assessment *see* suicide, risk, prevention/awareness; WorkKeys, NRF, industry certification assessments 198, 199
assimilation 281, *281*, *282*; *see also* multicultural competence and counseling
Association for Counselor Education and Supervision (ACES) 2, 4, 8, 306; *see also* Council for Accreditation of Counseling and Related Educational Programs (CACREP)
Association for Specialists in Group Work (ASGW) 110–111
Association of Multicultural Counseling and Development (AMCD) 279
ASVAB (Armed Services Vocational Aptitude Battery) **116**, 118–119
authoritative parenting style 187–188
autonomy 13, *41*, **42**, **44**, 46, **47**, 416
AYP *see* Adequate yearly progress

Bandura, Albert / social learning theory *41*, 52; modeling 52, 54; motivation 54; observational learning 52, 245; reciprocal determinism 52, 423
BASIC ID (behavior, affect, sensation, imagery, cognition, interpersonal factors, and drug/biological considerations) 120–121, *121*, **121**, 150
Beck, Aaron / cognitive behavioral theory/therapy (CBT) 245–246, **246**
behavior contract 51, 399, 416
behavior intervention plan (BIP) *102*, 151, 416
behavior modification and learning theory (Skinner) 49–51
behavioral counseling 49, 51, 244–245, **244**, **245**; case conceptualization: Yasmin **255**, 256; *see also* theories and techniques for school settings
behavioral rehearsal **244**, 256, 416
beliefs, vision, mission statements 85–86
beneficence 13, 416
Berne, Eric / transactional analysis (TA) theory 40, *41*, 45
biases: awareness and identification 280, 282; case conceptualization/responses (cultural/religious custom) **285**, 287; cultural 113; gender 36; personal bias, cultural self 280, 283
bibliotherapy 39, 47, 175, 208, 416

biological (BASIC ID) approach 120–121, *121*, **121**, 150
Bloom, Benjamin / Bloom's taxonomy of educational objectives 49, 52, **53**
Board of Education 82
Bridges' Paws in Jobland 203
Brown, Duane / Brown's values-based career development theory *193*, 196–197
Buckley Amendment *see* Family Education Rights and Privacy Act
bulimia 128, 416
bullying, cyber-bullying, violence 155–163, 180, 181–184, **305**, 308, 416, 418
burnout 38, 39

CACREP 3, 8–9, 81–82; *see also* Council for Accreditation of Counseling and Related Educational Programs
CAEP 3, 9–10
cards: as occupational choice support 203; school report cards 89
career and college transitions 197–202; ASCA position on 198, 199, 200–201; Goals 2000: Educate America Act, National Skills Standards Act, and the School-to-Work Opportunities Act 197; industry certifications 198–199; school-to-work movement, school-to-work initiatives 197–198; technical education 199, 199–200, 355, 409; *see also* career development
career and technical education 199, 200; ASCA position on 199, 201
career assessment instruments 202–203
career awareness 190, **195**, 416
career counseling 189, 191, 192, 196, 416
career development 189–203, 280, 416; ASCA position on 189, 198, 199, 200–201; career and college transitions 197–202; decision making, influences 190–191; RIASEC *see* Holland; RIASEC (Holland, John / Holland typology) 196, 202, 232, 424
career development inventories 190, 417
career development theories: Brown's values-based career development theory (Brown, Duane) *193*, 196–197; Cochran's narrative career counseling theory (Cochran, Larry) *193*, 196, 229; constructivist 192, *193*, 196–197; Frank Parsons, trait–job factor matching 1, 119, 192; John Holland / Holland's typology, RIASEC 192, *193*, 194, 196, 202, 232, 424; Krumboltz, John, social learning theory *193*, 197, 222, 224, **229**, **233**; Life Span Life Space approach (Donald Super) *193*, 194; Linda Gottfredson, self-creation / circumscription and compromise theories *193*, 194–195, **195**, 221, 230;

objectivist 1, 192, *193*, 194–196; Personality Development Theory (Anne Roe) *193*, **195**; Savickas, Mark / Savickas' narrative career construction approach *193*, 196, 224, 229; Susan Phillips, Developmental-Relational Theory *193*, 195–196; Tiedeman, David / Tiedeman's postmodern career construction theory *193*, 196
career exploration 190, 223, 227, **233**, 373, 417
career information delivery systems (CIDS) 194, 202–203
career planning, orientation, preparation 173, 190, 417
career readiness / Career Readiness Certificate 198, 226, 233, 355, 409
Career Trek 203
career-related interest inventories: Kuder occupational interest survey (KOIS) **115**, 119, 202; self-directed search (SDS) 194, 202; strong interest inventory (SII) **115**, 119, 202; *see also* Holland, John / Holland's typology, RIASEC
case conceptualization/responses: 504 plan (Kenneth) **35**, 61; access gap, college opportunities (Jameel) **277**, 286; anger management, ASCA-conform outcome goals **93–94**; assessment, appraisal (assessment tests, Jennifer) **114**, 149; assessment, appraisal, BASIC ID (Aymee) **121**, 150; assessment, appraisal, gifted children (Andre) **119**, 150; assessment, appraisal, SOAP notes (Geoffrey, divorce) **127**, 150–151; assessment, appraisal (special needs) **117**, 149; assessment, appraisal, college entrance (Carolyn) **118**, 149; career development, mental circumscription **195**, **221**; child abuse suspicion (Charlie) **26**, 60; cognitive development stages (Caryn) **49**, 62; conflict resolution, behavioral rehearsal **245**, 256; consultation stages/phases **136**, 153; counselor–parent alliances (Robert) **18**, 59; counselor–student privilege, case notes (Donna) **33**, 61; counselor–student privilege, confidentiality (Donna) **16**, 59; defiance (Kelly) **43**, 61–62; cultural sensitivity, encapsulation (Kwame) **281**, 286; developmental assets, motivation and self-esteem (Kafi) **252**, 256; cultural sensitivity, cultural customs (Michelle Obama) **285**, 286; cultural sensitivity, stereotyping (Maya) **281**, 286; dropout prevention **87**, 150; ego states (Eddie) **46**, 62; grief, play therapy (Yasmin) **255**, 256; group work **186**, 221; individual counseling, family deayj (Kyleigh) **109**, 152–153; internet safety, sexting (Steven)

*184*, 221; intrinsic motivation (Ronnie) *56*, 62; moonlighting (Stuart) *28*, 60; motivation, ability self-concept (John) *58*, 62–63; needs assessment target *90*; prevention techniques *186*, 221; professional development, parental trust *172*, 221; professional development, staff development *305*, 314; program assessment measures 151; program assessment measures (addiction programs, DARE, Just Say No) *145*, 152; program assessment measures (peer-helping program) *147*, 151; program assessment, outcomes, result demonstration *142*, 154; program assessment *143–144*; program assessment (Principal Shome) 151; rational emotive behavior therapy (Elijah) *248*, 256; reinforcement, motivation (Dr. Cantholdem) *51*, 62; RTI, ASCA tier levels (Whitney) *102*; sensitive counseling topics, disclosure (Kirbi) *29–31*, 60; student service types (April) *131*, 153; suicidal ideation prevention vs confidentiality (Patrick) *24*, 60; supervision, mentoring (Troy) *139–140*, 152; teambuilding *311–312*, 314; technological applications, digital technology access (Jeremiah) *271*, 286; vision vs mission statements *86*, 149; world view negotiation, consultation/collaboration *136–137*, 153
case simulations: child abuse, sexual abuse investigating (Ernesto) 68–75; collaboration 155–165; high school career development 224–236
CBT (cognitive behavioral theory/therapy) 245–246, *246*; *see also* theories and techniques for school settings
CDSCP-assessing (program/school counselor assessment/appraisal) 138–148; assessment design 146–147; classroom-group and closing-the-gap results reports 139–144; distal (over time) measures/evaluation 144–145, *145*, 152; proximal (immediate) measures/evaluation 144–145, *145*, 151, 152; school counselor assessment 147–148
CDSCP-defining (student/professional standards) 84–85; ethical standards for school counselors 85; *see also* ethical considerations and standards); mindsets and behaviors for student success 84; professional standards and competencies 84–85; *see also* competencies, school counselors; student standards and domains 84
CDSCP-delivery (direct student services) 99–129; appraisal and advising 112–128; *see also under own heading*; competencies, school counselors 148; counseling (individual, small groups) 106–113; *see also* group counseling, group work; *individual counseling*; crisis, crisis response 134; direct-indirect service ratio 99; instruction 104–107; prevention and intervention activities 100, 124, 126, 127, 130, 145, 150, 177, 180, 186, 423; relationship to MTSS 101–102, *101*, *102*, 152; *see also* Multitiered System of Supports (MTSS); Response to Intervention (RTI) programs 101–103, *102*, 152
CDSCP-delivery (indirect student services) 129–138; collaboration 129–134; consultation 134–137; referrals 129, 137–138; *see also each under their own heading*
CDSCP-managing (program focus/planning) 85–99; advisory council 98–99, *136–137*, 415; annual administrative conference 97; annual data review and student outcome goals 90–94; beliefs, vision, mission statements 85–86; data-informed/producing practices 86–87, *87*, 88, 150; lesson plans 95–96; use of time and calendars 97–98
Center for School Counseling Outcome Research and Evaluation (CSCORE) 97
certification, credentials (students): career readiness / Career Readiness Certificate 198, 226, 233, 355, 409; industry certifications 198–199; WorkKeys assessments 198, 199
certification, licensure, credentials (counselors/teachers) 11–12, 82; ASCA position on 11, 38–39; National Board for Certified Counselors (NBCC) 11–12, 21; National Board for Professional Teaching Standards (NBPTS) 12; National Certified Counselor exam (NCE) 12, 82; National Certified Counselor (NCC) credential, NBCC 11; National Certified School Counselor (NCSC) credential, NBCC 12; school counselors 11–12; supervision 38–39; teachers 39
character education 47, 176, 180–182, 235
child abuse and neglect 23, 24–27, 417; ASCA position on 24, 25; assessment, signs of 26, 124, 336, 337; case conceptualization: (Charlie) *26*, 60; case simulation (Ernesto) 73–75; Child Abuse and Neglect Training Modules 124; Child Abuse Prevention and Treatment Act (CAPTA) 24, 25; defining 24; identifying and mandatory reporting 24, 124; neglect prevention 25; parent/guardian indicators 122–124; practice exam (Timmy) 335–336, 376–378

Child Abuse Prevention and Treatment Act (CAPTA) 24
Child Protective Services (CPS) 23, 26, 60; case conceptualization: Charlie 60; case conceptualization: Ernesto 67, 73–74; case conceptualization: Timmy 378
child study team 34, 129, 417; case conceptualization/responses *213–214*, 222
choice theory 249
Choices Explorer 203
Choices Planner 203, **228**
CIDS (career information delivery systems) 194, 203
circumscription and compromise theory (Gottfredson) *193*, 195, **195**, 221, 230
classroom instruction 6, 7, 29, 95, 104, 145, *145*, 152, 176–177, 195
classroom management 6, 51, 105–106, 176, 277
classroom-group action plan 94–95
clinical diagnosis 128–129
clinical supervision 37–38
closed group 112, 417
closing-the-gap action plan, action plans 94, 95, 141, 210
Cochran, Larry / Cochran's narrative career counseling theory *193*, 196, 229
cognitive behavioral counseling/therapy (CBT) 245–246, **246**; *see also* theories and techniques for school settings
cognitive development and learning theories *41*, 46, 49–54; Bandura: social learning theory *41*, 52, 54, 423; Bloom, Benjamin / Bloom's taxonomy of educational objectives 49, 52, *53*; learning styles theories 52, 54; Marzano, Robert / Marzano's Nine Instructional Strategies 49, 52, **53–54**; Piaget: cognitive development stages *41*, 46, 49, **49**, **50**, 62; Skinner: behavioral learning theory *41*, 50–51, 244–245, **244**; Vygotsky: contextual perspectives (sociocultural theory) *41*, 49, 52; *see also under each name*
collaboration 129–134, 417; ASCA position on 132, 133, 310; in behavioral counseling **244**; case conceptualization/responses, April's IEP *131*, 153; case conceptualization/responses, collaboration or consultation **136–137**, 153; case simulation, Internet safety/cyberbullying 158–163; collaboration or consultation 136; collaborative approaches to consultation 134–135; collaborative leader, systemic change, teambuilding 311–313, 314; community collaboration / school-family-community partnerships 132–133, 182, 185, **274**, 310; *see also* school-family-community partnerships; confidentiality 200; during crisis response 132–134; peer-to-peer helping programs 133, 179; process 131, *131*
college access professionals 198; ASCA position on 198
college readiness, practice exam 325–328, 360–364
competencies, school counselors 147–148, 190; Advocacy Competencies (ACA) 274–275, **274**; ASCA standards and competencies 10–11, 84, 85, 111, 139; assessment and appraisal 147–148; direct/indirect student services behaviors 148; mindsets 148; multicultural *see* multicultural competence and counseling; National Certified School Counselor (NCSC) 12; planning and assessment behaviors 148; professional foundation behaviors 148; specific school counseling (CACREP) 421; spiritual 283; technology 305, **307**
comprehensive developmental school counseling program (CDSCP) model 4
comprehensive school counseling program (CDSCP), developmental domains 172–234; academic development 204–221; career development 189–203, 223–234; social emotional development 175–188; *see also each under their own heading*
comprehensive school counseling program, components 81–172; ASCA Position on 82; CDSCP defining (student/professional standards) 84–85, 138–148; CDSCP delivery (direct/indirect student services) 99–139; CDSCP managing (program focus, program planning) 85–99; CDSCP program and school counselor assessment/appraisal 138–148; *see also each under their own heading*
compromise and circumscription theory (Gottfredson) *193*, 195, **195**, 221, 230
computer-assisted career guidance systems (CACGS) 203, 417
confidentiality 15–21; *ASCA Ethical Standards for School Counselors* (2022) 15, 18, 19, 21; ASCA position on 15; assessment process 139; child abuse and neglect, mandatory reporting 24, 124; concept 15; Connors scale/test 51; counseling-related electronic communication 19–20; directory information disclosure 20–21; ethical/moral obligation 16, **16**; Family Educational Rights and Privacy Act (FERPA) 19–20; group counseling 18, 112; harm to self and others 21–23; informed consent 29–30, 36, 37, 61, 221, 339, 382–383; legal obligation,

Index ■ 445

legal consequences 7, 15, 16, *16*, 18; limits, breaches 16, 17, 21–22, 24, 124, 128; minors, emancipated minors 16, 419; parent, legal and social services involvement 17; parental concerns 16–19, *18*, 20, 59; privilege of counselor–student relationship 7, 15, 16, *16*; research 36; student records, counseling case notes 30–31, 32

conflict resolution 181, 417; case conceptualization/responses (small group sessions) *245*, 256

Connors scale/test 51

constructivist career development theories: Brown, Duane / Brown's values-based career development theory *193*, 196–197; Cochran, Larry / Cochran's narrative career counseling theory *193*, 196, 229; Krumboltz, John, social learning theory *193*, 197, 222, 224, *229*, *233*; Savickas, Mark / Savickas' narrative career construction approach *193*, 196, 224, 229; Tiedeman, David / Tiedeman's postmodern career construction theory *193*, 196

consultation 134–137, 417; collaboration or consultation 136, *136–137*, 153; cultural diversity 136; goal 134; parental 189; process, stages, phases 135, *135*, 136; triadic nature 134–135

control theory see reality counseling/therapy

corporal punishment 25; ASCA position on 25; see also child abuse and neglect

Council for Accreditation of Counseling and Related Educational Programs (CACREP) 3, 8–9, 81–82

Council for the Accreditation of Educator Preparation (CAEP) 3, 9–10

credentialing and licensure see certification, licensure credentials, (counselors/teachers)

crisis, crisis response 417; ASCA position on 133; collaboration 132–133; crisis planning 133; crisis-management teams 133; as direct student service 134; identity crisis *41*, 42, 61; post crisis follow-up 134; steps 134; see also safe schools

CSCORE 97

cultural competence see multicultural competence and counseling

cultural diversity; see also diversity

curriculum development 206–207, *207*; case simulation 223, 234

cyberbullying and internet safety 182–184, 308, 418; ASCA position: student safety and digital technology 183, 184; case simulation (Kenji / collaboration) 155–156, 157–160, 162; case simulation (Steven / social media misuse) *184*, 222

DARE (Drug Abuse Resistance Education) programs *145*, 152, 185

data analysis 418

data-driven programs, practices 419

data-informed, data-producing practices *87*, 88, 150

de Shazer, Steve / solution-focused brief counseling 250–251

developmental assets 251–252, *252*, 256; see also strengths-based counseling

diagnostic testing 34, 419

differentiated instruction 104–105, 212, 216–217

direct student services see CDSCP-delivery (direct student services)

disabilities 420; ASCA position on 214; Individuals with Disabilities Education Act (IDEA) and Section 504 plans 33, 34, 213–214, 421; case conceptualizations (April, Genita) *131*, 153, 213–214, *214*, 222; individualized education program/plan (IEP) 33, 35, 421; play therapy 254; programs for students with disabilities 213–215; testing, appraisal *118*, 150; see also special needs

discipline 7; ASCA position on 25, 176; corporal punishment 25; outcome measurements (group/school) 95, *94–95*, *152*; see also violence, school violence

DISCOVER 203

distal (over time) measures/evaluation 144–145, *145*, 152

diversity 180, 269–286, 272–273; advocacy and equity 270–275; anti-racist practice, ASCA position on 269–270, 271, 272; biases (cultural, gender, racial) 114, 272, 280; case conceptualization/responses (cultural/religious custom) *285*, 287; case conceptualization/responses (equal representation) *277*, 286; case conceptualization/responses (Kwame, Maya) *281*, *282*, 285; cultural diversity 269; equity see equity for all students, gender equity; gender equity, ASCA position on 271; LGBTQ+, ASCA position on 273; multicultural competence and counseling see under own heading; racial identity development 280–281, 282; socioeconomic status (SES) 272; School Counselor Multicultural Competence Checklist 281; spirituality and religion see spirituality and religion / spiritual development; see also cultural diversity

divorce 18–19, *127*, 150–151, 187–188, 339, 382

dropping out of school: case conceptualization/responses *87*, 150;

GED-track programs, alternative and specialty education programs *see under their own headings*; practice exam (alternative education) 356, 409; prevalence 219; prevention **87**, 150; risk factors for 217, 219–220

Drug Abuse Resistance Education (DARE) *145*, 152, 185

drug and alcohol: DARE program *145*, 152, 185; Just Say No program *145*; *see also* substance use, abuse, addiction

Dryden, W. / rational emotive behavior therapy (REBT) 248–249, **249**, 256

dual relationships 37, 402

dyadic counseling 109

early intervention: case simulation (Ernesto) 64–75; practice exam 337–340, 379–385; teams 34

Education Trust 4–5

educational diagnostician 34, 91, 132, 419

Elementary and Secondary Education Act (ESEA) 284

Ellis, Albert / rational emotive behavior therapy (REBT) 248–249, **249**, 256

emancipated minor 16, 419

encapsulation 280–281, *281*, *282*, 285, 419; *see also* multicultural competence and counseling

enculturation 281, *281*; *see also* multicultural competence and counseling

English as a second language (ESL) students 212, 214–215, **276**, 419; case simulation, Sabrina/ESL student 289, 294

English language learners (ELL) students 214–215, **275**

enrichment programs 150, 210, 216–218, 222

equity, diversity, advocacy, ethical considerations 269, 273–274, 276, 279, 280

equity: advocacy and equity 270–275; case conceptualization/response (college access gap) *277*, 286; and educational access 5, 8, 34, 146, 273; gender, ASCA position on 271

Erford, B. T. 303

Erikson, Erik / psychosocial theory of human development: eight stages of psychosocial development 40, 42–43; identity crisis *41*, 42, 61; psycho-social strength / virtue 42

ESEA 284

ESL 212, 214–215, **276**, 419; *see also* English as a second language

ethical codes and principles 13, *14*, 416, 419, 421, 422; autonomy 13, 416; beneficence 13, 416; fidelity 13, 419; justice 13, 421; nonmaleficence 13, 59, 422

ethical considerations and standards 12–38; *ASCA Ethical Standards for School Counselors see* ASCA ethical standards; assessment and interpretation 139, 147; career development, college transition 199, 200; confidentiality 15–17, 19–21, 184; core idea 85; diversity, equity, advocacy 269, 273–274, 276, 279, 280; dual relationships 37, 402; ethical-vs-legal standard conflicts 14; harm, suicide prevention 22; moral and spiritual development theories *see under own heading*; *NBCC Code of Ethics* 21; peer-to-peer support programs 132; research 36, 139; school counseling program assessment 139; scope of practice, referrals, moonlighting 28, 29, 60; *see also* referrals; scope of practice; social responsibility 425; spirituality 283, 284; student records, case notes 32; supervision, counselor self-care 38, 39; technological applications, digital technology 183, 184

ethical decision-making model 13

ethical standards, *NBCC Code of Ethics* 21

expressive toys 254–255, 256; *see also* play therapy techniques

extrinsic motivation 55, 419

Family Educational Rights and Privacy Act (FERPA) 19–20, 31, *33*, 36, 200, 419; *see also* confidentiality

FERPA *see* Family Education Rights and Privacy Act

fidelity 13, 42, 419

formal and informal appraisal 115–122, 425; 504 plans 34, **35**, 61, 129, 212–213, 214, 414; *see also* 504 plans, 504 committee/team; Americans with Disabilities Act (ADA, 1990), Section 504 33–34, 34, 212, 414, 415, 424; appraisal categories 115, **115**; appraisal instruments **115**; ASCA position on 116; BASIC ID 120–121, *121*, **121**, 150; counseling communication as informal appraisal 120; formal 112–113, 114, 115–119, **115**; high-stakes testing 116; informal 120–122, **121**, **122**; instruments and cultural bias 113; Kaufman Assessment Battery for Children **115**, 117–118; Kuder occupational interest survey (KOIS) **115**, 119, 202, 373; measurement concepts 113, **113–114**; Peabody Individual Achievement Test (PIAT) **115**, 117; practice exam 348–351; Preliminary Scholastic Aptitude Test (PSAT) 115, 118, 217, 347, 396; SAT (Scholastic Aptitude Test) 115, 118, 149, 294, 346; self-directed search (SDS) 194, 202; SOAP notes 121–122,

122, *127*; special needs assessments, 504 plans 34, *35*, 61, 116, 129, 212–213, 214, 414; *see also* 504 plans, 504 committee/team; standardized tests and their controversy 112, 115, 116, 205, 420; Stanford Achievement Test Series **115**, 117; Stanford–Binet Intelligence Scales (Stanford–Binet) **115**, 119, 224, 229, 334, 373, 374; strong interest inventory (SII) **115**, 202; Vineland Adaptive Behavior Scales (Vineland) **115**, 119; Wechsler adult intelligence scale (WAIS) intelligence tests **115**, 119; Wechsler intelligence scale for children (WISC) intelligence tests **115**, 119; Woodcock–Johnson Test of Achievement **115**, 117; Woodcock–Johnson Test of Achievement (Woodcock–Johnson) **115**, 117, 334, 335, 374, 375

formal case notes 30, 31–32

foster care, supporting students in 26–27; ASCA position on 27

Fowler, James / Fowler's stages of faith *41*, 47, *48*

free appropriate public education (FAPE) 212, ***213–214***, 222, 419

Freud, Sigmund / five-stage psychosexual theory *41*, 43–44, 45; erogenous zones *41*, 43; pleasure principle *41*, 43–44; reality principle 44; stages **45**

Gardner, Howard /multiple intelligence theory 207–208, **208**, 421

GATB (General Aptitude Test Battery) 115, 117–118

GED-track programs 218, **276**, 419–420; case conceptualization/responses (Reginald) **219**, 222; practice exam 355–357, 409–410, 411–413; *see also* alternative educational programs

gender equity 271; ASCA position on 271

general equivalency diploma (GED) programs 218, **219**, 222, 355, 356–357, 409–412, 419–420

Gestalt counseling, Gestalt theory 246–247, **247**; case conceptualization (Joshua) 384

gifted and talented student test/programs 117, 118, 119, 210, 216–218, **276**; ASCA position on 216

Glasser, William 249, **250**

*Goals 2000. Educate America Act, National Skills Standards Act,* and the *School-to-Work Opportunities Act* (1994) 197

Gottfredson, Linda (self-creation / circumscription and compromise theories) *193*, 194–195, ***195***, 221, 230

group activities 104, 111

group counseling, group work 106–107, 109–112; ASCA position on 109; Association for Specialists in Group Work (ASGW) 110–111; children of divorce 188; confidentiality 18, 112; dyadic counseling 109; group composition and member screening 109, 111; homogeneous and heterogeneous groups 111; informed consent 29; open group 112, 423; parental consent 111, 112; psychoeducational groups 109–110

group mindsets & behaviors actions plans 141

guidance counselor 2, 3, 420

gun violence 181; ASCA position on prevention of school-related gun violence 182

harm to self or others 16, 21–24, 60; aggression 415; bullying, cyberbullying *see* bullying, cyberbullying and internet safety; gun violence 181, 182; harm to others 22, 100; harm to self, suicidal ideation *see* suicide, risk, prevention/awareness; mandatory reporting 21–22, 23; school violence 181–183; *see also* violence, school violence

Havighurst, Robert / six-stage developmental task model *41*, 43, **44**

Health Insurance Portability and Accountability Act (HIPAA) 31

high stakes testing 420; ASCA position on 116, 420; *see also* achievement tests

history of school counseling 1–3

Holland, John / Holland typology, RIASEC 196, 202, 232, 424

homelessness 35–36

homeschooling 210–211

human development theories: cognitive development and learning *41*, 46, 49–54, **53–54**; *see also* cognitive development and learning theories; moral and spiritual development *41*, 46–49, *47*, *48*; *see also* moral and spiritual development theories; psychosocial development 40–46, **45**, *46*, **46**; *see also* psychosocial development theories

human resources leadership 303, 420

IDEA (Individuals with Disability Education Act) 33–34, 212, 213, 420

IEP *see* individualized education program/plan (IEP)

in loco parentis 14, 420

inclusion classroom 420

indirect student services *see* CDSCP-delivery (indirect student services)

individual counseling 107–110, 316–317, 321, 420; career development decision 173;

case conceptualization/responses, family deayj (Kyleigh) *109*, 152–153; nonmedical model (Rogers, Carl) 2, person-centered counseling techniques 151, 247–249, *248*; trauma, grief and trauma-informed practices 107–109
individualized education plan/program (IEP) 33, 35, 132, 214, 215, 438; case conceptualizations (April, Genita) *131*, 153, 213–214, *214*, 222
individualized education program 420
Individuals with Disability Education Act (IDEA) 33–34, 212, 213, 420
industry certifications, students 198–199
informal assessments 121
informed consent 29–30, 36, 37, 61, 221, 339, 382–383
in-home drug testing 186
instruction 104–107; classroom 6, 7, 29, 95, 104, 145, *145*, 152, 176–177, 195; instructional strategies / Marzano, Robert 49, 52, *53–54*, 54; school counseling lesson 104; small group *35*, *101*, 176–177
instructional strategies 52, *53–54*, 105, 212, 213, 277; case conceptualization/response *90*, 152
intelligence development level, intelligence quotient (IQ) 49, 118; *see also* cognitive development and learning theories
intelligence testing 420; problematic nature 28; test instruments **115**; Wechsler adult intelligence scale (WAIS) intelligence tests **115**, 119; Wechsler intelligence scale for children (WISC) intelligence tests **115**, 119; Woodcock–Johnson Test of Achievement **115**, 117; Woodcock–Johnson Test of Achievement (Woodcock–Johnson) **115**, 117, 334, 335, 374, 375
intelligences, multiple, theory (Gardner, Howard) 207–209, *208*, 421
internet safety and cyberbullying 182–184, 308; ASCA position: student safety and digital technology 183, 184; case simulation, Kenji / collaboration 155–156, 157–160, 162; case simulation, Steven *184*
intervention plan 420; academic 65, 71; behavioral *102*, 151, 416; practice exam (early intervention, section 504) 338–339, 381–383
intrinsic motivation 55, *56*, 62, 420
IQ *see* intelligence quotient

Job Corps 218, **276**; case conceptualization/responses (Reginald) *219*, 222; practice exam 355, 410
*Journal of School Counseling* (JSC) journal 96

Just Say No to Drugs campaign 37, *145*, 152, 185
justice 421; Kitchener ethical principle 13, 421; Kohlberg stages of moral development *41*; social (ASCA positions, ethical standards, National Model) 36, 269, 273, 304; social justice (transformative leadership) 5, 426

Kaufman Assessment Battery for Children **115**, 117–118
Kitchener, K. S. / Kitchener's five ethical principles 13, *14*, 416, 419, 421, 422; autonomy 13, 416; beneficence 13, 416; fidelity 13, 419; justice 13, 421; nonmaleficence 13, 59, 422
Kohlberg, Lawrence /Kohlberg's stages of moral development *41*, 46–47, *47*
KOIS (Kuder occupational interest survey) **115**, 119, 202
Krumboltz, John / Krumholtz's social learning theory *193*, 197, 222, 224, *229*, *233*
Kuder occupational interest survey (KOIS) **115**, 119, 202, 373

LBGTQ youth, ASCA position on 273
leadership 301–324; approaches 304; functions, characteristics and practices 301–302; program management *see* comprehensive developmental school counseling program (CDSCP); school, family, community partnerships 304, 305; school counseling websites 308–309; school-family-community partnerships 309–310; skills, attributes, practices 303–306; staff development, team building *305*, 311–312, *311–312*; strategies *305*; systemic change 311–313; technological competencies, technology use 5, 19, 184, 306–308, *307*; term 421
leadership, styles: human resources leadership 303, 420; political leadership 303, 422; structural leadership 303, 425; symbolic leadership 303–304, 425
leadership frameworks: distributed 304, 422; participatory 304, 422; servant 304, 424; transformational 304, 311, 426; transformative 304, 426
learning profile 421
learning styles theories 52, 54
learning theories *see* cognitive development and learning theories
least restrictive environment 213, *214*, 222, 421
legal obligation, legal consequences 14, 22; child abuse and neglect prevention *see* child abuse and neglect; Child Abuse Prevention and Treatment Act (CAPTA) 419; confidentiality 7, 15, 16–17, *16*, 18, 19;

electronic communication, technological applications 182–183, 184; Elementary and Secondary Education Act (ESEA) 284; Family Educational Rights and Privacy Act (FERPA) 19–20, 31, *33*, 36, 200, 419; Goals 2000: Educate America Act, National Skills Standards Act, and the School-to-Work Opportunities Act 197; Health Insurance Portability and Accountability Act (HIPAA) 31; Individuals with Disabilities Education Act (IDEA) 33–34, 212, 213, 420; informed consent 29–30, 36, 37, 61, 221, 339, 382–383; in loco parentis 14, 420; National Defense Education Act 2; No Child Left Behind Act (NCLB) 209, 421; privilege of counselor–student relationship 7, 15, *16*; Section 504, Rehabilitation Act 33–34, 61, 212–214, 414, 424; student record keeping/access 20, 32–33; substance abuse, screening and prevention 186

lesson plans 95–96

letters of recommendation 200; ASCA position on 200

LGBTQ+, ASCA position on 273

licensure *see* certification, licensure credentials, (counselors/teachers)

Life Span Life Space approach (Super) *193*, 194

life stages (Super) *193*, 194, 196

life-saving appraisal 122–129; behavioral, emotional, attitudinal clues 122–123; child abuse and neglect, family problems 123–124; self-injurious behaviors, self-mutilation 128; sexual abuse 124; substance abuse, addiction 124; suicidal ideation 125–127; timeliness needs 122–123

Limited English proficient (LEP) students 212, 214–216, 421

Marzano, Robert / Marzano's Nine Instructional Strategies 49, 52, **53–54**, 54; instructional strategies 53, 54, 152

Maslow, Abraham / Maslow's theory of motivation 56–57, *56*

MBTI (Myers-Briggs Type Indicator) **115**, 119

medical plan 213, **293**, 421

mental health, students: ASCA position on 27; collaboration 130, 311; individual-and mental health–focused paradigm (TSCI) 4, 204; life-saving appraisal 122–129; *see also under own heading*; mental health movements 2; referrals 138; suicide, suicidal ideation *see* suicide, risk, prevention/ awareness

metaphorical expression, toys for 254

Metropolitan Life Insurance Company (MetLife) 5

military-connected students, ASCA position on 110

mission, vision, belief statements 85–86

modeling *41*, 52, 54, 180, 197, 245, 246, 303, 421

moonlighting **28**, 60

moral and spiritual development theories: Fowler's stages of faith *41*, 47, *48*; Kohlberg's stages of moral development *41*, 46–47, **47**; Piaget, stage model of moral development *41*, 46, **47**, 55; Piaget, theory of moral development 46

moral development 46, **47**, 175

motivation 54–55, 421; case simulation, Ernesto 68, 70, 71; case simulation, John **58**, 62–63; case simulation, Kafi 252; dissonance, cognitive discomfort experience 54–55; extrinsic 55, 419; intrinsic 55, **56**, 62, 420; modeling 52, 54; praise 55–56, **56**; reinforcement (extrinsic rewards, punishments) 54–55; standardized personality assessments 119

motivation, theories: achievement motivation theory (McClelland) 57–58, **58**; behavioral (Skinner, Bandura) 54–55; cognitive (Piaget) 54; humanistic / Maslow's theory of motivation 54, 56–57, *56*

Multicultural Career Counseling Minimal Competencies (NCDA) 190

multicultural competence and counseling 273, 278–282, 285, 421; acculturation 281, *281*, *282*; anti-racist practice, ASCA position on 272; ASCA position on 269, 272; Association of Multicultural Counseling and Development (AMCD) 279; case conceptualization/responses (cultural/religious custom) **285**, 287; case conceptualization/responses (Kwame, Maya) *281*, *282*, 285; case simulation, Sabrina/ESL student 288–297; competence categories **279**, 418; cultural blindness **279**, 418; cultural ineptness **279**, 418; cultural sensitivity **279**, 285, 286, 418; culturally competent school counseling program, categories **279**; encapsulation 280–281, *281*, *282*, 285, 419; multicultural responsiveness **249**; personal bias, cultural self 280, 283; racial identity development 280–281, *282*; *School Counselor Multicultural Competence Checklist* 280; stereotyping 280

multiple intelligences (theory, types, school counseling strategies) 207–208, **208**, 421

Multitiered System of Supports (MTSS) 100–101, **101**, 103; ASCA Position on 101, 103

Myers-Briggs Type Indicator (MBTI) **115**, 119

National Board for Certified Counselors (NBCC) 11–12, 21, 82; *NBCC Code of Ethics* 21; National Certified Counselor exam (NCE) 11; National Certified School Counselor (NCSC) credential 12
National Board for Professional Teaching Standards (NBPTS) 12
National Career Development Association (NCDA) 190
National Center for Transforming School Counseling (NCTSC) 5
National Defense Education Act 2
National Model (ASCA) *see* ASCA National Model
National Occupational Competency Testing Institute (NOCTI) assessment 198
National School Counselor Training Initiative (NSTCI) 5
national specialty counseling credentials 12
needs assessment 89–90, **90**, 151, 421
negative/positive reinforcement *41*, 50, 421, 423
new vision school counseling (TSCI) 3–4, 9, 204, 421
No Child Left Behind Act (NCLB, 2001), schools' responsibility 209, 421
NOCTI 198
nonmaleficence 13, 59, 422
non-standardized tests/assessments *114*, 120, **121**, 150, 335, 375; *see also* BASIC ID; informal assessments
nontraditional occupation 192, 228, 422; case conceptualization/response (I want to be a nurse) **196**, 222
nurturing toys 253; *see also* play therapy techniques

objectivist career development theories 192, *193*, 196; Anne Roe, Personality Development Theory *193*, 195; Donald Super, Life Span Life Space approach *193*, 194; Frank Parsons, trait–job factor matching 1, 192, *193*; John Holland / Holland's typology, RIASEC 192, *193*, 194, 196, 202, 232, 424; Linda Gottfredson, self-creation / circumscription and compromise theories *193*, 194–195, **195**, 221, 230; Susan Phillips, Developmental-Relational Theory *193*, 195–196
observation, subjective/objective 121, **122**; case simulation, Geoffrey 150
observational learning 52, 245; *see also* modeling
Occupational Information Network (O*Net) 203, 422
*Occupational Outlook Handbook* (OOH) 203, 422

open group 112, 422; *see also* group counseling, group work
operant conditioning *41*, 50–51, 244–245, **244**, 423
outcome measurement and evaluation 95, **94–95**, *152*, 406, 422; annual data review and student outcome goals 90–94; Center for School Counseling Outcome Research and Evaluation (CSCORE) 97
outcome goal plan, annual, and statement 92–93, **92–93**, **93–94**, 141, 152

paraphrasing, counseling technique 249, 422
parent involvement, school-family-community partnerships 309–310
parents: attitude types, towards/away from children 196; child abuse and neglect *see under own heading*; confidentiality 16–19, **18**; counselor-parents alliances 59; disabilities, IDEA and Section 504 plans 34, 213–214; divorce 18–19, **127**, 150–151, 187–188, 339, 382; educational programming for 304–306; electronic communication 19–20; elementary-/middle-/high-school children 172–174; guardians and noncustodial parents 19; homeschooling 210–211; informed consent 29–30, **30**; learning motivation, encouraging **58**; in loco parentis 14; parental consent 20, 29, 61; *see also* informed consent; parent–child interactions, parent attitudes 195; parenting styles 188–189; referral, students to counseling 137–138; school dropout 219–220; school-family-community partnerships 309–310; student case notes, access to 32–33; student harm to self and others, parent communication 21–23, **24**, 127–129; substance abuse and addiction, students' 185, 186; trust **174**
Parent–Teacher Association (PTA) 18
*Parent–Teacher–Student Resource Center* (PTSRC) 310
Parsons, Frank 1, 192, *193*
participatory leadership 304, 422
Peabody Individual Achievement Test (PIAT) **115**, 117
peer helping programs, peer support 104, 132, 179, 181, 245, 422; ASCA position on 132, 422; case conceptualization/responses **147**, 151; peer mediation 181, 422; peer tutoring 132
peer supervision 38, 39
peer-reviewed research and journals 96
Perls, Fritz 246, **247**
personality development *see* psychosocial development

personality development theory / transactional analysis (TA) theory 40, *41*, 45
Personality Development Theory (Roe), objectivist career development theories *193*, 195
person-centered (humanistic) counseling 247–248, **248**
Phillips, Susan, Developmental-Relational Theory *193*, 195–196
Piaget, Jean: cognitive development stages *41*, 46, 49, **49**, **50**, 62; Piaget, stage model of moral development *41*, 46, **47**, 55
PIAT (Peabody Individual Achievement Test) **115**, 117
play therapy 215, 422; Adlerian counseling 243, **243**; case conceptualization: Esther **258**, 262; case conceptualization: Yasmin **255**, 256; techniques 253–255
political leadership 303, 422
positive role models 47, 54, 175
positive/negative reinforcement *41*, 50, 421, 423
positivistic career development theories 196
practice exam: academic achievement 341–344, 386–391; alternative educational programs 355–357, 409–413; assessment 345–347, 392–396; college readiness 325–328, 360–364; early intervention 337–340, 379–385; program evaluation 352–354, 403–408; school violence 329–332, 365–371; scope of practice 348–351, 397–402; special needs 348–351, 397–402; student appraisal 333–336, 372–378
praise 55–56, **56**; *see also* motivation
preparation, training programs 8–10; ASCA position on 10; ASCA standards for school counselor preparation programs 10; CACREP standards for the specialized practice area of school counseling 8–9; CAEP standards for educator preparation 9–10
prevention 423; anorexia and bulimia 128; collaboration 130; dropout 150; drug and alcohol 145; screening and prevention education 126; secondary 186; sexually transmitted disease 177; suicide 126, 127; tertiary 186; violence, bullying 124, 180
preventive services 216; *see also* responsive services
primary developmental domains 172–234; academic development 204–221; career development 189–203, 223–234; social/emotional development 175–188; *see also each under their own heading*
primary prevention 100, 102, 130, 185–186, 423; substance use, abuse, addiction 185–186

process addiction 185, 186, 423
professional associations 2–3, 12, 14, 110, 309, 423
professional identity 5–11; dual roles (educator, counselor) 6–8; licensing and advanced voluntary credentials 10–12; preparation, training programs 8–10
*Professional School Counseling* (PSC) journal 96
program assessment, evaluation 138, 139–140, 141–142, 144, 423; program evaluation, practice exam 352–354, 403–408; *see also* assessments and appraisals
program delivery *see* CDSCP-delivery (direct student services), CDSCP-delivery (indirect student services)
proximal (immediate) measures/evaluation 144–145, **145**, 151, 152
proximal development zone *41*, 52
PSAT (Preliminary Scholastic Aptitude Test) 115, 118, 217, 347, 396
psychoeducational groups 109–110
psychosocial development theories 40–44, *41*; Berne's transactional analysis (TA) theory 40, *41*, 45; Erikson's eight stages of psychosocial development 40–43, *41*; Freud's five-stage psychosexual theory *41*, 43–44, 45, **45**; Havighurst, Robert / six-stage developmental task model *41*, 43, **44**
PTSRCs *see* Parent–teacher–student resource centers

racial identity development 280–281, 282
racism, anti-racist practice, ASCA position on 272
RAMP *see* Recognized ASCA model program
rational emotive behavior therapy (REBT) 248–249, **249**, 256; case conceptualization (Elijah) *248*, 256; case conceptualization (Esther) 256, 262, 264
Reagan, Nancy 37, 185
reality counseling 249, **250**, 264, 400
reality counseling/therapy 249–250, **250**
reality principle 44
REBT *see* Rational emotive behavior therapy
reciprocal determinism *41*, 52, 423
Recognized ASCA Model Program (RAMP) 4
referrals from school counseling 27, 28, 60, 129, 137–138
Rehabilitation Act (1973) 33–34, 212, 414, 424
reinforcement/reinforcer *41*, 50, 55, **229**, 244–245, **244**; positive/negative reinforcement *41*, 50, 421, 423; schedules of reinforcement 8, *41*, 51, **244**
religion *see* spirituality and religion / spiritual development

research, in-school 36–37, 139
research-based counseling practices 423
resilience 8, 175, 188, 251, 423
Response to Intervention (RTI) programs/teams 101–103, *102*, 423
responsive services 7, 100, 106–107, 134, 172, 216, 278, 423; *see also* preventive services
retention 277–278
RIASEC test, Holland typology 196, 202, 232, 424
Roe, Anne (Personality Development Theory) *193*, 195
Rogers, Carl / Rogerian counseling 2, 247, **248**
role diffusion, role confusion 42, **42**
RTI *see* Response to Intervention (RTI) programs/teams

safe schools 133; ASCA position on 133, 176, 179, 182; *see also* bullying, cyber-bullying; violence
SAP (student assistance programs) 107
SAT (Scholastic Aptitude Test) 115, 118, 149, 294, 346
Savickas, Mark / Savickas' narrative career construction approach *193*, 196, 224, 229
scaffolding 52
SCALE (School Counseling Analysis, Leadership, and Evaluation) Research Center 83–84
scary toys 254; *see also* play therapy techniques
schedules of reinforcement 8, *41*, 51, **244**
school counseling lesson 104, *143*, 151
school counseling program *see* comprehensive school counseling program
school counselor assessment 147–148; *see also* CDSCP-assessing (program/school counselor assessment/appraisal)
school counselor certification, licensing 11–12; ASCA Position on 11
School Counselor Performance Appraisal Template 148
school counselor preparation programs: ASCA Position on 10; standards 10
school leadership team 98, 313
school nurse 26, 60, 129, 130, 131, 424
school psychologist *102*, 129, 131, 424
school resource officer 331, 370
school social worker *102*, 129, 131, 424
school violence *see* violence, school violence
school-community partnerships 309–310
school-family-community partnerships 309–310
school-to-work movement, school-to-work initiatives 197–198
School-to-Work Opportunities Act (1994) 197, 424
scope of practice, practice exam 348–351, 397–402

scope of practice, extend and limitations 27–29, 107, 129, 137; areas of expertise and training, acknowledging 27–28; ASCA position on student mental health 27; counselor-agency cooperation 28; moonlighting **28**, 60; referrals 27, 28, 129; student evaluation, assessment, interpretation 28–29
SDS (self-directed search) 194, 202
Search Institute 251–252
secondary prevention 100, 102, 185, 186, 221, 424
Section 504, ADA 33–34, 212, 414, 424
self-care, counselor 38, 39
self-directed search (SDS) 194, 202
self-esteem 206, 252, **252**, 256
self-harm *see* harm to self or others
Seligman, Martin 251, **252**
servant leadership 304, 424
sexual abuse 124, 138
sexually transmitted disease, prevention 177; ASCA position on 177
SFBC (solution-focused brief counseling) 250, **250**, 264
short-term nature of school counseling 107
SIGI Plus 203
SII (strong interest inventory) **115**, 119, 202
simulations 119
Skinner, B. F. *41*, 54–55, 244, **244**; behavior modification and learning theory 49–51; behavioral counseling 49, 244, **244**; motivation 54–55; operant conditioning, schedules of reinforcement *41*, 50–51, 244–245, **244**; *see also* cognitive development and learning theories
SMART goals 94
SOAP notes 121–122, **122**, *127*
social justice 5, 35–36, 269, 272, 273, 275, 302, 304; *see also* transformational leadership
social learning theory *see* Krumboltz, John / Krumboltz's social learning theory
social promotion 277–278
social responsibility 44, 243, 272, 425
social-cognitive counseling approach 245, 256; *see also* modeling
social/emotional development *41*, 42, 61, 172–189, 425; Adlerian counseling 243, **243**; ASCA position on 175, 176; behavioral counseling 49, 51, 244–245, **244**, *245*, *255*, 256; bullying, cyber-bullying 155–163, 180, 180–184, 181–184, *305*, 308, 416, 418; character education 47, 176, 180–182, *181*, 235; cognitive behavioral counseling 245–246, **246**; conflict resolution 181, **245**, 256, 417; crisis, crisis response *41*, 42, 61, 132–134, 417; curriculum development

206–207, **207**, 223, 234; divorce 18–19, ***127***, 150–151, 187–188, 339, 382; dropping out of school *see under own heading*; Gestalt counseling 246–247, **247**, 384; group counseling, group work 18, 29, 106–107, 109–112; Just Say No to Drugs 37, ***145***, 152, 185; parenting styles 188–189; *see also* parents; peer-to-peer helping programs, support. mediation 104, 132, ***147***, 151, 179, 181, 245, 422; person-centered counseling 151, 247–248, **248**; play therapy 215, 243, ***243***, 253–255, ***255***, 256, **258**, 262, 422; prevention (primary, secondary, tertiary) *see* prevention; psychoeducational groups 109–110; rational emotive behavior therapy (REBT) 248–249, **248**, **249**, 256, 262, 264; reality counseling 249–250; responsive services 7, 100, 106–107, 134, 172, 216, 278, 423; sexually transmitted infections, ASCA position on 177; solution-focused brief counseling 250–251; strengths-based counseling 251–253; substance use, abuse, addiction 185–187; transitioning 178–179, 202–203; violence 32, 122, 124, ***136***, 138, 155–163, 179–187, ***305***, 308, 329–332, 365–371, 416, 418; *see also* violence, school violence; violence, school violence *see* violence
socioeconomic status (SES), potential achievement impact 272
Socrates 283
sole possession records 30–32
solution-focused brief counseling (SFBC) 250, **250**, 264
special needs: ASCA School Counselor Specialty Standards 8, 9; 504 plans 34, 34, ***35***, 61, 116, 129, 212–213, 214, 414; case conceptualization/response (Kenneth, 504 plan) ***35***, 61; practice exam 397–402; *see also* alternative and specialty education programs
spiritual development theories *see* moral and spiritual development theories
spirituality and religion / spiritual development 283–285; ASCA *Ethical Standards for School Counselors* 283; case conceptualization/ responses (cultural/religious custom) ***285***, 287; Fowler's stages of faith *41*, 47, *48*; homeschooling 210–211; personal bias identification 283; School Counselor Spiritual and Religious Competencies (Kimbel, Schellenberg) 283; spirituality vs religion 284; student-organized events 284; teaching vs preaching approach 284
staff development: professional development 306; teambuilding 311–312, ***311–312***, 426

standardized tests 112, 115, 205, 420; *see also* formal and informal appraisal; intelligence testing
Stanford Achievement Test Series **115**, 117
Stanford–Binet Intelligence Scales (Stanford–Binet) **115**, 119, 224, 229, 334, 373, 374
STEPS (solutions to ethical problems in schools) model 13
stereotyping 161, 272, 280, 282, ***282***, 286
strengths-based counseling 151, 187, 251, **252**, 262, 264, 425
strokes *41*, 45
strong interest inventory (SII) **115**, 119, 202
structural leadership 303, 425
student assistance programs (SAPs) 107
student records, counseling case notes 30–31, 32
substance use, abuse, addiction 124–125, 138, 185–187, 304–305, 415, 425; biological model 187; case conceptualization/ responses, prevention techniques ***186***, 221; case conceptualization/responses, program assessment measures ***145***, 152; DARE (Drug Abuse Resistance Education) programs ***145***, 152, 185; disease model 187; etiology of addiction models 187; family model 187; in-home drug testing 186; Just Say No to Drugs campaign 37, 145, 152, 185; primary prevention 100, 102, 130, 185–186, 423; psychological model 187; secondary prevention 100, 102, 185, 186, 221, 424; sociocultural model 187; tertiary prevention 102, 185, 186, 426
suicide, risk, prevention/awareness 22–24; ASCA Position on 22, 100, 127; suicide assessment 127, 425; suicide ideation 23–24, ***24***, 60, 425
summarizing, counseling technique 53, *53*, 425
Super, Donald / Life Span Life Space approach ***193***, 194
supervision 37–39; ASCA position on 38–39; Association for Counselor Education and Supervision (ACES) 2, 4, 8, 306; clinical 37–38; developmental models of 38; peer supervision or consultation 38, 39, 132
symbolic leadership 303–304, 425
systemic change 129, **279**, 311–313
systems-focused school counseling program paradigm and service delivery 3, 4, 9, 176–177, 275, 302, 311–312, 425

TA *see* Theory of personality development
teacher education, standards and accreditation 9–10; *see also* CAEP
teambuilding, skills and strategies 311–312, ***311–312***, 426

technical education 199, 199–200, 200, 355, 409; ASCA position 199, 201; ASCA position on 199
technological competencies, counselor 5, 19, 184, 306–308, **307**
technological competencies, students 182–184; ASCA position on digital technology, student safety 183; *see also* internet safety and cyberbullying
technology use, purposes 306
tertiary prevention 102, 185, 186, 426
The National Technology Institute for School Counselors 96, 407
theories and techniques for school settings 246–247, **247**, 384; Adlerian counseling 243, **243**; behavioral counseling 51, 244–245, **244**, **245**, **255**, 256; case conceptualization: Esther **255**, 257–265; case conceptualization: Yasmin **255**, 256; cognitive behavioral counseling/therapy (CBT) 245–246, **246**; person-centered counseling 151, 247–248, **248**; play therapy techniques 215, 243, **243**, 253–255, **255**, 256, **258**, 262, 422; rational emotive behavior therapy (REBT) 248–249, **248**, **249**, 256, 262, 264; reality counseling 249, **250**, 264, 400; solution-focused brief counseling (SFBC) **250**, **250**, 264; strengths-based counseling 151, 187, 251, **252**, 262, 264; *see also each under own name*
theory of personality development / transactional analysis (TA) theory 40, *41*, 45
Tiedeman, David / Tiedeman's postmodern career construction theory *193*, 196
toys 253–255, 256, 258, 262; *see also* play therapy techniques
traditional career development theories *see* objectivist career development theories
transactional analysis (TA) 40, *41*, 45
transactional stimulus, transactional response *41*, 45
transformational leadership 304, 311, 426
transformative leadership 304, 426
Transforming School Counseling Initiative (TSCI) 4–5, 209, 426; and NCLB objectives 209
*Transforming School Counseling Initiative* (TSCI) 4–5, 209
transgender and nonbinary youth, ASCA position on 273
transitioning 178–179, 202–203
trauma and trauma-informed practices 107–109; ASCA Position on 108; play therapy techniques 253, 254; PTSD 108, 134; *see also* child abuse and neglect; crisis; MTSS

TSCI *see* Transforming School Counseling Initiative

undocumented status students, ASCA position on 271
Universal Academic Achievement 426
universal screening 103; ASCA position on 103; *see also* Multitiered System of Supports (MTSS); Response to Intervention (RTI) programs/teams
use of time and calendars 97–98
*Use of Time Calculator* (ASCA) 97–98, 99

Vineland Adaptive Behavior Scales (Vineland) **115**, 119
violence, school violence 179–182; ASCA position on 180, 181, 182, 183; bullying, cyber-bullying 155–163, 180, 181–184, **305**, 308, 416, 418; gun 181, 182; life-saving appraisal 122; practice exam 329–332, 365–371; prevention, reduction 124, *136*, 180, 181; record keeping, reporting 32, 124; referrals 138; sexual *see* sexual abuse; *see also* child abuse and neglect
vision, belief, mission statements 85–86
virtual classrooms and learning environments / virtual school counseling 211–214; ASCA's position on virtual school counseling 212
Vocation Bureau 1
vocational guidance: as origins of school counseling 1–2; Parsons, Frank, as father of 1
Vygotsky, Lev S.: cognitive development/learning theory *41*, 49; cultural mediation 52; scaffolding *41*, 52; zone of proximal development 52

Wechsler adult intelligence scale (WAIS) intelligence tests **115**, 119
Wechsler intelligence scale for children (WISC) intelligence tests 115, 119
Woodcock–Johnson Test of Achievement (Woodcock–Johnson) **115**, 117, 334, 335, 374, 375
WorkKeys assessments 198, 199
worldviews, students': (multi)cultural competent assessment/counseling 112, 136, 202, 243, **247**, **250**, **251**, 278, 280, 421; career beliefs, career decision making 196, 233; counselor–student collaboration 163; spiritual/faith development *48*, 283, 284; term 426

zeitgeist 426
zone of proximal development *41*, 52

Printed in the United States
by Baker & Taylor Publisher Services